W9-DCX-430

FIXING YOUR HOUSE TO SELL

Other Publications:

FIXING YOUR HOUSE TO SELL

TIME-LIFE BOOKS
ALEXANDRIA, VIRGINIA

Fix It Yourself was produced by

ST. REMY PRESS

MANAGING EDITOR	Kenneth Winchester
MANAGING ART DIRECTOR	Pierre Léveillé

Staff for *Fixing Your House To Sell*

Series Editor	Brian Parsons
Series Assistant Editor	Kent J. Farrell
Editors	Fiona Gilsenan, Nancy D. Kingsbury
Series Art Director	Diane Denoncourt
Art Director	Solange Pelland
Research Editor	Naomi Fukuyama
Designers	Normand Boudreault, Julie Léger, Nicolas Moumouris
Editorial Assistant	Frances Slingerland
Contributing Writers	Mavis Hogan Assad, Robert J. Eyre, Jennifer Henderson, Cynthia Jervis, Christopher Little, Michael R. MacDonald
Contributing Illustrators	Gérard Mariscalchi, Jacques Proulx
Cover	Robert Monté
Index	Christine M. Jacobs
Administrator	Denise Rainville
Accounting Manager	Natalie Watanabe
Production Manager	Michelle Turbide
Systems Manager	Shirley Grynspan
Systems Analyst	Simon Lapierre
Studio Director	Maryo Proulx

Time-Life Books Inc. is a wholly owned subsidiary of

THE TIME INC. BOOK COMPANY

President and Chief Executive Officer	Kelso F. Sutton
President, Time Inc. Books Direct	Christopher T. Linen

TIME-LIFE BOOKS INC.

EDITOR	George Constable
Executive Editor	Ellen Phillips
Director of Design	Louis Klein
Director of Editorial Resources	Phyllis K. Wise
Editorial Board	Russell B. Adams Jr., Dale M. Brown, Roberta Conlan, Thomas H. Flaherty, Lee Hassig, Jim Hicks, Donia Ann Steele, Rosalind Stubenberg
Director of Photography and Research	John Conrad Weiser
PRESIDENT	John M. Fahey Jr.
Senior Vice Presidents	Robert M. DeSena, James L. Mercer, Paul R. Stewart, Curtis G. Viebranz, Joseph J. Ward
Vice Presidents	Stephen L. Bair, Stephen L. Goldstein, Juanita T. James, Andrew P. Kaplan, Susan J. Maruyama, Robert H. Smith
Supervisor of Quality Control	James King
Publisher	Joseph J. Ward

Editorial Operations

Copy Chief	Diane Ullius
Production	Celia Beattie
Library	Louise D. Forstall
Correspondents	Elisabeth Kraemer-Singh (Bonn); Christina Lieberman (New York); Maria Vincenza Aloisi (Paris); Ann Natanson (Rome).

THE CONSULTANTS

Consulting editor **David L. Harrison** served as an editor for several Time-Life Books do-it-yourself series, including *Home Repair and Improvement, The Encyclopedia of Gardening* and *The Art of Sewing.*

Richard Day, a do-it-yourself writer for nearly a quarter of a century, is a founder of the National Association of Home and Workshop Writers and is the author of several home repair books.

Joseph Truini is Senior Editor of Home Mechanix Magazine. He specializes in how-to articles for do-it-yourselfers and has worked as a cabinetmaker, home improvement contractor and carpenter.

Mark M. Steele, a professional home inspector and construction consultant in the Washington D.C. area, is an editor of home improvement articles and books.

Library of Congress Cataloging-in-Publication Data
Fixing your house to sell.
p. cm. – (Fix it yourself)
Includes index.
ISBN 0-8094-6284-2.
ISBN 0-8094-6285-0 (lib. bdg.)
1. Dwellings–Maintenance and repair–Amateurs' manuals.
I. Time-Life Books. II. Series.
TT14817.3.F58 1989
683'.7—dc20 89-27411
CIP

For information about any Time-Life book, please write:
Reader Information
Time-Life Customer Service
P.O. Box C-32068
Richmond, Virginia
23261-2068

First printing. Printed in U.S.A.
Published simultaneously in Canada.
School and library distribution by Silver Burdett Company, Morristown, New Jersey.

CONTENTS

HOW TO USE THIS BOOK

Fixing Your House To Sell is divided into three sections. The Emergency Guide on pages 8 to 13 provides information that can be indispensable, even lifesaving, in the event of a household repair emergency. Take the time to study this section *before* you need the important advice it contains.

The Repairs section—the heart of the book—is a comprehensive system for troubleshooting and repairing common, small problems in the average home that can detract from its appeal to a potential buyer. Pictured below are four sample pages from the chapter entitled Kitchen and Bathrooms, with captions describing the various features of the book and how they work. For example, if a ceramic tile in the kitchen or a bathroom is loose or cracked, the Troubleshooting Guide will direct you to page 59 for step-by-step directions on removing and replacing it. Or, if the toilet seat in a bathroom is loose or broken, you will be sent to page 59 for procedures to tighten or replace it.

Each job has been rated by degree of difficulty and by the average time it will take for a do-it-yourselfer to complete; keep in mind that this rating is only a suggestion. Before

Introductory text
Describes common problems found in a particular part of the house as well as what house inspectors and home buyers look for.

Illustration checklist
Provides a checklist of the features to inspect as well as hints on how to quickly enhance the appearance of your home before showing it.

KITCHEN AND BATHROOMS

The condition of your kitchen and bathrooms can make or break the sale of your home. While a kitchen and bathroom are exposed to more relentless use and daily abuse than any other room in the house, a potential buyer wants to see a kitchen and bathrooms that are clean, comfortable and efficient. Before you put your house on the market, inspect your kitchen and bathrooms thoroughly and fix flaws that the choosy buyer will be on the lookout for. Use the Troubleshooting Guide *(below)* and the checklist diagrams *(page 53)* to help identify common problems you might easily overlook; then, refer to the pages indicated to make the appropriate repairs.

Constant use, exposure to water and steam, repeated spot-cleaning and temperature fluctuations all take their toll on kitchen and bathroom surfaces. The first "fix" is therefore the most basic: a thorough cleaning—including sinks, bathtubs, countertops, cabinets, fixtures and appliances. A solution of mild household detergent and water can remove many stains from most surfaces; a stubborn stain or a special surface may require special treatment. Refer to the cleaning guide on page 54 for advice on making any surface shine. After cleaning, make all necessary surface repairs. Resecure any lifted laminate or edging tape on a counter *(page 57)*. Cover a scratch in an enamel, porcelain, wood or laminate surface and fill a nicked surface *(page 55)*; to ensure that the repair will not be visible, first test the color of any filler on an inconspicuous part of the surface.

A minor flaw in a kitchen or bathroom drawer or cabinet is common; a drawer or cabinet is exposed to temperature and humidity extremes as well as moisture, and may be opened and closed many times a day. Repair a sticking drawer so that it slides smoothly and repair a crooked cabinet door so that it hangs straight *(page 56)*. Clean door and drawer hardware; replace missing or damaged pieces.

In a bathroom, clean ceramic tile surfaces and the grouted joints between tiles. Replace a damaged ceramic tile and repair damaged grout *(page 58)*. Inspect the caulk between the wall and the bathtub; missing or damaged caulk is not only unsightly but can create leak problems. If necessary, recaulk any faulty joint *(page 57)*.

Some kitchen and bathroom furnishings may be worth replacing before you show the house. For example, a soiled or stained shower curtain can detract from a bathroom's appearance; consider replacing it with an inexpensive new one. Or, if a toilet seat is worn, replace it *(page 59)*.

TROUBLESHOOTING GUIDE

SYMPTOM	PROCEDURE
Plumbing fixture faulty	Service plumbing system *(p. 107)*
Electrical outlet, switch or lighting fixture faulty	Service electrical system *(p. 95)*
Wall or ceiling dirty, dingy or faded	Service walls and ceilings *(p. 38)*
Surface dirty or stained	Clean surface *(p. 54)* □○
Enamel-coated surface scratched or nicked	Repair enamel-coated surface *(p. 55)* □○
Porcelain surface scratched or nicked	Repair porcelain surface *(p. 55)* □○
Plastic laminate surface scratched or nicked	Repair plastic laminate surface *(p. 55)* □○
Wood surface scratched or nicked	Repair wood surface *(p. 55)* □○
Plastic laminate corner or edge lifted from countertop	Resecure plastic laminate *(p. 57)* □○
Drawer sticking or binding	Service drawer *(p. 56)* □○
Cabinet door loose or crooked	Service cabinet door *(p. 56)* ⬓○
Drawer or cabinet door hardware loose, damaged or missing	Tighten loose hardware; replace damaged or missing hardware
Caulk between bathtub and wall damaged or missing	Recaulk joint *(p. 57)* □○
Ceramic tile grout damaged or missing	Regrout ceramic tile joint *(p. 58)* □◒
Ceramic tile grout dirty or stained	Clean grout *(p. 54)* □○; seal grout *(p. 58)* □○
Ceramic tile damaged or missing	Replace ceramic tile *(p. 58)* ⬓◒
Bathtub anti-slip decal worn	Soften decal with mineral spirits, nail polish remover or lacquer thinner, then gently scrape from surface with a razor-blade tool; clean bathtub surface *(p. 54)* □○
Toilet seat loose or damaged	Service toilet seat *(p. 59)* □○

DEGREE OF DIFFICULTY: □ Easy ⬓ Moderate ■ Complex
ESTIMATED TIME: ○ Less than 1 hour ◒ 1 to 3 hours ● Over 3 hours
(Does not include drying time)

52

KITCHEN AND BATHROOMS

KITCHEN CHECKLIST
Clean windows *(page 74)*.
Open curtains and install high-wattage light bulbs to brighten room.
Service electrical outlets, switches and lighting fixtures *(page 95)*.
Clean or paint walls and ceilings *(page 38)*.
Clean appliances inside and outside *(page 54)*.
Organize and clean drawers; repair any sticking drawer *(page 56)*.
Polish fixtures and hardware *(page 54)*.
Clear and clean countertops; repair any scratch or nick *(page 55)*.
Organize and clean cupboards and cabinets; repair any loose or sticking door *(page 56)*.
Clean and polish floor *(page 60)*.

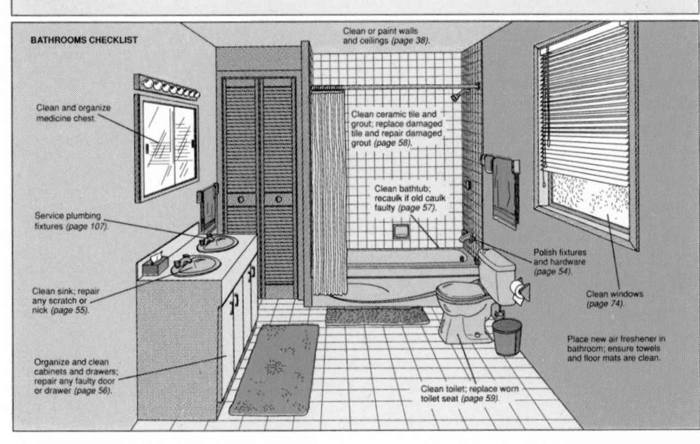

53

Degree of difficulty and time
Rate the complexity of each repair and how much time the job should take for a homeowner with average do-it-yourself skills.

Troubleshooting Guide
To use this chart, locate the symptom that most closely describes your problem and then follow the recommended procedures in the other column. Simple fixes may be explained on the chart; in most cases, you will be directed to an illustrated step-by-step procedure.

deciding whether you should attempt a repair, read all the instructions carefully. Then, be guided by your own confidence, and the tools and time available to you; for complex or time-consuming repairs, you may wish to seek professional help. Most repairs in *Fixing Your House To Sell* can be made with a basic set of screwdrivers, putty knives and readily-available cleaning supplies. For information on hand tools, power tools and rental tools, refer to Tools & Techniques *(page 126)*; if you are a novice at home repair, read this section before making any repairs.

Work logically and follow the safety precautions presented in each chapter. Wear safety goggles when working on a ceiling or when chipping ceramic tiles or cutting fiberglass insulation. Rubber gloves can protect your hands from caustic chemicals and cleaning solutions; heavy work gloves can prevent cuts and scratches from sharp materials. Exercise caution when using power tools or working on the roof. Do not mix together different types of cleaning solutions unless you are specifically instructed; safely store and dispose of leftover cleaning solutions and chemicals *(page 141)*.

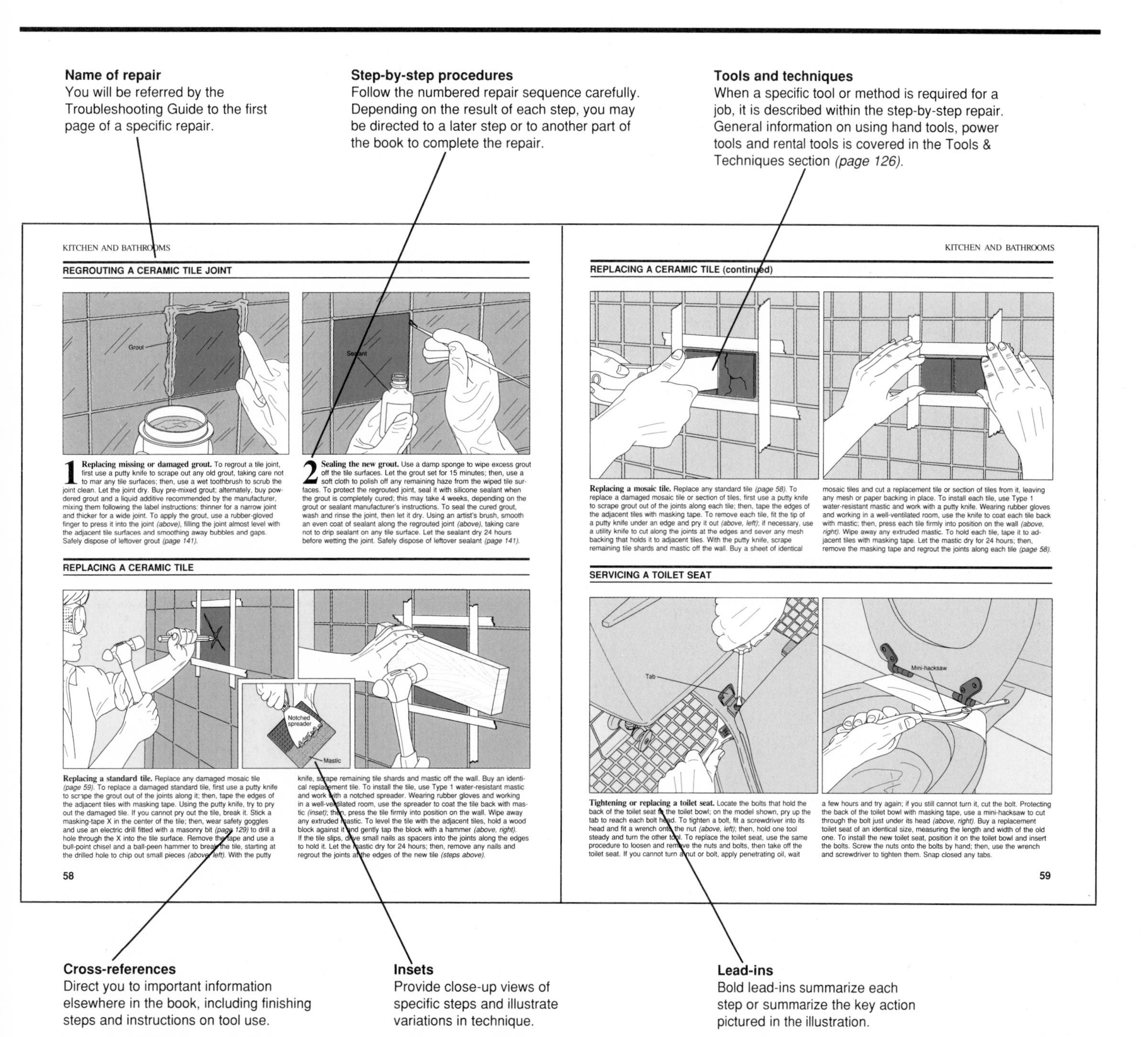

KITCHEN AND BATHROOMS

REGROUTING A CERAMIC TILE JOINT

1 Replacing missing or damaged grout. To regrout a tile joint, first use a putty knife to scrape out any old grout, taking care not to mar any tile surfaces; then, use a wet toothbrush to scrub the joint clean. Let the joint dry. Buy pre-mixed grout; alternately, buy powdered grout and a liquid additive recommended by the manufacturer, mixing them following the label instructions: thinner for a narrow joint and thicker for a wide joint. To apply the grout, use a rubber-gloved finger to press it into the joint *(above)*, filling the joint almost level with the adjacent tile surfaces and smoothing away bubbles and gaps. Safely dispose of leftover grout *(page 141)*.

2 Sealing the new grout. Use a damp sponge to wipe excess grout off the tile surfaces. Let the grout set for 15 minutes; then, use a soft cloth to polish off any remaining haze from the wiped tile surfaces. To protect the regrouted joint, seal it with silicone sealant when the grout is completely cured; this may take 4 weeks, depending on the grout or sealant manufacturer's instructions. To seal the cured grout, wash and rinse the joint, then let it dry. Using an artist's brush, smooth an even coat of sealant along the regrouted joint *(above)*, taking care not to drip sealant on any tile surface. Let the sealant dry 24 hours before wetting the joint. Safely dispose of leftover sealant *(page 141)*.

REPLACING A CERAMIC TILE

Replacing a standard tile. Replace any damaged mosaic tile *(page 59)*. To replace a damaged standard tile, first use a putty knife to scrape the grout out of the joints along it; then, tape the edges of the adjacent tiles with masking tape. Using the putty knife, try to pry out the damaged tile. If you cannot pry out the tile, break it. Stick a masking-tape X in the center of the tile; then, wear safety goggles and use an electric drill fitted with a masonry bit *(page 129)* to drill a hole through the X into the tile surface. Remove the tape and use a bull-point chisel and a ball-peen hammer to break the tile, starting at the drilled hole to chip out small pieces *(above, left)*. With the putty knife, scrape remaining tile shards and mastic off the wall. Buy an identical replacement tile. To install the tile, use Type 1 water-resistant mastic and work with a notched spreader. Wearing rubber gloves and working in a well-ventilated room, use the spreader to coat the tile back with mastic *(inset)*; then, press the tile firmly into position on the wall. Wipe away any extruded mastic. To level the tile with the adjacent tiles, hold a wood block against it and gently tap the block with a hammer *(above, right)*. If the tile slips, drive small nails as spacers into the joints along the edges to hold it. Let the mastic dry for 24 hours; then, remove any nails and regrout the joints at the edges of the new tile *(steps above)*.

58

KITCHEN AND BATHROOMS

REPLACING A CERAMIC TILE (continued)

Replacing a mosaic tile. Replace any standard tile *(page 58)*. To replace a damaged mosaic tile or section of tiles, first use a putty knife to scrape grout out of the joints along each tile; then, tape the edges of the adjacent tiles with masking tape. To remove each tile, fit the tip of a putty knife under an edge and pry it out *(above, left)*; if necessary, use a utility knife to cut along the joints at the edges and sever any mesh backing that holds it to adjacent tiles. With the putty knife, scrape remaining tile shards and mastic off the wall. Buy a sheet of identical mosaic tiles and cut a replacement tile or section of tiles from it, leaving any mesh or paper backing in place. To install each tile, use Type 1 water-resistant mastic and work with a putty knife. Wearing rubber gloves and working in a well-ventilated room, use the knife to coat each tile back with mastic; then, press each tile firmly into position on the wall *(above, right)*. Wipe away any extruded mastic. To hold each tile, tape it to adjacent tiles with masking tape. Let the mastic dry for 24 hours; then, remove the masking tape and regrout the joints along each tile *(page 58)*.

SERVICING A TOILET SEAT

Tightening or replacing a toilet seat. Locate the bolts that hold the back of the toilet seat to the toilet bowl; on the model shown, pry up the tab to reach each bolt head. To tighten a bolt, fit a screwdriver into its head and fit a wrench onto the nut *(above, left)*; then, hold one tool steady and turn the other tool. To replace the toilet seat, use the same procedure to loosen and remove the nuts and bolts, then take off the toilet seat. If you cannot turn a nut or bolt, apply penetrating oil, wait a few hours and try again; if you still cannot turn it, cut the bolt. Protecting the back of the toilet bowl with masking tape, use a mini-hacksaw to cut through the bolt just under its head *(above, right)*. Buy a replacement toilet seat of an identical size, measuring the length and width of the old one. To install the new toilet seat, position it on the toilet bowl and insert the bolts. Screw the nuts onto the bolts by hand; then, use the wrench and screwdriver to tighten them. Snap closed any tabs.

59

EMERGENCY GUIDE

Preventing problems when fixing your house to sell. Fixing your house to sell is not dangerous; with safe work habits, an emergency situation is unlikely to arise. Accidents, however, can befall even the most careful of workers. Prepare yourself to handle an emergency by reading the instructions in this chapter thoroughly *before* you need them. The list of safety tips at right covers basic guidelines for performing the repairs in this book. The Troubleshooting Guide on page 9 puts emergency procedures at your fingertips; it provides quick-action steps to take and refers you to pages 10 through 13 for detailed instructions.

Take the time to set up properly for a repair, assembling the tools, equipment and materials you need; wear appropriate clothing and use any safety gear recommended. Always work methodically; never rush through a job. Read Tools & Techniques *(page 126)* for valuable information on the proper use of tools indoors and outdoors, as well as on using ladders and working on the roof. Keep on hand a well-equipped first-aid kit; stock it with mild antiseptic, sterile gauze dressings and bandages, adhesive tape and bandages, scissors, tweezers, and a packet of needles. Also keep on hand a fire extinguisher rated ABC; know how to use it *(page 11)*.

Familiarize yourself with the utilities of your home, knowing where and how to shut off the electricity, the water supply and the gas supply *(page 10)*; in the event of an electrical, water or gas emergency, you will need to respond quickly. Keep in mind the potential dangers of any substance you use. Sharp tools can cut skin and rough materials can cause splinters. Many cleaners and solvents, glues, adhesives and patching compounds, and finishing products contain chemicals that can burn skin and eyes, and emit toxic vapors that can cause dizziness, faintness and nausea; work carefully with them, always following the manufacturer's instructions. When disposing of any substance, keep in mind its possible impact on the environment; see page 141 for information on the safe disposal of hazardous substances and consult your local fire department or environmental protection agency for specific regulations in your community.

When you are in doubt about your ability to handle an emergency, do not hesitate to call for help. Post the telephone numbers for your local fire department, hospital emergency room and poison control center as well as your physician near the telephone; in most areas, dial 911 in the event of a life-threatening emergency. Also seek technical help when you need it. If you are ever uncertain about the nature or safety of a repair, consult a qualified professional; even in a non-emergency situation, a building inspector in your community can answer questions about the condition of your home.

SAFETY TIPS

1. Before attempting any repair in this book, read the entire procedure; familiarize yourself with specific safety information.

2. Ensure that you know where and how to shut off your home's electricity, water supply and gas supply *(page 10)*.

3. Wear the proper safety gear for the job: safety goggles to protect your eyes from flying particles or chemical splashes; rubber gloves to protect your hands from chemical products; work gloves to protect your hands from sharp materials.

4. Keep a first-aid kit on hand; stock it with mild antiseptic, sterile gauze dressings and bandages, adhesive tape and bandages, scissors, tweezers and a packet of needles.

5. When working with flammable chemicals or power tools, have a fire extinguisher rated ABC nearby; be prepared to use it if necessary *(page 11)*.

6. Keep children and pets away from your work area.

7. When you are using any product that emits hazardous fumes or vapors, ensure that the work area is well ventilated. Do not smoke while using any flammable product.

8. Carefully read the label on any cleaner, solvent, glue, adhesive, patching compound or finishing product you use. Follow the manufacturer's instructions to the letter, paying special attention to any hazard warnings and storage information.

9. Hang rags soaked with a chemical product outdoors to dry or seal them in airtight metal or glass containers. Dispose of and store chemical products safely *(page 141)*.

10. Do not pour chemical products down a house drain or into a septic system. When disposing of leftover chemical products or empty chemical containers, put them out for pick-up on designated Household Hazardous Waste Clean-up Days. (Call your local department of public works for specific information.) Should the service not exist in your community, package the products separately and seal the containers securely before putting them out for regular trash collection.

11. Follow basic safety rules for working on ladders *(page 137)* and on the roof *(page 138)*. Work with a helper or within earshot of someone else and only in good weather conditions—never when it is wet or windy. Do not attempt any repair on a roof if it is wet or laden with snow or ice.

12. When working outdoors with power tools, use only heavy-duty, three-prong extension cords rated for outdoor use. Inspect the extension cord closely before each use; if it is damaged, replace it. To secure the connection of the power tool, loop its power cord loosely together with the extension cord before plugging it in.

13. Do not use power tools in damp or wet conditions. Plug a power tool only into an outlet protected by a GFCI (ground-fault circuit interrupter) and never cut off or bypass the third, or grounding, prong on the plug of its power cord; a power tool with a two-prong plug must be labeled "double insulated".

14. Take periodic breaks from your work to rest and inspect what you have done. Never undertake repairs when you are tired. When thirsty, drink a non-alcoholic beverage. Wear a hat when working outdoors in hot, sunny weather.

15. Post the telephone numbers of your local fire department, hospital emergency room and poison control center as well as your physician near the telephone.

TROUBLESHOOTING GUIDE

SYMPTOM	PROCEDURE
Electrical fire: flames or smoke from power tool or outlet	Have someone call fire department immediately
	If fire not small and contained or if flames or smoke coming from wall or ceiling, leave house immediately and call fire department from home of neighbor
	Control fire using ABC fire extinguisher *(p. 11)*
	Shut off electrical power *(p. 10)*
Chemical fire: flames or smoke from cleaning, finishing or other chemical product	Have someone call fire department immediately
	If fire not small and contained or if flames or smoke coming from wall or ceiling, leave house immediately and call fire department from home of neighbor
	Control fire using ABC fire extinguisher *(p. 11)*
Electrical shock	If victim immobilized by live current, knock him free of source using wooden implement *(p. 11)*
	Have someone call for medical help immediately
	If victim not breathing, administer artificial respiration; if victim has no pulse, administer cardiopulmonary resuscitation (CPR) only if qualified
	If victim breathing and has pulse, and has no back or neck injury, place in recovery position *(p. 11)*
Power tool, extension cord or outlet sparks, shocks or hot to touch	Shut off electrical power *(p. 10)*
	Locate and repair cause of problem before using power tool, extension cord or outlet again
Fall from roof or ladder	Have someone call for medical help immediately
	Treat victim of fall *(p. 12)*; **Caution:** Do not move victim
Head injury	Have someone call for medical help immediately
	If victim not breathing, administer artificial respiration; if victim has no pulse, administer cardiopulmonary resuscitation (CPR) only if qualified
	If victim breathing and has pulse, and has no back or neck injury, place in recovery position *(p. 11)*
Dizziness, faintness, nausea or blurred vision	If indoors, leave work area immediately and get fresh air *(p. 12)*
	If outdoors, lie down in shade with feet elevated; apply cool, wet cloth to forehead and drink non-alcoholic beverages
	If symptoms persist, seek medical attention
Large object embedded under skin	Support object in place with loose bandages and seek medical help immediately; **Caution:** Removing object can cause hemorrhage
Splinter	Use sterilized needle and tweezers to open wound and pull out splinter *(p. 12)*
	If splinter lodged deeply or if wound becomes infected, seek medical attention
Skin scratch or puncture from rusted metal	Wash wound using soap and water; seek medical attention concerning need for tetanus shot
Cut or minor wound	Apply pressure to stop bleeding *(p. 12)*
	If bleeding persists or if wound is deep, seek medical attention
Bruise	Apply ice pack immediately to reduce swelling
	If pain does not diminish or swelling persists, seek medical attention
Particle or chemical product in eye	Flush eye with water *(p. 12)* and seek medical help immediately; **Caution:** Do not rub eye
Burn	If burn severe, seek medical help immediately
	If burn not severe, flush with gentle flow of cool water, then cover lightly with clean cloth soaked in water; **Caution:** Do not apply antiseptic spray or ointment, butter, oil, baking soda or alcohol
Chemical product on skin	Wash skin thoroughly with soap and water; refer to product label for additional instructions
	If skin irritation develops, seek medical attention and take product with you
Chemical product swallowed	Call local poison control center; follow emergency instructions on product label and take product with you to hospital
Chemical product spilled	Clean up chemical spill *(p. 13)*
Water supply pipe or plumbing fixture leaking	Shut off water supply *(p. 10)*
Gas supply pipe or fixture leaking; odor of rotten eggs detected	Shut off gas supply *(p. 10)*; leave house immediately and call fire department from home of neighbor

SHUTTING OFF ELECTRICAL POWER

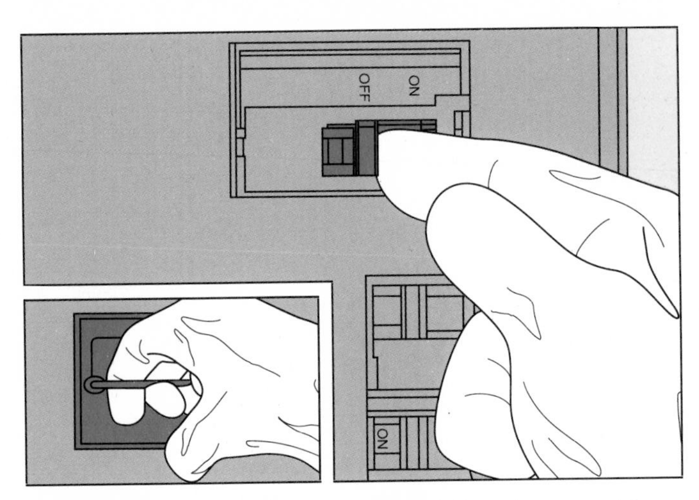

Shutting off power at the service panel. If the floor around the service panel is wet, stand on a dry board or a rubber mat or wear rubber boots. Wear heavy, dry rubber gloves and use only one hand; keep your other hand in your pocket or behind your back. At a circuit breaker panel, flip off the main breaker *(above)*—as an added precaution, use your knuckle; any shock will then jerk your hand away from the panel. At a fuse panel, remove the main fuse block by gripping its metal handle and pulling it out of the box *(inset)*. On a panel with more than one fuse block, remove them all. If the panel has a shutoff lever, shift it to OFF to turn off power.

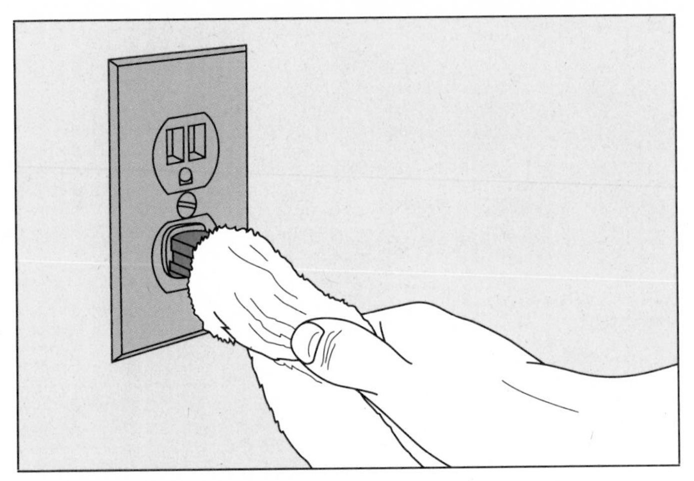

Pulling the power cord plug from the wall outlet. If the floor around the wall outlet is wet, or if the wall outlet itself is sparking or burning, do not touch the power cord or the electrical tool; instead, shut off power at the service panel *(step left)*. Otherwise, protect your hand with a thick, dry towel or a heavy work glove. Without touching the wall outlet or the electrical tool, grasp the power cord several inches from the plug and pull the plug out of the wall outlet *(above)*. Locate and repair the problem before using the wall outlet or the electrical tool again.

SHUTTING OFF THE WATER AND GAS SUPPLY

Shutting off the water supply. If water is leaking from a plumbing fixture, close its shutoff valve *(inset)*. If water is leaking from an undetermined source, turn off the water supply at the main shutoff valve *(above)*, usually located near the water meter or where the main water supply pipe enters the house. If your water supply is provided by a well, look for the main shutoff valve on the main water supply pipe near the pressure gauge or pump.

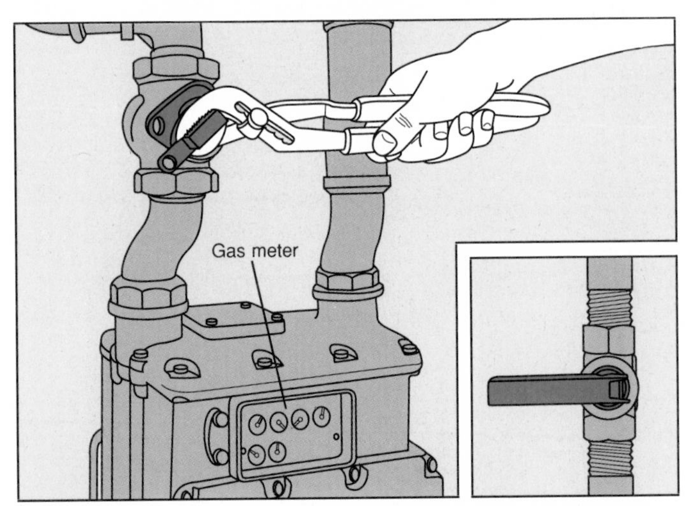

Shutting off the gas supply. The main shutoff valve is located on the main gas supply pipe for the house at the gas meter, usually in the basement. Use an adjustable wrench to shut off the gas supply, turning the valve handle *(above)* until it is perpendicular to the supply pipe. To shut off the gas at the boiler or furnace, grip the valve handle on the supply pipe leading to the unit and turn it until it is perpendicular to the supply pipe *(inset)*.

EXTINGUISHING A FIRE

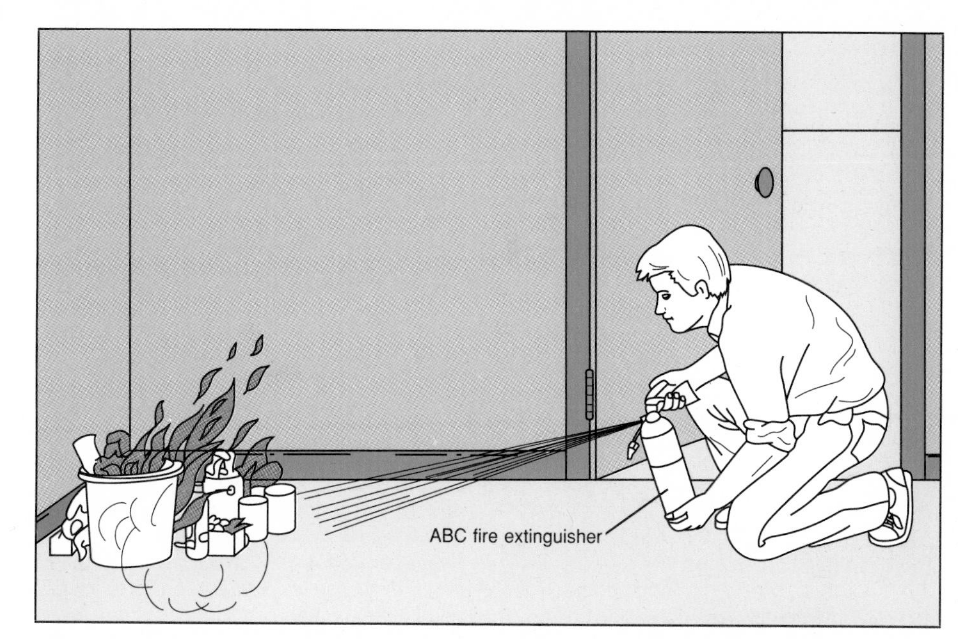

Fighting a fire. Call the fire department immediately. If the fire is inside the chimney or flames or smoke come from the walls or ceiling, evacuate the house; go to a neighbor's home to call for help. To extinguish a small fire in paints or solvents, in a power tool or outlet, or in furnishings near a fireplace, use a dry-chemical fire extinguisher rated ABC. Note the nearest exit and position yourself 6 to 10 feet from the fire. Holding the extinguisher upright, pull the lock pin out of the handle and aim the nozzle at the base of the flames. Squeeze the handle and spray in a quick side-to-side motion *(left)* until the fire is completely out. Watch for "flashback," or rekindling, and be prepared to spray again. If the fire spreads, leave the house. Dispose of any burned waste by following the advice of your local fire department. Have your extinguisher recharged professionally after every use or replace it if it is non-rechargeable.

RESCUING AND TREATING A VICTIM OF ELECTRICAL SHOCK

Freeing someone from a live current. Usually a person who contacts live current is thrown back from the source, but sometimes muscles contract involuntarily around a power tool or its cord. Do not touch the victim or the tool. Immediately stop the flow of electricity, shutting off power at the main service panel or unplugging the tool *(page 10)*. If the power cannot be cut immediately, use a wooden broom handle, a board or another non-conducting object to knock the victim free of the electrical source *(above)*.

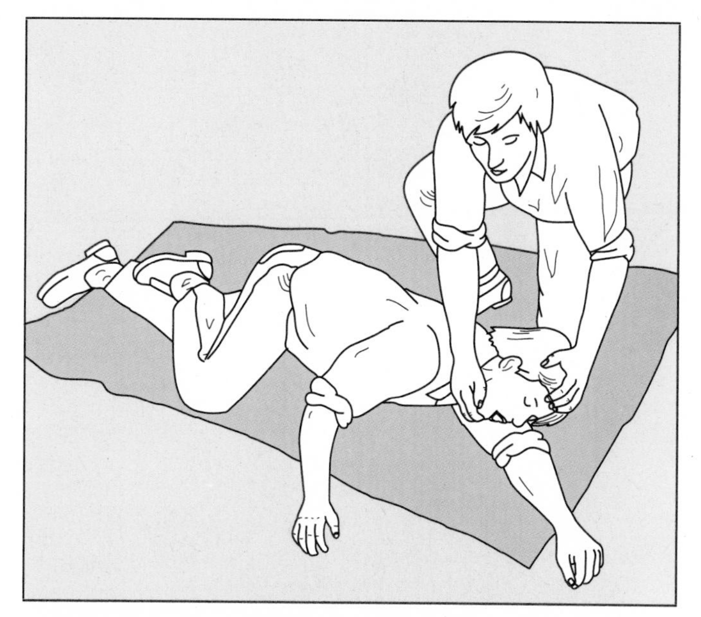

Handling a victim of electrical shock. Call for medical help immediately. Check the victim's breathing and pulse. If there is no breathing, give mouth-to-mouth resuscitation; if there is no pulse, give cardiopulmonary resuscitation (CPR) only if you are qualified. If the victim is breathing and has no neck or back injuries, place him in the recovery position *(above)*. Tilt the head back with the face to one side and the tongue forward to maintain an open airway. Keep the victim calm until help arrives.

PROVIDING FIRST AID

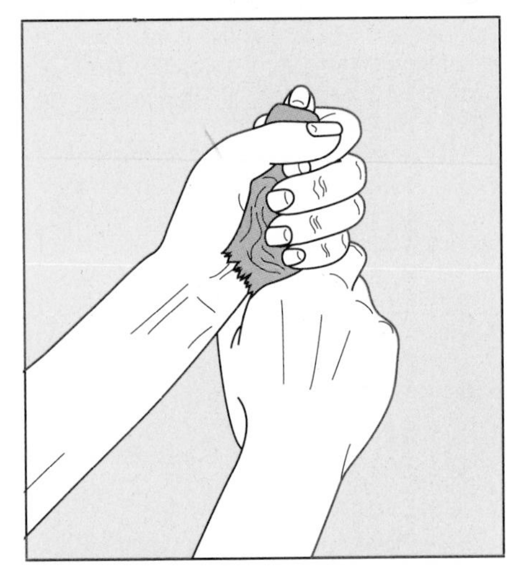

Treating a cut. To stop the bleeding, wrap a clean cloth around the wound and apply direct pressure with your hand, elevating the limb *(above)*. If the cloth becomes blood-soaked, add a second cloth over the first one. Continue applying pressure and elevating the limb until the bleeding stops. Wash the wound with soap and water, then bandage it. Seek medical attention if bleeding persists or the wound is deep.

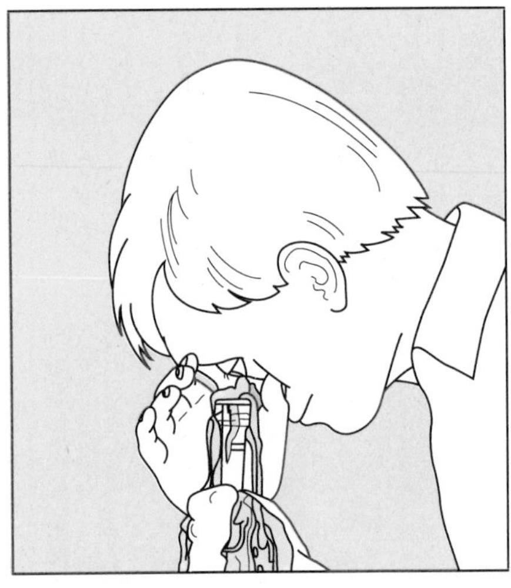

Flushing particles or chemicals from the eye. Immediately hold the eyelids apart and position the injured eye under a steady, gentle flow of cool water from a garden hose *(above)* or faucet. **Caution:** Remove any nozzle from the garden hose to prevent an eye injury from a strong jet of water. Flush the eye for 10 minutes, then cover it with a sterile gauze bandage and seek medical attention.

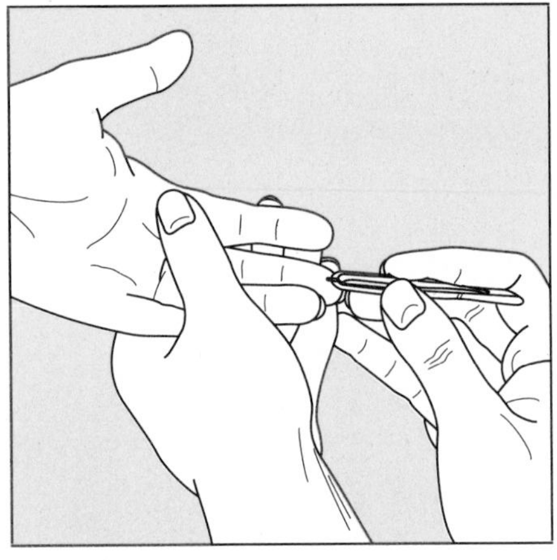

Treating a splinter. Wash your hands and the area around the wound with soap and water. A metal splinter may require treatment for tetanus; seek medical attention. For other splinters, use the point of a needle that is sterilized in a flame or with alcohol to loosen the splinter; pry it up until it can be pulled out with tweezers *(above)*. Wash the area again with soap and water to prevent infection, then bandage it. If the splinter is lodged too deeply for removal, seek medical attention.

Treating dizziness or faintness. At the first sign of dizziness, faintness, fatigue or nausea, leave the work area and get fresh air; if you are outdoors, move to the shade. Loosen your clothing at the waist, chest and neck; if you feel faint, sit with your head lowered between your knees *(above)*. Before continuing work indoors, have someone ventilate the work area and close all containers; before continuing work outdoors, drink a cool, non-alcoholic beverage. If the symptoms persist, seek medical attention.

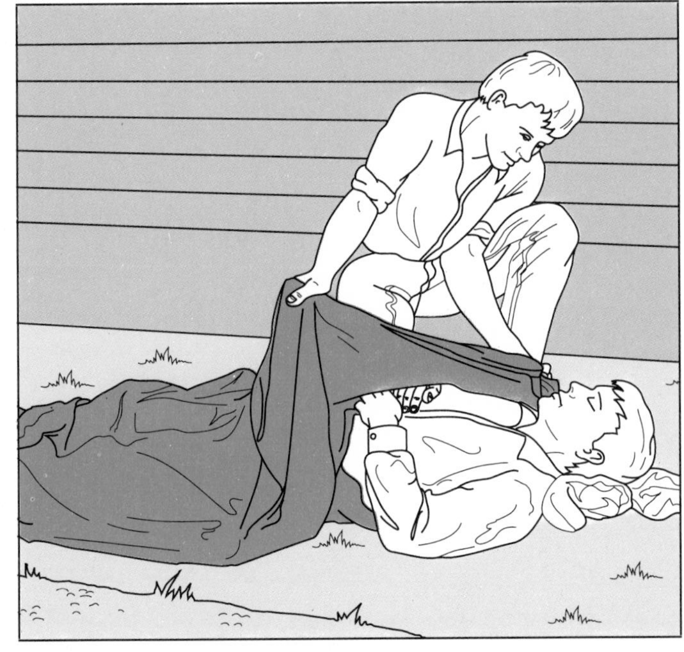

Treating the victim of a fall. Have someone call for medical help immediately. **Caution:** Do not move the victim until qualified medical help arrives, especially if there is pain in the areas of the neck or back, or if clear spinal fluid can be seen flowing from the ears or nose. Cover the victim to help regulate body temperature in case of shock *(above)*. Help the victim to stay calm and keep others from crowding around. When qualified medical help arrives, make sure that they are advised of possible spinal cord injury.

CLEANING UP A CHEMICAL SPILL

1 Soaking up the spill. If the spill is more than 1 quart of a product that is flammable or more than 1 gallon of a product that emits toxic fumes, leave the work area and call the fire department. Otherwise, work quickly to clean up the spill. Open windows and doors to the outdoors and turn on fans to increase air circulation. If the spill is small, use a clean rag dipped in the appropriate solvent *(chart below)* to wipe it up. Otherwise, pour a generous amount of cat litter on the spill *(above)* and wait until it is absorbed. Use an old putty knife or dustpan to scoop the saturated cat litter into a metal container.

2 Cleaning up the spill area. To clean up any remaining traces of the spill, choose an appropriate solvent *(chart below)* and apply it with a clean rag or a scrub brush; wear rubber gloves and safety goggles. Wash the spill area with a solution of household detergent and warm water, scrubbing with an old broom *(above)*. Then, rinse the area thoroughly and wipe it dry with clean rags. To dispose of the waste materials, place them in an airtight metal container, then call your local fire department or environmental protection agency for the regulations on the safe disposal of hazardous materials in your community.

MATERIAL SPILLED	CLEANING SOLVENT REQUIRED
Paint or stain	For water-based type, use a solution of household detergent and water
	For oil-based type, use mineral spirits or turpentine, then a solution of household detergent and water
Urethane or polyurethane	Use mineral spirits or turpentine, then a solution of household detergent and water
Varnish	Use mineral spirits or turpentine, then a solution of household detergent and water
Shellac	Use denatured alcohol
Linseed or tung oil	Use mineral spirits or turpentine, then a solution of household detergent and water
Contact cement	For water-based type, use a solution of household detergent and water
	For non-flammable solvent-based type, use contact cement cleaner or thinner or 1,1,1 trichloroethane
	For flammable solvent-based type, use contact cement cleaner or thinner or acetone
Wood glue, carpet glue or vinyl floor adhesive	If glue or adhesive has not set, use a solution of household detergent and water
	If glue or adhesive has set, soak it with mineral spirits for about 20 minutes, then scrape it off
Epoxy glue	If glue has not set, use denatured alcohol or acetone
	If glue has set, soak it with denatured alcohol or acetone for about 20 minutes, then scrape it off
Wood floor wax	Use mineral spirits
Muriatic acid	Use water
Wallcovering remover	Use water
Plastic laminate filler	If filler has not set, use acetone
	If filler has set, soak it with acetone for about 20 minutes, then scrape it off
Machine or motor oil	Use mineral spirits, then a solution of household detergent and water

SELLING YOUR HOME

There can be many reasons for selling your home—a change of job, a growing family or investment needs. Whatever your reason is for selling your home, a variety of small repairs and general cleaning tasks can make the house easier to sell—at the price you ask. Real estate professionals from realtors to appraisers and inspectors cite two factors as most often determining whether a buyer stops his search for a home at a particular house or walks off to continue house-hunting: a realistic asking price and the cleanliness of the home.

From the moment a prospective buyer drives up to the door, your house is on display. Take the time before you put your house on the market to give it a thorough cleaning and inspection—inside and outdoors. Make the easy repairs and catch up on the regular maintenance that you have put off. Minor irritants you can overlook or comfortably ignore while living in the house are likely to stand out as detracting focal points to a potential buyer. Fix the minor problems; however, do not attempt to disguise any major problem.

Use the illustration at right as a guide to the areas and systems of your home important to its sale, then refer to the specific chapters indicated. Each chapter pinpoints common problems, and directs you through basic cleaning and repair jobs. Taking care of these tasks can increase the likelihood of your house selling quickly at your original selling price. The longer a house is listed on the market, the less chance there is that it will sell at the asking price.

Make use of real estate professionals to ease the business of selling your home. The first step for many vendors is contacting an inspector who can examine the entire house, determining its condition and offering advice on the repairs it needs. An appraiser can help you set a fair asking price by evaluating your property in relation to comparable properties in the neighborhood. Although many vendors choose to sell their homes by themselves, saving the commission of an agent, most vendors opt for employing an agent.

If you decide to become a FIZZBO (coined from the "For Sale by Owner" yard signs), be aware of the responsibilities entailed. Refer to page 16 for information on when and how to obtain the services of qualified real estate professionals. Before signing contracts with a real estate agent, appraiser or inspector, consult a lawyer specializing in real estate transactions. Selling your home is a legal matter; refer to page 17 for information on the legal responsibilities and liability of the vendor.

Just as a few weekend projects can take care of small problems, small touches when showing your house can convince prospective buyers that this is the home they would like to live in. The tips on page 17 will help you show your house at its best, and help you deal efficiently and pleasantly with potential buyers. Remember that any effort you make in repairing, cleaning and showing your home is likely to be returned in a fast sale at a favorable price.

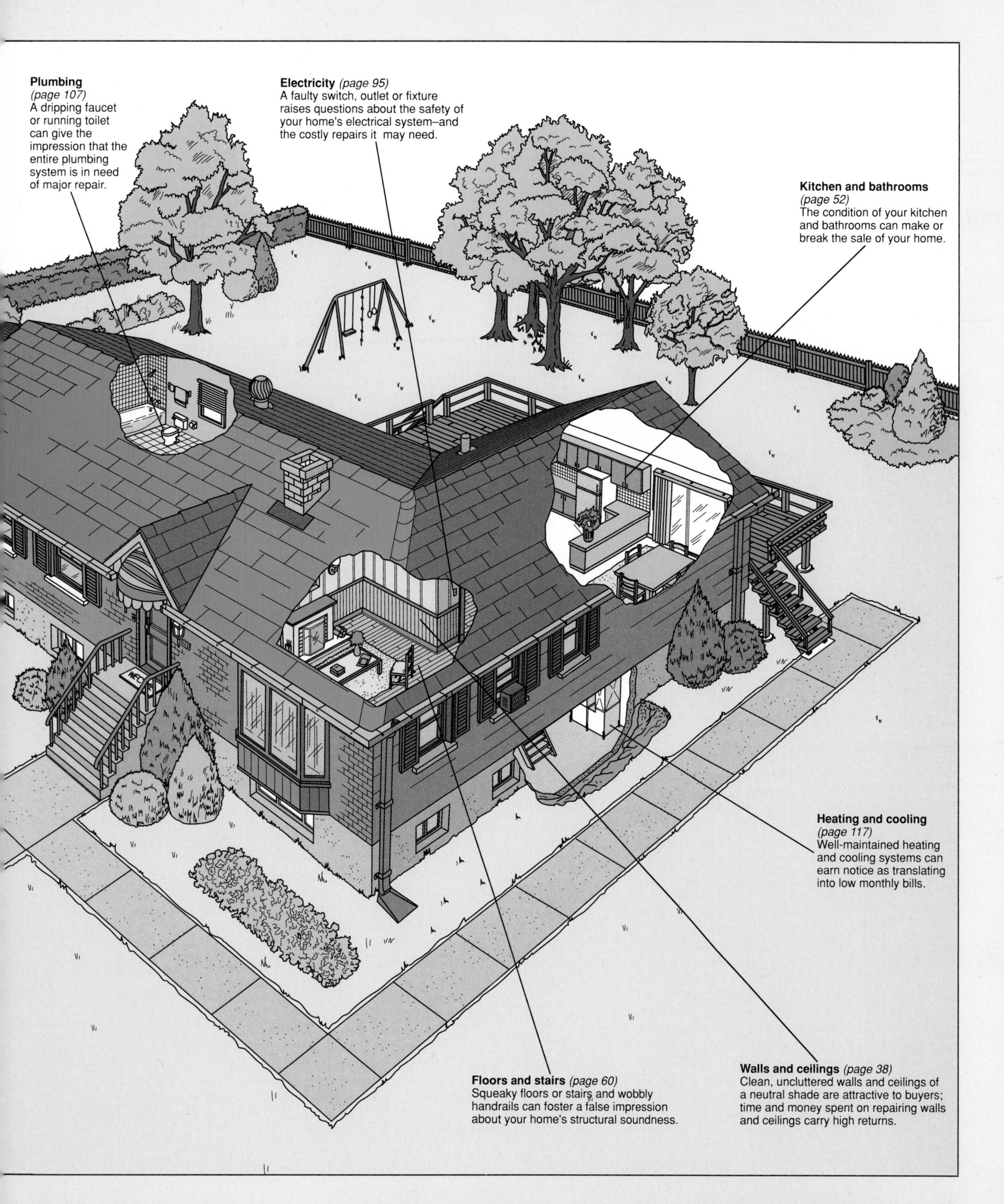
Plumbing
(page 107)
A dripping faucet or running toilet can give the impression that the entire plumbing system is in need of major repair.
Electricity *(page 95)*
A faulty switch, outlet or fixture raises questions about the safety of your home's electrical system–and the costly repairs it may need.
Kitchen and bathrooms
(page 52)
The condition of your kitchen and bathrooms can make or break the sale of your home.
Heating and cooling
(page 117)
Well-maintained heating and cooling systems can earn notice as translating into low monthly bills.
Floors and stairs *(page 60)*
Squeaky floors or stairs and wobbly handrails can foster a false impression about your home's structural soundness.
Walls and ceilings *(page 38)*
Clean, uncluttered walls and ceilings of a neutral shade are attractive to buyers; time and money spent on repairing walls and ceilings carry high returns.

PREPARING TO MAKE A SUCCESSFUL SALE

Having the house inspected. Any defect in your house, whether large or small, can affect its marketability. If you are selling an older house, have made major repairs, or suspect a defect, have your home evaluated by a house inspector. A good house inspector can help identify major defects and pinpoint minor problems that might affect the sale of the house. A thorough house inspection covers both the house exterior and interior, from the basement floor to the roof ridge, including the electrical, plumbing, and heating and cooling systems.

To find a reputable house inspector, ask a friend or neighbor who has recently bought or sold property. Alternately, consult a local realtor, a mortgage company or your local consumer affairs office for a recommended house inspector. Ensure that your house inspector is listed with a national- or state-level professional house-inspection organization. Before you hire a house inspector, find out what kind of documentation and guarantee is provided; in general, choose a house inspector who will provide you with a full written report of the inspection and is willing to guarantee the report in the event of a future problem.

If you suspect or you are informed by a house inspector that there is a major structural defect in your home, hire a professional engineer to evaluate it and document the inspection results. If at any time you have had a pest infestation in the house, ask a house inspector or a real estate agent about your legal obligations; some states have laws that require a seller to obtain a certificate of non-infestation within 30 days of a property transfer.

Having the house appraised. A fair asking price is one of the most important factors in ensuring a prompt house sale; and a quick sale saves you time and money. With careful initial pricing, you can avoid the protracted negotiations involved in later lowering your asking price. Never use your local tax assessment appraisal as the basis for setting your asking price; it often bears little relation to the market value of the house. Instead, hire a good appraiser who can help you determine the best asking price for your home. Have your house appraised before you approach a real estate agent and before you deal with potential buyers; dealing with an agent or a buyer is easier if you are confident about your asking price and can back it up with a certified appraisal report. By having your own appraisal done, a potential buyer or the buyer's mortgage company or bank is less likely to hire an appraiser and your initial asking price is more likely to stand.

To find a reputable appraiser, ask the local branch of a national or regional residential real-estate appraisal organization. Although appraisers have no legal qualifications and are not formally certified, many appraisal organizations have clear standards covering professional ethics, required training and work experience, and peer review. Hire an appraiser who is a member of a national or regional organization; ask about the organization's standards. Find an appraiser who works for a flat fee—not a percentage of the final appraised value, which can lead to an inflated appraisal and an asking price that is unrealistically high. Choose an appraiser who will provide a full written report, backed by data gathered through careful research on your local real estate market; some appraisers guarantee their reports. Finally, get a copy of the appraisal report; have the appraiser explain it to you carefully and correct any misrepresentations or omissions.

Having the house sold. If you have the time, the interest and the energy, consider selling your house yourself; while there can be much work involved, you will eliminate the need to hire and pay a real estate agent. For information and advice about selling your house yourself, ask the local real estate board to recommend a good real estate consultant. A good consultant can guide you through the selling process; the fee of a consultant is negotiable, but is usually about two percent of the house selling price—compared to the six or seven percent fee of a real estate agent.

To sell a house yourself, you will need to have the house inspected and appraised. Your job will include the handling of newspaper and word-of-mouth advertising, the screening of prospective buyers by checking their references thoroughly, as well as the arranging and managing of visits and open houses. You also will need to consult a lawyer who specializes in real estate transactions to obtain information and papers for the legal work involved.

If you fail to sell your own house after two months or if you prefer to avoid the work involved in selling your house yourself, hire a good real estate agent to sell the house for you. A good real estate agent will list the house, promote it, screen buyers, arrange showings and open houses, and organize all the paperwork up to and including the sale closing. While a real estate agent cannot handle any legal matters involved in the sale of the house, a good agent will advise you on when, how and where to obtain the services of a lawyer who specializes in real estate transactions. Some agents will also help you obtain a home warranty or the services of a house inspector. An agent's fee for these services is usually six or seven percent of the house selling price, but this may vary and is often negotiable.

To find a reputable real estate agent, ask a friend or neighbor who has recently bought or sold property. Then, shop around, comparing the services, experience and fees of different agents. A qualified real estate agent must be licensed by a state authority and may be certified by a state or national association. Ask the agent about his certification and qualifications; if he works for a brokerage company, ask the company about the qualifications it requires of its agents. Also ask the agent and the company about their experience in selling homes in your area. A good agent or company will happily disclose this information.

Evaluate a potential agent's knowledge of your neighborhood. A good agent should be able to sell your neighborhood, as well as your house. Ensure that the agent knows about local health and community services, shopping facilities, schools, and recreational programs. A good agent should also be able to provide you with tips on how to get your home into the best possible shape for showing to prospective buyers.

Determining your liability for a house defect. While no house is ever in perfect condition, concealing a serious defect when you sell a house can mean a lawsuit. Long after the sale of your house, you or your real estate agent can be held liable by the buyer for a house defect that was concealed by one of you, or that could have been discovered by one of you had you taken reasonable care to look for it. The liability of a house seller or agent is determined by state law; while past law proclaimed that it was the buyer who had to beware *(caveat emptor),* state law now often holds the seller or agent responsible for the sale of a defective house—whether the defect was known or unknown to the seller or agent.

Disputes among sellers, buyers and their agents typically involve a defective roof, basement or foundation, or plumbing system; pest infestation and inaccurate property documentation are other common causes of legal action. If you make a major structural repair or you suspect structural damage, have the house evaluated by a professional engineer. If there is a defect or if you correct one, tell your agent and make a note of the conversation; it is then your agent's responsibility to inform the house buyer. If you are selling the house yourself, it is your responsibility to inform the buyer. If you are in doubt about your legal obligations, consult a lawyer who specializes in real estate transactions.

Showing the house. Once you have fixed your house to sell and made your arrangements with inspectors, appraisers and real estate agents, it is time for you or your agent to show the house to prospective buyers. Use the tips below to help prepare for and conduct a successful sales visit. The tidiness of the house, the behavior of you and other family members, and your ability to provide quick, pleasant answers to a prospective buyer's questions can make a strong impression on anyone visiting—and can mean the difference between a visitor who takes one look and leaves, and one who wants the house.

1. Make sure the house is clean and tidy before a sales vist; consult the checklist diagrams in each chapter of this book for specific tips.

2. Avoid sales visits when you are entertaining your own guests or when you are busy—a prospective buyer should have your complete attention.

3. Ensure that an open house is planned for an opportune time, such as a holiday weekend, and that it will not conflict with a major event such as a televised sport competition.

4. Let the real estate agent show the house even if you are not at home; a hard-to-see house is a hard-to-sell house.

5. Determine in advance which household items and fixtures are to be included in the sale price and which are not; for an item not included, but which you are willing to sell, have a price for it in mind should a prospective buyer express an interest in it.

6. Add a few decorator touches before a sales visit—fresh flowers, pleasant aromas from the kitchen, an attractive furniture arrangement or a special lighting effect might help make the sale.

7. For a sales visit during the cold, winter months, light a fire in the fireplace, if you have one, to brighten and warm the house.

8. During a daytime sales visit, open drapes and curtains to make the house bright and cheerful; at night, turn on bright lights.

9. Eliminate distracting noise during a sales visit by turning off any running televisions, radios, stereos and unnecessary appliances.

10. Keep pets out of the way during a sales visit; they can be distracting and troublesome.

11. Let the real estate agent do the selling when you are home during a sales visit. Be prepared to answer questions, but be brief.

12. During a sales visit, have copies of recent utility bills and property tax assessments handy for quick reference if an interested buyer asks for information about house expenses.

13. During a sales visit, keep handy a neighborhood map, a copy of the community newspaper, and any information on local services and organizations about which an interested prospective buyer might have questions.

14. If a prospective buyer wants to discuss the house sale at length during a visit, choose a comfortable area to sit, and provide refreshments.

15. Have on hand a small information packet on the house for an interested prospective buyer to take after a visit; include a recent photograph of the house and a floor plan, scaled to size.

GROUNDS AND EXTERIOR

The condition of your home's grounds and the house exterior makes an immediate, strong impression on a prospective house buyer. The moment a buyer drives up to the house, he or she forms an opinion about your home. This all-important first impression, created by what realtors call the "curb appeal" of your home, can mean the difference between a buyer eager to see the rest of the house and one who will not even bother to visit. Nothing will create a negative impression more quickly than rot or mildew on an exterior house wall, or an overgrown and unkempt lawn. Before putting the house up for sale, take time to carefully inspect the grounds and exterior. Use the Troubleshooting Guide *(page 20)* and checklist diagram *(right)* to help identify easy-to-overlook damage that a buyer will be on the lookout for; then, refer to the pages indicated to make the needed repair.

Start with the yard. Keep the lawn watered and mowed; in the autumn, rake up leaves. Trim an overgrown lawn edge or hedge *(page 22)* and prune damaged or unruly branches from shrubs and trees *(page 23)*. Pull out the weeds from your gardens *(page 22)* and walkways *(page 24)*. Check your fencing; replace any damaged fence board *(page 31)* and reinforce a leaning post or sagging gate *(page 32)*.

Inspect the asphalt or masonry surfaces of the driveway, walkways, steps and patio. Clean any dirty or stained surface *(page 24)*. Fill any cracks or potholes in asphalt *(page 27)*, and repair any cracks, chips or crumbled edges on concrete surfaces *(page 25)*. In warm weather, keep the driveway and walkways swept clean of debris; in the winter, clear them of snow and ice.

If an exterior house wall is dirty or dingy, consider cleaning it with a pressure washer *(page 29)* or painting it with an airless sprayer *(page 37)*. While these are time-consuming and somewhat costly jobs, they can make a house look like new. Pay close attention to exterior wood surfaces such as siding and trim, as well as deck and porch floors, stairs and railings. If wood is dirty or stained, clean it *(page 28)*. Check wood for signs of rot and insect damage, and repair minor damage *(page 29)*; for major damage, call a professional. If paint or finish on wood is faded, apply a new coat *(page 36)*.

Check the condition of gutters and downspouts. If a gutter or downspout is clogged with leaves or debris and drains poorly, clean it *(page 33)*. Resecure a sagging gutter *(page 33)* or a loose downspout *(page 34)*. Inspect the roofing on the house. Working on a ladder or using a pair of binoculars, check the condition of asphalt shingles and flashings. Seal open flashing joints *(page 34)* and patch holes in flashing *(page 35)*; repair torn or lifted asphalt shingles *(page 35)*.

Most grounds and exterior repairs can be made with basic gardening tools and workshop tools such as a hammer, a screwdriver, a putty knife and a caulking gun; rent special tools such as a pressure washer or airless sprayer at a tool rental center. Refer to Tools & Techniques *(page 126)* for advice on using any tools required and for directions on safely working on ladders *(page 137)* or the roof *(page 138)*.

GROUNDS AND EXTERIOR CHECKLIST

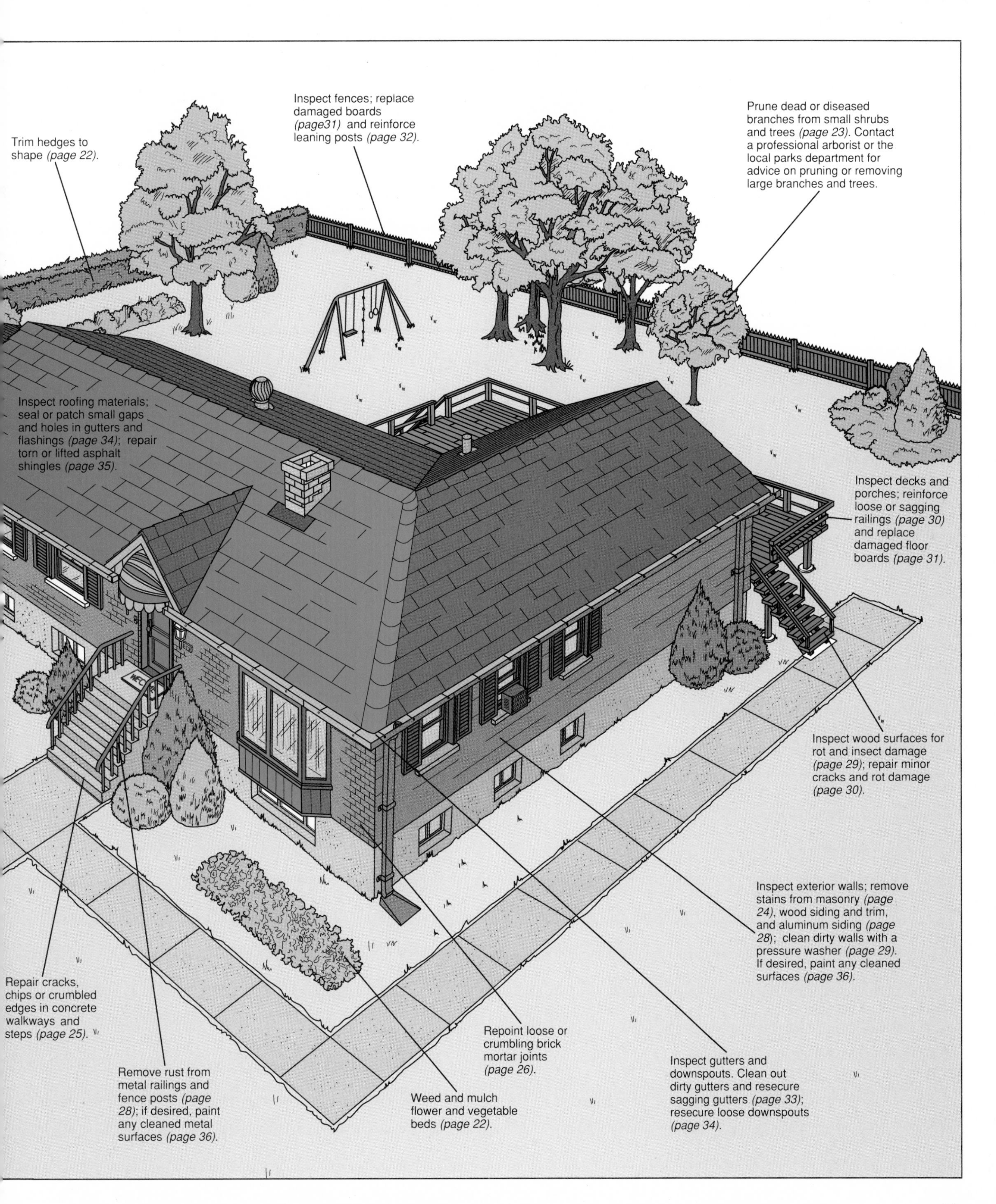
Trim hedges to shape (page 22).
Inspect fences; replace damaged boards (page31) and reinforce leaning posts (page 32).
Prune dead or diseased branches from small shrubs and trees (page 23). Contact a professional arborist or the local parks department for advice on pruning or removing large branches and trees.
Inspect roofing materials; seal or patch small gaps and holes in gutters and flashings (page 34); repair torn or lifted asphalt shingles (page 35).
Inspect decks and porches; reinforce loose or sagging railings (page 30) and replace damaged floor boards (page 31).
Inspect wood surfaces for rot and insect damage (page 29); repair minor cracks and rot damage (page 30).
Inspect exterior walls; remove stains from masonry (page 24), wood siding and trim, and aluminum siding (page 28); clean dirty walls with a pressure washer (page 29). If desired, paint any cleaned surfaces (page 36).
Repair cracks, chips or crumbled edges in concrete walkways and steps (page 25).
Remove rust from metal railings and fence posts (page 28); if desired, paint any cleaned metal surfaces (page 36).
Weed and mulch flower and vegetable beds (page 22).
Repoint loose or crumbling brick mortar joints (page 26).
Inspect gutters and downspouts. Clean out dirty gutters and resecure sagging gutters (page 33); resecure loose downspouts (page 34).

TROUBLESHOOTING GUIDE

SYMPTOM	PROCEDURE
YARD AND GARDENS	
Lawn overgrown	Mow lawn
Lawn edge growing over driveway, walkway, patio or garden edge	Trim lawn edge *(p. 22)* □○
Garden overgrown with weeds; littered with debris	Weed and mulch garden *(p. 22)* □◒
Hedge overgrown	Trim hedge *(p. 22)* □◒
Shrub or tree branch dead, damaged or diseased	Prune shrub or tree branch *(p. 23)* □◒
Insect hive or nest	Control pest infestation *(p. 140)*
FENCES	
Wood surface dirty or stained	Clean wood *(p. 28)* □○
Wood dark and spongy or crumbling; paint or finish on surface lifting	Check for rot and insect damage, and repair minor damage *(p. 29)* □○; if damage extensive, consult a professional
Wood fencing damaged	Replace fence board *(p. 31)* □○
Wood fence post leaning or wobbling	Reinforce fence post *(p. 32)* □◒
Wood gate sagging	Reinforce gate *(p. 32)* □○
Metal surface dirty, stained or rusted	Clean metal *(p. 28)* □○
Paint or finish peeling or faded	Paint or finish surface *(p. 36)* □◒
DRIVEWAY, WALKWAYS AND PATIO	
Asphalt or masonry dirty; littered with debris	Sweep asphalt or masonry
Asphalt or masonry overgrown with weeds or moss	Remove weeds or moss from asphalt or masonry *(p. 24)* □○
Asphalt or masonry stained	Remove stains from asphalt or masonry *(p. 24)* □○
Crack in asphalt	Fill crack in asphalt *(p. 27)* □○
Pothole in asphalt	Fill pothole in asphalt *(p. 27)* □○
Asphalt patched extensively	Seal asphalt *(p. 27)* □●
Shallow surface holes (popouts) in concrete	Repair concrete popouts *(p. 92)* □○
Crack in concrete; edge chipped or crumbling	Repair concrete *(p. 25)* □○
Exterior drain clogged or sluggish	Clean exterior drain *(p. 23)* □○
EXTERIOR HOUSE WALLS	
Crack in concrete foundation wall	Evaluate any crack in concrete *(p. 91)*; caulk hairline crack *(p. 91)* □○ or patch small, open crack *(p. 92)* □○; for crack that indicates structural problem, consult a professional
Brick mortar joint damaged or missing	Repoint brick *(p. 26)* □◒
Masonry stained	Clean masonry *(p. 24)* □○

DEGREE OF DIFFICULTY: □ Easy ⬓ Moderate ■ Complex
ESTIMATED TIME: ○ Less than 1 hour ◒ 1 to 3 hours ● Over 3 hours
(Does not include drying time)

TROUBLESHOOTING GUIDE

SYMPTOM	PROCEDURE
EXTERIOR HOUSE WALLS (continued)	
Aluminum siding stained, scratched or rusted	Clean aluminum siding *(p. 28)* □○
Wood siding or trim stained	Clean wood *(p. 28)* □○
Wood dark and spongy or crumbling; paint or finish on surface lifting	Check for rot and insect damage, and repair minor damage *(p. 29)* □○; if damage extensive, consult a professional
Wall dirty or dingy	Clean wall using a pressure washer *(p. 29)* ⬓●
Paint or finish peeling or faded	Paint or finish wall using an airless sprayer *(p. 37)* ⬓●
DECKS AND PORCHES	
Wood surface dirty or stained	Clean wood *(p. 28)* □○
Wood dark and spongy or crumbling; paint or finish on surface lifting	Check for rot and insect damage, and repair minor damage *(p. 29)* □○; if damage extensive, consult a professional
Wood railing sagging	Reinforce rail or handrail *(p. 30)* □○
Metal surface dirty, stained or rusted	Clean metal *(p. 28)* □○
Deck floor board damaged	Replace deck floor board *(p. 31)* □◒
Paint or finish peeling or faded	Paint or finish surface *(p. 36)* □◒
Crack in concrete step; edge chipped or crumbling	Repair concrete *(p. 25)* □○
GUTTERS AND DOWNSPOUTS	
Gutter or downspout clogged with leaves and debris	Clean gutter and downspout *(p. 33)* □◒
Gutter sagging	Resecure gutter *(p. 33)* □○
Gutter joint open	Seal gutter joint *(p. 34)* □○
Gutter torn or punctured	Patch gutter *(p. 35)* □○
Downspout swaying or rattling	Resecure downspout *(p. 34)* □○
Metal surface stained or rusted	Clean metal *(p. 28)* □○
Paint peeling or faded	Paint surface *(p. 36)* □◒
ROOFING	
Flashing joint open	Seal flashing joint *(p. 34)* □○
Flashing torn or punctured	Patch flashing *(p. 35)* □○
Asphalt shingle torn, cracked or perforated	Seal asphalt shingle *(p. 35)* □○
Asphalt shingle edge lifted or curled	Resecure asphalt shingle *(p. 35)* □○

DEGREE OF DIFFICULTY: □ Easy ⬓ Moderate ■ Complex
ESTIMATED TIME: ○ Less than 1 hour ◒ 1 to 3 hours ● Over 3 hours
(Does not include drying time)

SPRUCING UP THE YARD

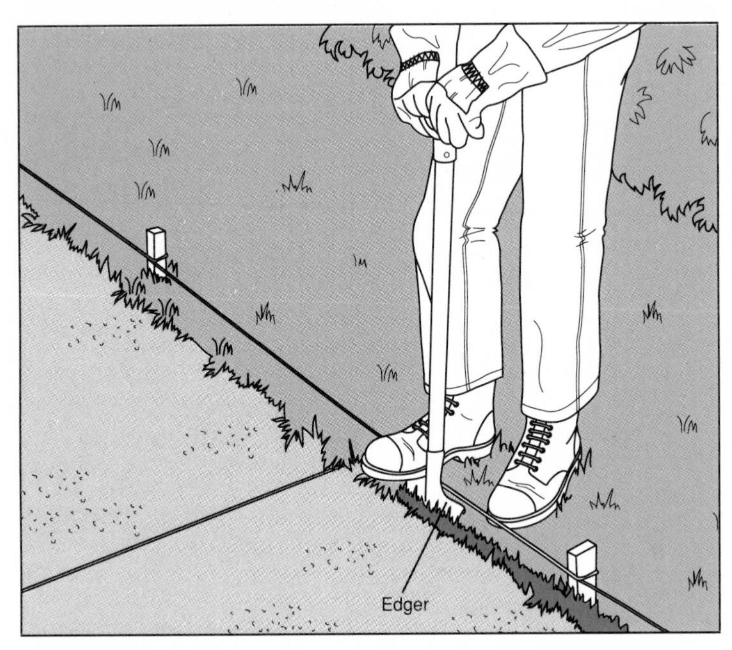

Trimming a lawn edge. If a lawn edge is growing untidily over the edge of a driveway, walkway, patio or garden, cut it back to form a neat border. Water the area a day before cutting the sod to moisten the soil. Set up a guideline of stakes and string a few inches from and parallel to the edge to be trimmed. Wear work gloves and sturdy shoes. Starting at one end of the edge to be trimmed, use an edger to make a cut in the sod about 2 to 3 inches deep; continue, making overlapping cuts along the guideline *(above)* until the entire edge is cut. If necessary, move the guideline as you go. When the cut is complete, remove the loose sod by hand and dispose of it. Sweep up debris along the cut lawn edge.

Trimming a hedge. If a hedge is overgrown, trim it to a neat, uniform shape. Set up a guideline of stakes and string, running the string along the hedge a few inches above the top. Wear work gloves and safety goggles. Starting at one end and following the guideline, use a hedge trimmer to make a straight cut along the hedge top *(above)*; then, cut the sides of the hedge, sloping them slightly so the hedge base is slightly wider than the top. If the trimmer catches on a thick branch, prune the branch *(page 23)*, then continue. After the hedge is cut, use the trimmer to round off any square-cut corners. Shake the hedge to dislodge clippings; then, rake them up and dispose of them.

Weeding and mulching a garden. If a flower or vegetable garden is littered with debris and overgrown with weeds, weed and mulch it to give it a tidy, well-tended appearance. Water the garden the day before weeding to moisten the soil. Collect any debris lying on the ground, and any torn leaves, broken tips and damaged fruits and flowers from plants, bagging and disposing of them as you go. Hand-pull as many weeds as possible. Wearing work gloves, grasp a weed near the base of its stem; pulling gently, work the stem from side to side to dislodge as much of the root system as possible; for stubborn weeds, use a weeding fork *(inset)* or a dandelion weeder to dig down and lever up the roots. Bag and dispose of the pulled weeds. Once the ground is clean, buy a commercial mulch such as peat moss, wood chips or pine nuggets at a garden supply center. Using a spade, carefully spread a 1/2-inch layer of mulch over the ground and under any plants *(above)*; then, using the back of the spade, lightly tamp down the mulch. Water the garden regularly and watch it carefully, hand-pulling weeds whenever they push through the mulch.

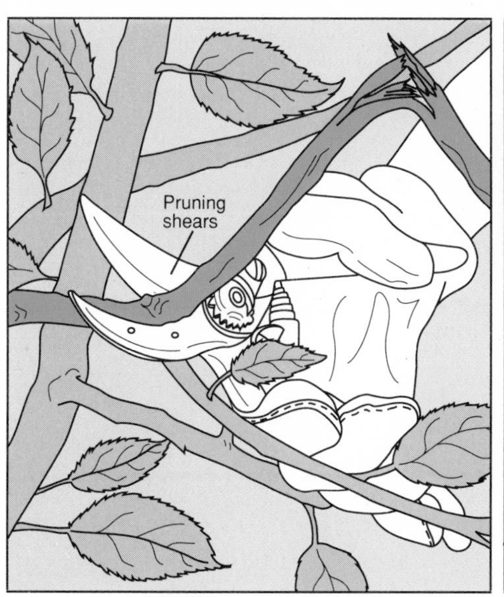

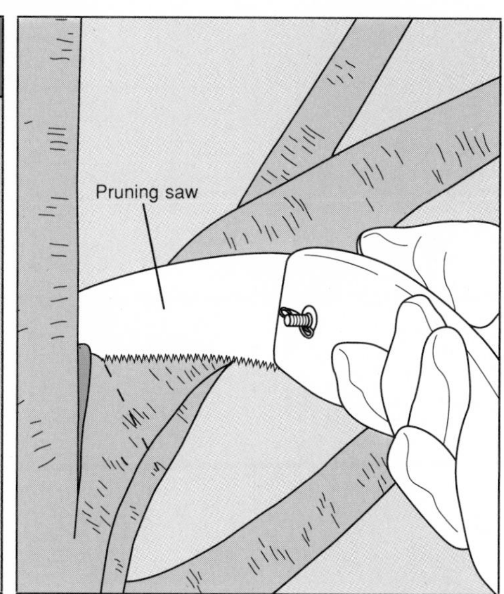

Pruning shrub and tree branches. If a shrub or tree branch is dead, damaged or diseased, remove it to give the plant a natural, healthy appearance. Wear work gloves and safety goggles. To remove a very small branch less than 3/4 inch in diameter, use pruning shears. Fit the shears around the branch at a point 1/4 to 1/2 inch from the nearest healthy branch, angling the cutting blades in the direction of growth of the healthy branch. Then, pressing the blades firmly against the branch, squeeze the handles to make a clean cut, taking care not to twist the shears and tear the bark. If you prune a diseased branch, wipe the blades of the shears with rubbing alcohol before making another cut. Bag and dispose of pruned branches.

To remove a small branch between 3/4 and 1 inch in diameter, or any overhead branch less than 1 inch in diameter, use lopping shears. Standing well to one side if you are working overhead, position the shears and make the cut *(above, center)* as you would with pruning shears.

To remove a branch between 1 and 2 inches in diameter, use a pruning saw; if necessary, work on a ladder *(page 137)*. Hold the saw blade against the branch at a point 1/2 inch from the nearest healthy branch or the trunk, angling the blade away from the branch or trunk. Then, using steady back-and-forth strokes, saw through the branch in a clean, straight line *(above, right)*. If you accidentally tear the bark, use a sharp knife to trim off the torn material.

CLEANING AN EXTERIOR DRAIN

Removing debris from a drain. If an exterior drain in a driveway or walkway is clogged and drains poorly, clean it. Wearing rubber gloves, remove leaves and debris from around the drain; then, remove the drain cover and pull any debris from the mouth of the drainpipe. If the cover is rusted or broken, buy an identical replacement. Reposition the cover, ensuring that it is seated flat. If the drain continues to work poorly, remove the cover and try flushing the drain. Holding the end of a garden hose at the drainpipe opening, turn on the water slowly, gradually increasing the flow *(above)*; flush the drain until any debris is washed down through the pipe, then recover the drain. If you cannot flush the drain and water begins to back up, stop. Have a professional drain-cleaning company service the drain; do not use a chemical drain cleaner to try and unblock it.

CLEANING ASPHALT AND MASONRY

Removing weeds. Remove unsightly weeds from cracks and joints in an asphalt or masonry driveway, walkway or patio. Slightly moisten the soil in the crack or joint. Wearing work gloves, grasp the weed near the base of its stem; pulling gently, work the stem from side to side *(above)* to dislodge as much of the root system as possible; for stubborn weeds, use a weeding fork or a dandelion weeder to dig down and lever up the roots. Bag and dispose of the weeds, then brush dislodged dirt off the asphalt or masonry surface. Repair any cracks in the concrete *(page 25)* or asphalt *(page 27)* through which weeds have been growing.

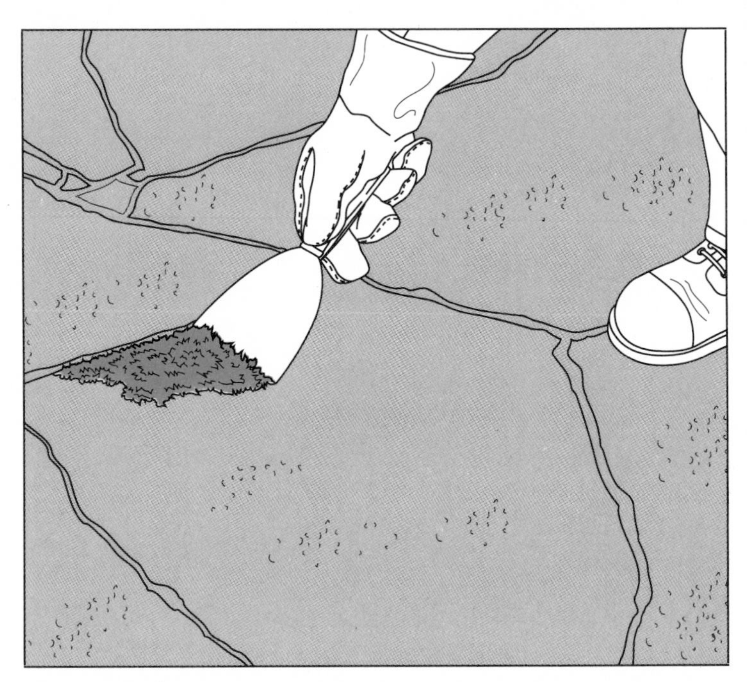

Removing moss. Remove unsightly moss and lichen from the surface of a driveway, walkway, patio or wall. Slightly moisten the affected surface. Wearing work gloves, use a putty knife to scrape the growth off the surface *(above)*; use the knife edge to pry growth out of cracks and crevices in the surface. Bag and dispose of the debris, then brush remaining material and dirt off the surface. Remove any organic stains from the surface *(step below)*. Consider trimming back nearby hedges *(page 22)* and branches *(page 23)* to increase air circulation and sunlight, inhibiting future moss and lichen growth.

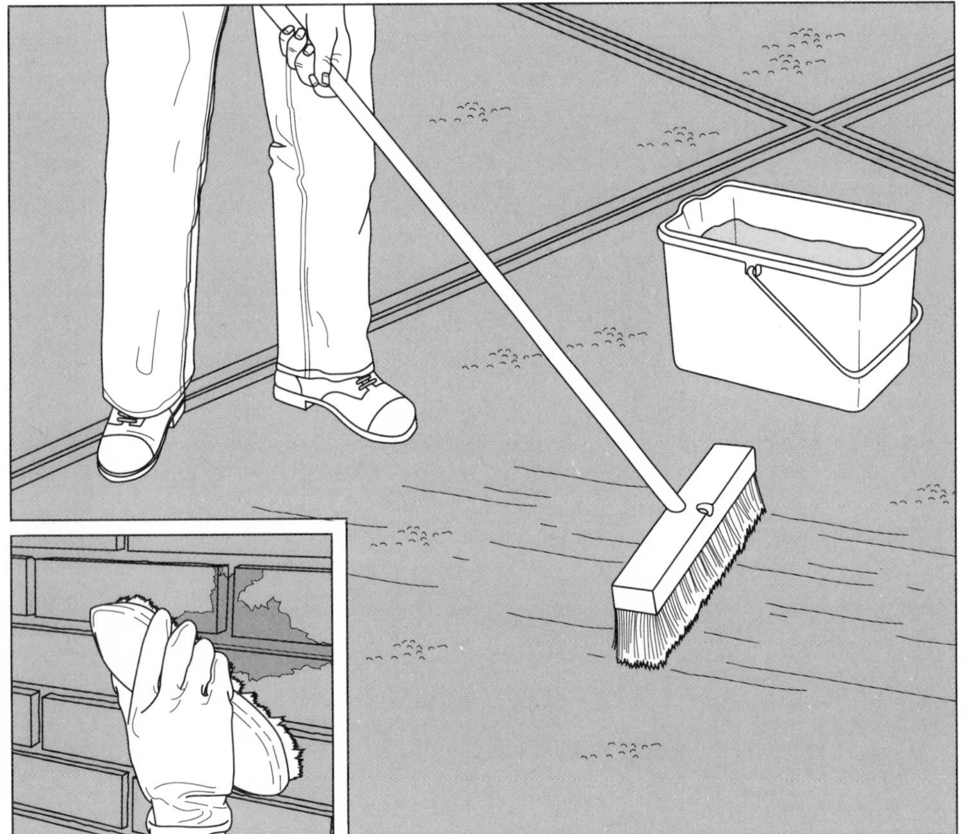

Removing stains. To clean a large, badly-stained brick, stone, concrete or asphalt surface, use a pressure washer *(page 29)*. Remove a small grease or oil stain from exterior masonry as you would from interior concrete *(page 88)*. To remove other small stains, wear rubber gloves and safety goggles to mix as many gallons of cleaner as needed in a plastic bucket. For most light stains, mix a little scouring powder or 1/2 cup of trisodium phosphate (TSP) and 1/2 cup of household detergent per gallon of water. For light efflorescence—white, powdery mineral deposits on concrete or brick—mix 1 cup of TSP per gallon of water; for heavy efflorescence, buy muriatic acid at a building supply center and mix it with water according to the manufacturer's instructions. **Caution:** Always pour acid into water; never pour water into acid.

To remove a stain from a patio, walkway or driveway, use a stiff-bristled broom soaked with cleaner to vigorously scrub the stain *(left)*; on a wall, use a stiff-bristled scrub brush *(inset)*. Then, rinse the scrubbed surface with fresh water; if you are cleaning with muriatic acid, wait for any fizzing action to stop before rinsing. After removing stains from asphalt, consider sealing the surface *(page 27)*.

REPAIRING CONCRETE

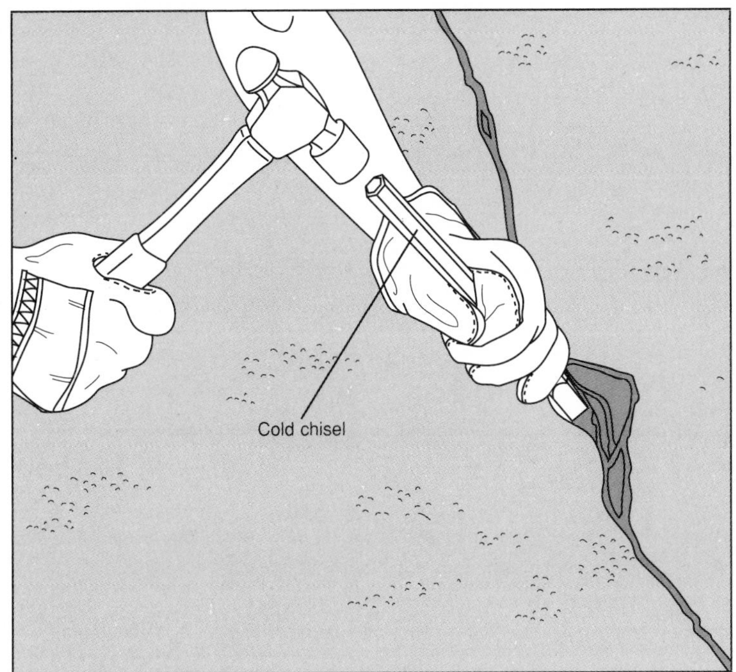

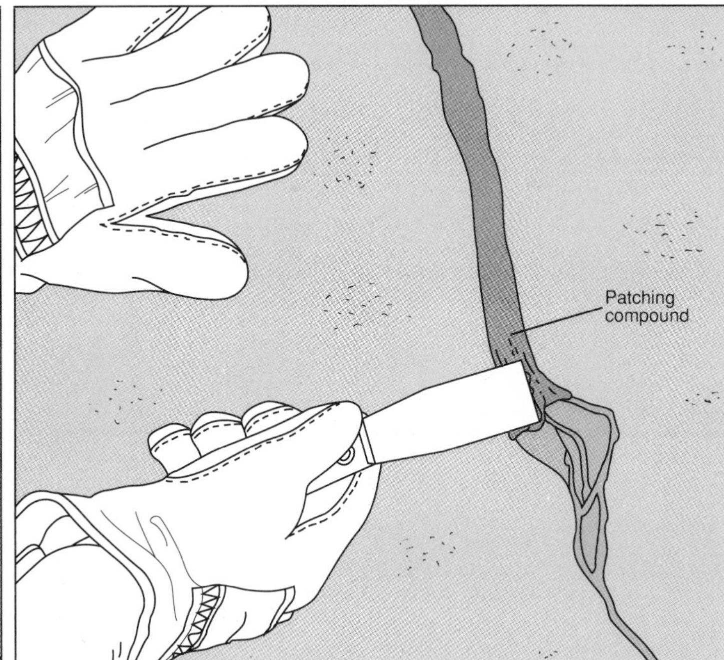

Patching cracked concrete. If a concrete surface is cracked, patch it. Wearing work gloves, use a cold chisel and a ball-peen hammer to undercut the edges of the crack, widening it slightly *(above, left)*; then, use a stiff-bristled scrub brush and fresh water to clean the crack thoroughly. Let the crack dry. Buy pre-mixed latex-based concrete patching compound that contains a bonding agent at a building supply center. Prepare the patching compound following the manufacturer's instruc-

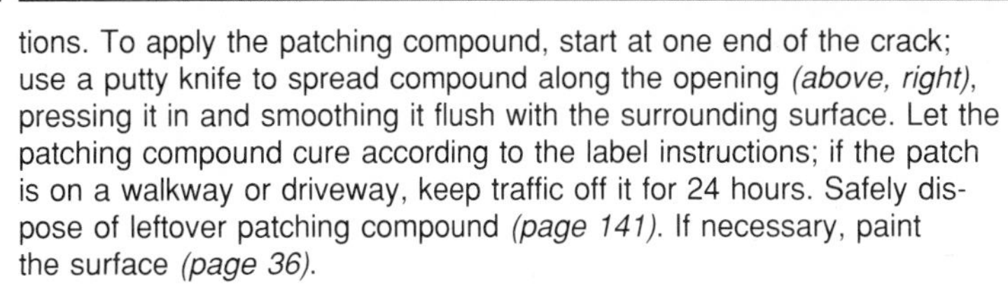

tions. To apply the patching compound, start at one end of the crack; use a putty knife to spread compound along the opening *(above, right)*, pressing it in and smoothing it flush with the surrounding surface. Let the patching compound cure according to the label instructions; if the patch is on a walkway or driveway, keep traffic off it for 24 hours. Safely dispose of leftover patching compound *(page 141)*. If necessary, paint the surface *(page 36)*.

Gluing chipped concrete. If a concrete edge or corner has crumbled or broken in small pieces, rebuild the edge *(step right)*; if the edge or corner has broken off in one piece, glue the chip back into place. Using a stiff-bristled brush, clean the damaged surfaces. Buy concrete glue at a building supply center and prepare it following the label instructions. Wearing rubber gloves, use an old paintbrush to apply an even coat of the glue on the bottom of the chip *(above)* and the top of the surface. Press the chip into position on the surface, then secure it with duct tape. Let the glue cure for the length of time recommended by the manufacturer, then remove the tape; if the repair is on a step or walkway, keep traffic off the surface for 24 hours. Safely dispose of leftover glue *(page 141)*. If necessary, paint the surface *(page 36)*.

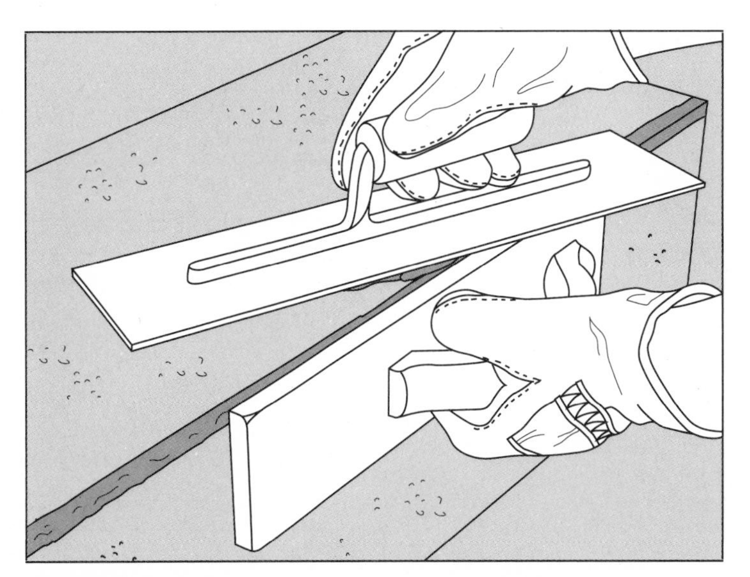

Rebuilding a concrete edge. Using a stiff-bristled brush, clean off the damaged edge. Buy pre-mixed latex-based concrete patching compound that contains a bonding agent at a building supply center. Prepare the compound following the manufacturer's instructions. Wearing work gloves, use a putty knife to spread patching compound along the damaged edge. To square the edge, hold a wooden float against one side of the edge and use a rectangular trowel to spread the patching compound over the surface on the other side of the edge, smoothing it out flush with the float *(above)*. Let the patching compound cure according to the manufacturer's instructions; if the edge is on a step or walkway, keep traffic off it for 24 hours. Safely dispose of leftover patching compound *(page 141)*. If necessary, paint the surface *(page 36)*.

REPOINTING BRICK

1 Removing damaged mortar. If you are making a repair high on an exterior wall, use a ladder *(page 137)*. Wearing work gloves and safety goggles, use a bull-point chisel and a ball-peen hammer to chip loose and crumbling mortar from the joint between bricks *(above)*, cutting to a depth of 1/2 to 3/4 inch. Use a stiff-bristled brush to clean dust and debris out of the cut-back joint, then flush the joint with fresh water.

2 Filling the joint. Purchase pre-mixed mortar at a building supply center. Wearing work gloves, follow the manufacturer's instructions to mix a batch of mortar on a mason's hawk; mix the mortar to a consistency at which it holds its shape. Holding the hawk just below the joint to catch any spilled mortar, use a pointing trowel to work mortar into the joint *(above)*, packing it as tightly as possible. Scrape off excess mortar from surrounding bricks with the edge of the trowel.

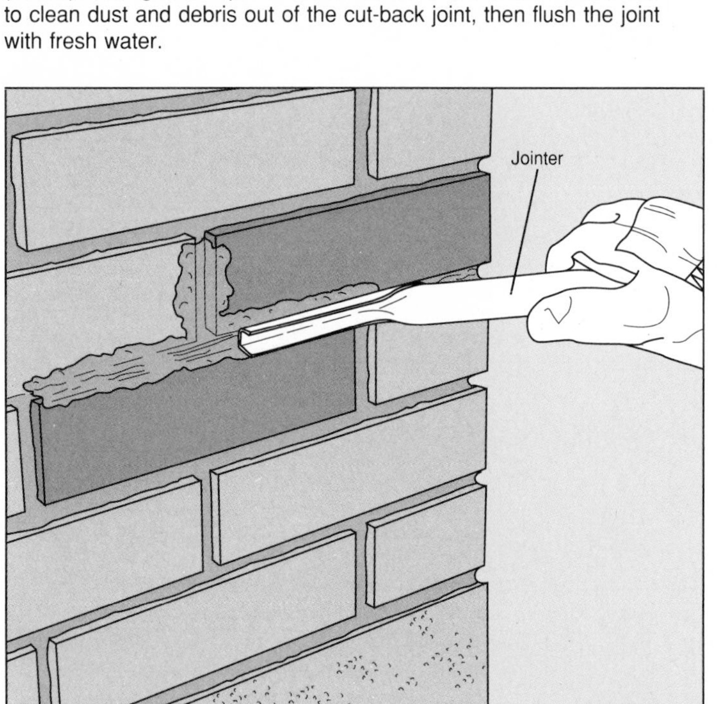

3 Striking the joint. Wait 30 minutes or until the mortar has set enough to hold a thumbprint. Then, use a jointer with a shape that matches the shape and depth of the original mortar joint to strike the joint, or press it to form a watertight seal; for the neatest appearance, strike vertical joints before striking horizontal joints. To strike a joint, wet the jointer with water; then, using firm, steady pressure, draw the jointer smoothly along the wet mortar in the joint *(above)*.

4 Smoothing the joint. Using the edge of a pointing trowel, scrape away mortar extruded from the joint by the presssure of the jointer *(above)*; then, use a wet, rough cloth or stiff-bristled brush to scrub mortar residue off surrounding brick surfaces. Safely dispose of leftover mortar *(page 141)*. Following the manufacturer's instructions, allow the new mortar to cure. Keeping the curing mortar damp for at least 3 days; mist the surface occasionally with water.

REPAIRING ASPHALT

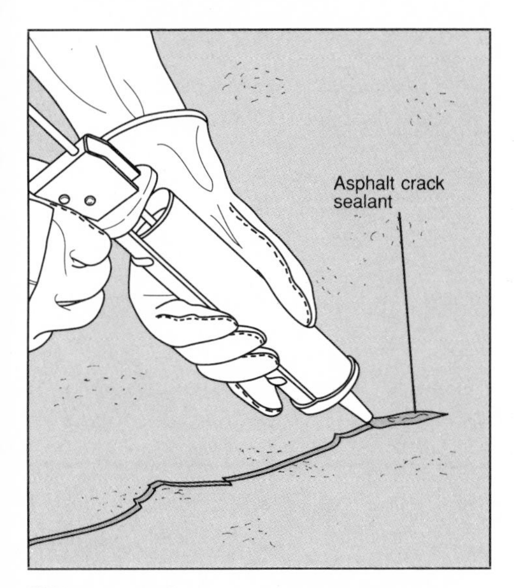

Filling a crack. Use a stiff-bristled brush to clean the crack, then flush it with water and let it dry. Wearing work gloves, load a caulking gun with asphalt crack sealant *(page 133)*. Starting at one end of the crack and holding the gun at a 45-degree angle to the surface, squeeze the trigger to eject a continuous bead of caulk along the crack *(above, right)*. Let the caulk dry. If the caulk does not completely fill the crack, follow the same procedure to apply a second layer of caulk and let it dry. If desired, seal the surface if it has been patched extensively *(step below)*.

Filling a pothole. Use a stiff-bristled brush to clean out the pothole. Then, if the hole is more than 1 inch deep, fill it with gravel so it is only 1 inch deep. Buy asphalt patching compound (blacktop patch) at a building supply center and follow the label instructions to prepare it. Wearing work gloves, use a pointing trowel to pack the patching compound into the hole *(above, left)*, filling it to a level just below the surrounding surface; then, use a 4-by-4 to tamp down the patching compound *(above, right)*. Wait 30 minutes. Add more patching compound, overfilling the hole slightly; then, tamp it flush with the surrounding surface. Let the patching compound cure, keeping traffic off it for 12 hours. Safely dispose of leftover patching compound *(page 141)*. If desired, seal the surface if it has been patched extensively *(step below)*.

SEALING ASPHALT

Applying an asphalt sealer. After cleaning asphalt or if an asphalt driveway or walkway surface has been patched extensively, seal the surface to provide a uniform, new-looking finish. Work on a dry day in a temperature between 50 and 85 degrees Fahrenheit. Set up a temporary barrier around the surface to keep traffic away. Purchase a commercial asphalt sealer at a building supply center; follow the label directions to prepare it and the asphalt surface—in some cases the surface must be dampened. Wear work gloves, sturdy shoes and safety goggles. Starting at one end of the surface, pour sealer from the container directly onto a section of asphalt; avoid pouring or splashing the sealer onto adjacent vegetation. Then, use a stiff-bristled broom to spread the sealer evenly over the surface. Continue, section by section *(left)*, and without overlapping the sections, until the entire surface is covered. Let the sealer dry, keeping it free of traffic for at least 12 hours.

CLEANING METAL

Cleaning a fence or railing. For stains on wrought iron or galvanized steel, wear rubber gloves and safety goggles to mix as many gallons of cleaner as needed in a plastic bucket. For common dirt, mix 1/3 cup of household detergent per gallon of water and scrub with a stiff-bristled brush, then dry the surface. For stubborn dirt and stains, use the same procedure, mixing 1 cup of trisodium phosphate (TSP) per gallon of water. Safely dispose of leftover cleaner *(page 141)*. For rust, wear work gloves and scrub the surface with a wire brush *(above)*; then, smooth the surface clean with medium steel wool, and wipe off any dust. Finish the surface *(page 36)*.

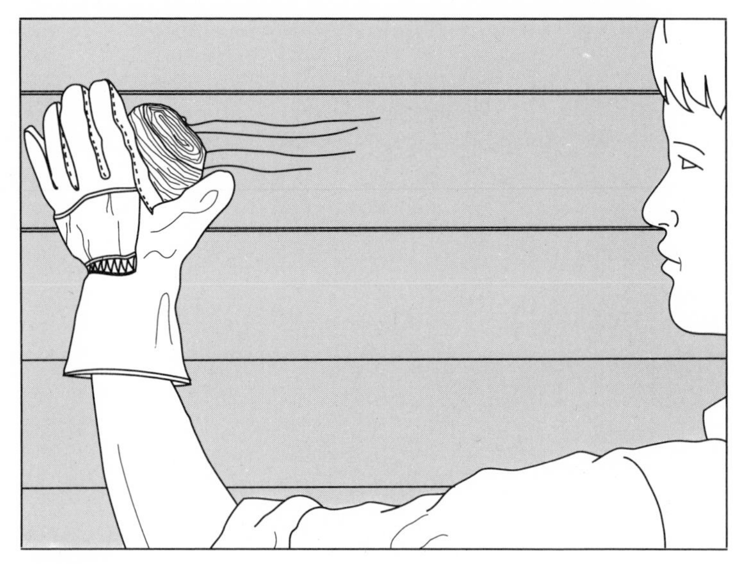

Cleaning aluminum siding. For stains, wear rubber gloves and safety goggles to mix as many gallons of cleaner as needed in a plastic bucket. For common dirt and stains, mix 1/3 cup of household detergent per gallon of water and scrub gently with a soft cloth; to avoid streaks, work from the bottom up and rinse immediately. For mildew, use the same procedure, mixing 1/3 cup of household detergent and 1/3 cup of trisodium phosphate (TSP) per 1 quart of household bleach and 3 quarts of water. Safely dispose of leftover cleaner *(page 141)*. For surface scratches and corrosion, wear work gloves to smooth the surface with fine steel wool *(above)*; then, finish the surface *(page 36)*.

CLEANING WOOD

Removing dirt and stains. To clean a large surface, use a pressure washer *(page 29)*. To remove small stains, wear rubber gloves and safety goggles to mix as many gallons of cleaner as needed in a plastic bucket. For common dirt, mix a little household detergent per gallon of water and scrub vigorously with a stiff-bristled scrub brush *(above, left)*; then, rinse the area with fresh water. For stubborn dirt or stains, use the same procedure, mixing 1/2 cup of trisodium phosphate (TSP) per gallon of water. For mildew and rust stains, mix 2 cups of household bleach per gallon of water; wait 30 minutes after scrubbing the area before rinsing it. For exuded pitch, use a paint scraper or putty knife to scrape the pitch off the surface; to clean any stain remaining, buy a commercial wood-brightening product, then mix and apply it according to the label instructions. Safely dispose of leftover cleaner *(page 141)*. For rusted fastener heads, wear work gloves and smooth the heads with fine steel wool; then, select a metal primer *(page 136)* and use a paintbrush to dab primer on each head *(above, right)*.

USING A PRESSURE WASHER

Using a pressure washer. To wash a large exterior surface such as a wall, a driveway, a deck or a patio, rent a gas-powered pressure washer rated 1000 to 1500 pounds per square inch (psi) at a tool rental center *(page 128);* and follow the manufacturer's instructions to set it up. Protect nearby surfaces not to be washed; to wash a wall, as shown, tape plastic sheeting over lighting fixtures, outlets and vents, close windows and doors, and cover nearby vegetation. Wearing rubber boots, rubber gloves and safety goggles, wash successive 5-foot-wide sections of the surface; on a wall, work from top to bottom and do not point the spray wand at windows or doors. Starting at one end of the surface, grip the wand firmly with both hands and brace it against you to steady it; then, keeping the wand almost perpendicular to the surface with the nozzle 12 to 18 inches from it, squeeze the trigger to start. To stop the water flow, release the trigger. Work to the other end of the surface *(left)*, then stop the water flow and turn off the pressure washer. After washing a driveway, deck or patio, keep traffic off it until it is dry. If necessary, clean any remaining stains off the asphalt, masonry *(page 24)*, metal or wood *(page 28)*.

REPAIRING MINOR WOOD ROT AND INSECT DAMAGE

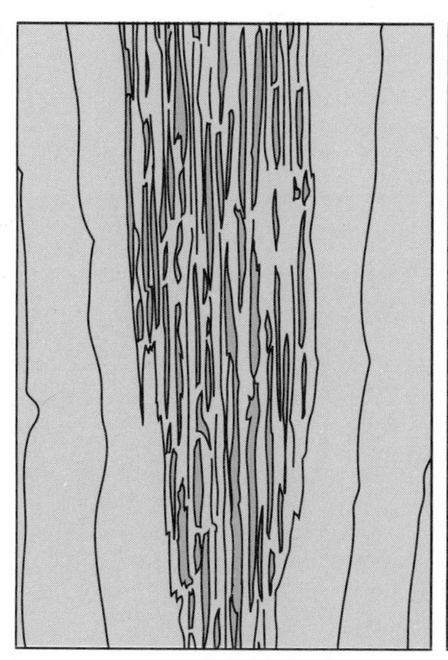

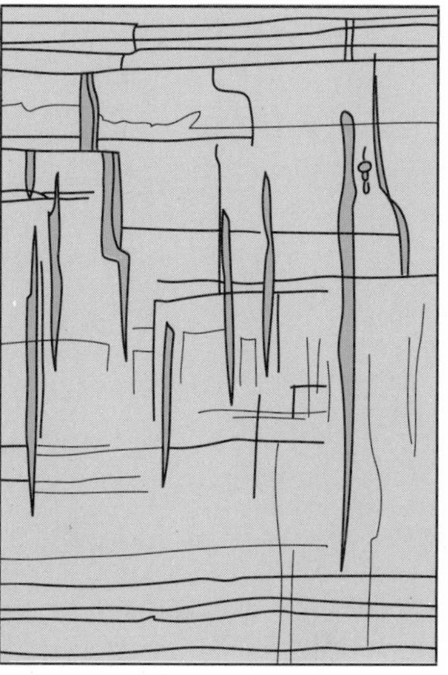

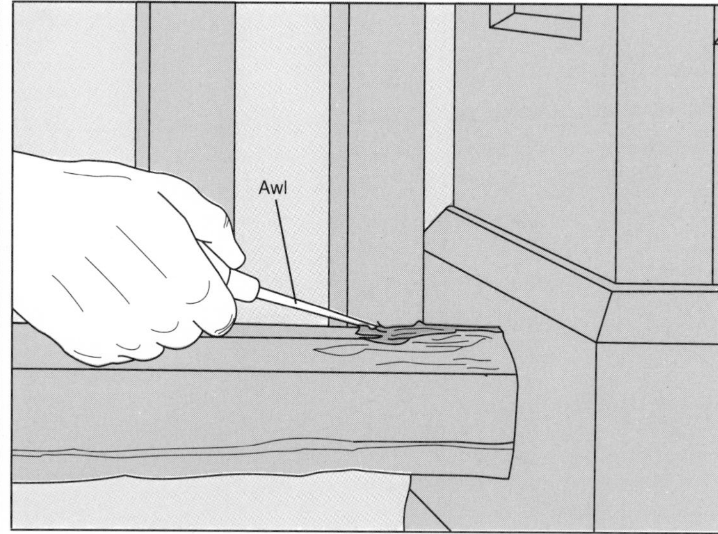

1 Identifying rot and insect damage. To check for rot and insect damage, closely inspect joints, surfaces where water can collect, and surfaces on or near the ground. Chipped, peeling or lifting finish, spongy wood fibers and gray or dark discoloration are telltale signs of rot or insect damage.

If the wood is pitted or powdery, or riddled with tiny holes or tunnels *(above, left)* and there are insect remains, suspect insect damage and consult a pest control professional. If the damage to the wood is minor, patch it *(step 2)*. Wood that is rotted may be split or cracked *(above, center)*, but it may also exhibit no visible signs of a problem. To test for rot, poke the wood using an awl, pressing it in as deeply as possible *(above, right)*. If the wood is soft and gives way, crumbling instead of splintering, it is weakened by rot. If the damage to the wood is minor, patch it *(step 2)*; otherwise, call a building professional.

REPAIRING MINOR WOOD ROT AND INSECT DAMAGE (continued)

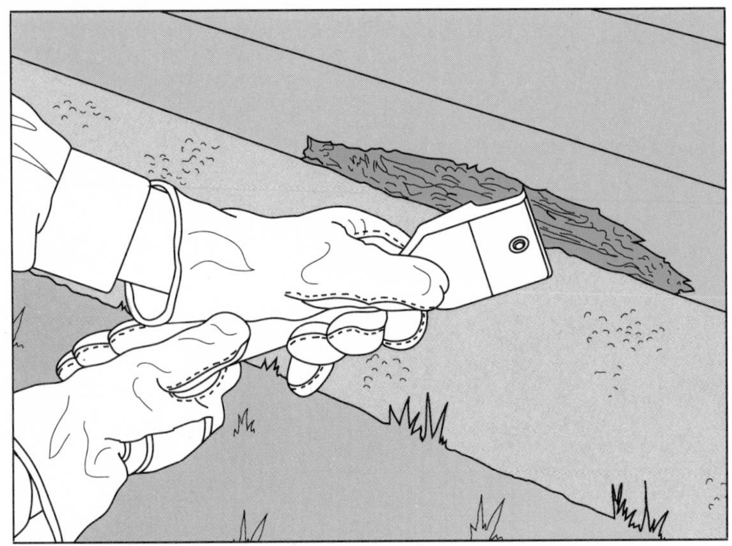

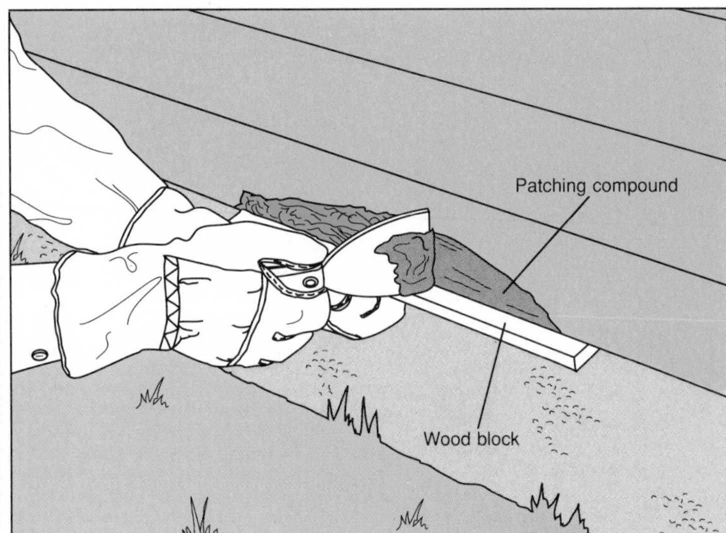

2 Patching the damaged wood. Wearing work gloves and safety goggles, remove all soft, damaged wood down to firm, healthy wood, digging out the damage with a paint scraper *(above, left)*. Buy epoxy patching compound at a building supply center and prepare it following the label instructions. Use a putty knife to pack patching compound into the damage, overfilling it slightly. Then, scrape off the excess patching compound, leveling it with the surrounding surface; if necessary, position a wood block along the edge of the surface as a guide *(above, right)*. To replicate any texture in the surface, rake the wet compound with the tip of the putty knife blade. Allow the patching compound to cure. Using medium-grit sandpaper, lightly sand the surface, then wipe it clean. Finish the surface *(page 36)*.

REINFORCING A WOOD RAILING

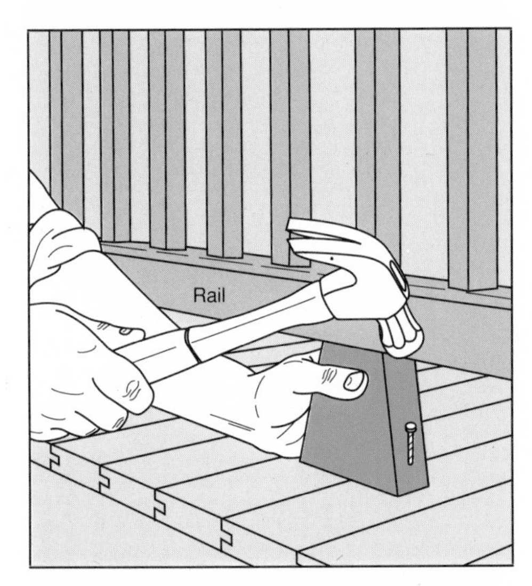

Bracing the length of a rail. If the rail along the bottom of a railing is sagging, reinforce it by installing 2-by-4 or 2-by-6 braces under it. To mark a brace for size, position it on the floor against the rail; prop up the rail at its correct height or have a helper support it. Saw the brace to length, angling the sides for drainage, then paint or finish the brace to match the railing. Fit the brace under the rail. Use an electric drill *(page 129)* to bore a pilot hole through each side of the brace into the floor; then, drive nails into the holes *(above)*. Also nail the rail to the brace.

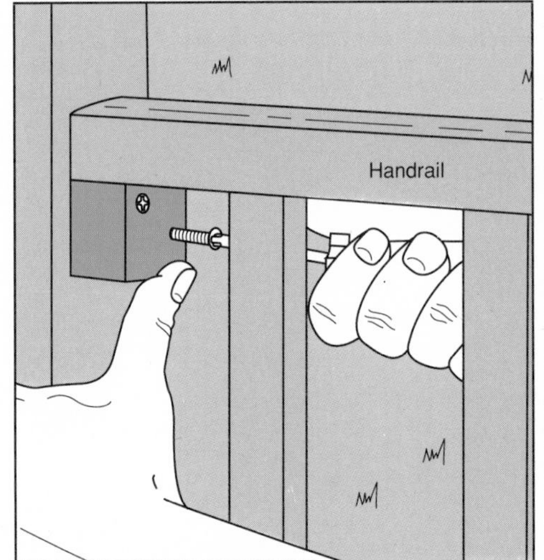

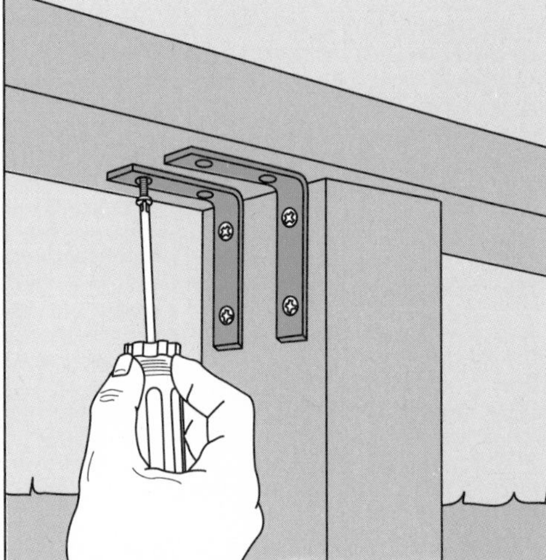

Bracing the end of a handrail or rail. If the end of a handrail or rail on a railing is loose or sagging, reinforce it by installing a wood brace or hardware. For a wood brace, use lumber of the same dimensions as the handrail or rail, and saw it to a length equal to the width of the handrail or rail; then, paint or finish the brace to match the railing. Prop up the handrail or rail at its correct height or have a helper support it. Position the brace under the handrail or rail and against the column or post. Use an electric drill *(page 129)* to bore pilot holes through the brace into the column or post, then drive screws into the holes *(above, left)*; for best results, use two screws, offsetting them slightly.

For a hardware brace, use galvanized steel L-braces. Prop up the handrail or rail at its correct height or have a helper support it. Position a brace under the handrail or rail and against the column or post. Use an electric drill *(page 129)* to bore through the holes in the brace into the handrail or rail and the column or post, then drive screws into the holes *(above, right)*; for best results, use two braces.

REPLACING A DECK FLOOR BOARD

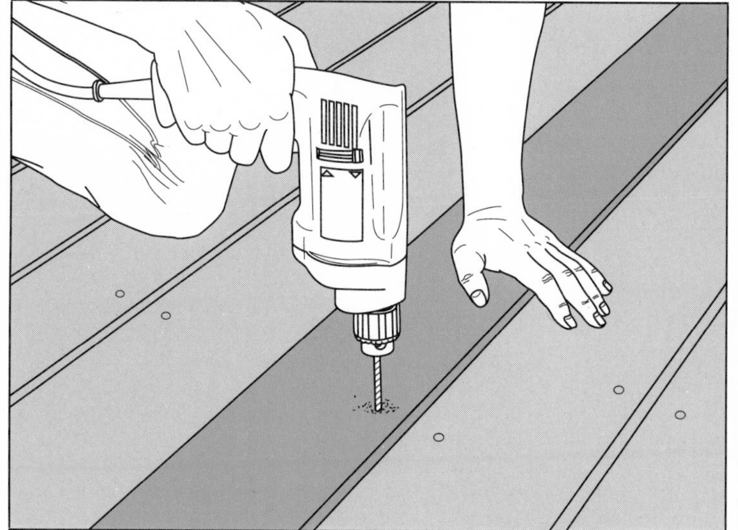

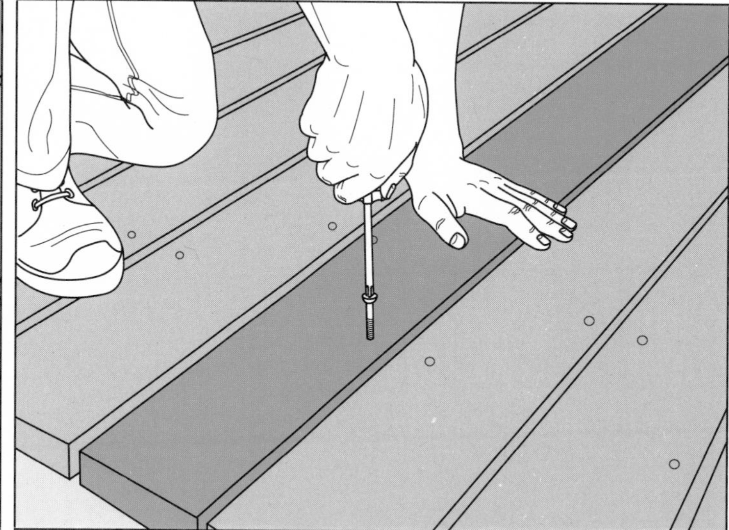

Removing and installing a deck board. If a deck floor board is damaged, replace it. To remove a board, first remove any fasteners holding it. To remove nails, use the notched end of a crowbar to pry up, then pull out the nails; to remove screws, use a reversible electric drill fitted with a screwdriver bit *(page 129)*. After removing all the fasteners, lift out the board; if you cannot remove a fastener, loosen it by hammering up on the bottom of the damaged board near the joist, then use the crowbar to pry up the board from above. Purchase replacement wood at a building supply center and mark it using the original flooring as a template; then, saw it to size and paint or finish it to match the floor. To install a board, lay it or have a helper hold it in the space from which you removed the old board, ensuring it is properly spaced from adjacent boards and its ends are properly aligned with the deck edges. Using an electric drill fitted with a twist bit *(page 129)*, drill pilot holes through the board into each joist under it *(above, left)*, numbering and spacing the holes to follow the pattern used on the rest of the flooring. Use a screwdriver to drive screws into the pilot holes *(above, right)* and secure the board to the joists.

REPLACING A FENCE BOARD

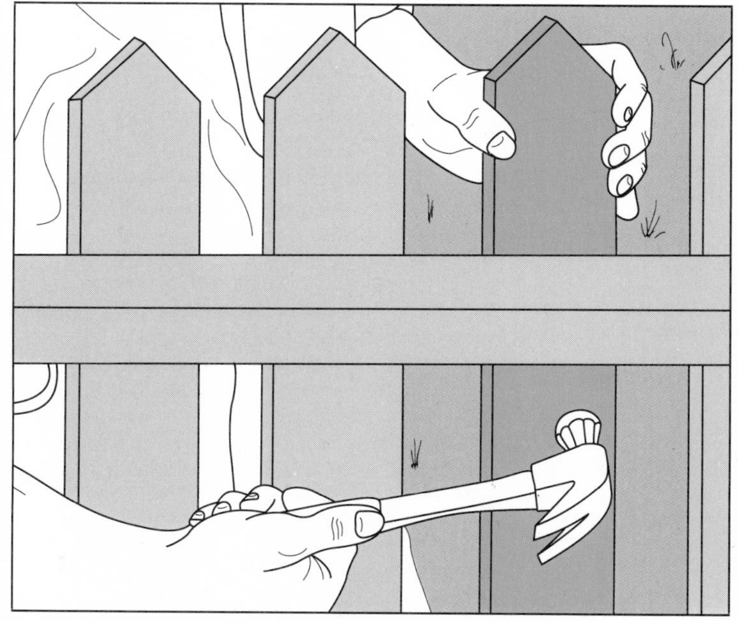

Removing and installing a fence board. If a fence board is damaged, replace it. To remove a board, hammer on the back of it near the rails *(above, left)* to lift the nails holding it; then, pull out the nails and lift off the board. Purchase replacement wood at a building supply center and mark it using the original fencing as a template; then, saw it to size and paint or finish it to match the fence. To install a board, prop it or have a helper hold it in position against the rails, then partially drive a galvanized nail through it into the top rail. Steadying the rail with a sledgehammer, finish driving the nail; then, drive in another nail *(above, right)*. Nail the board to the bottom rail the same way.

REINFORCING A WOOD FENCE POST

Installing sister posts or shims. If a wood fence post is loose and leaning, reinforce it. To reinforce a post set in soil, install a sister post on each side of it. Purchase pressure-treated 2-by-4s at a building supply center and saw them to a length at least half the height of the post with a 45-degree bevel at one end; finish them to match the fence *(page 36)*. Wearing work gloves, position a sister post bevel-out against the post and drive it halfway into the ground with a sledgehammer *(left)*. Saw off the top of the sister post at a 45-degree angle 18 to 24 inches from the ground. Repeat this procedure to install the other sister post. Then, drive at least two 4-inch galvanized spiral nails through each sister post into the fence post *(inset)*.

To reinforce a post set in concrete, force wood shims into any spaces between the post and the concrete footing. To make the shims, saw wood pieces to a length at least one-third the height of the post; finish them to match the fence *(page 36)*. Drive in each shim as far as possible with a rubber mallet, then use a chisel to cut it off at ground level. Select a caulk *(page 133)* and use a caulking gun to caulk around the base of the post.

REINFORCING A WOOD GATE

Installing a turnbuckle. Inspect the gate and gate posts. If a hinge is loose, tighten its fasteners; if it is damaged, replace it. If a gate post is leaning, reinforce it *(step above)*. Otherwise, reinforce a sagging gate by installing a turnbuckle assembly that extends from the end of the top rail near the hinge to the end of the bottom rail diagonally opposite. Buy a turnbuckle assembly at a hardware store or a building supply center: 1/8-inch woven cable with a turnbuckle, two U-bolt clips and two eye screws.

Using an electric drill fitted with a twist bit *(page 129)*, bore pilot holes for the eye screws in the rails, and install the eye screws in the holes. Using diagonal-cutting pliers, cut two lengths of cable, each 5 to 6 inches longer than the distance between the eye screws on the rails. Loop a cable through an eye screw and pull the two ends 5 to 6 inches through a U-bolt clip; then, loop the ends through one end of the turnbuckle and double them back through the clip. Tighten the clip with a wrench *(inset)*. Repeat the procedure to install the other length of cable. To tighten the cable, adjust the turnbuckle; using an old screwdriver for leverage, turn the turnbuckle until the cable is taut *(left)*.

CLEANING GUTTERS AND DOWNSPOUTS

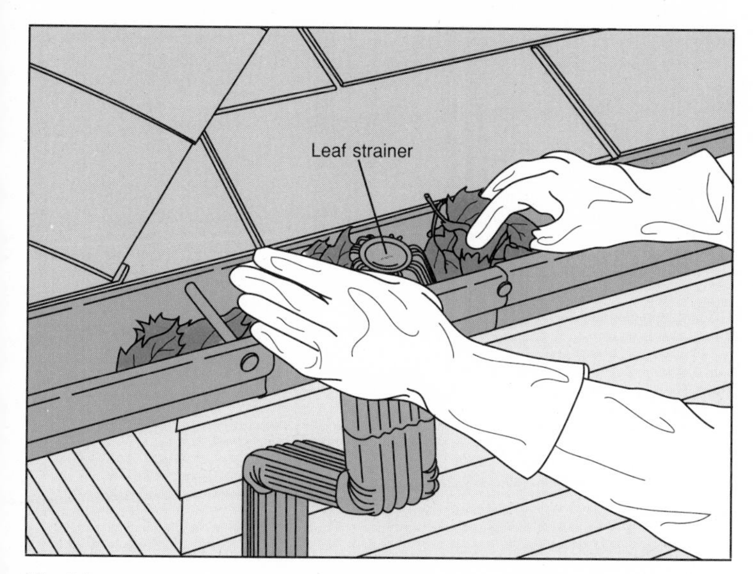

Flushing a gutter. Wearing rubber gloves and working on a ladder *(page 137)*, handpick *(above)* and bag leaves as well as other debris at the roof edge and in the gutter; work from end to end of the gutter. Then, flush the gutter. Starting at one end, use a garden hose to wash away dirt and grit, brushing it toward a downspout with a whisk broom; use a putty knife to scrape off any adhered material. Inspect the gutter. If water drains poorly, clean the downspout *(step right)*. If water pools in the gutter because of a sag, resecure the gutter *(step below)*. If the gutter leaks, seal any open joint *(page 34)* or patch any hole *(page 35)*.

Flushing a downspout. If water collects in a gutter and drains poorly through the downspout, clean the downspout. Wear rubber gloves and work on a ladder *(page 137)*. If there is a leaf strainer covering the downspout opening, remove it. Reach down the drop outlet and pull out as much debris as possible, bagging it for disposal. Then, aiming the end of a garden hose into the drop outlet, turn on the water slowly, gradually increasing the flow *(above)* to flush debris through the elbow and out the bottom of the downspout. Reinstall any leaf strainer you removed; if there is no leaf strainer, buy one for your model of gutter and install it to prevent a future blockage.

RESECURING A GUTTER

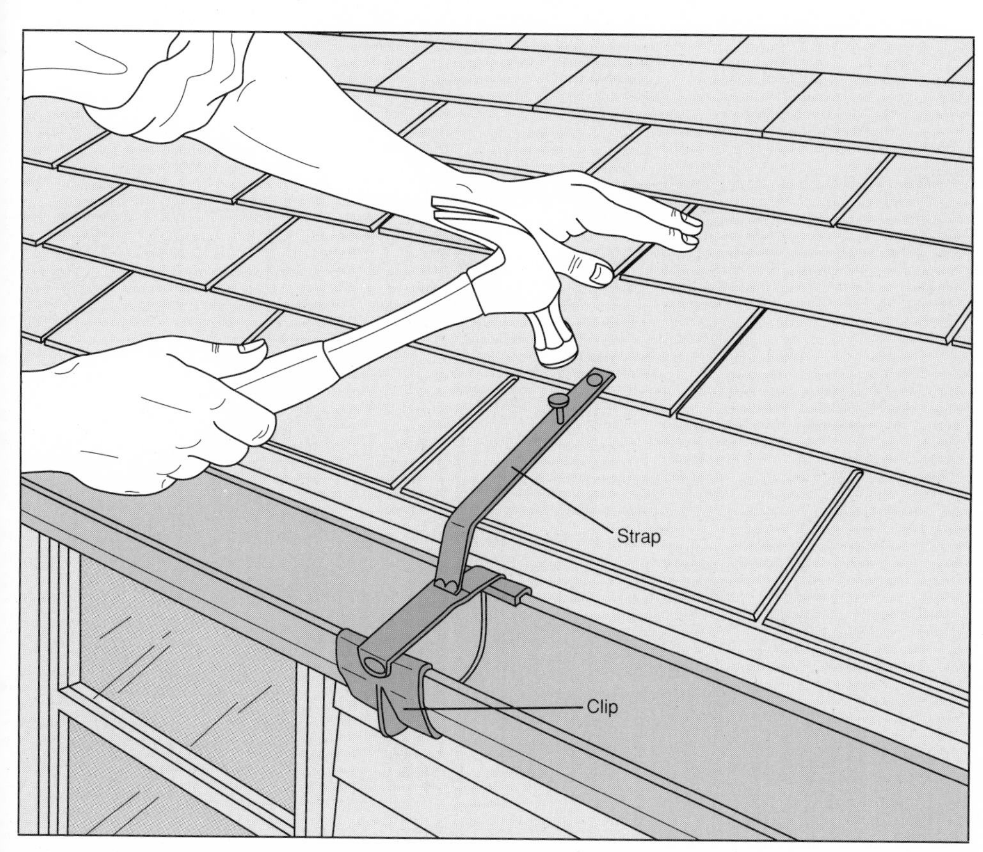

Installing a strap hanger. If a gutter section sags, check for a faulty or missing gutter hanger; work on a ladder *(page 137)*. If a hanger is damaged, remove it: using a pry bar and pliers to pry out and pull off a spike hanger; using tin snips to cut off a strap hanger or bracket hanger. To replace a hanger or add on an extra hanger, buy a strap hanger to fit your model of gutter at a building supply center. Follow the manufacturer's instructions to install the new hanger on the gutter. For the vinyl gutter shown, snap the hanger clips over the gutter edges. Position the hanger strap on or under the edge of a shingle, raising or lowering the strap until the gutter sag is corrected. Then, drive roofing nails through the strap to secure it *(left)*. Load a caulking gun with a cartridge of roofing cement and apply a dab of cement on each nail head. If necessary, use the same procedure to install other hangers, installing at least one strap hanger every 24 or 32 inches along the gutter until the sag is corrected.

RESECURING A DOWNSPOUT

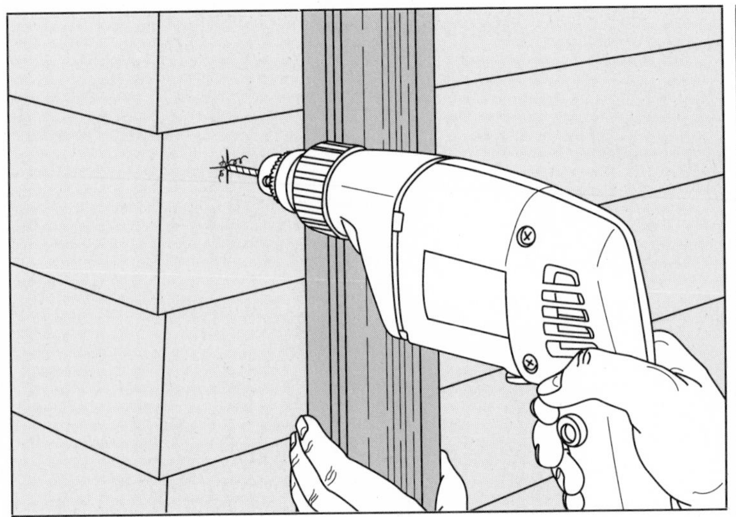

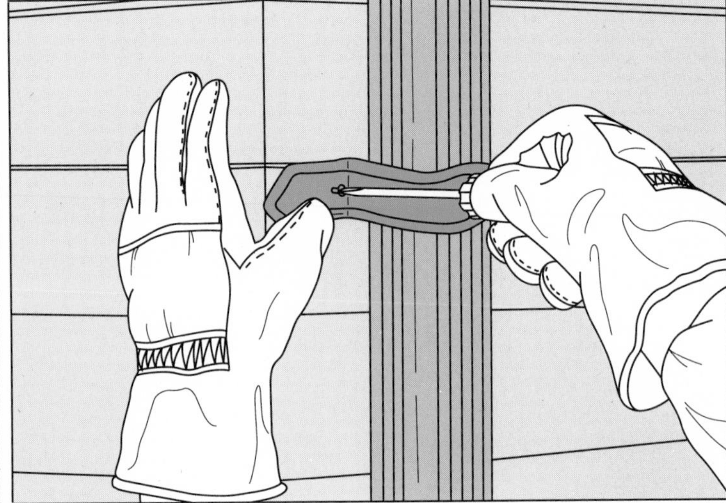

Installing a downspout bracket. If a downspout is loose, and it sways or rattles, install additional brackets to secure it. Buy a downspout bracket to fit your model of downspout, and fasteners to secure the bracket to your type of wall surface at a building supply center. If necessary, prepare to work on a ladder *(page 137)*. Prop the downspout in its correct position or have a helper steady it. Follow the manufacturer's instructions to install a bracket. On the metal downspout shown, position the bracket over the downspout and mark position points for fasteners. Using an electric drill fitted with an appropriate bit *(page 129)*, bore pilot holes for the fasteners at the marked points *(above, left)*. Holding the bracket in position over the downspout, drive screws through the bracket holes and into the pilot holes *(above, right)* to secure the bracket.

REPAIRING MINOR DAMAGE TO ROOFING MATERIALS

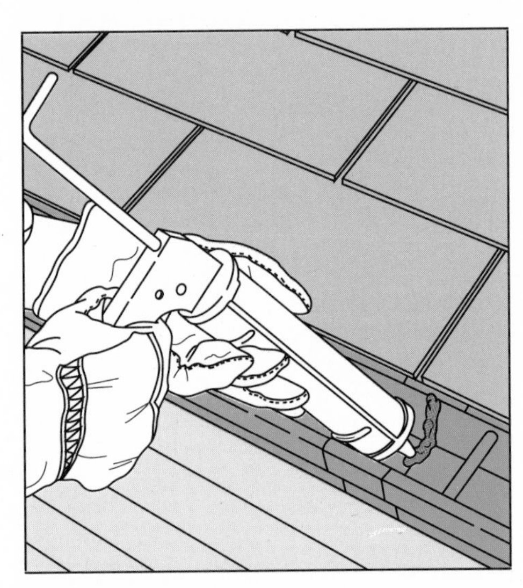

Sealing a gutter joint. If a gutter joint has separated and leaks, reseal it when the gutter is dry. Prepare to work on a ladder *(page 137)* or on the roof *(page 138)*. Wearing work gloves, use a clean, damp rag to wipe dirt and grit off the inside of the gutter along the joint. Load a caulking gun with silicone-based caulk *(page 133)* and apply a continuous bead of it along the joint *(above)*; use a small putty knife to smooth the caulk into the joint. If the joint leaks again, patch the gutter *(page 35)*.

Sealing a flashing joint. If a joint between overlapping pieces of flashing or between a flashing and another roofing material is open, reseal it when the roof is dry. Prepare to work on a ladder *(page 137)* or on the roof *(page 138)*. To reseal flashing to masonry, wear work gloves and safety goggles and carefully pull the flashing away from the surface or out of the mortar to which it was attached. Use a putty knife to scrape away old sealant, then use a wire brush to clean away grit and debris. Using a caulking gun loaded with roofing cement, fill the joint *(above, left)*. Then, push the flashing firmly back against the surface or into the mortar to bond it to the roofing cement.

To reseal a joint between pieces of flashing, wear work gloves and use a putty knife to scrape away old sealant from the joint; then, use a wire brush to clean away grit and debris. Using a caulking gun loaded with silicone-based caulk *(page 133)*, apply a continuous bead of it along the joint *(above, right)*. Then, use the putty knife to smooth the caulk, forcing it into the joint.

REPAIRING MINOR DAMAGE TO ROOFING MATERIALS (continued)

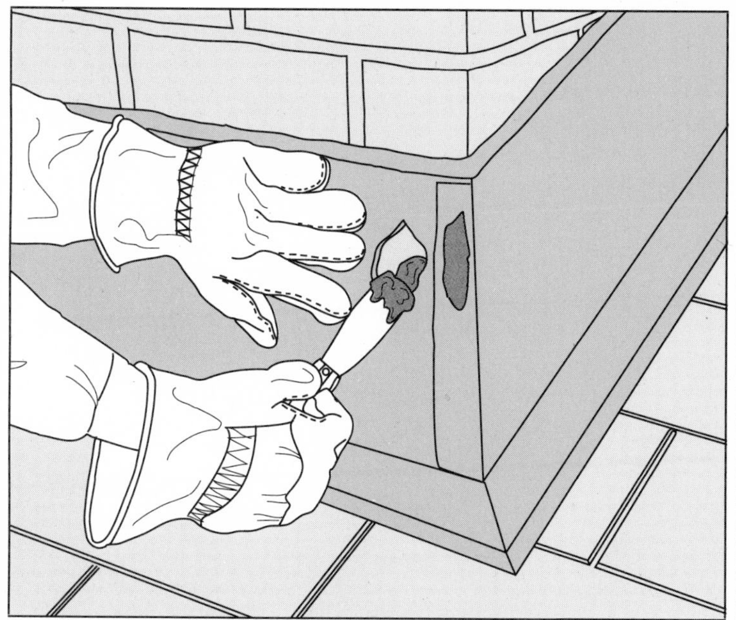

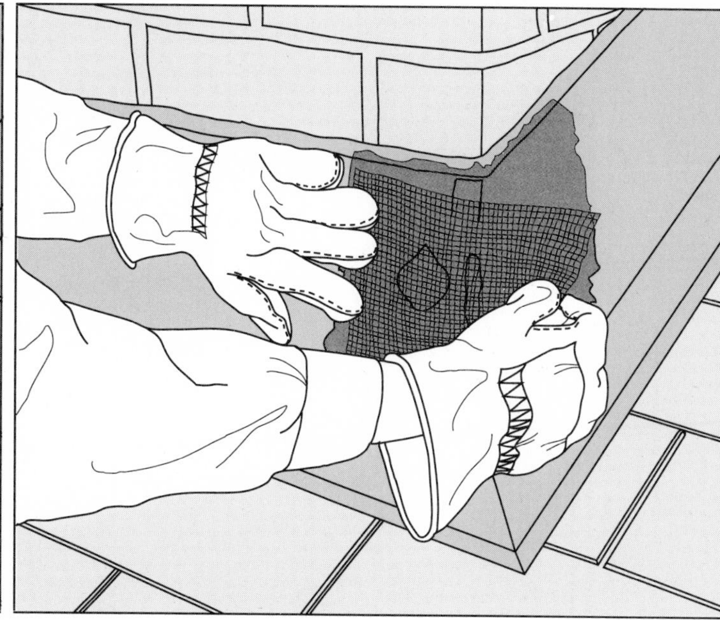

Patching a hole in a gutter or flashing. Buy fiberglass tape and epoxy at a building supply center. Prepare to work on a ladder *(page 137)* or on the roof *(page 138)*. Wearing work gloves and safety goggles, clean off the damaged surface with a wire brush and wipe it with a clean rag dampened with paint thinner. Use medium-grit sandpaper to remove rust spots and smooth the surface, then wipe it with a clean, dry rag. Using scissors, cut a piece of fiberglass tape: for a flashing, 3 inches wider and longer than the damage: for a gutter, 1 inch. Mix the epoxy following the manufacturer's instructions, then use a putty knife to spread it over the damage *(above, left)*, covering an area the size of the patch. Center the patch over the damage and press it firmly into place *(above, right)*, embedding it in the epoxy. Then, use the putty knife to apply epoxy on the patch, saturating it completely. Let the epoxy cure. If desired, paint the surface *(page 36)*.

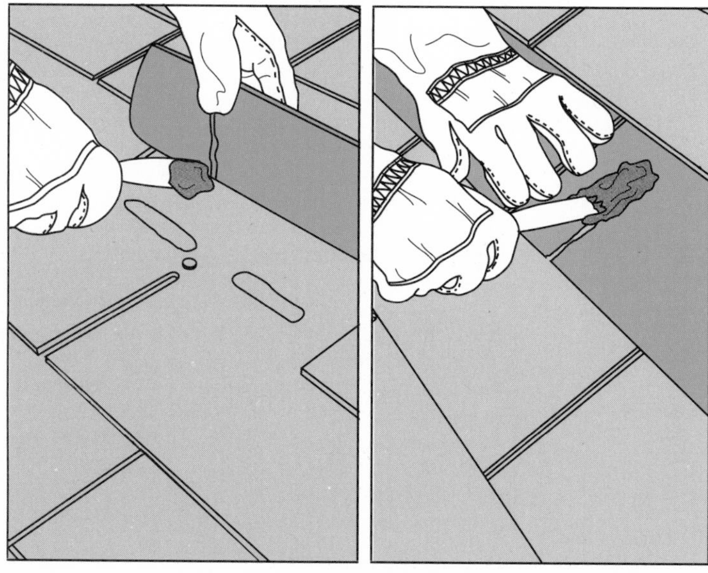

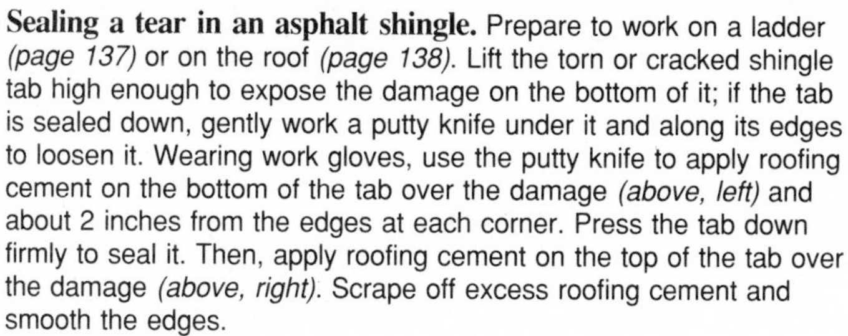

Sealing a tear in an asphalt shingle. Prepare to work on a ladder *(page 137)* or on the roof *(page 138)*. Lift the torn or cracked shingle tab high enough to expose the damage on the bottom of it; if the tab is sealed down, gently work a putty knife under it and along its edges to loosen it. Wearing work gloves, use the putty knife to apply roofing cement on the bottom of the tab over the damage *(above, left)* and about 2 inches from the edges at each corner. Press the tab down firmly to seal it. Then, apply roofing cement on the top of the tab over the damage *(above, right)*. Scrape off excess roofing cement and smooth the edges.

Resecuring a lifted asphalt shingle edge. Prepare to work on a ladder *(page 137)* or on the roof *(page 138)*. To seal a lifted or curled edge, raise the lifted or curled shingle tab high enough to reach under it. If the tab is partly sealed down, gently work a putty knife under it and along its edges to loosen it. Wearing work gloves, hold up the tab and use the putty knife to apply roofing cement on the bottom of it about 2 inches from the edges at each corner *(above)*. Press the tab down firmly to seal it. Lay a brick on top of the tab to help the bonding of the roofing cement; remove the brick when the cement is cured.

FINISHING AN EXTERIOR SURFACE

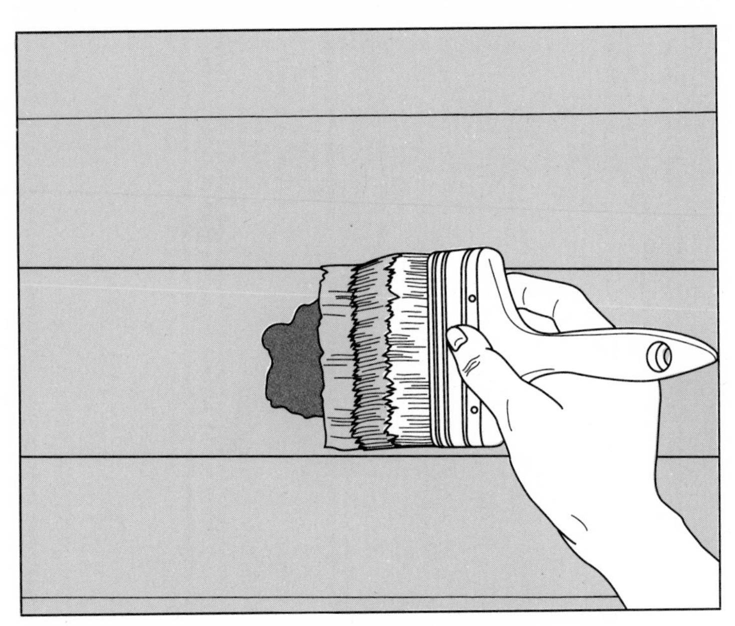

Preparing to paint or finish. To paint or finish a large exterior surface, use an airless sprayer *(page 37)*. Before painting or finishing a small surface, prepare it; if necessary, clean the masonry *(page 24)*, metal or wood *(page 28)*. On a concrete surface, repair any cracks, chips or crumbled edges *(page 25)*; on wood, repair any rot or insect damage *(page 29)*. Select an exterior paint or finish; for bare masonry, metal or wood or a patched surface, also a primer recommended by the paint or finish manufacturer *(page 135)*. Cover nearby surfaces and vegetation with drop cloths or plastic sheeting. Use a paintbrush to apply any primer necessary *(above)*; let the primer dry. Then, paint or finish the surface: using a paint mitt for a decorative surface *(step right)*; a paintbrush for trim *(step below)*; and a roller for a flat surface *(page 37)*.

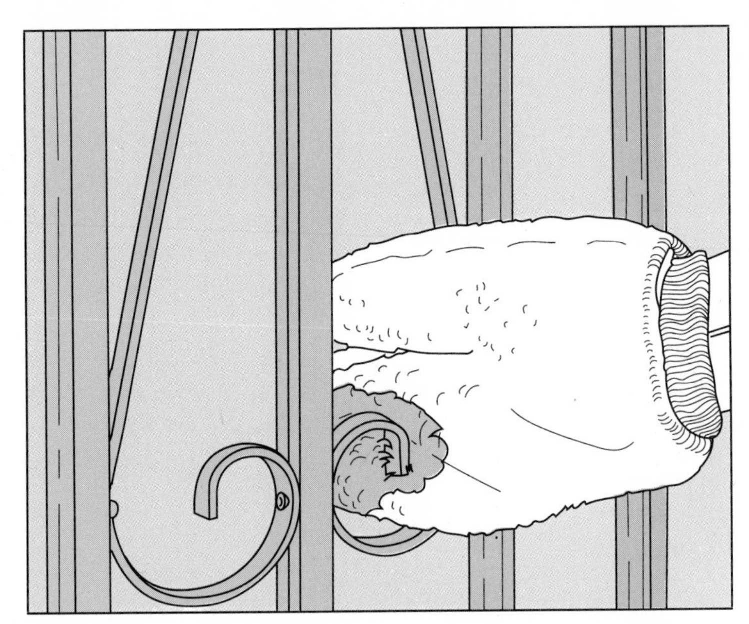

Using a paint mitt on a decorative surface. Use a paint mitt for decorative metal or wood surfaces, and in tight spots. To apply paint or finish with a paint mitt, pour some paint or finish into a roller tray, then put on the mitt; if desired, put on a rubber glove first for extra protection. Dip the paint mitt into the paint or finish, dampening but not soaking the palm. For a narrow surface, wrap the paint mitt around it *(above)* and rub up and down. For a wide surface, press the paint mitt flat against it and rub back and forth. For a crevice, use the tip of the paint mitt to work in the paint or finish. Reload the paint mitt and continue the same way until the surface is covered, then let it dry. If necessary, apply a second coat, first sanding the surface lightly with fine-grit sandpaper and wiping it clean. Safely dispose of leftover paint or finish *(page 141)*.

Using a paintbrush on trim. Use a paintbrush for exterior trim and in any corners or recesses of a flat surface that a roller cannot reach. To apply paint or finish with a paintbrush, pour some paint or finish into a container. Dip the paintbrush bristles into the paint or finish, coating one-third of their length for precise work; half their length otherwise. Start at one end of the surface and work along it; on wood, work in the direction of the grain. Brush paint or finish onto the surface using a smooth back-and-forth stroke *(left)*; then, reverse the direction of the stroke to brush back lightly over the paint or finish and smooth it. If necessary, use a paint shield *(inset)* to protect any adjacent surface while you work, regularly wiping dripped paint or finish off the edge of the shield with a cloth to prevent smears. Reload the paintbrush and continue, section by section, until the surface is covered. Let the paint or finish dry. If necessary, apply a second coat, first sanding the surface lightly with fine-grit sandpaper and wiping it clean. Safely dispose of leftover paint or finish *(page 141)*.

Using a roller on a flat surface. Use a roller to paint or finish a flat horizontal or vertical exterior surface—for masonry, use a long-nap roller cover; for wood, a medium-nap one. If you are working overhead, wear a hat and safety goggles. If necessary, first use a paintbrush *(page 36)* to paint or finish any corners or recesses of the surface that a roller cannot reach. To apply paint or finish with a roller, pour some paint or finish into a roller tray. Dip the roller into the paint or finish, rolling it to coat the cover completely and evenly. Start at a corner; on a vertical surface, start at a top corner. Working slowly to avoid splattering, roll paint or finish out onto a 3-foot section of the surface; then, reverse the pattern to roll back over the paint or finish and smooth it. Reload the roller and continue *(left)*, section by section, until the surface is covered. Let the paint or finish dry. If necessary, apply a second coat, first sanding the surface lightly with fine-grit sandpaper and wiping it clean. Safely dispose of leftover paint or finish *(page 141)*.

USING AN AIRLESS SPRAYER

Using an airless sprayer. To paint or finish a large surface such as an exterior wall, rent an airless sprayer at a tool rental center *(page 128)*; follow the manufacturer's instructions to set it up. Work on a calm, dry and cloudy day. Select an exterior paint or finish; for bare masonry or wood or a patched surface, also a primer recommended by the paint or finish manufacturer *(page 135)*. Then, fill the airless sprayer. Protect nearby surfaces; on a wall, tape plastic sheeting over lighting fixtures, outlets and vents, close windows and doors, and cover nearby vegetation.

Wearing work gloves, use a paintbrush to apply primer to any patched area and let it dry. Wearing safety goggles and a respirator, use the airless sprayer to paint or finish successive 3-foot-wide sections of the surface; on a wall, work from top to bottom. Starting at one end of the surface, hold the spray nozzle at a 60-degree angle to the surface and 10 inches from it; then, squeeze the trigger to start, moving the nozzle in a steady back-and-forth motion. To stop the spray, release the trigger. Work to the other end of the surface, then stop the spray and turn off the airless sprayer; if you are working on a wall, use a cardboard shield to protect a window or door as you spray around it *(left)*. After painting or finishing a deck, keep traffic off it until it dries. If necessary, apply a second coat. Safely dispose of leftover paint or finish *(page 141)*.

WALLS AND CEILINGS

To a potential buyer, your home's walls and ceilings are the most visible, impression-forming parts of its interior. Small investments of time and money in maintaining and repairing walls and ceilings can be returned many times over—real estate surveys indicate that few things influence a buyer's opinion of a house more than their appearance. A simple repair such as cleaning off a painted surface *(page 40)*, a wood surface *(page 44)* or a wallcovering *(page 46)* can quickly and dramatically enhance the appearance of any wall or ceiling. Alternately, applying a new coat of paint to a wall or ceiling and refinishing the trim *(page 50)* can make any room seem like new.

Day-to-day living inevitably inflicts minor damage to the walls and ceilings of even the most carefully-maintained home. Take the time to look for wall and ceiling flaws, and repair them before showing the house. Look behind your furniture, wall hangings and draperies for minor damage to the walls and trim of each room, and examine the ceiling, putting yourself in the shoes of a potential buyer. Hairline cracks around stress points such as doors and windows, popped drywall nails and faded paint may be the normal results of age and wear, but to the eyes of a buyer they can become unsightly focal points. Use the Troubleshooting Guide *(page 39)* and the checklist diagram *(below)* to help identify small, easy-to-fix problems; then, refer to the pages indicated to make the appropriate repair.

On drywall or plaster walls and ceilings, it is typically a simple matter to fill cracks and holes, whether they are large *(page 42)* or small *(page 41)*, and to repair minor damage to the outside corner of a wall *(page 42)*. Repairs may differ

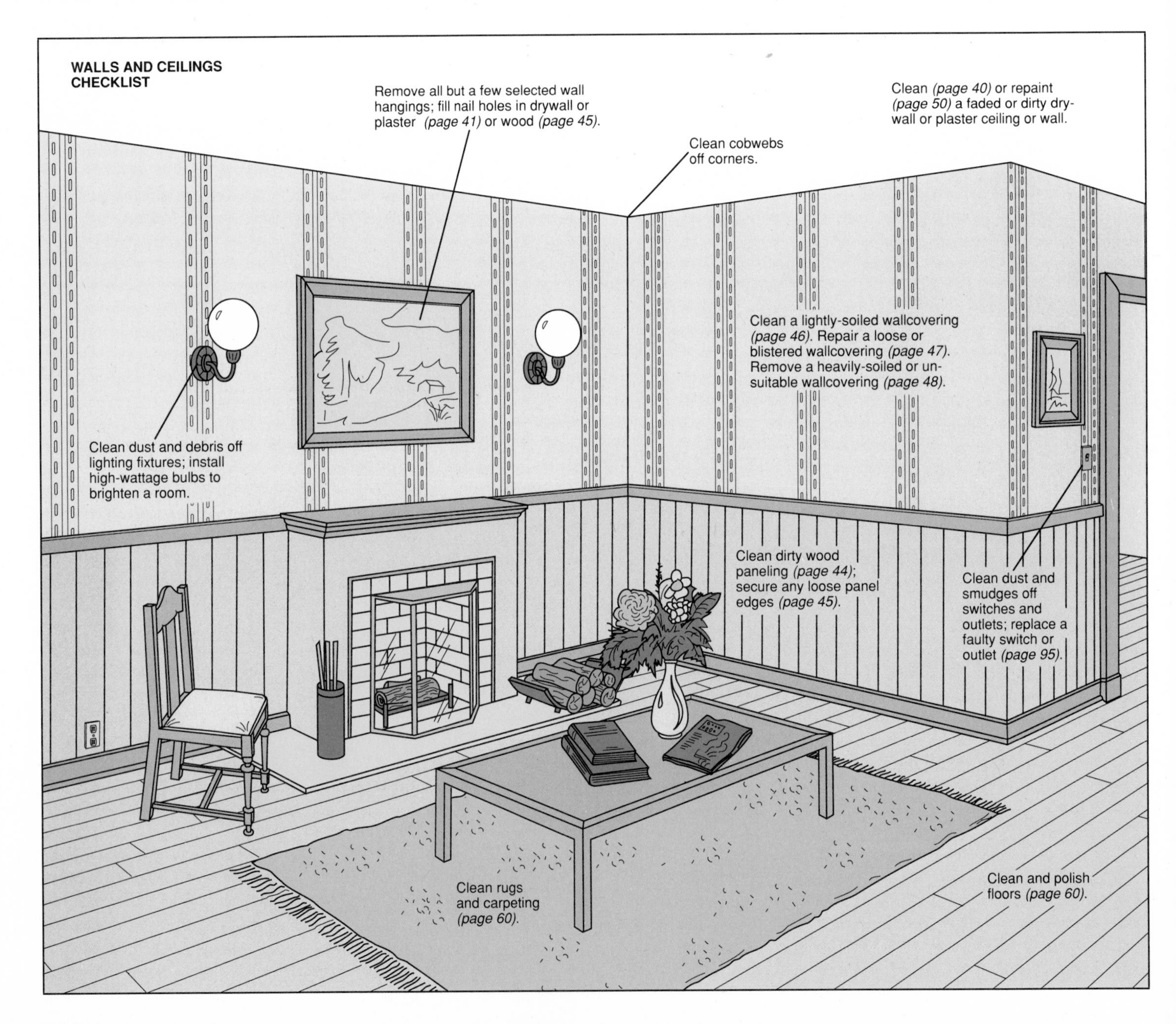

somewhat for drywall and plaster; read the repair instructions carefully and follow any specific advice for your particular wall or ceiling surface. If your home was built after 1940, it is most likely to have walls and ceilings of drywall.

On walls that are covered with wood paneling and on any wood trim, you can easily repair minor damage to the surface *(page 44)*. And on a wall finished with a wallcovering, it takes little time to repair a loose corner or seam or a blister *(page 47)*. Pay special attention to any wallcoverings in the house; the appeal of any wallcovering pattern is a matter of personal taste, and the covering that sends you into a reverie may drive a potential buyer out the door. Your best bet is to remove all but the most muted and subdued wallcoverings as well as any that are heavily soiled *(page 48)*, then follow up with a coat of fresh paint that is a neutral color.

Before painting a wall or ceiling, prepare for the job properly *(page 49)*, covering up surfaces and items not to be painted. Make any necessary repair to the surface, then clean it well. If you are painting an entire room, paint the ceiling, then the walls, and finish with any trim. Work methodically and carefully, ensuring that you have good lighting and ventilation. Clean and store your tools properly, and safely dispose of leftover cleaning and finishing products.

Most repairs to walls and ceilings can be made with a small number of cleaning, patching, smoothing and finishing tools such as a putty knife, a sanding block and a paintbrush. Refer to Tools & Techniques *(page 126)* for advice on using any tools required and consult the charts on caulks and paints for help in choosing the appropriate products for patching and finishing your home's walls and ceilings.

TROUBLESHOOTING GUIDE

SYMPTOM	PROCEDURE
Paint on wall, ceiling or trim dirty, dingy or faded	Clean painted surface *(p. 40)* □◒;
	If desired, prepare to paint *(p. 49)* and paint surface *(p. 50)* ⬓◒
Paint on wall, ceiling or trim peeling or chipped	Remove peeling paint *(p. 40)* □○; prepare to paint *(p. 49)* and paint surface *(p. 50)* ⬓◒
Nail popped in drywall wall or ceiling	Reset or remove popped nail *(p. 41)* □○
Small hairline crack or hole in drywall or plaster wall or ceiling	Fill crack or hole *(p. 41)* □○; prepare to paint *(p. 49)* and paint surface *(p. 50)* ⬓◒
Large, open crack in drywall or plaster wall or ceiling	Fill crack *(p. 42)* □○; prepare to paint *(p. 49)* and paint surface *(p. 50)* ⬓◒
Damaged outside corner in drywall or plaster wall	Repair outside corner *(p. 42)* □○; prepare to paint *(p. 49)* and paint surface *(p. 50)* ⬓◒
Wood panel or trim dirty or dingy	Clean wood panel or trim *(p. 44)* □○
	If desired, prepare to paint *(p. 49)* and paint or refinish surface *(p. 51)* ⬓◒
Scratch, gouge or dent in wood panel or trim	Cover minor scratch; fill gouge or dent *(p. 44)* □○
Small crack or hole in wood panel or trim	Fill crack or hole *(p. 45)* □○
	If desired, prepare to paint *(p. 49)* and paint or refinish surface *(p. 51)* ⬓◒
Wood panel edge loose or bowed	Secure wood panel *(p. 45)* ⬓○
Gap between wood trim and wall	Reseat trim; if unsuccessful, seal gap *(p. 45)* □○
Wallcovering dirty or soiled	Test wallcovering for washability and clean wallcovering *(p. 46)* □◒
	If desired, remove wallcovering *(p. 48)* ⬓◒; prepare to paint *(p. 49)* and paint surface *(p. 50)* ⬓◒
Wallcovering corner or seam lifted	Secure loose wallcovering *(p. 47)* □○
Blister in wallcovering	Repair blistered wallcovering *(p. 47)* □○
Wallcovering unsuitable	Remove wallcovering *(p. 48)* ⬓◒; prepare to paint *(p. 49)* and paint surface *(p. 50)* ⬓◒
Ceiling tile dirty or damaged	Clean or replace ceiling tile *(p. 51)* □○

DEGREE OF DIFFICULTY: □ Easy ⬓ Moderate ■ Complex
ESTIMATED TIME: ○ Less than 1 hour ◒ 1 to 3 hours ● Over 3 hours
(Does not include drying time)

CLEANING A PAINTED SURFACE

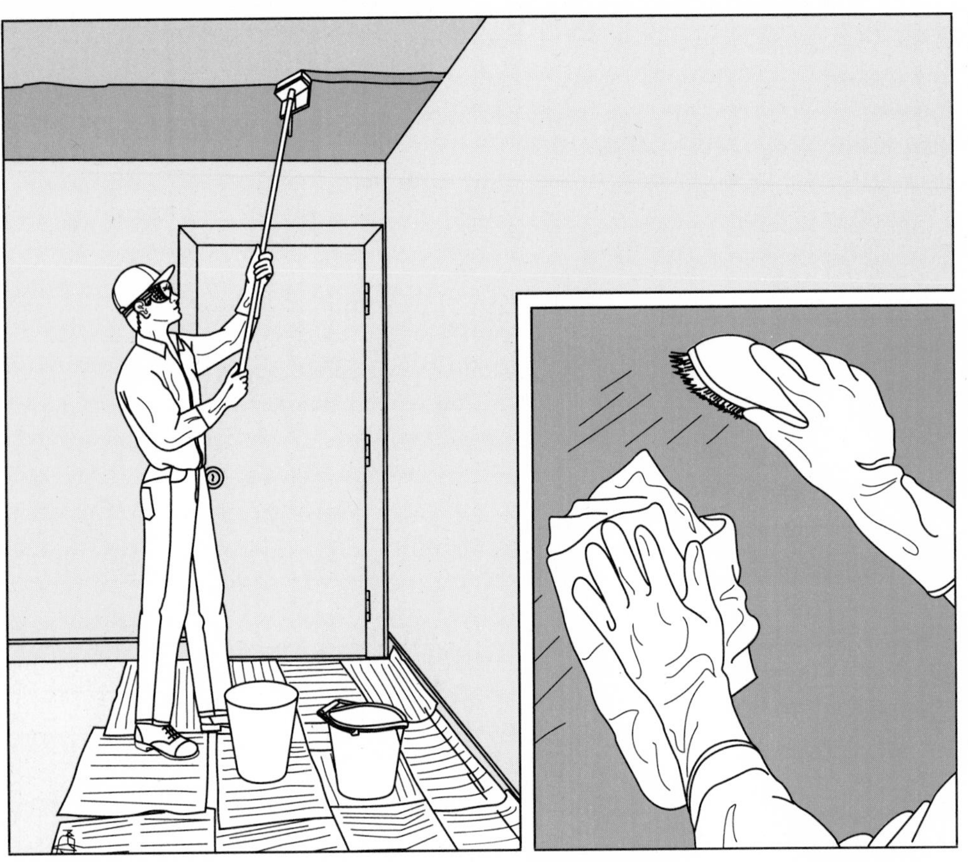

Washing a ceiling or wall. To clean a textured surface, vacuum it with a brush attachment. Otherwise, prepare to wash the ceiling or wall as you would to prepare for painting *(page 49)*. Wearing rubber gloves and safety goggles, mix as many gallons of cleaner as needed in a plastic bucket. For a lightly-soiled surface, mix a little mild household detergent in 1 gallon of water. For stubborn dirt or grease, mix 2 to 3 tablespoons of trisodium phospate (TSP) in 1 gallon of warm water; if you are not repainting, use less TSP to avoid deglossing the paint. For mildew, open a window for ventilation and mix 1 cup of household bleach in 1 gallon of warm water.

To clean a ceiling, soak a sponge mop in the cleaner, then squeeze out excess. Starting in one corner *(left)*, mop a small section of the ceiling; then, rinse and reload the mop. If the mopped section is not completely clean, mop it again; otherwise, mop the next section. Continue the same way until the entire ceiling is clean. To clean a wall, follow the same procedure, using a soft-bristled scrub brush and a supply of clean cloths. Starting in a bottom corner and working up, scrub a small section of the wall, then wipe it dry with a cloth *(inset)*; when the cloth is soiled, use a clean one. If stains remain after cleaning, apply an appropriate solvent *(page 134)*. Safely dispose of leftover cleaner *(page 141)*.

REMOVING PEELING PAINT

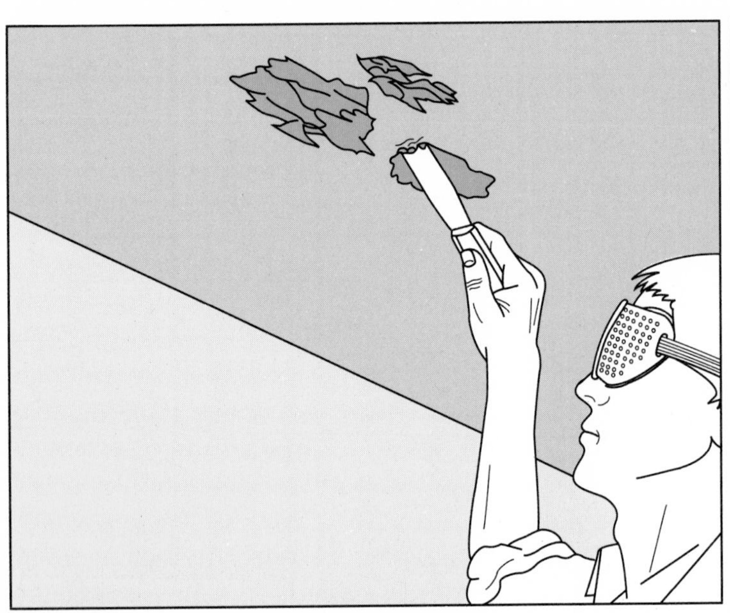

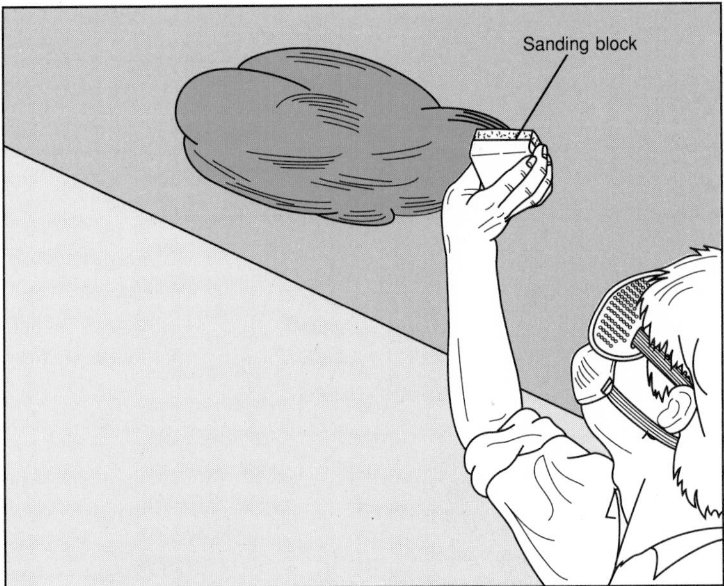

Scraping and sanding a painted surface. To remove loose or peeling paint from a surface, use a putty knife; if you are working overhead, wear safety goggles and use a stepladder *(page 137)*. Slip the blade of the putty knife under the edge of the peeling paint *(above, left)*, then push to dislodge it; work carefully to avoid gouging the surface. To remove stubborn paint, twist the blade slightly to break it. Continue the same way until all the loose and peeling paint is removed. If there are rough edges left by missing paint, wear a dust mask and use medium-grit sandpaper on a sanding block to smooth them *(above, right)*; then, wipe or brush any dust off the surface. Paint the surface *(page 50)*.

RESEATING A POPPED DRYWALL NAIL

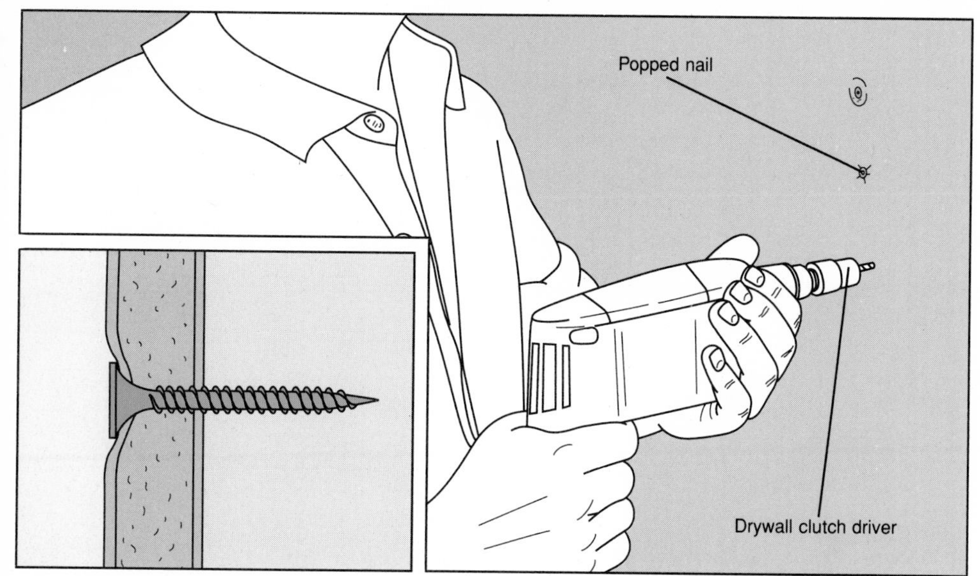

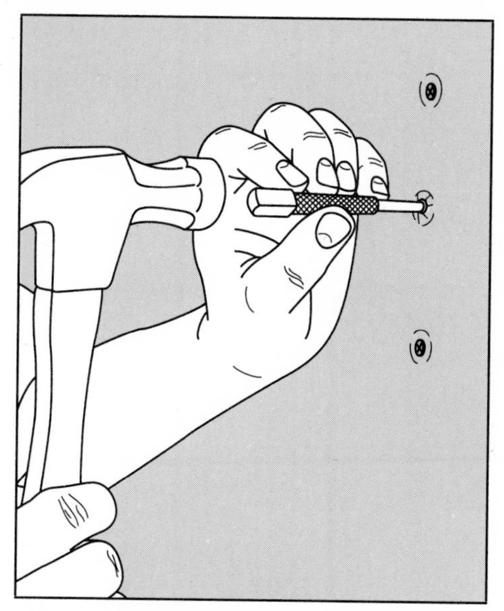

1 Installing drywall screws. Refasten the drywall panel to the stud or joist with drywall screws; if you are working overhead, use a stepladder *(page 137)*. If the popped nail is in the ceiling, find the direction in which the joist runs *(page 130)*; with a popped nail in a wall, as shown, the stud always runs vertically. Prepare to use an electric drill *(page 129)*, fitting it with a drywall clutch driver attachment. Seat a 1 1/4-inch drywall screw in the driver tip. Holding the drill perpendicular to the surface, press the screw tip into it about 2 inches to one side of the popped nail at the stud or joist. Applying moderate pressure, squeeze the trigger switch of the drill to start, slowly guiding the screw through the drywall panel and into the stud or joist. As the screw takes hold, increase the drill speed; continue until the clutch driver just touches the surface, then stop. The screw should be set just below the surface, slightly dimpling the drywall panel *(inset)*. Drive in another screw 2 inches to the other side of the popped nail *(above)*.

2 Hiding the popped nail. If the head of the popped nail protrudes from the surface, carefully try to pull the nail out with pliers and install a drywall screw in the hole *(step 1)*. Otherwise, sink the popped nail below the surface using a nail set and a hammer. Hold the nail set on the head of the popped nail and strike the top of it lightly with the hammer *(above)*, driving the head about 1/16 inch below the surface. Fill the nail and screw holes *(step below)*.

FILLING A SMALL CRACK OR HOLE

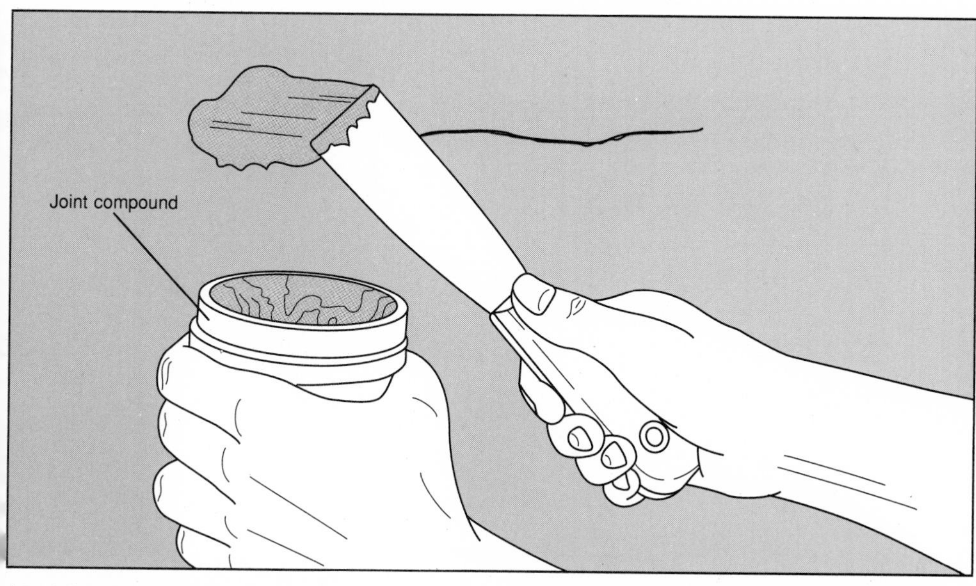

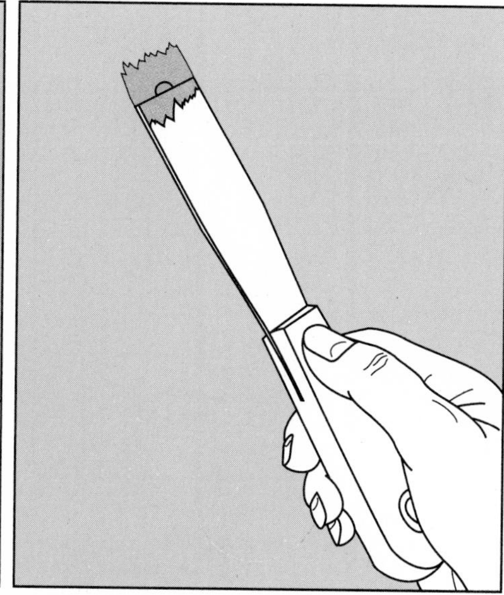

Applying joint compound. To fill a hairline crack or small hole in drywall or plaster, use pre-mixed joint compound; if you are working overhead, use a stepladder *(page 137)*. Using coarse-grit sandpaper on a sanding block, roughen the surface around the damage, then wipe or brush off the dust. Moisten the surface with water from a spray bottle. To fill a hairline crack, use a putty knife to press the compound into the crack, smoothing it flush with the surface *(above, left)*. To fill a small hole, press in the compound with a finger, then use a putty knife to smooth it flush with the surface *(above, right)*. If necessary, texture the wet joint compound *(page 43)*; otherwise, let the joint compound dry. Using medium-grit sandpaper, lightly sand the surface, then wipe or brush off the dust. Paint the surface *(page 50)*.

FILLING A LARGE CRACK

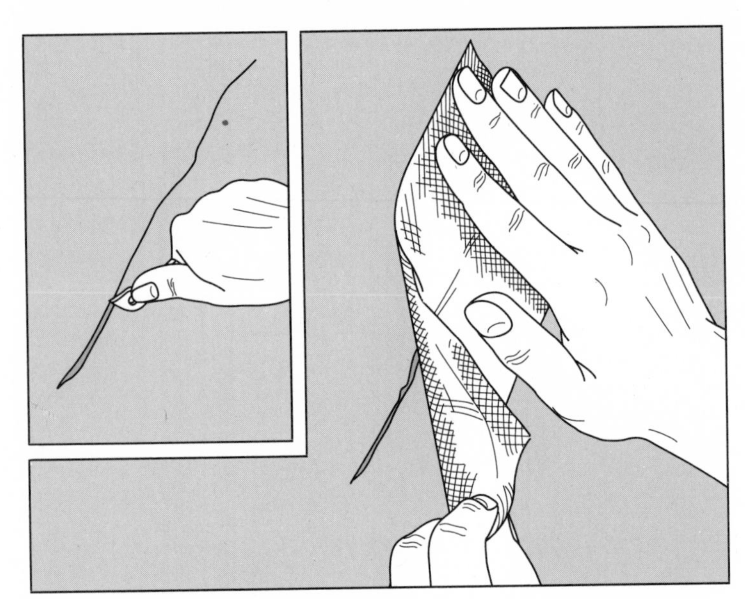

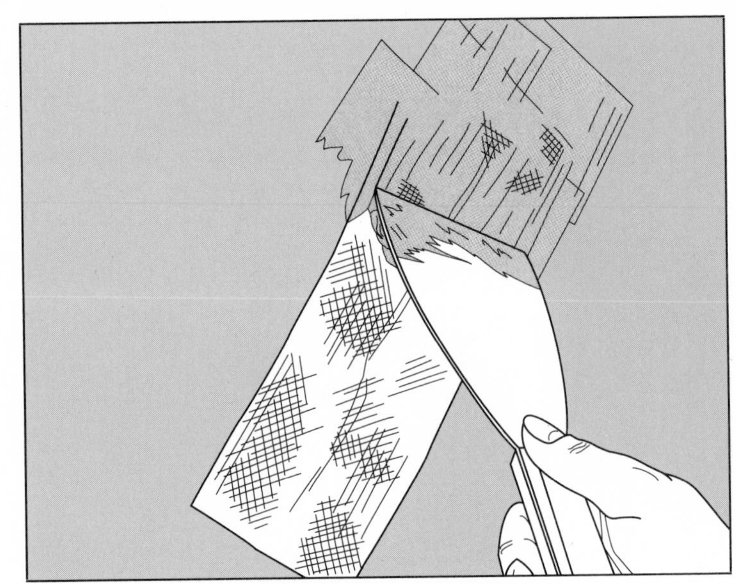

1 Applying fiber-mesh tape. To fill an open crack up to 1/4 inch wide in drywall or plaster, use fiber-mesh joint tape and pre-mixed joint compound; if you are working overhead, use a stepladder *(page 137)*. Open the edges of the crack by lightly drawing the tip of a can opener along it *(inset)*. Brush away loose particles with a soft-bristled brush. Moisten the surface with water from a spray bottle. Cut a length of tape slightly longer than the crack and press it over the crack *(above)*; if the crack is crooked or branched, apply several short lengths of tape without overlapping the ends.

2 Applying joint compound. To fill the taped crack, use a putty knife to spread a thin layer of joint compound over the tape *(above)*, pushing it into the mesh and the crack. Let the compound dry. Next, spread a second, wider layer of compound over the first in one long stroke; then, smooth down the edges of the patch so they are level with the surrounding surface. If necessary, texture the wet compound *(page 43)*; otherwise, let the compound dry. Using medium-grit sandpaper on a sanding block, lightly sand the surface, then wipe or brush off any dust. Paint the surface *(page 50)*.

REPAIRING AN OUTSIDE CORNER

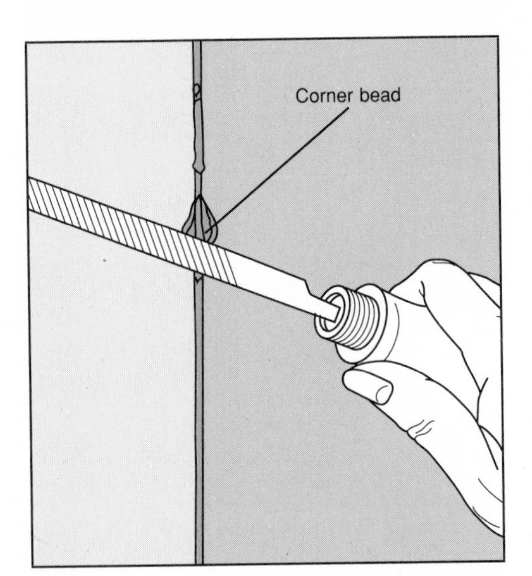

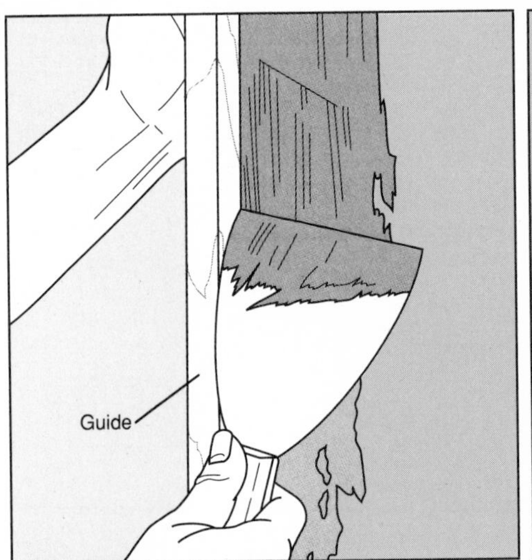

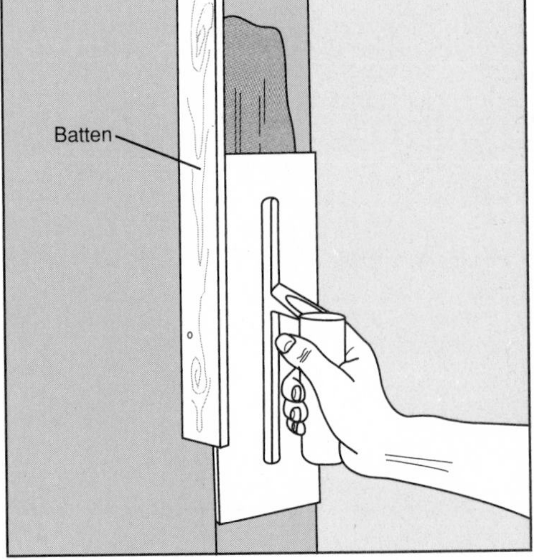

1 Preparing to patch the corner. Using a putty knife, chip away any loose drywall or plaster from the corner. Inspect any exposed metal of the corner bead behind it. If a damaged edge of the corner bead protrudes, use a file to smooth it flush with the corner *(above)*. Using coarse-grit sandpaper on a sanding block, roughen the wall surface around the edges of the opening, then wipe or brush off any dust. Moisten the opening with water from a spray bottle.

2 Patching the corner. To patch the outside corner, use pre-mixed joint compound. For drywall, work with a putty knife and use a board as a guide. Holding the guide against one side of the corner, use the putty knife to work compound into the opening on the opposite side of the corner; then, smooth the compound flush with the surrounding surface *(above, left)*. Let the compound dry, then use the same procedure to patch the other side of the corner.

For plaster, work with a trowel and use a wooden batten as a guide; nail the batten to one side of the corner with its edge protruding beyond the corner. Use the trowel to work a thin layer of compound into the opening on the opposite side of the corner; let the compound dry. Continue applying compound the same way until the opening is filled, smoothing the final layer flush with the surrounding surface *(above, right)*. Remove the batten and use the same procedure to patch the other side of the corner. Remove the batten and fill the nail holes *(page 41)*.

REPAIRING AN OUTSIDE CORNER (continued)

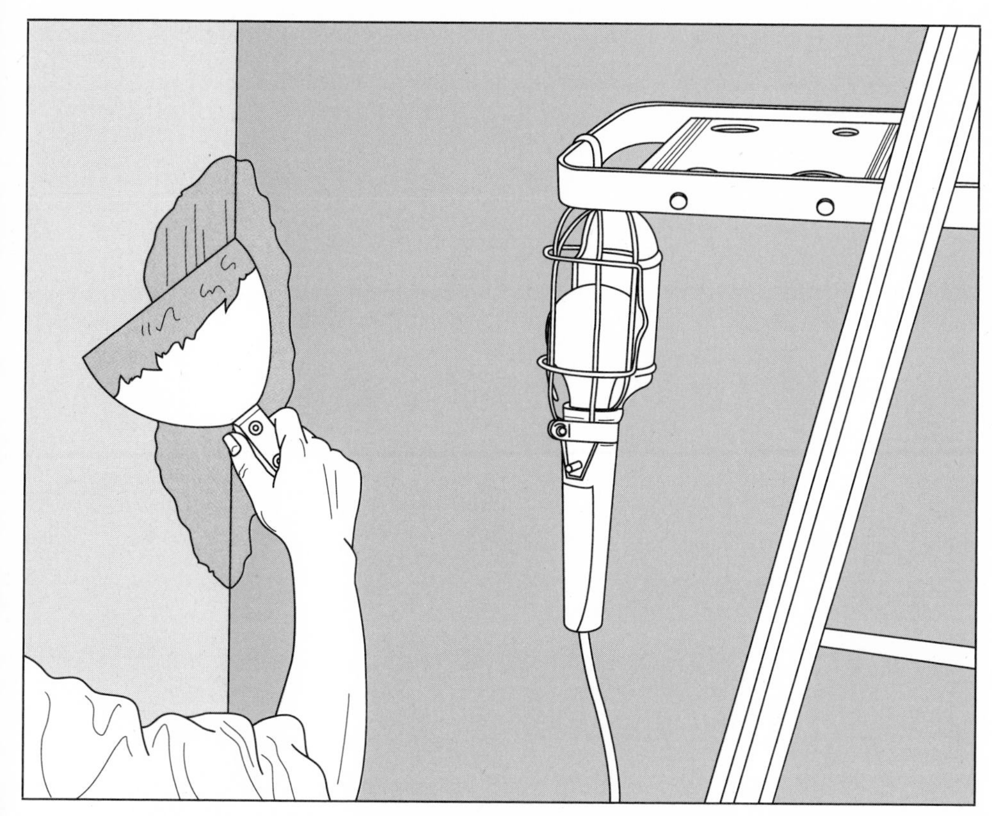

3 Finishing the corner. For a professional-looking corner, use a putty knife to apply a finishing layer of compound to the patched corner. Work with a good light source. Lightly load the putty knife with compound. Starting at the top of the patch on one side of the corner, hold the putty knife so the blade extends past the edge of the corner; then, lightly draw it down the patch *(left)* to smooth on a thin layer. Repeat the procedure on the opposite side of the corner. Wipe the putty knife clean, then feather the compound on each side of the corner. Draw the putty knife over the compound away from the corner, tapering the edges flush with the surrounding surface. If necessary, texture the wet compound *(page 43)*; otherwise, let the compound dry. Using medium-grit sandpaper on a sanding block, lightly sand the surface, then wipe or brush off any dust. Paint the surface *(page 50)*.

DUPLICATING A TEXTURED SURFACE

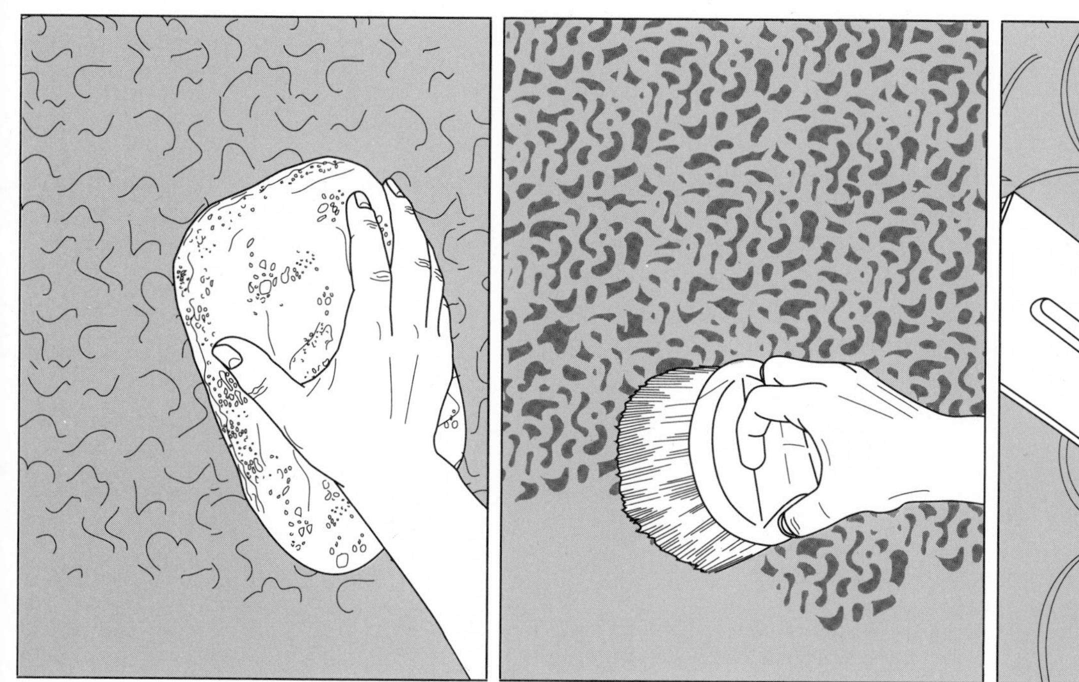

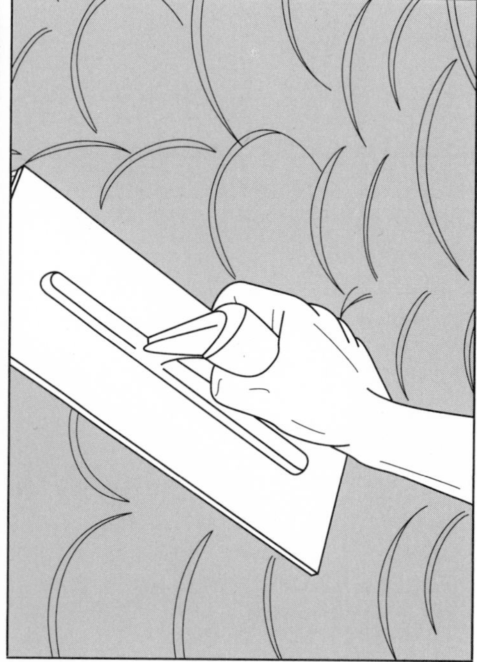

Texturing a patch. To replicate the texture of a surface in the wet joint compound of a patch, practice first on a piece of scrap material; only texture the patch when you are satisifed with your technique. If you are working overhead, use a stepladder *(page 137)*. For an orange-peel type of texture, lightly press a dry sponge into the compound *(above, left)*. For a stippled effect, use a stippling brush *(above, center)*, a whisk broom or a wire brush to gently strike the surface of the compound. For a ridged-adobe effect, pull a trowel in short semicircular passes across the compound *(above, right)*. After texturing the patch, let the compound dry. If the peaks or ridges of the patch are sharper than those of the surrounding surface, use fine-grit sandpaper on a sanding block to lightly sand them. Wipe or brush off any dust, then paint the surface *(page 50)*.

CLEANING A WOOD SURFACE

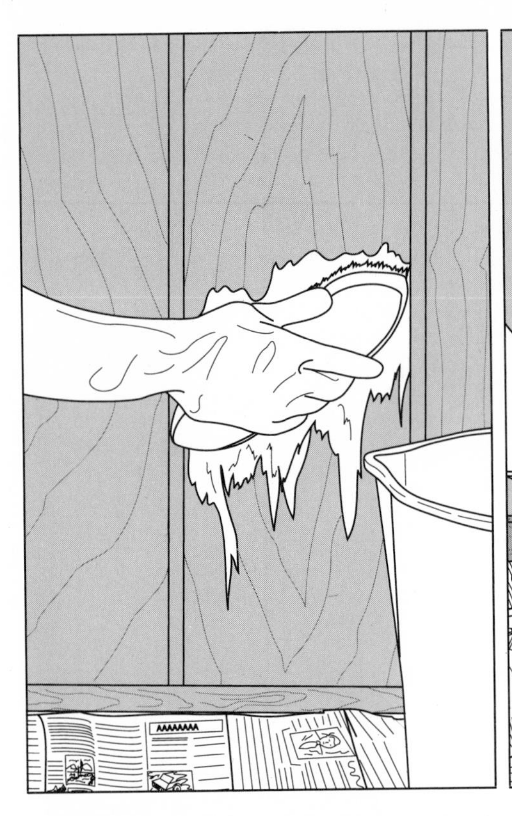

Cleaning wood paneling and trim. Clean painted wood as you would any other painted surface *(page 40)*. For unfinished wood, use a commercial lemon oil. For clear-finished wood, test a soution of mild household detergent and water on an inconspicuous area of the surface. If the finish dulls, use a commercial lemon oil; otherwise, use the solution of detergent and water. If you are working overhead, use a stepladder *(page 137)*.

Prepare to clean as you would to paint *(page 49)*; wear rubber gloves. If you are using a solution of detergent and water, mix as many gallons as needed in a plastic bucket and work with a soft-bristled scrub brush. On a panel, start at a bottom corner and work up, scrubbing a small section *(far left)*; then, rinse and reload the brush. If the section is not completely clean, scrub it again; otherwise, scrub the next section. Continue until the entire panel is clean. On trim, work from end to end the same way. If you are using a commercial lemon oil, work with a lint-free cloth. Following the manufacturer's directions, dampen the cloth with cleaner and wipe it onto the wood, working in the direction of the grain *(near left)*. If stains remain after cleaning, apply an appropriate solvent *(page 134)*. Safely dispose of leftover cleaner *(page 141)*.

REPAIRING A WOOD SURFACE

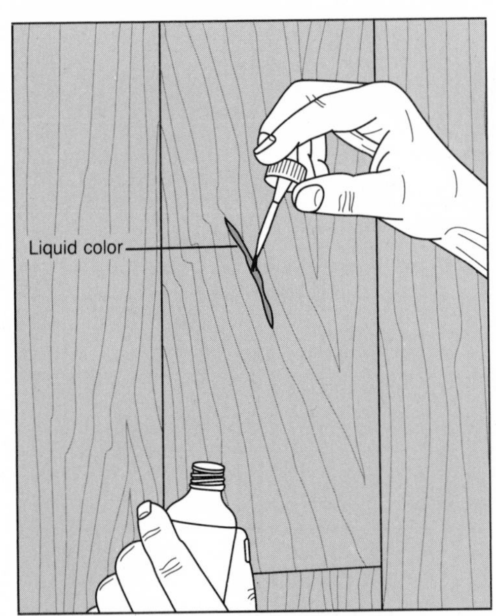

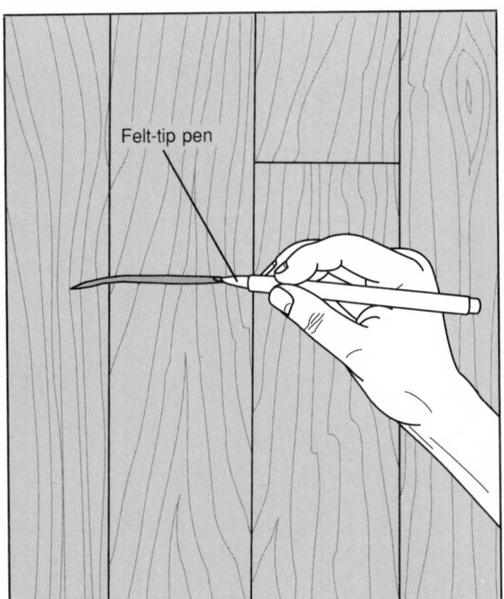

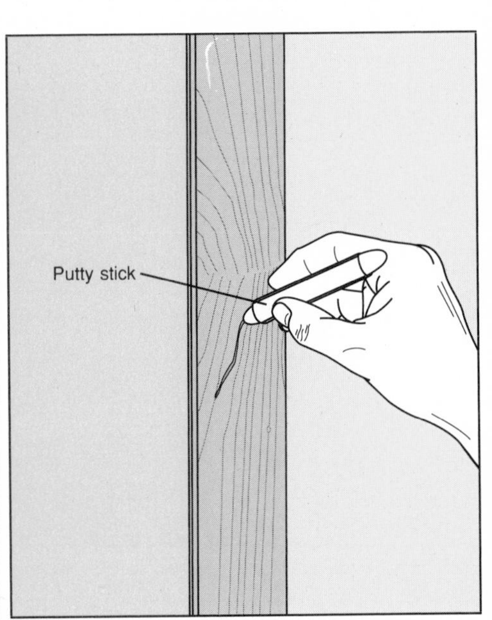

Covering a minor scratch, gouge or dent. To cover a scratch in a wood surface, use liquid color (furniture dye) or a special wood-tone felt-tip pen. To ensure the color matches the wood, test it first on an inconspicuous area of the surface. To apply liquid color, follow the manufacturer's directions to lightly load the applicator and brush the color over the scratch *(above, left)*; then, wipe it with a dry cloth. To use a felt-tip pen, draw it lightly along the scratch *(above, center)*.

To fill a minor gouge or dent or cover a nail head in a wood surface, use a putty stick of a color that matches the wood. Warm the tip between your fingers to soften the putty; then, rub the tip back and forth across the depression *(above, right)* to fill it level with the surrounding surface. Or, use a knife to cut a small piece of putty from the tip, then smooth it into the depression with a finger. Use a wax crayon or wax-based shoe polish to fill the depression the same way.

REPAIRING A WOOD SURFACE (continued)

Filling a small crack or hole. To patch a small hole or crack in a wood surface, use pre-mixed wood patching compound of a color that matches the wood; on painted wood, use white-colored compound. Work with a putty knife. To fill the crack or hole, load the tip of the putty knife with compound and smooth it over the damage *(above)*, overfilling the crack or hole slightly to allow for shrinkage. Let the compound dry; if the patch shrinks and dries below the surface level, fill it again. Use medium-grit sandpaper on a sanding block to sand the patch flush with the surrounding surface, then wipe or brush off any dust. If necessary, paint or refinish the surface *(page 50)*.

Sealing a gap. If trim springs, leaving a gap along the wall, use a rubber mallet padded with a cloth to tap it back into place. Then, drive finishing nails through the trim into the studs behind; use a nail set to set the nail heads, then fill the holes with a putty stick *(page 44)*. To fill any remaining gap, use a caulk *(page 133)* of a color that matches the wood; on painted wood, use clear or white-colored caulk. Load a caulking gun with the caulk. Starting at one end of the gap, squeeze the trigger to eject a continuous bead of caulk along it *(above)*. Wearing a rubber glove, run a wet finger along the caulk to press it down. Let the caulk dry. If necessary, paint or refinish the surface *(page 50)*.

SECURING A WOOD PANEL

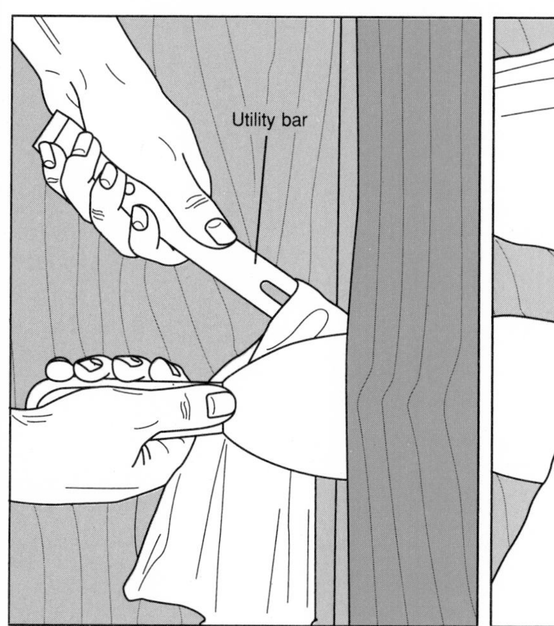

1 Gluing the edge. If the edge of a wood panel is loose or bowed, resecure it by using wood glue to hold it in place, then using nails to fasten it. To apply the glue, use a putty knife and a pry bar padded with a cloth to carefully pry out the panel edge *(above, left)*. Holding the edge out with a wood stick, insert the tip of the glue bottle; squeeze the bottle to eject a continuous bead of glue along the stud or furring strip behind the edge *(above, right)*. Following the directions on the glue bottle label, wait for the glue to become tacky, then firmly push the panel edge back into place. Using a damp cloth, wipe away any extruded glue.

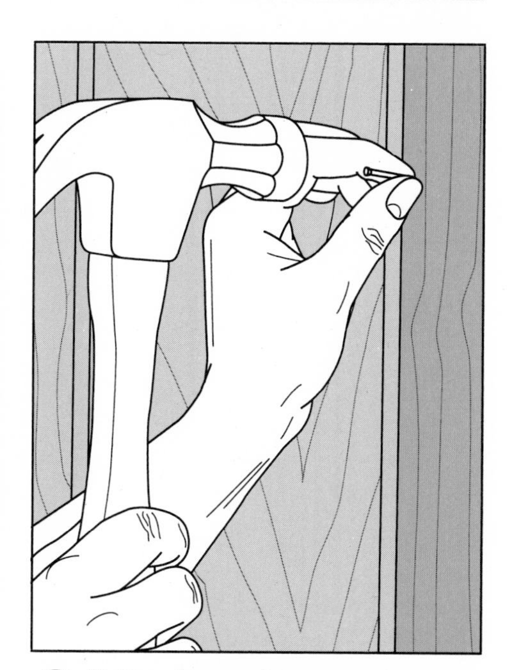

2 Nailing the panel. Drive finishing nails along the glued panel edge *(above)*. If the panel bulges in the middle, locate a stud or furring strip behind the bulge and drive nails through the panel grooves into it. Use a nail set to set the nail heads, then fill the holes with a putty stick *(page 44)*.

TESTING A WALLCOVERING FOR WASHABILITY

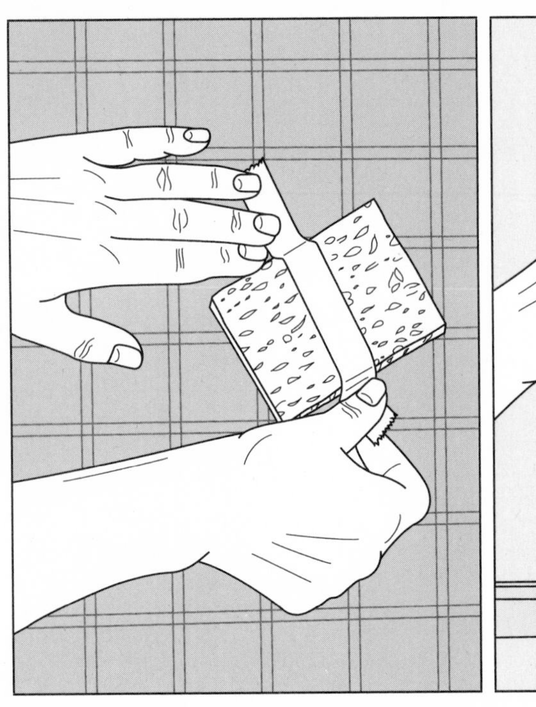

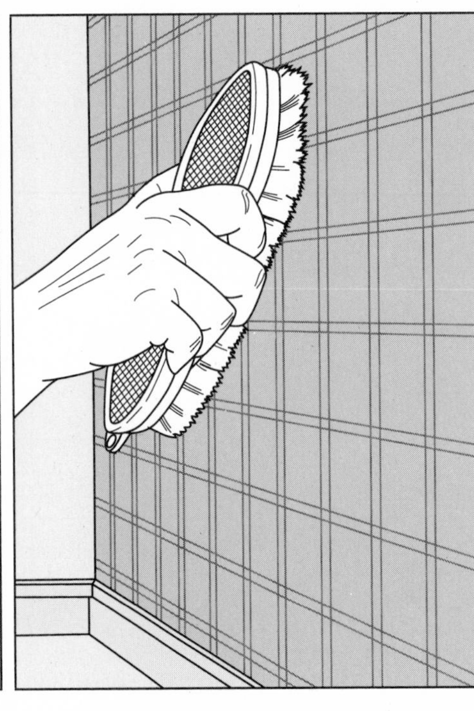

Choosing a cleaning method. To clean a stubborn stain from a wallcovering, buy a commercial wallcovering cleaning product recommended for the type of wallcovering and stain, and follow the manufacturer's directions to use it. To clean a soiled wallcovering, first determine whether it should be washed or dry-cleaned by testing it for water and abrasion resistance on an inconspicuous area of the surface. Attach a water-dampened sponge to the wallcovering with masking tape *(far left)*. Leave it for several minutes, then remove it. If water has penetrated the wallcovering, dry-clean it; if water has not penetrated the wallcovering, wash it. If the wallcovering can be washed, check whether it can be scrubbed by rubbing a soft-bristled scrub brush over the damp area *(near left)*. If the wallcovering does not tear or wear away, use a scrub brush to wash it; if it does tear, use a sponge to wash it. Wash or dry-clean the wallcovering as necessary *(step below)*.

CLEANING A WALLCOVERING

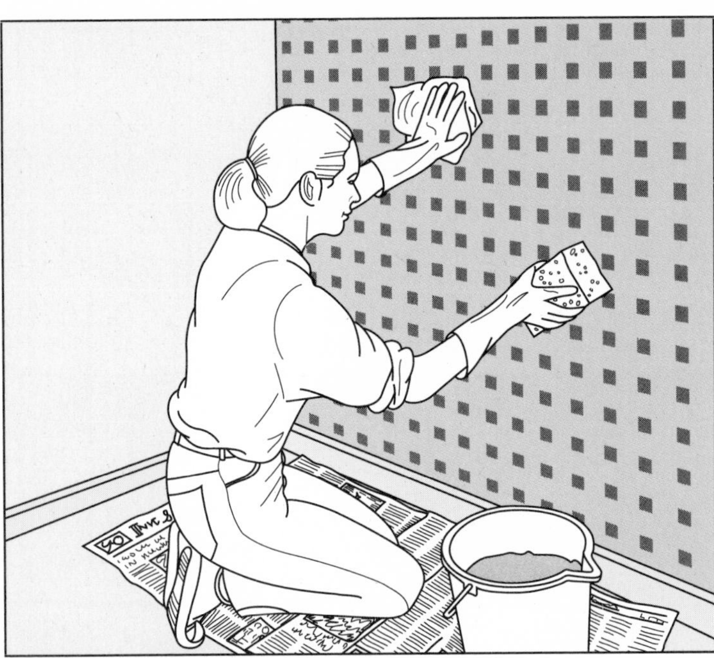

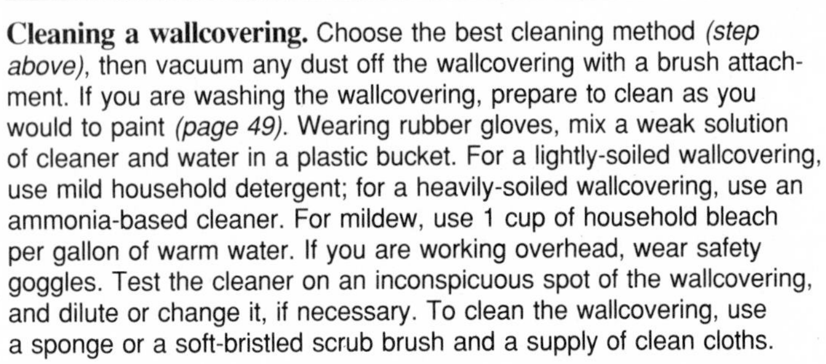

Cleaning a wallcovering. Choose the best cleaning method *(step above)*, then vacuum any dust off the wallcovering with a brush attachment. If you are washing the wallcovering, prepare to clean as you would to paint *(page 49)*. Wearing rubber gloves, mix a weak solution of cleaner and water in a plastic bucket. For a lightly-soiled wallcovering, use mild household detergent; for a heavily-soiled wallcovering, use an ammonia-based cleaner. For mildew, use 1 cup of household bleach per gallon of warm water. If you are working overhead, wear safety goggles. Test the cleaner on an inconspicuous spot of the wallcovering, and dilute or change it, if necessary. To clean the wallcovering, use a sponge or a soft-bristled scrub brush and a supply of clean cloths. Starting in a bottom corner and working up, wash a small section, wiping it dry with a cloth *(above, left)*. Continue, section by section, until the entire wallcovering is clean, ensuring that water does not seep into any seams. Safely dispose of leftover cleaner *(page 141)*.

If you are dry-cleaning the wallcovering, use grade K-1 kerosene and a large cloth. Working outdoors and wearing rubber gloves, dampen the cloth in kerosene, then air it until it is nearly dry. To clean the wallcovering, tie the cloth securely around the head of a mop or broom. Start at a bottom corner and work up, passing the cloth over a strip from floor to ceiling *(above, right)*. Continue, strip by strip, until the entire wallcovering is clean. Safely dispose of the cloth *(page 141)*.

SECURING A LOOSE WALLCOVERING

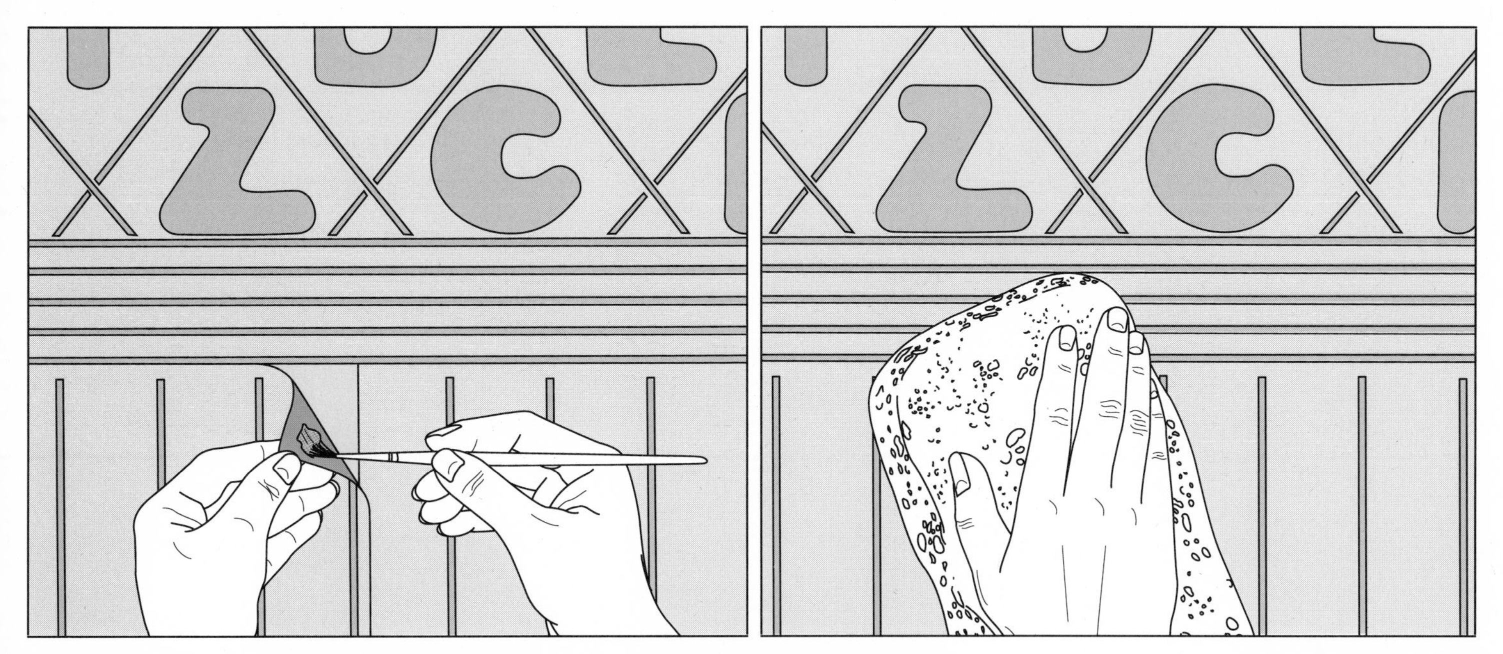

Pasting a corner or seam. To resecure a lifted wallcovering corner or seam, use acrylic seam paste and work with an artist's brush. Using a wet sponge, dampen the lifted wallcovering, then carefully pull it out as far as possible. Load the brush and use it to smooth the adhesive onto as much of the lifted wallcovering and exposed wall as possible *(above, left)*. Let the adhesive dry a few minutes until it is tacky, then gently press the wallcovering back into place. Wait a few minutes more, then use a large sponge *(above, right)* or a seam roller to flatten and smooth the wallcovering. Wipe away any extruded glue with a slightly damp sponge.

REPAIRING A WALLCOVERING BLISTER

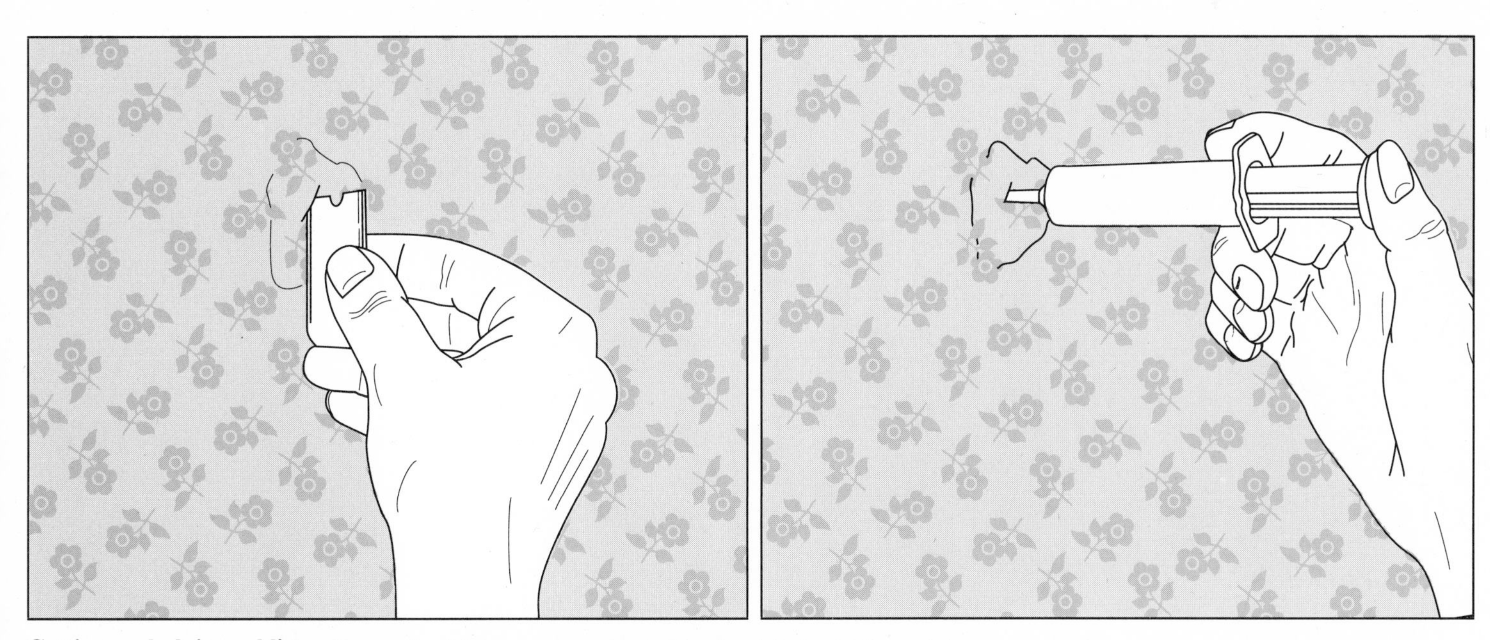

Cutting and gluing a blister. To repair a blister, use a syringe-style glue injector sold specially for wallcovering repairs. Using a wet sponge, dampen the lifted wallcovering. Using a single-edge razor blade or a utility knife, cut a slit in the blister *(above, left)* no larger than the tip of the injector; if possible, make the cut along a pattern line on the wallcovering. Push the tip of the injector tip through the slit and press gently on the plunger to inject a small amount of glue *(above, right)*. Remove the injector, then use a slightly damp sponge to flatten and smooth the wallcovering, and wipe away any extruded glue.

REMOVING A WALLCOVERING

1 Loosening the wallcovering. To remove a wallcovering, check whether it is strippable. Use the tip of a putty knife to loosen the top corner of a wallcovering strip, then pull down on the corner. If the strip pulls away easily, remove it; continue, strip by strip, to remove the wallcovering, then clean the wall *(step 3)*. If the wallcovering is not strippable, use wallcovering remover to loosen it; prepare for the job as you would to paint *(page 49)*. Using a wire brush, lightly score the surface of the wallcovering, taking care not to damage the wall behind. Wearing rubber gloves and opening a window for ventilation, follow the manufacturer's directions to mix as much wallcovering remover and water as needed. If you are working overhead, wear safety goggles. Using a large sponge, wet the wallcovering with remover *(left)*, soaking any scored cuts, seams and edges; repeat several times over a 30-minute period until the remover penetrates. Work the tip of a putty knife under a seam at the bottom of a strip and push upwards. If the strip lifts easily, remove the wallcovering *(step 2)*; if not, apply more remover until it does.

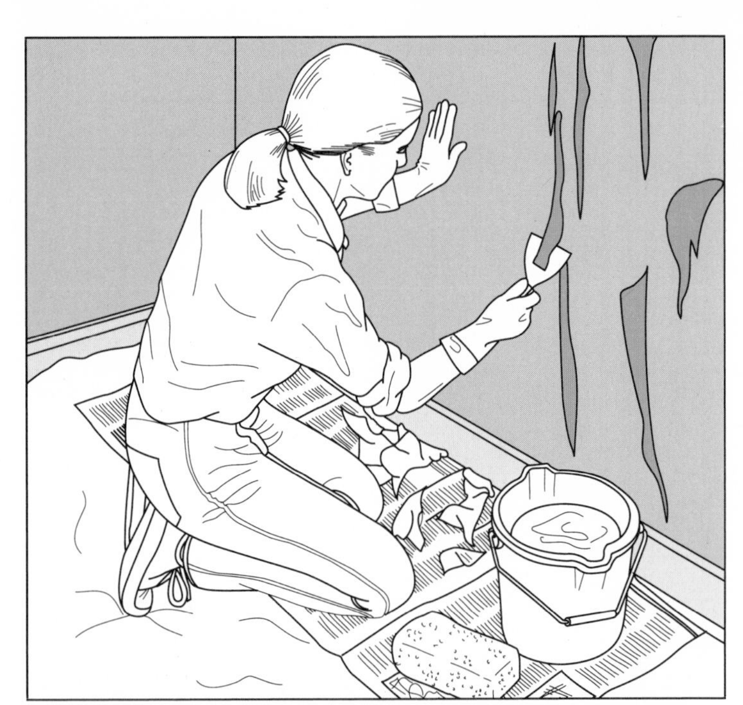

2 Removing non-strippable wallcovering. To remove the wallcovering, use a supply of disposable plastic bags for collecting sodden debris and work with a flexible putty knife. Work the tip of the putty knife under and along a seam at the bottom of a strip of wallcovering and carefully push upwards *(above)*, taking care not to damage the wall behind. As the wallcovering lifts, pull it up and off the wall. Continue, strip by strip, until the wallcovering is removed. If a strip of wallcovering is hard to peel off, do not force it; apply more wallcovering remover *(step 1)*, then continue.

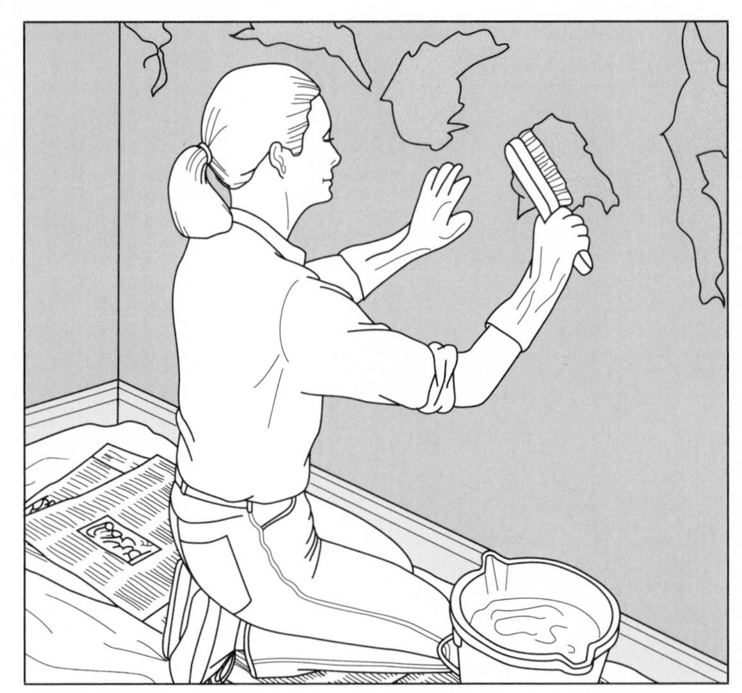

3 Cleaning the wall. Strippable wallcovering may leave a fuzzy residue on the wall—follow the wallcovering manufacturer's instructions to clean it. To clean adhesive left by a non-strippable wallcovering, wear rubber gloves and use a stiff-bristled brush to apply more wallcovering remover *(step 1)*, scrubbing off the residue *(above)*. If mildew remains on the wall, open a window for ventilation and mix a solution of 1 cup of household bleach per gallon of warm water, then scrub it onto the wall. Let the surface dry. Safely dispose of leftover cleaner *(page 141)*. If necessary, paint the surface *(page 50)*.

PREPARING TO PAINT

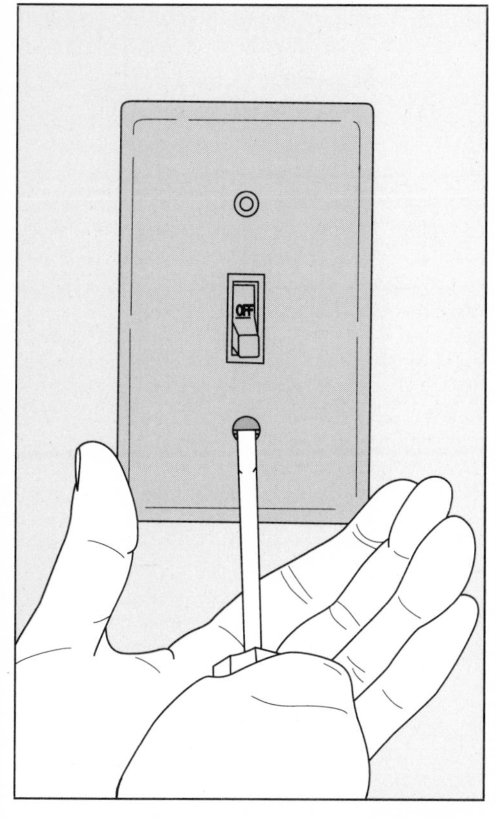

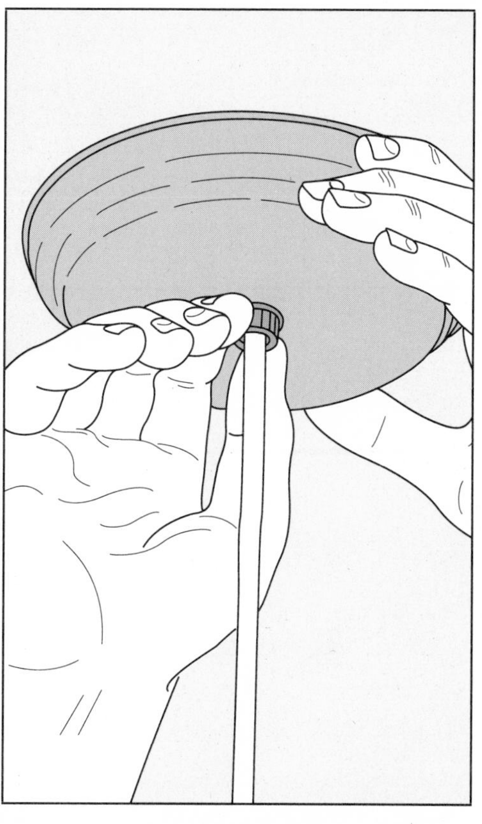

1 Removing obstructions. To prepare for painting, washing or removing a wall-covering, start by moving any freestanding furniture away from the surface. Then, detach from the surface any mounted furnishings: wall hangings, window coverings and bookshelves. Finally, remove any hardware such as brackets, hangers and cover plates fastened to the surface. Before removing the cover plate of a switch, outlet or fixture, shut off electricity to the circuit at the service panel *(page 96)*.

To remove the cover plate of a switch or outlet, unscrew it *(far left)*, then lift it off; tape the screws to the cover plate for safekeeping. To remove the cover plate of a lighting fixture, follow the manufacturer's instructions for your model. On the typical swag fixture shown, unscrew the lock nut *(near left)*, then slide it and the cover plate down the cable; wrap the lighting fixture, cover plate and lock nut together in plastic.

2 Protecting adjacent surfaces. Ensure that any surfaces not to be painted or washed are well protected from splashes and debris before starting work. Store any freestanding furniture as well as detached furnishings and hardware as far from the work surface as is practical—if possible, in another room. Cover and protect large furnishings and immovable fixtures such as radiators or banisters near the work surface with newspapers, fabric drop cloths or plastic sheets. Cover and protect the floor or stairs below the work surface with newspapers or fabric drop cloths—do not use a plastic sheet; it may slip when walked on. For a carpeted floor or stairs, do not use newspaper; the ink may stain the carpeting. Use masking tape to cover and protect the edges of any wall, ceiling, trim, window pane and immovable fixture or hardware adjacent to the work surface; plan to remove the tape as soon as you finish working to prevent any damage from the adhesive.

PAINTING A SURFACE

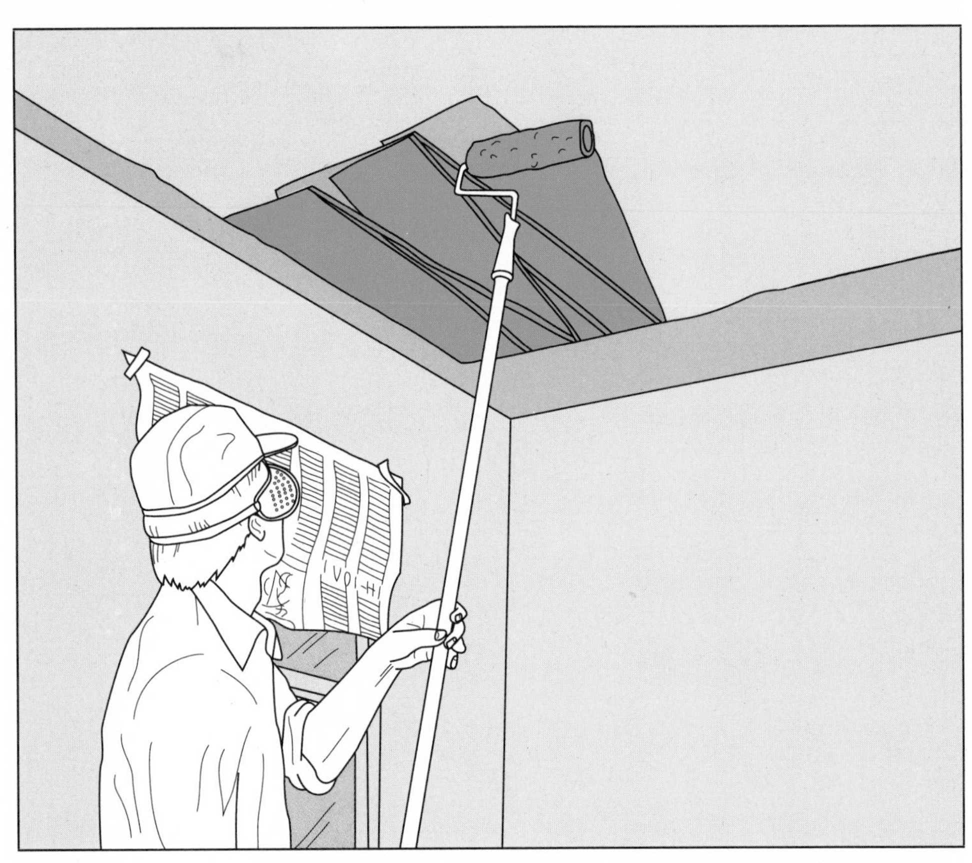

Painting a ceiling. Prepare to paint *(page 49)*. If necessary, clean the ceiling *(page 40)* and make necessary repairs, removing any peeling paint *(page 40)*, reseating any popped nails *(page 41)*, and filling any small cracks or holes *(page 41)* or large cracks *(page 42)*. Select a paint; for a patched surface, also a primer recommended by the paint manufacturer *(page 135)*. Wear a hat and safety goggles. Using a paintbrush, apply primer to any patched area and let it dry.

To paint the ceiling, use a 2-inch trim paintbrush and a short-nap roller fitted with an extension pole; for a textured surface, use a long-nap roller. Use the trim brush to paint a 2-inch strip along the edges of the ceiling at walls and obstructions. Then, use the roller to paint the surface. Starting at a corner, roll paint out onto a 3-foot section, using a W or M pattern *(left)*; then, reverse the pattern to roll back over the paint and smooth it. Reload the roller and continue, section by section, until the ceiling is painted; roll slowly to avoid spraying and splattering. Let the paint dry; if necessary, apply another coat. Safely dispose of leftover paint *(page 141)*.

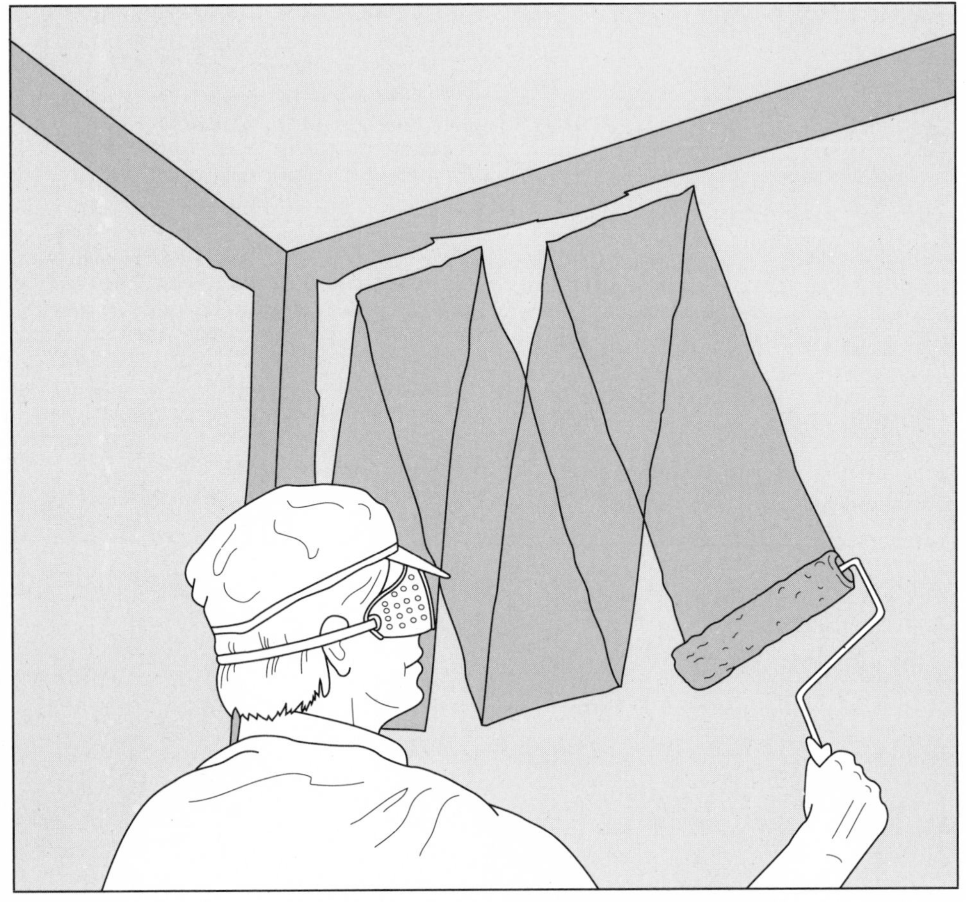

Painting a wall. Prepare to paint *(page 49)*. If necessary, clean the wall *(page 40)*. Remove any peeling paint *(page 40)*. Reseat any popped nails *(page 41)*. Fill any small cracks or holes *(page 41)* or large cracks *(page 42)*. Repair any damaged outside corner *(page 42)*. Select a paint; for a patched surface, also a primer recommended by the paint manufacturer *(page 135)*. Wear a hat and safety goggles. Using a paintbrush, apply primer to any patched area and let it dry.

To paint the wall, use a 2-inch trim paintbrush and a short-nap roller fitted with an extension pole; for a textured surface, use a long-nap roller. Use the trim brush to paint a 2-inch strip along the edges of the wall at the ceiling, other walls and obstructions. Then, use the roller to paint the surface. Starting at a top corner, roll paint out onto a 3-foot section, using a W or M pattern *(left)*; then, reverse the pattern to roll back over the paint and smooth it. Reload the roller and continue, section by section, until the wall is painted; roll slowly to avoid spraying and splattering. Let the paint dry; if necessary, apply another coat. Safely dispose of leftover paint *(page 141)*.

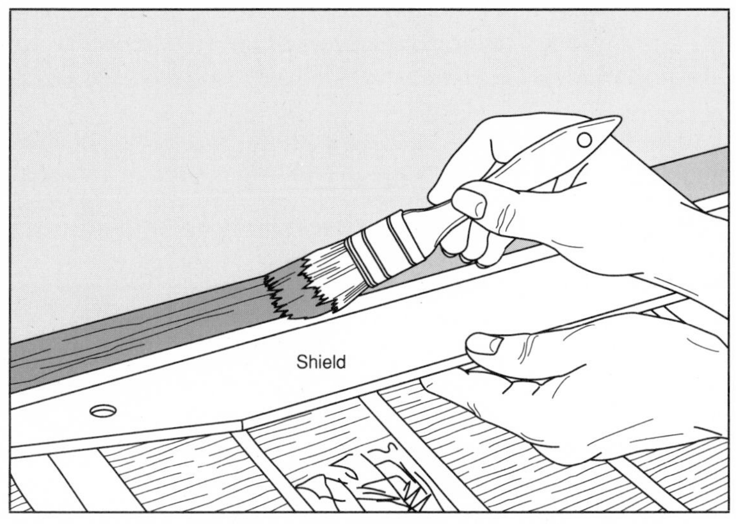

Painting or refinishing wood trim. Prepare to paint or refinish the surface *(page 49)*. If necessary, clean the trim *(page 44)*. Remove any peeling paint *(page 40)* and make any necessary repairs to the surface *(page 44)*. Select a paint or finish; for a patched surface, also a primer recommended by the paint manufacturer *(page 135)*. Using medium-grit sandpaper on a sanding block, smooth old paint or remove old clear finish, then wipe or brush off any dust. Use a paintbrush to apply primer to any patched area; let it dry.

To paint trim, use a 2-inch trim paintbrush and work with a shield. Start at one end of the trim and work along it in the direction of the wood grain. Holding the shield against the edge of the trim to protect the adjacent wall *(above, left)* or floor *(above, right)*, brush paint onto a section of trim using a smooth back-and-forth stroke; then, reverse the direction of the stroke to brush lightly back over the paint and smooth it. Reload the paintbrush and continue, section by section, until the trim is painted; regularly wipe dripped paint off the edge of the shield with a clean cloth to prevent smears. Let the paint dry; if necessary, apply another coat. Safely dispose of leftover paint *(page 141)*.

To apply clear finish to trim, follow the same procedure, wiping the sanded wood with mineral spirits before applying the first coat. Use fine-grit sandpaper on a sanding block to lightly sand a dried coat of finish before applying an additional coat.

CLEANING OR REPLACING A CEILING TILE

Removing a ceiling tile. If a grid-mounted ceiling tile is damaged or dirty, remove it. Wearing safety goggles and working on a stepladder *(page 137)*, push up the tile to free it, then turn and tilt it sideways *(left)* to slide it out. Replace a badly damaged tile with an exact duplicate. To clean a dusty tile, vacuum it with a brush attachment. To clean a lightly-soiled tile, wipe the tile with a cloth dampened with a solution of mild household detergent and water; then, wipe it with a damp sponge and dry it with a clean cloth. To clean a fingerprint or smoke stain from a tile, use a natural-rubber "dry sponge" or artist's gum eraser to gently rub it off. To refurbish a heavily-soiled tile, paint it. Use a spray can of latex paint of a color that matches the tile; if the tile is water-stained, also an oil-based primer *(page 135)*. Use a paintbrush to apply primer to any water stain and let it dry. Then, spray-paint the tile following the paint manufacturer's instructions and let it dry. To install a tile, slide it short- side first through the grid opening; then, turn and lower it into place, ensuring that it is securely seated. Examine the metal grid; if it is rust-stained, use a cloth dampened with denatured alcohol to clean it.

KITCHEN AND BATHROOMS

The condition of your kitchen and bathrooms can make or break the sale of your home. While a kitchen and bathroom are exposed to more relentless use and daily abuse than any other room in the house, a potential buyer wants to see a kitchen and bathrooms that are clean, comfortable and efficient. Before you put your house on the market, inspect your kitchen and bathrooms thoroughly and fix flaws that the choosy buyer will be on the lookout for. Use the Troubleshooting Guide *(below)* and the checklist diagrams *(page 53)* to help identify common problems you might easily overlook; then, refer to the pages indicated to make the appropriate repairs.

Constant use, exposure to water and steam, repeated spot-cleaning and temperature fluctuations all take their toll on kitchen and bathroom surfaces. The first "fix" is therefore the most basic: a thorough cleaning—including sinks, bathtubs, countertops, cabinets, fixtures and appliances. A solution of mild household detergent and water can remove many stains from most surfaces; a stubborn stain or a special surface may require special treatment. Refer to the cleaning guide on page 54 for advice on making any surface shine. After cleaning, make all necessary surface repairs. Resecure any lifted laminate or edging tape on a counter *(page 57)*. Cover a scratch in an enamel, porcelain, wood or laminate surface and fill a nicked surface *(page 55)*; to ensure that the repair will not be visible, first test the color of any filler on an inconspicuous part of the surface.

A minor flaw in a kitchen or bathroom drawer or cabinet is common; a drawer or cabinet is exposed to temperature and humidity extremes as well as moisture, and may be opened and closed many times a day. Repair a sticking drawer so that it slides smoothly and repair a crooked cabinet door so that it hangs straight *(page 56)*. Clean door and drawer hardware; replace missing or damaged pieces.

In a bathroom, clean ceramic tile surfaces and the grouted joints between tiles. Replace a damaged ceramic tile and repair damaged grout *(page 58)*. Inspect the caulk between the wall and the bathtub; missing or damaged caulk is not only unsightly but can create leak problems. If necessary, recaulk any faulty joint *(page 57)*.

Some kitchen and bathroom furnishings may be worth replacing before you show the house. For example, a soiled or stained shower curtain can detract from a bathroom's appearance; consider replacing it with an inexpensive new one. Or, if a toilet seat is worn, replace it *(page 59)*.

TROUBLESHOOTING GUIDE

SYMPTOM	PROCEDURE
Plumbing fixture faulty	Service plumbing system *(p. 107)*
Electrical outlet, switch or lighting fixture faulty	Service electrical system *(p. 95)*
Wall or ceiling dirty, dingy or faded	Service walls and ceilings *(p. 38)*
Surface dirty or stained	Clean surface *(p. 54)* □○
Enamel-coated surface scratched or nicked	Repair enamel-coated surface *(p. 55)* □○
Porcelain surface scratched or nicked	Repair porcelain surface *(p. 55)* □○
Plastic laminate surface scratched or nicked	Repair plastic laminate surface *(p. 55)* □○
Wood surface scratched or nicked	Repair wood surface *(p. 55)* □○
Plastic laminate corner or edge lifted from countertop	Resecure plastic laminate *(p. 57)* □○
Drawer sticking or binding	Service drawer *(p. 56)* □○
Cabinet door loose or crooked	Service cabinet door *(p. 56)* ⬓○
Drawer or cabinet door hardware loose, damaged or missing	Tighten loose hardware; replace damaged or missing hardware
Caulk between bathtub and wall damaged or missing	Recaulk joint *(p. 57)* □○
Ceramic tile grout damaged or missing	Regrout ceramic tile joint *(p. 58)* □◒
Ceramic tile grout dirty or stained	Clean grout *(p. 54)* □○; seal grout *(p. 58)* □○
Ceramic tile damaged or missing	Replace ceramic tile *(p. 58)* ⬓◒
Bathtub anti-slip decal worn	Soften decal with mineral spirits, nail polish remover or lacquer thinner, then gently scrape from surface with a razor-blade tool; clean bathtub surface *(p. 54)* □○
Toilet seat loose or damaged	Service toilet seat *(p. 59)* □○

DEGREE OF DIFFICULTY: □ **Easy** ⬓ **Moderate** ■ **Complex**
ESTIMATED TIME: ○ **Less than 1 hour** ◒ **1 to 3 hours** ● **Over 3 hours**
(Does not include drying time)

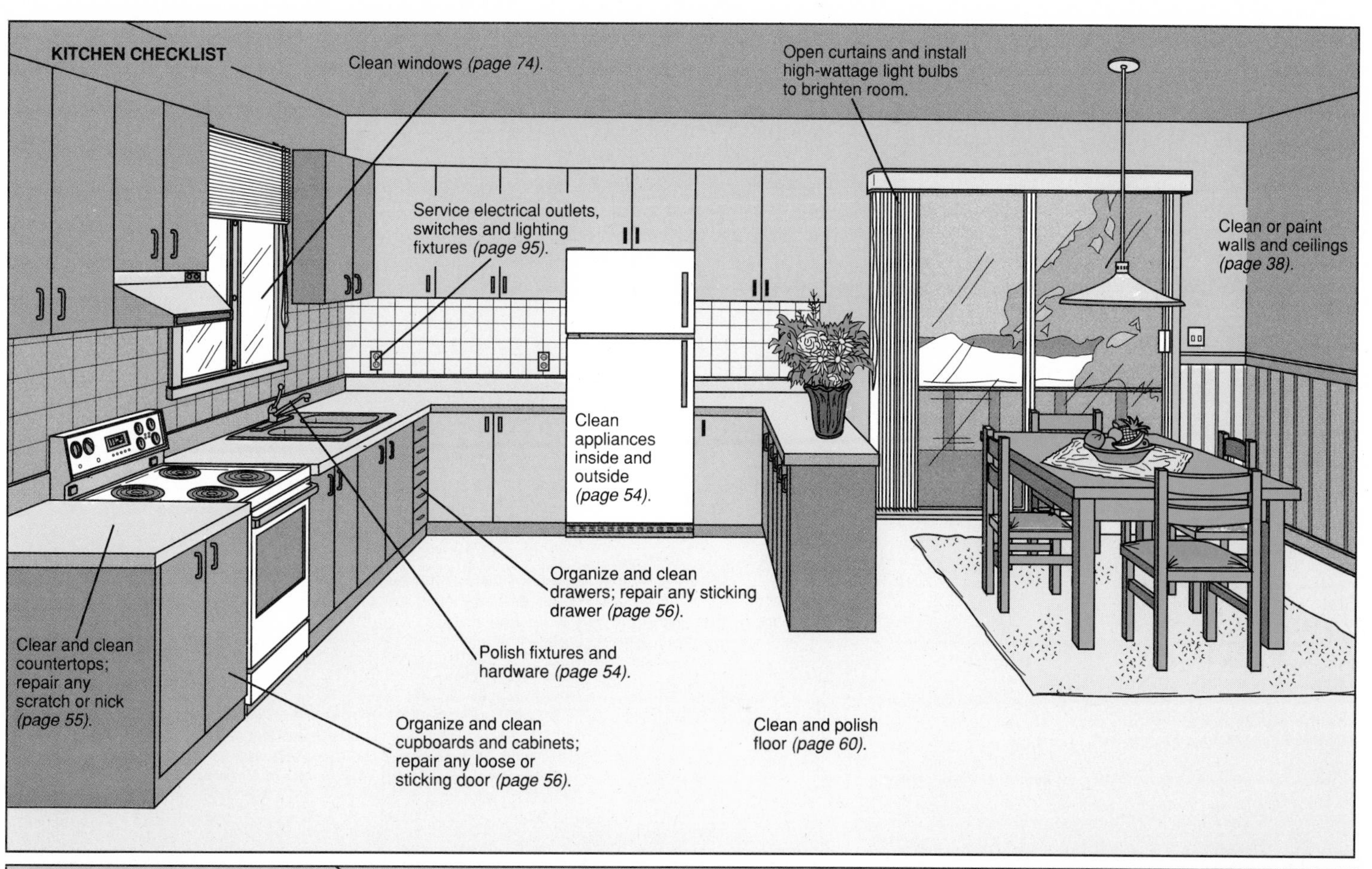
KITCHEN CHECKLIST
Clean windows (page 74).
Open curtains and install high-wattage light bulbs to brighten room.
Service electrical outlets, switches and lighting fixtures (page 95).
Clean or paint walls and ceilings (page 38).
Clean appliances inside and outside (page 54).
Organize and clean drawers; repair any sticking drawer (page 56).
Polish fixtures and hardware (page 54).
Clear and clean countertops; repair any scratch or nick (page 55).
Organize and clean cupboards and cabinets; repair any loose or sticking door (page 56).
Clean and polish floor (page 60).

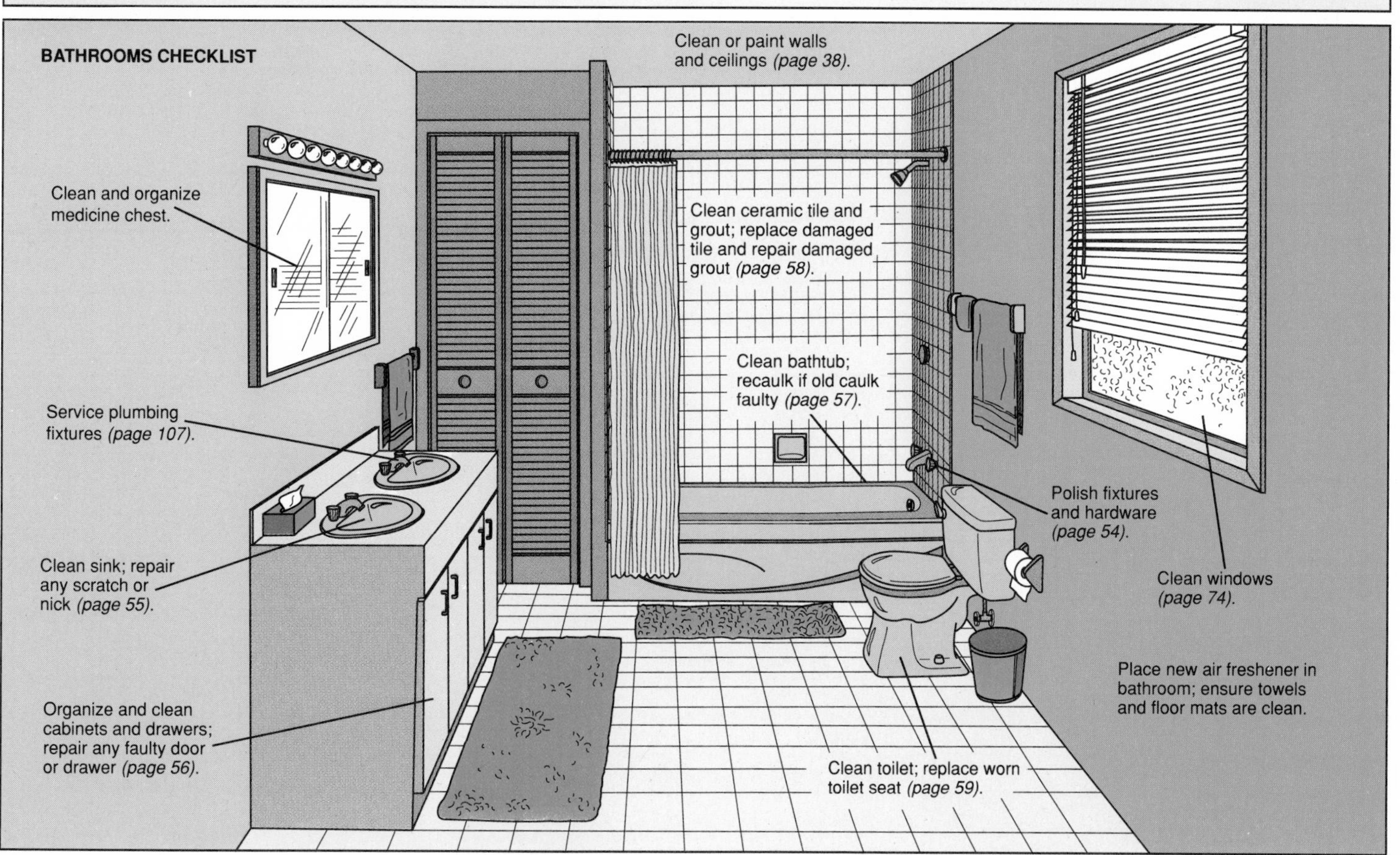
BATHROOMS CHECKLIST
Clean or paint walls and ceilings (page 38).
Clean and organize medicine chest.
Clean ceramic tile and grout; replace damaged tile and repair damaged grout (page 58).
Clean bathtub; recaulk if old caulk faulty (page 57).
Service plumbing fixtures (page 107).
Polish fixtures and hardware (page 54).
Clean sink; repair any scratch or nick (page 55).
Clean windows (page 74).
Place new air freshener in bathroom; ensure towels and floor mats are clean.
Organize and clean cabinets and drawers; repair any faulty door or drawer (page 56).
Clean toilet; replace worn toilet seat (page 59).

CLEANING A KITCHEN OR BATHROOM SURFACE

Removing dirt, stains and deposits. To clean most kitchen and bathroom surfaces, a solution of mild household detergent and water or an all-purpose household cleaner is usually sufficient. For a stubborn stain, a special cleaner or method may be necessary; refer to the cleaning guide below for instructions on removing typical stains.

Always start with the mildest cleaner; change to a stronger one only if necessary. When possible, use a common household product such as household bleach, baking soda or white vinegar instead of a commercial cleaner. Buy a special product such as rottenstone or trisodium phosphate (TSP) at a grocery store or a building supply center; buy automative body polish at an auto parts supply store.

Exercise caution when you are using any cleaner; keep it away from children and pets. Never mix together different cleaners unless you are specifically instructed by the manufacturer. Also avoid using an abrasive unless you are specifically instructed; you may scratch the surface. Wear rubber gloves when working with a cleaner. To prepare a paste or a poultice, use a clean container. Start with a small amount of any dry ingredient, then slowly add liquid, stirring constantly, until you achieve the consistency desired: batter-like for a paste and putty-like for a poultice. If you leave a poultice on a surface overnight, cover it with plastic; tape the plastic to the surface using duct tape or masking tape. Safely dispose of any leftover cleaner *(page 141)*.

SURFACE	CLEANING METHOD
Porcelain or porcelain-enamel bathtub or sink	For mineral deposits, use a stiff-bristled brush loaded with a paste of baking soda and white vinegar; then, rinse with water and let dry. For common stains, use a paste of cream of tartar and hydrogen peroxide. For stubborn stains, line the surface with paper towels and saturate the towels with household bleach; leave for 30 minutes, then remove the towels and rinse with water.
Fiberglass shower or bathtub	For stubborn stains, use a cloth dampened with a non-abrasive commercial cleaner; then, wipe clean with a damp sponge. To polish, use a cloth loaded with automotive body polish.
Stainless steel sink or fixture	For rust stains, use a cloth dampened with white vinegar, rubbing in the direction of any steel grain; then, dry immediately with a cloth.
Stainless steel or chrome shower head	For mineral deposits, remove shower head *(page 109)*. Use a toothpick to clean out holes; then, soak head overnight in white vinegar and rinse with water.
Porcelain toilet bowl	For common stains, pour in commercial toilet bowl cleaner; scrub with a stiff-bristled brush, then flush. For stubborn stains, pour in 1 cup of household bleach.
Enamel-coated appliance	For common stains, use a sponge or a soft scrub pad dampened with a non-abrasive commercial cleaner; then, rinse with water and let dry. For stubborn stains, use undiluted household bleach. To polish, use a cloth loaded with automotive body polish.
Brass fixture	For tarnish, use a cloth loaded with a commercial brass cleaner or a paste of equal parts of salt, flour and white vinegar; then, rinse with water and let dry. Polish with a cloth. To prevent tarnish, apply a commercial acrylic spray according to the manufacturer's instructions.
Chrome fixture	For mineral deposits, use a stiff-bristled brush dampened with white vinegar—never a metal cleaner or an abrasive cleaner; then, dry and polish immediately with a cloth.
Unpainted wood	For common dirt and stains, use a soft-bristled brush dampened with mineral oil, gently rubbing in the direction of the wood grain. For stubborn dirt and stains, use a brush loaded with a paste of rottenstone and mineral oil; then, wipe clean with a damp sponge and dry with a cloth. To polish, use a cloth dampened with lemon oil or wood polish.
Painted wood	For stubborn dirt and stains, mix 2 to 3 tablespoons of trisodium phosphate (TSP) in 1 gallon of warm water and scrub with a soft-bristled brush; then, rinse with water.
Wood chopping block or cutting board	For deposits and greasy coatings, use a soft-bristled brush loaded with a paste of baking soda and water; then, wipe clean with a damp sponge and rub with cooking oil.
Plastic laminate countertop	For stubborn stains, use a cloth loaded with a paste of baking soda and water; then, rinse with water and dry immediately with a cloth. For ink stains, use a cloth dampened with rubbing alcohol. To polish, use a cloth loaded with acrylic floor polish.
Marble countertop	For stubborn stains, mix a poultice of talcum powder or whiting (calcium carbonate) and household bleach, and apply with a rubber-gloved hand; leave overnight, then scrape off by hand. Rinse with water, and dry immediately with a cloth.
Ceramic tile and grout	For stubborn stains, mix 2 teaspoons of white vinegar or heavy-duty laundry detergent in 1 quart of water, and scrub with a stiff-bristled brush; then, rinse with water, and dry immediately wth a cloth. For mildew, mix 1/2 cup of household bleach in 1 quart of water; for stubborn mildew, use undiluted household bleach. For a permanent stain on grout, apply a commercial grout colorant.
Plastic shower curtain	For dirt and mildew, use a sponge loaded with a paste of baking soda and water; then, wipe clean with a sponge dampened with lemon juice. Rinse with water.
Cloth shower curtain	For dirt and mildew, machine-wash without spinning dry; use laundry detergent and 1/2 cup of baking soda in the wash cycle and white vinegar in the rinse cycle, then hang up to dry.
Glass shower door	For filmy deposits, use a sponge dampened with white vinegar; then, dry with a cloth.
Acrylic shower door	For stubborn stains, use a cloth dampened with lemon juice; then, dry immediately with a cloth.
Mirror	For filmy deposits, use a sponge dampened with white vinegar; then, dry with a cloth.

REPAIRING A SCRATCH OR NICK

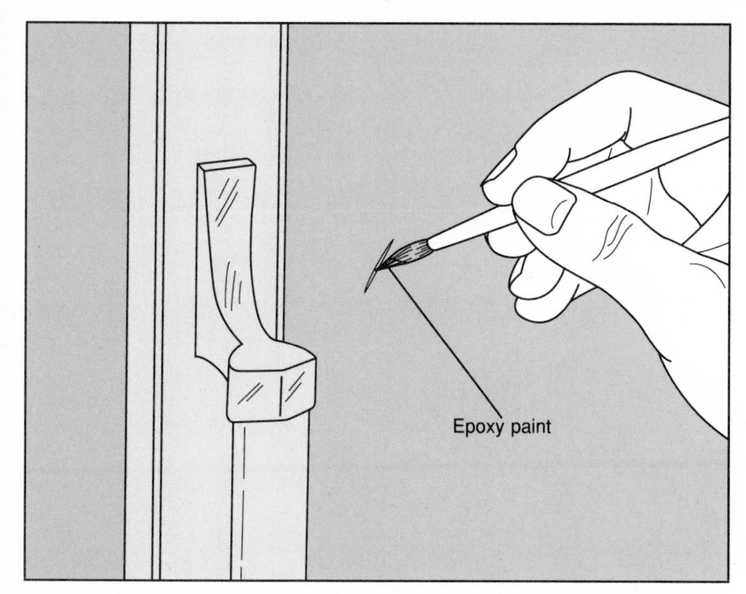

Repairing an enamel-coated surface. To repair a gouge in an enamel surface such as that of an appliance, consult a professional about recoating the surface. To cover a scratch or surface nick in an enamel surface, use epoxy paint; ensure the color matches the enamel by testing it first on an inconspicuous area of the surface. To apply epoxy paint, follow the manufacturer's directions to lightly load an artist's brush and brush the paint onto the scratch or nick *(above)*. Let the paint dry. If desired, polish the surface using a soft cloth and automotive body polish. Safely dispose of leftover paint *(page 141)*.

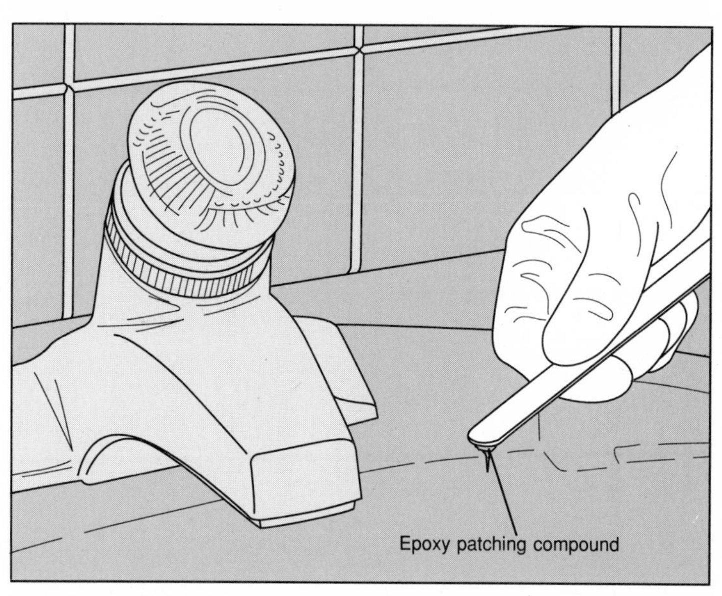

Repairing a porcelain surface. To cover a scratch or fill a nick in a porcelain surface such as that of a sink, use an epoxy patching compound; ensure the color matches the porcelain by testing it first on an inconspicuous area of the surface. Wearing rubber gloves, follow the manufacturer's directions to mix the resin and hardener into a compound. Then, working quickly and carefully, use a lightly-loaded disposable stick to dab the compound onto the damage *(above)*, smoothing it flush with the surrounding surface. Wipe off drips using a cloth dampened with mineral spirits. Safely dispose of leftover compound *(page 141)*.

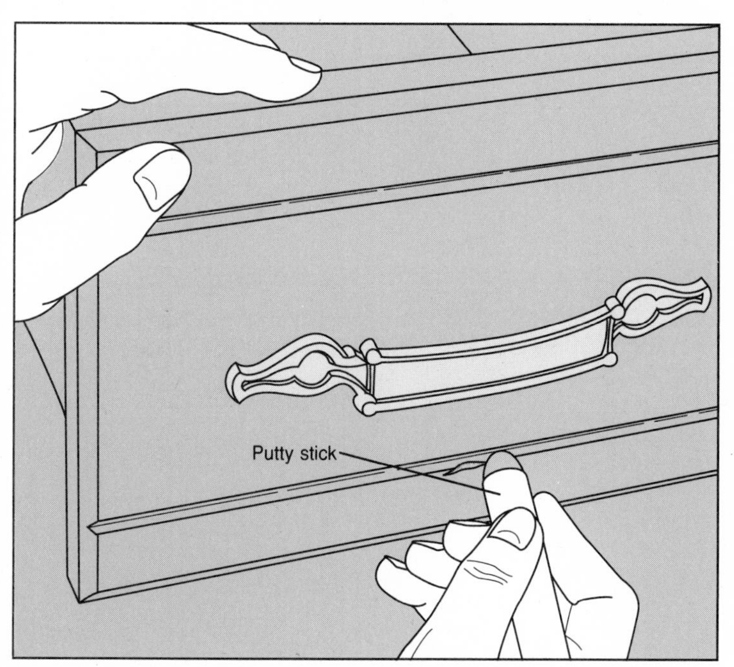

Repairing a wood surface. To cover a scratch in wood, use liquid color (furniture dye) or a special wood-tone felt-tip pen; ensure the color matches the wood by testing it first on an inconspicuous area of the surface. To apply liquid color, follow the manufacturer's directions to brush the color over the scratch; then, wipe it with a dry cloth. To use a felt-tip pen, draw it lightly along the scratch. To fill a nick in wood, use a putty stick of a color that matches the wood. Warm the tip between your fingers to soften the putty; then, rub the tip back and forth across the nick *(above)* to fill it level with the surface. Alternately, use a knife to cut a piece of putty off the tip, then smooth it into the nick with a finger.

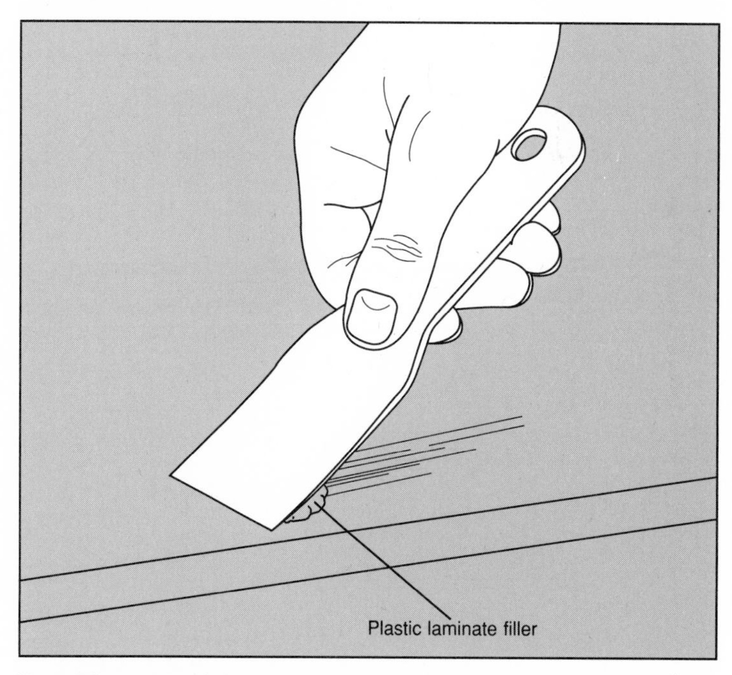

Repairing a plastic laminate surface. To repair a gouge in a plastic laminate surface such as that of a countertop, consult a professional about replacing the surface. To cover a scratch or fill a surface nick in a plastic laminate surface, use a pre-mixed plastic laminate filler; ensure the color matches the laminate by testing it first on an inconspicuous area of the surface. To apply the filler, lightly load the tip of a plastic putty knife and smooth it over the damage *(above)*, leveling the filler flush with the surface. Wipe off drips using a cloth dampened with mineral spirits. Let the filler dry. If desired, polish the surface using a soft cloth and acrylic floor polish. Safely dispose of leftover filler *(page 141)*.

SERVICING A DRAWER

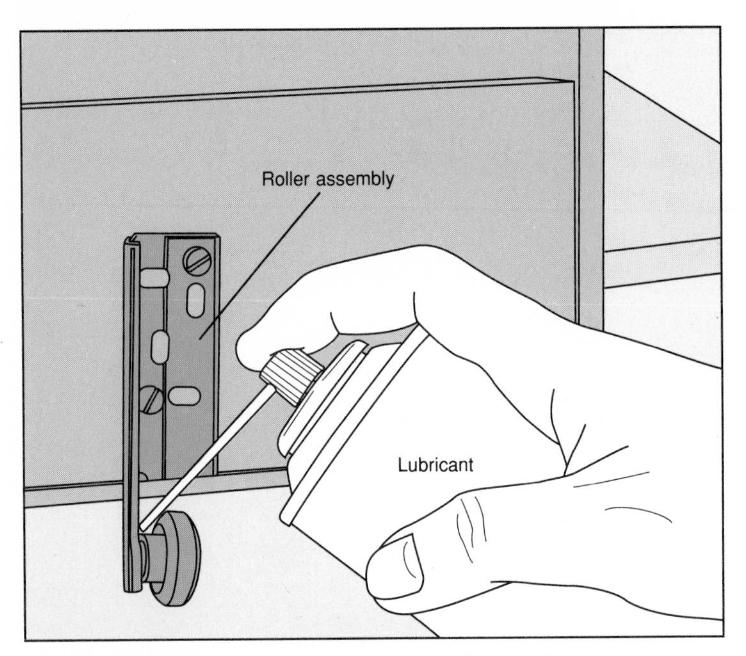

Servicing a metal roller assembly and guide track. Remove the drawer from the cabinet. If the drawer has wood guides and the cabinet has wood runners, service them *(step right)*. If the drawer has a roller assembly and there is a guide track in the cabinet, clean them with a solution of mild household detergent and water; then, dry them thoroughly. Tighten any loose screws, then reinstall the drawer. If the drawer still sticks, spray a little silicone-based lubricant on the roller assembly *(above)* and the guide track.

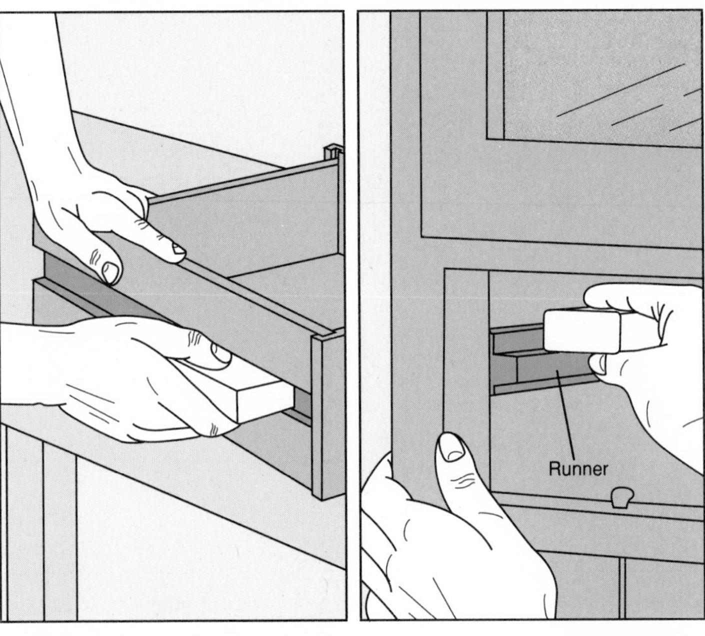

Servicing a wood guide and runner. Remove the drawer from the cabinet. If the drawer has a metal roller assembly and the cabinet has a metal guide track, service them *(step left)*. If the drawer has wood guides and there are runners in the cabinet, use a putty knife to gently scrape old wax and debris off them; then, lubricate them using a bar of soap or paraffin wax, rubbing a new coat of material along each sliding surface of the drawer guides *(above, left)* and the cabinet runners *(above, right)*. Tighten any loose screws, then reinstall the drawer.

SERVICING A CABINET DOOR

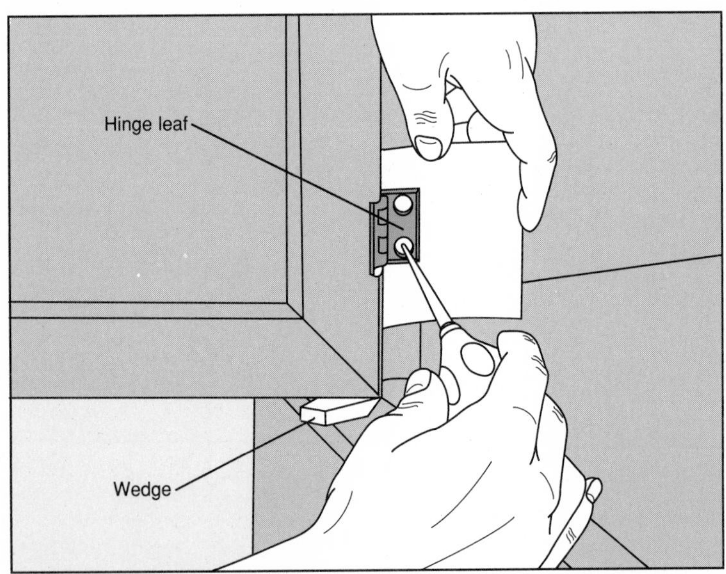

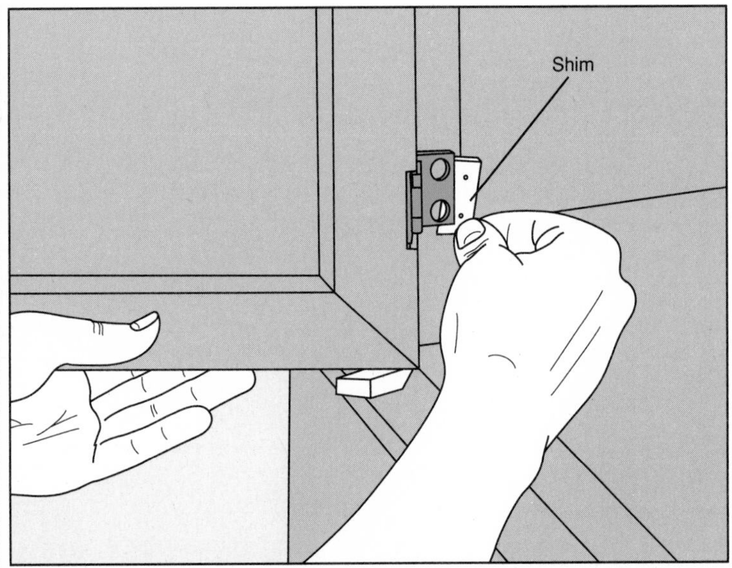

Repairing a loose or crooked door. Open the door to inspect the hinges and the cabinet frame. If a hinge is damaged, replace it. If a hinge is loose, tighten its screws; if a screw cannot be tightened, remove it and install a longer one of the same diameter. If the door is loose or crooked because a hinge is attached to a warped part of the cabinet frame, shim the hinge. Insert a wedge under the bottom corner of the open door to straighten it and unscrew the hinge leaf from the cabinet frame. Slide a piece of cardboard behind the hinge leaf, then use an awl to trace its outline on the cardboard and punch screw-hole positions *(above, left)*. Remove the cardboard and use a utility knife or scissors to cut the shim slightly smaller than the traced outline. Insert the shim behind the hinge leaf *(above, right)*, aligning the punched holes in it with the screw holes in the hinge leaf. Using screws of the same diameter but slightly longer than the old hinge screws, screw the hinge leaf and shim to the cabinet frame. Remove the wedge and close the door.

RESECURING PLASTIC LAMINATE

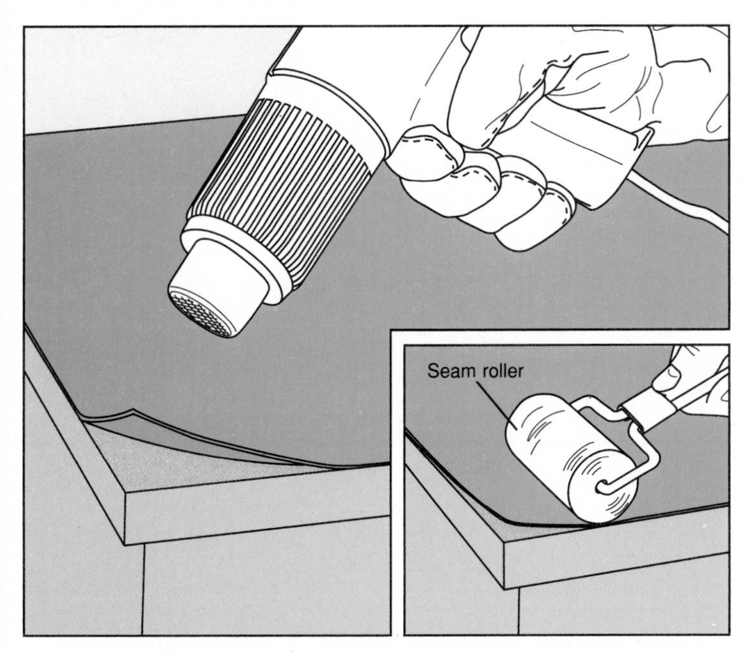

Securing a lifted corner. To secure a lifted corner, wear work gloves and use a heat gun set to its lowest heat setting. Keeping the nozzle 6 inches from the surface, move the gun back and forth over the lifted section *(above)* until the glue on the bottom is tacky; then, use a seam roller to roll down the section *(inset)*. If the section lifts again, glue it. Using a putty knife, lift the section and scrape old glue off the bottom of it and the surface under it. Apply contact cement to both surfaces, following the manufacturer's instructions; then, without letting the surfaces touch, allow the cement to dry until it is no longer tacky. Roll down the section with a seam roller and wipe away any extruded cement. Safely dispose of any leftover cement *(page 141)*.

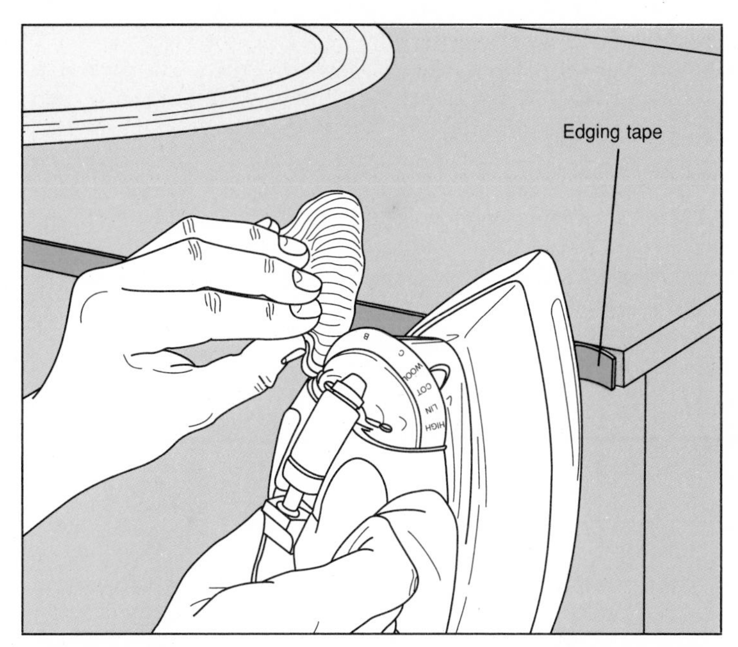

Securing a lifted edge. To secure lifted edging tape, first use a putty knife to pry back the lifted section and scrape old glue off the back of it and the surface behind it. Set a household iron to medium-high and wait for it to warm. Starting at the adhered end of the edging tape, pass the iron over the lifted section, pressing it down with a cloth as you go *(above)*. Hold down the pressed edging tape with masking tape for 24 hours, then remove the masking tape. If the edging tape lifts again, glue it. Apply wood glue to the surface behind the edging tape, following the manufacturer's instructions; then, press the edging tape back onto the surface. Wipe away any extruded glue. Hold down the glued edging tape with masking tape until the glue dries, then remove the masking tape.

RECAULKING A JOINT

Replacing damaged or missing caulk. To recaulk a joint, first pull out any loose caulk by hand, then use a putty knife to scrape out adhered caulk. Use a wet toothbrush and a non-abrasive commercial cleaner to scrub the joint clean, then rinse the joint with fresh water. Let the joint dry. To remove any remaining soap film, wipe the joint with a soft cloth dampened with rubbing alcohol; for any remaining mildew, use household bleach. Before caulking the joint between a bathtub and wall as shown, fill the bathtub with water to expand the joint; then, tape the edge of the wall above the joint and the bathtub below the joint with masking tape. To caulk the joint, select a caulk *(page 133)* of a suitable color. Load a caulking gun with the caulk. Starting at one end of the joint, hold the gun at a 45-degree angle to the surface and squeeze the trigger to eject a continuous bead of caulk along the joint *(left)*. Remove the masking tape; then, wear a rubber glove and run a wet finger along the caulk, pressing it into the joint. Let the caulk set for 24 hours before draining the bathtub.

REGROUTING A CERAMIC TILE JOINT

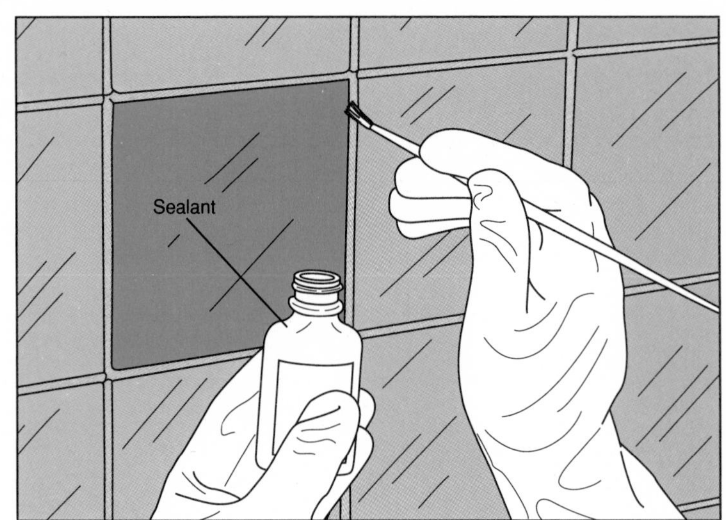

1 Replacing missing or damaged grout. To regrout a tile joint, first use a putty knife to scrape out any old grout, taking care not to mar any tile surfaces; then, use a wet toothbrush to scrub the joint clean. Let the joint dry. Buy pre-mixed grout; alternately, buy powdered grout and a liquid additive recommended by the manufacturer, mixing them following the label instructions: thinner for a narrow joint and thicker for a wide joint. To apply the grout, use a rubber-gloved finger to press it into the joint *(above)*, filling the joint almost level with the adjacent tile surfaces and smoothing away bubbles and gaps. Safely dispose of leftover grout *(page 141)*.

2 Sealing the new grout. Use a damp sponge to wipe excess grout off the tile surfaces. Let the grout set for 15 minutes; then, use a soft cloth to polish off any remaining haze from the wiped tile surfaces. To protect the regrouted joint, seal it with silicone sealant when the grout is completely cured; this may take 4 weeks, depending on the grout or sealant manufacturer's instructions. To seal the cured grout, wash and rinse the joint, then let it dry. Using an artist's brush, smooth an even coat of sealant along the regrouted joint *(above)*, taking care not to drip sealant on any tile surface. Let the sealant dry 24 hours before wetting the joint. Safely dispose of leftover sealant *(page 141)*.

REPLACING A CERAMIC TILE

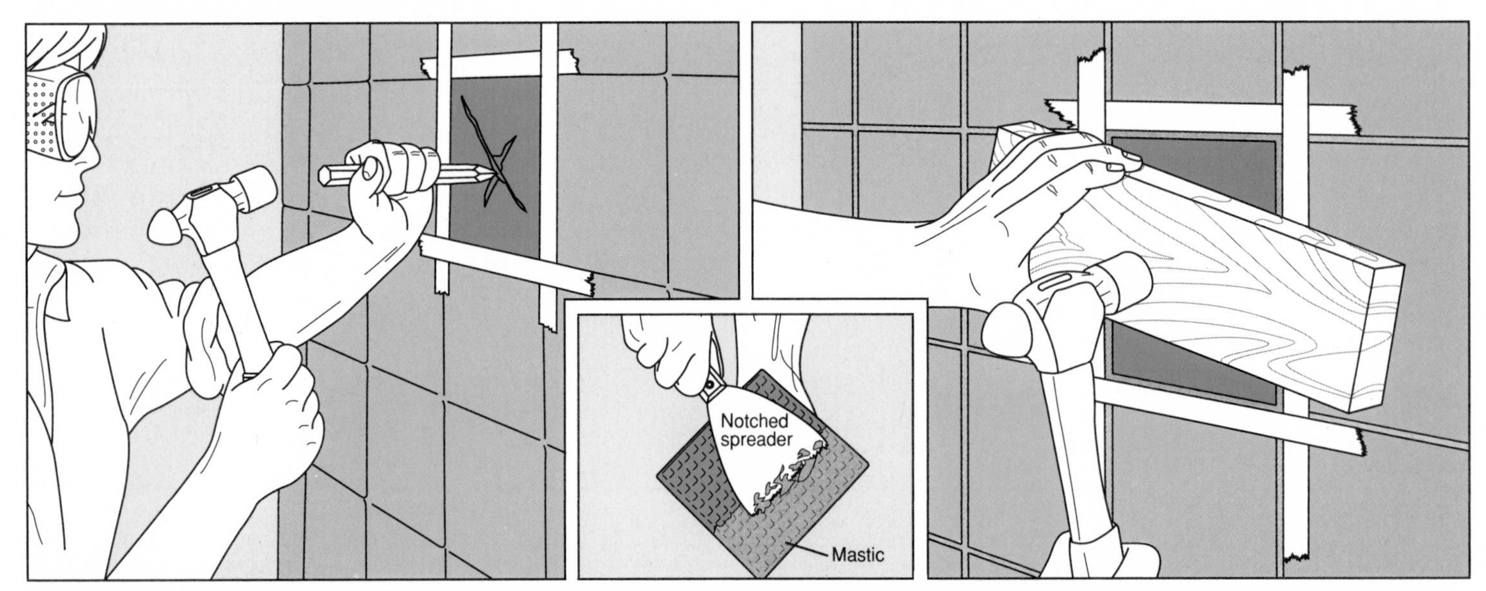

Replacing a standard tile. Replace any damaged mosaic tile *(page 59)*. To replace a damaged standard tile, first use a putty knife to scrape the grout out of the joints along it; then, tape the edges of the adjacent tiles with masking tape. Using the putty knife, try to pry out the damaged tile. If you cannot pry out the tile, break it. Stick a masking-tape X in the center of the tile; then, wear safety goggles and use an electric drill fitted with a masonry bit *(page 129)* to drill a hole through the X into the tile surface. Remove the tape and use a bull-point chisel and a ball-peen hammer to break the tile, starting at the drilled hole to chip out small pieces *(above, left)*. With the putty knife, scrape remaining tile shards and mastic off the wall. Buy an identical replacement tile. To install the tile, use Type 1 water-resistant mastic and work with a notched spreader. Wearing rubber gloves and working in a well-ventilated room, use the spreader to coat the tile back with mastic *(inset)*; then, press the tile firmly into position on the wall. Wipe away any extruded mastic. To level the tile with the adjacent tiles, hold a wood block against it and gently tap the block with a hammer *(above, right)*. If the tile slips, drive small nails as spacers into the joints along the edges to hold it. Let the mastic dry for 24 hours; then, remove any nails and regrout the joints at the edges of the new tile *(steps above)*.

REPLACING A CERAMIC TILE (continued)

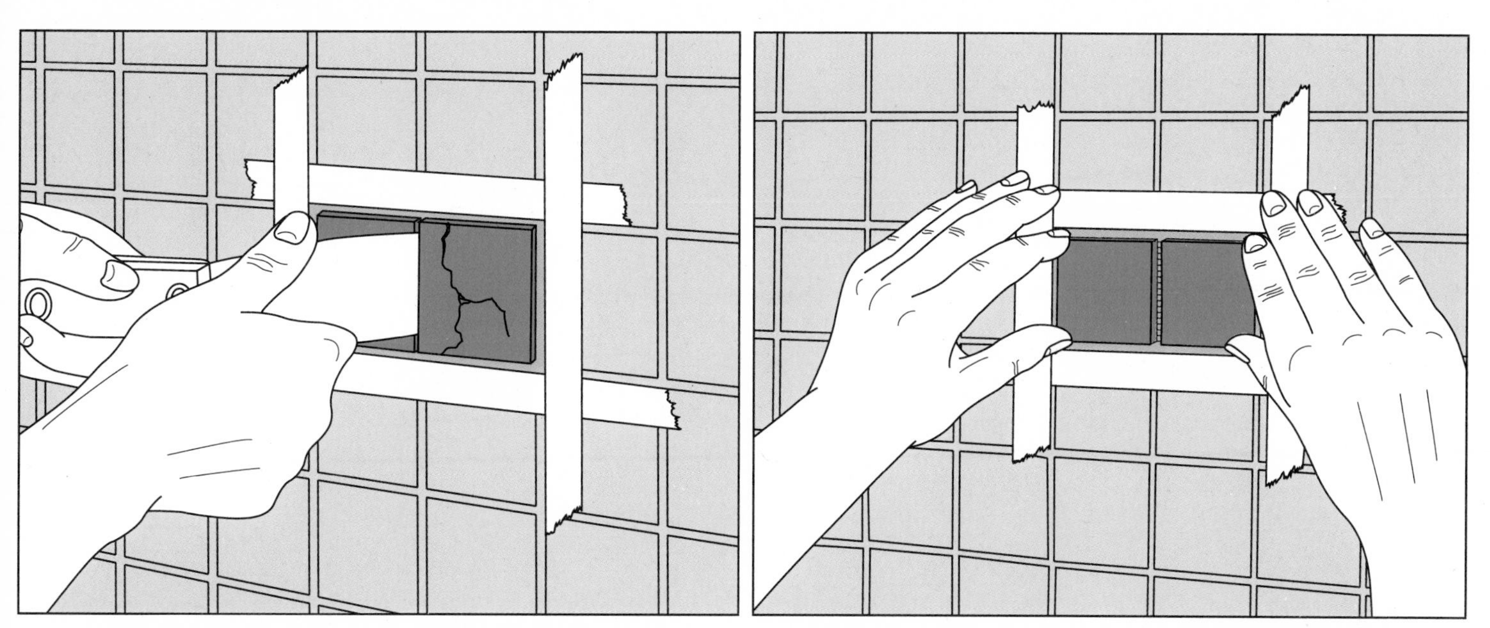

Replacing a mosaic tile. Replace any standard tile *(page 58)*. To replace a damaged mosaic tile or section of tiles, first use a putty knife to scrape grout out of the joints along each tile; then, tape the edges of the adjacent tiles with masking tape. To remove each tile, fit the tip of a putty knife under an edge and pry it out *(above, left)*; if necessary, use a utility knife to cut along the joints at the edges and sever any mesh backing that holds it to adjacent tiles. With the putty knife, scrape remaining tile shards and mastic off the wall. Buy a sheet of identical mosaic tiles and cut a replacement tile or section of tiles from it, leaving any mesh or paper backing in place. To install each tile, use Type 1 water-resistant mastic and work with a putty knife. Wearing rubber gloves and working in a well-ventilated room, use the knife to coat each tile back with mastic; then, press each tile firmly into position on the wall *(above, right)*. Wipe away any extruded mastic. To hold each tile, tape it to adjacent tiles with masking tape. Let the mastic dry for 24 hours; then, remove the masking tape and regrout the joints along each tile *(page 58)*.

SERVICING A TOILET SEAT

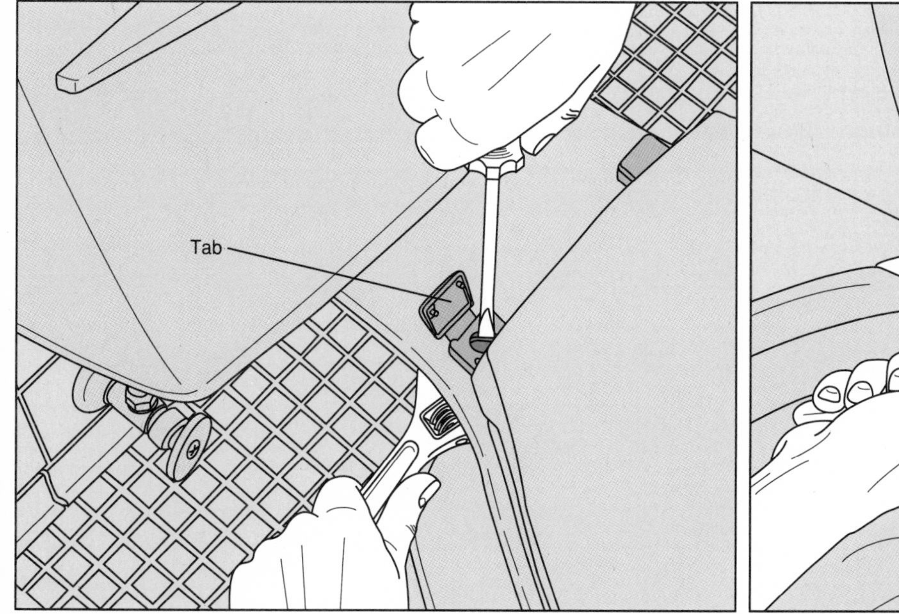

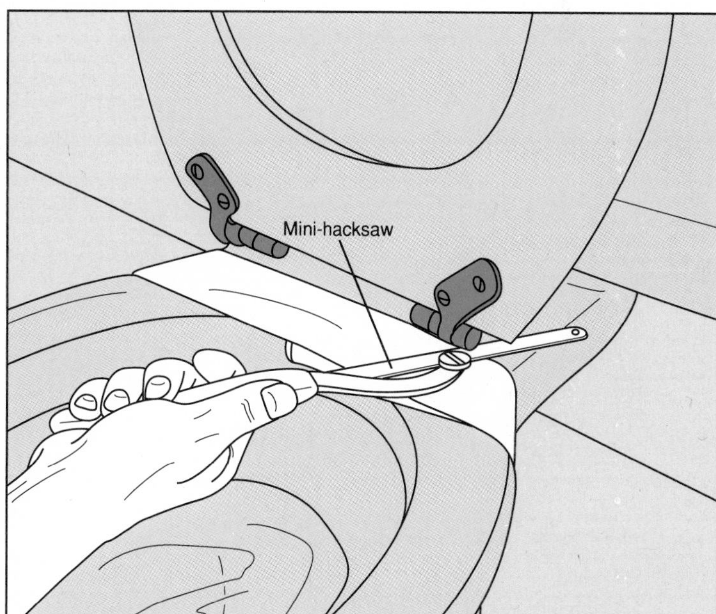

Tightening or replacing a toilet seat. Locate the bolts that hold the back of the toilet seat to the toilet bowl; on the model shown, pry up the tab to reach each bolt head. To tighten a bolt, fit a screwdriver into its head and fit a wrench onto the nut *(above, left)*; then, hold one tool steady and turn the other tool. To replace the toilet seat, use the same procedure to loosen and remove the nuts and bolts, then take off the toilet seat. If you cannot turn a nut or bolt, apply penetrating oil, wait a few hours and try again; if you still cannot turn it, cut the bolt. Protecting the back of the toilet bowl with masking tape, use a mini-hacksaw to cut through the bolt just under its head *(above, right)*. Buy a replacement toilet seat of an identical size, measuring the length and width of the old one. To install the new toilet seat, position it on the toilet bowl and insert the bolts. Screw the nuts onto the bolts by hand; then, use the wrench and screwdriver to tighten them. Snap closed any tabs.

FLOORS AND STAIRS

The condition of your floors and stairways plays a critical role in the overall evaluation of your home by a prospective buyer. A clean, properly-finished floor will shine with an inviting glow; a sturdy, silent staircase with a firm balustrade will encourage confidence in the structural soundness of the house. Real estate agents and home buyers look for well-maintained floors and carpets, and listen for squeaks that could indicate problems. Scratched or dull wood surfaces, torn or stained wall-to-wall carpeting and shaky stairway handrails can reduce the resale value of your home.

Before showing your home, clean the floors. If you are not sure what the finish on a wood floor is, check by dropping a bead of water in an inconspicuous spot and leaving it for an hour. If the water causes a white mark, the finish is wax; if not, the finish is polyurethane. Do not wash a waxed wood floor; when washing a polyurethaned wood floor, thoroughly squeeze out the sponge mop. After cleaning, rejuvenate vinyl flooring *(page 62)*, a waxed wood floor *(page 67)* or a polyurethaned wood floor *(page 68)* if it is still dull or dingy. Silence squeaky floors *(page 69)* and stairs *(page 70)*; resecure a wobbly newel post or handrail *(page 71)*.

Remove stains from your carpets *(page 64)*. Use a water-extraction cleaning machine to steam clean an entire wall-to-wall carpet *(page 64)*; send valuable scatter rugs for professional dry-cleaning, and roll up and store worn rugs prior to a viewing of your house. Carpeting with minor damage usually can be easily repaired by patching it with a leftover piece of the original material *(page 65)* or by resecuring it *(page 66)*. Patch damaged vinyl flooring *(page 62)* as well with leftover pieces of the original material.

Read label directions and warnings before using cleaning, stripping or refinishing products. Adequate ventilation and protective work or rubber gloves are essential when working with chemical solutions. Always test a cleaning or refinishing product on an out-of-the-way spot before using it; properly dispose of used or leftover chemical solutions *(page 141)*. A floor polisher for rejuvenating vinyl flooring or wood floors and a water-extraction cleaning machine for cleaning carpets can be rented at a tool rental center; refer to the chapter on Tools & Techniques *(page 126)* for information on what to look for and be sure that you always follow the manufacturer's set-up and operating instructions.

TROUBLESHOOTING GUIDE

SYMPTOM	PROCEDURE
Vinyl or ceramic-tiled flooring dirty	Wash flooring with a solution of 1/2 cup vinegar per gallon of water
Vinyl flooring dull or dingy	Rejuvenate flooring *(p. 62)* □◒
Vinyl flooring damaged	Patch vinyl flooring *(p. 62)* □○
Ceramic-tiled flooring damaged	Replace ceramic floor tile *(p. 63)* □○
Wood floor dirty	Sweep or vacuum waxed wood floor; wash polyurethaned wood floor with a solution of 1/2 cup vinegar per gallon of water
	If necessary, spot-clean wood floor *(p. 67)* □○
Wood floor stained	Spot-clean wood floor *(p. 67)* □○
Wood floor dull or dingy	Rejuvenate waxed wood floor *(p. 67)* □◒ polyurethaned wood floor *(p. 68)* □◒
Wall-to-wall carpet dirty or dingy	Steam-clean carpet *(p. 64)* □◒
Wall- to-wall carpet stained	Spot-clean carpet *(p. 64)* □○
	If necessary, repair carpet *(p. 65)* ⬓○
Wall-to-wall carpet buckled, wrinkled or loose	Resecure carpet *(p. 66)* ⬓◒
Wall-to-wall carpet damaged	Repair carpet *(p. 65)* ⬓○
Floor squeaks	Apply liquid floor wax or talcum powder to squeaky board joints and work in with a clean cloth; silence squeaky floor board *(p. 69)* □○
Stair squeaks	Silence squeaky stair *(p. 70)* □○
Newel post wobbles	Secure newel post *(p. 71)* □○
Handrail wobbles	Secure handrail *(p. 71)* □○
Baluster damaged	Replace baluster *(p. 72)* ⬓○
Small gouge or crack in wood floor or stairway	Repair minor wood damage *(p. 73)* □○

DEGREE OF DIFFICULTY: □ **Easy** ⬓ **Moderate** ■ **Complex**
ESTIMATED TIME: ○ **Less than 1 hour** ◒ **1 to 3 hours** ● **Over 3 hours**
(Does not include drying time)

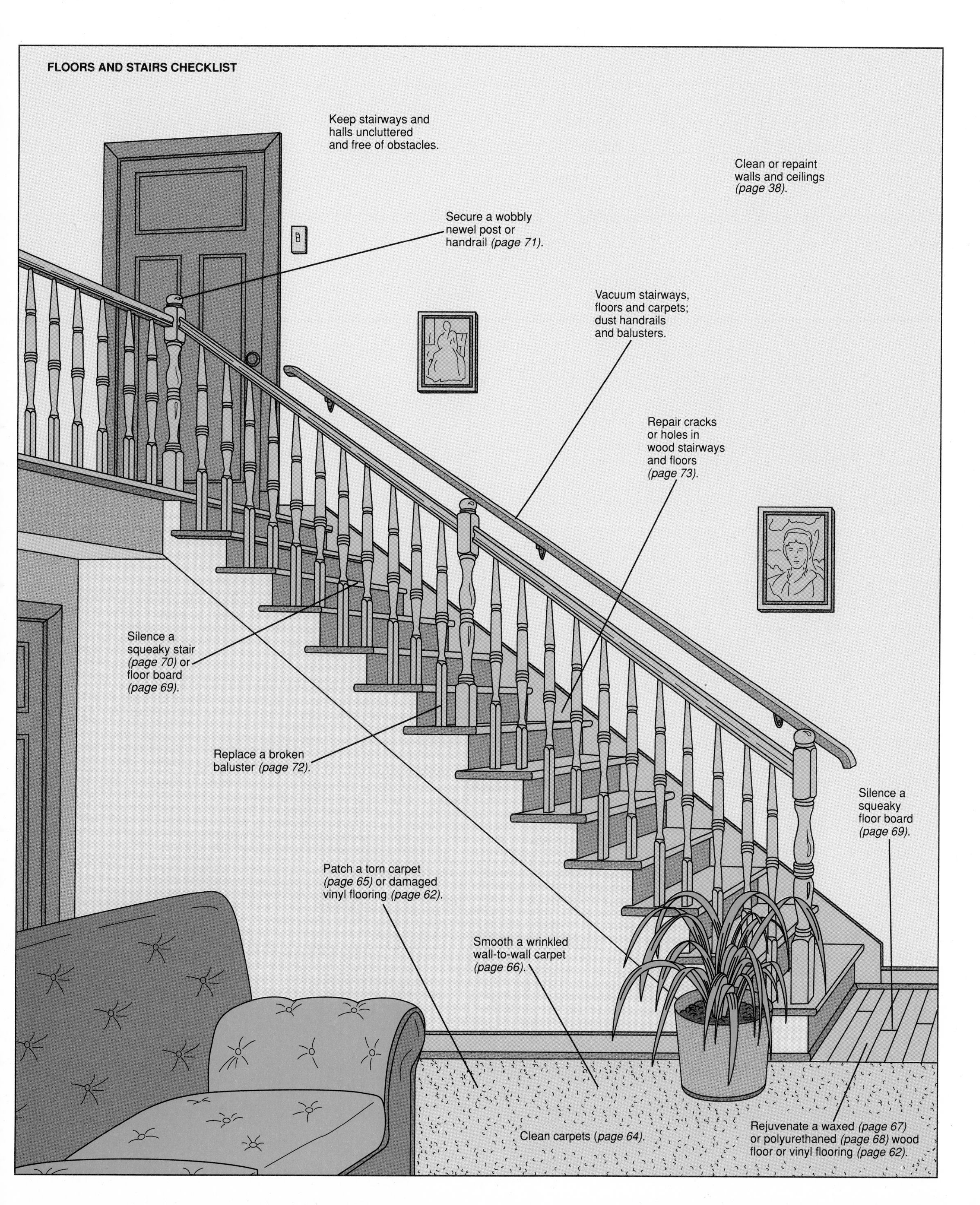
FLOORS AND STAIRS CHECKLIST
Keep stairways and halls uncluttered and free of obstacles.
Clean or repaint walls and ceilings (page 38).
Secure a wobbly newel post or handrail (page 71).
Vacuum stairways, floors and carpets; dust handrails and balusters.
Repair cracks or holes in wood stairways and floors (page 73).
Silence a squeaky stair (page 70) or floor board (page 69).
Replace a broken baluster (page 72).
Silence a squeaky floor board (page 69).
Patch a torn carpet (page 65) or damaged vinyl flooring (page 62).
Smooth a wrinkled wall-to-wall carpet (page 66).
Clean carpets (page 64).
Rejuvenate a waxed (page 67) or polyurethaned (page 68) wood floor or vinyl flooring (page 62).

REJUVENATING VINYL FLOORING

1 Stripping the old finish. To strip old finish off vinyl flooring, rent a floor polisher *(page 128)* and buy stripping pads at a tool rental center; set up according to the manufacturer's instructions. Move the furniture out of the room, then sweep or vacuum the flooring. Apply a vinyl-flooring finish stripper with a sponge mop. Use the floor polisher to work the stripper into the finish *(above)*, beginning at the center of the room and moving out to the edges in a star pattern. Check the pad periodically; if it clogs, replace it. For hard-to-reach corners, use the sponge mop. Remove the stripper-and-finish mixture with a wet-dry vacuum or a squeegee and dustpan.

2 Applying a fresh coat of acrylic finish. Clean residue off the flooring using a solution of 1/2 cup vinegar per gallon of water and a sponge mop; rinse the mop frequently in clean water. Let the flooring dry, then seal any small gouges or scratches using a water-based sealer. Working with a clean sponge mop, apply a light, even coat of sealant; let it dry. Then, apply an acrylic vinyl-flooring finish, following the manufacturer's instructions. Work with a squeegee to apply the finish *(above)*, beginning at a corner of the room and moving toward a door. Avoid walking on the flooring until the finish is dry. When the finish is dry, move the furniture back into place.

PATCHING VINYL FLOORING

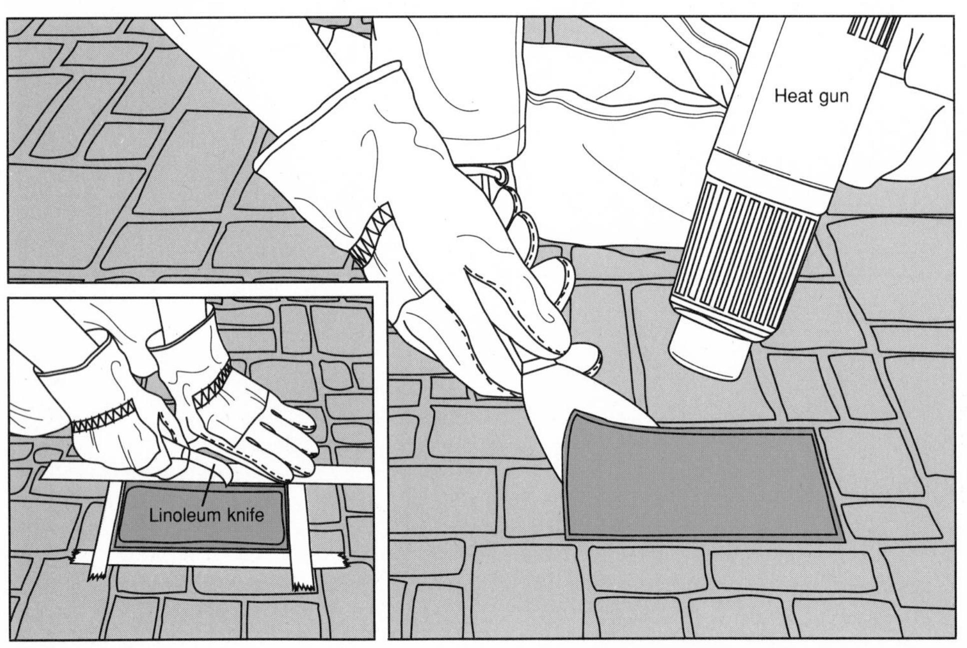

1 Removing the damaged flooring. Buy flooring adhesive and a seam sealing kit at a building supply center. To patch sheet flooring, use a piece of matching sheet flooring that is at least 2 inches longer and wider than the damaged section. Place the patch on the damaged section, aligning its pattern; then, tape it in place using masking tape. Wearing work gloves, use a straightedge and a linoleum knife or a utility knife to slice through both layers of vinyl *(inset)*, simultaneously trimming the patch to size and cutting the damaged section. Remove the patch, discarding the excess bits and masking tape. To soften the flooring adhesive securing the damaged section, use a heat gun. Setting the heat gun to its lowest heat setting, keep the nozzle about 6 inches from the surface and move the gun back and forth over the damaged section; work a putty knife under the edges of the damaged section to pry it up *(left)*. To patch tile flooring, use the same procedure to remove each damaged tile.

PATCHING VINYL FLOORING (continued)

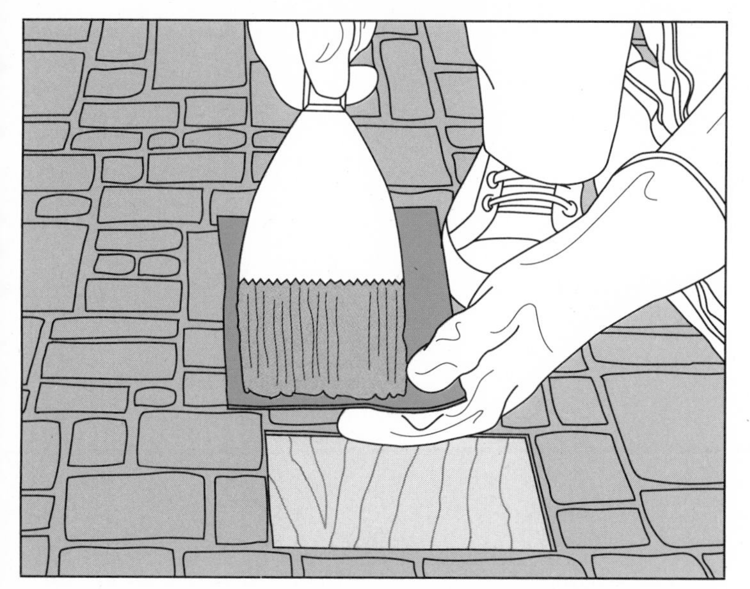

2 Applying the adhesive. Use a paint scraper to remove old adhesive from the floor; if necessary, soften it first with a heat gun as you did to remove the damaged flooring *(step 1)*. Wearing rubber gloves, use a notched spreader to apply flooring adhesive on the back of the patch *(above)* or new tile. Set the patch or new tile into place, carefully aligning its pattern. Press the patch or new tile down firmly, then wipe away any extruded adhesive using a cloth dampened with water. Let the adhesive dry; if necessary, weigh down the patch or new tile with a brick or other heavy object.

3 Sealing the patch joints. Carefully read and follow the instructions accompanying the seam sealing kit. Work in a well-ventilated room, opening windows and doors to the outdoors. Wearing rubber gloves, draw a continuous bead of sealant along each joint between the patch or new tile and the original flooring in one smooth stroke *(above)*. Wipe away excess sealant using a cloth dampened with water. Do not walk on the repaired section of flooring until the sealant has dried for the time specified by the manufacturer.

REPLACING A CERAMIC FLOOR TILE

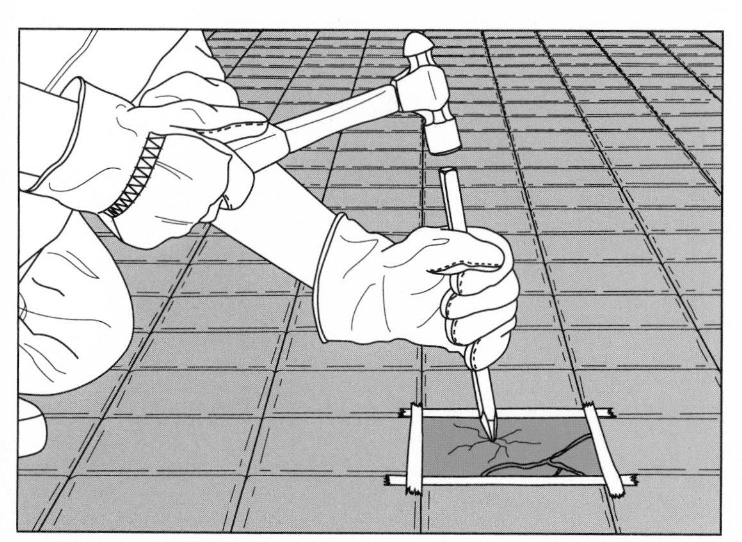

1 Removing the damaged tile. To remove a damaged tile, use a putty knife to scrape the grout out of the joints along it. Tape the edges of the adjacent tiles with masking tape and try to pry out the damaged tile with the putty knife. If you cannot pry out the tile, break it. Stick a masking-tape X in the center of the tile; then, wear safety goggles and use an electric drill *(page 129)* fitted with a masonry bit to drill a hole through the X into the tile. Remove the tape and use a bull-point chisel and a ball-peen hammer to chip out small pieces of the tile, starting at the drilled hole and working out toward the edges *(above)*. Scrape remaining tile shards and mastic off the floor with the putty knife.

2 Installing a new tile. To install a new tile, use Type 1 water-resistant mastic and pre-mixed grout. Wearing rubber gloves and working in a well-ventilated room, use a notched spreader to coat the back of the tile with mastic; then, press the tile firmly into position. To level the tile, center a wood block across it and gently tap the block with a hammer *(inset)*. Let the mastic dry for 24 hours. Then, use a rubber-gloved finger to press grout into each tile joint *(above)*, filling it and smoothing away bubbles and gaps. Wipe off excess grout using a damp sponge and let the grout cure; if necessary, then apply a silicone sealant, following the manufacturer's instructions. Safely dispose of leftover mastic, grout and sealant *(page 141)*.

SPOT-CLEANING A CARPET

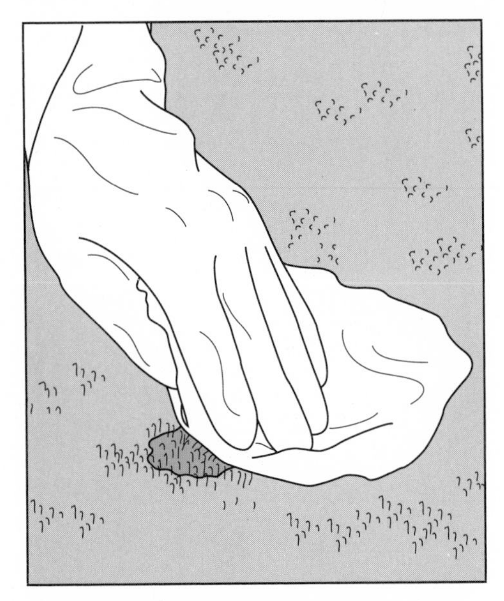

Lifting a stain. Gently blot the stain using a clean, white cloth dampened with a solution of mild household detergent and water *(above)*. If the stain does not lift, try mineral spirits, testing first on an inconspicuous spot. If mineral spirits darkens the carpet or does not lift the stain, use a commercial spot-cleaner.

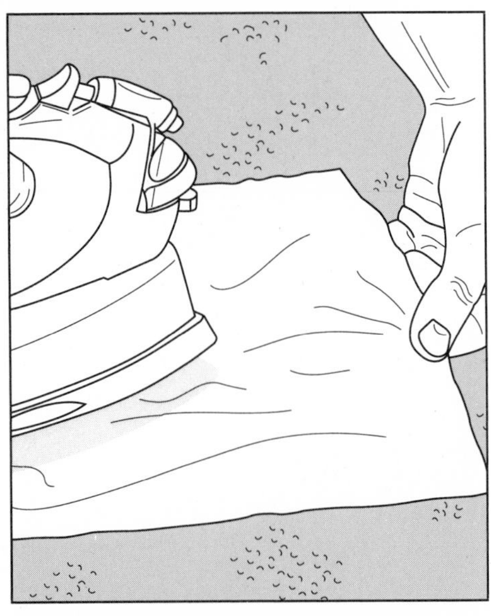

Removing dried wax. Place a double thickness of brown paper on the wax. Set an iron on low and touch it to the paper, slowly pulling out the paper to lift the wax *(above)*; do not let the iron touch the carpet. Continue until the wax is lifted. Brush the area to restore the nap.

Removing gum. Press an ice cube wrapped in a piece of thin cotton against the gum *(above)* until it hardens and becomes brittle. Then, gently pull the gum off the carpet, being careful not to damage the nap. Let the area dry, then brush it to restore the nap.

CLEANING A WALL-TO-WALL CARPET

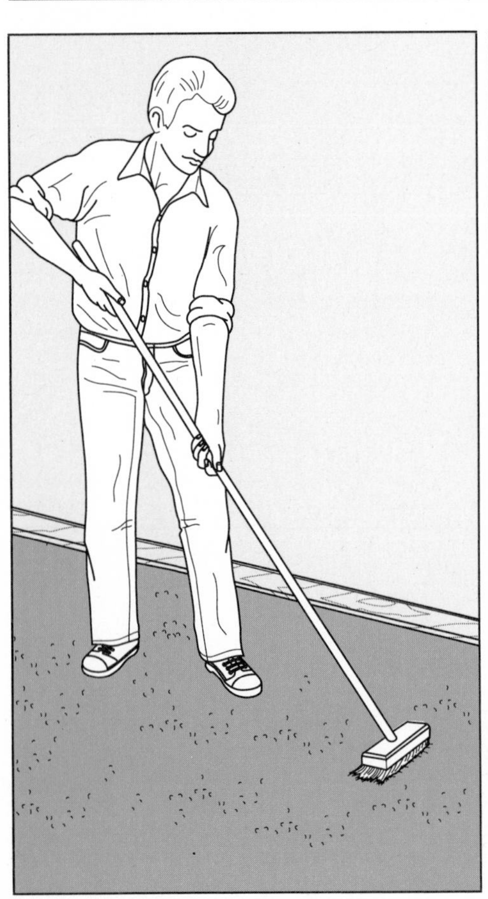

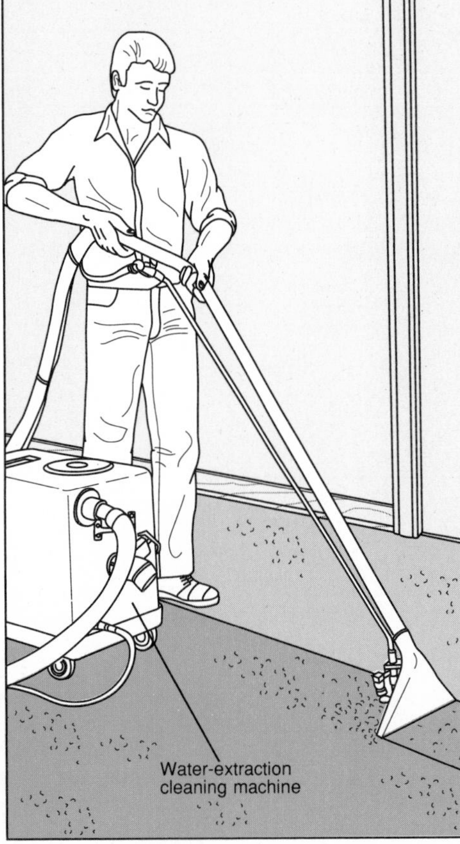

Steam-cleaning a carpet. Rent a water-extraction cleaning machine *(page 128)* and buy carpet shampoo at a tool rental center; set up according to the manufacturer's instructions. Test the shampoo by applying a small amount on an inconspicuous spot of the carpet; if the carpet dye runs, dilute the shampoo with water or use a milder shampoo. Move your furniture out of the room, then vacuum the carpet thoroughly; spot-clean it, if necessary *(steps above)*.

Raise the nap of a deep-pile carpet before cleaning it by brushing against the nap with a long-handled brush *(far left)*. Begin cleaning the carpet in a corner of the room and work toward a door. Apply shampoo to a 3-foot section of the carpet by depressing the spray trigger as you move the nozzle *(near left)*; do not use more shampoo than recommended by the manufacturer and avoid over-soaking the carpet. To extract the shampoo and dirt from the section of carpet, release the spray trigger and move the nozzle back and forth over it. Continue cleaning the carpet the same way, overlapping each 3-foot section slightly.

Raise the nap of a deep-pile carpet again after cleaning it. Allow the carpet to dry overnight before you move the furniture back into place. To prevent furniture legs from staining a slightly-damp carpet, slip small pieces of aluminum foil or waxed paper under them; leave the foil or paper for several days until the carpet is completely dry.

REPAIRING A WALL-TO-WALL CARPET

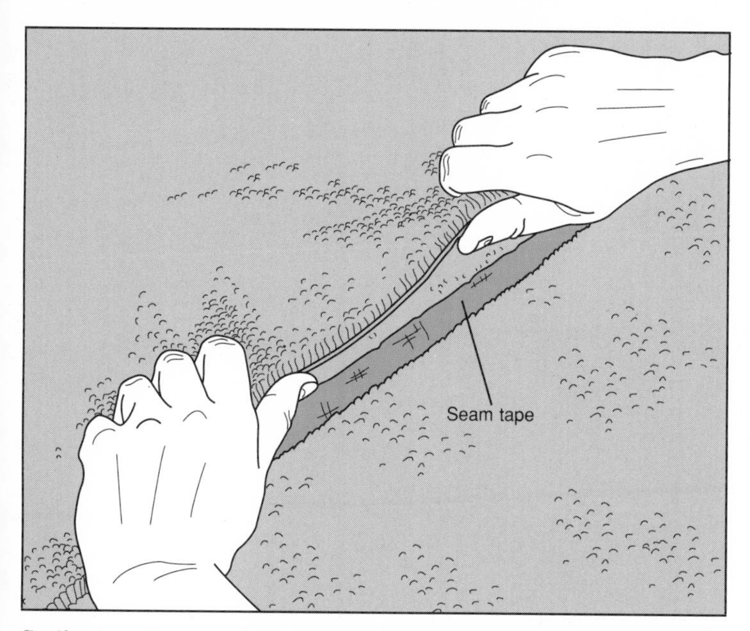

Sealing a split. Use scissors to carefully snip off any frayed edges of the carpet backing along the split. Then, cut a strip of self-adhesive carpet seam tape 2 inches longer than the split; peel the paper off one side of it. Working with a helper if necessary, lift the edges of the carpet along the split and center the tape under them with the adhesive side facing up. Pull one edge of the carpet along the split toward the other edge and press it down firmly onto the tape. Then, pull the other edge of the carpet along the split *(above)* until it meets the first edge and press it down firmly onto the tape.

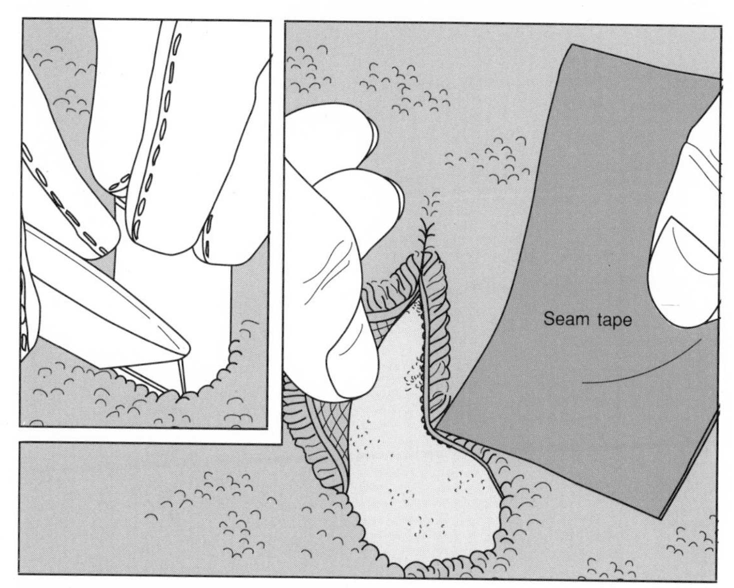

Patching a small tear, burn or stain. Wearing work gloves, cut out the damaged carpet with a utility knife, using the rim of a small container as a guide *(inset)*; avoid damaging the underpadding. Then, cut a patch of matching carpet equal to the size of the damaged carpet on a work table the same way; use scissors to carefully snip any frayed edges off its backing. Cut a strip of self-adhesive carpet seam tape slightly larger than the patch; peel the paper off one side of it. Use the utility knife and a straightedge to cut a slit at an edge of the undamaged carpet large enough to fit the tape. Lift the edges of the undamaged carpet and center the tape under them with the adhesive side facing up *(above)*. Then, position the patch on the tape, aligning its pile direction, and press it down firmly into place. Run a dull knife along the patch edges to free any stuck threads.

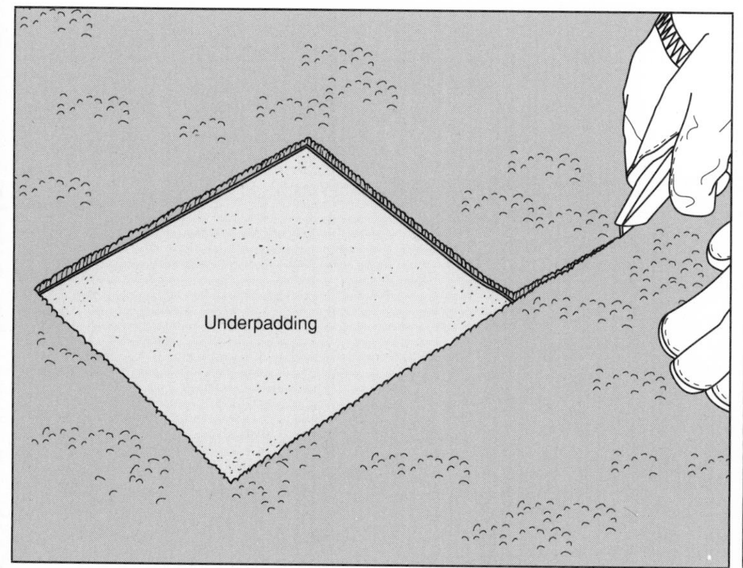

Patching a large tear, hole or stain. Wearing work gloves, cut out the damaged carpet with a utility knife, using a straightedge as a guide; try as much as possible to cut along rows of threads. Work carefully to avoid damaging the underpadding. Lay a patch of matching carpet on a work table and place the damaged carpet on top of it; make sure the pile of both pieces runs the same way. Using the damaged carpet as a guide, cut the patch to size with the utility knife; also cut a piece of burlap 4 to 6 inches longer and wider than the patch. Use scissors to carefully snip off any frayed edges of the backing on the undamaged carpet and the patch. Then, center the burlap under the edges of the undamaged carpet; if you have difficulty fitting it into place, use the utility knife to cut a flap at a corner of the undamaged carpet large enough for it *(above, left)*. Lift the edges of the undamaged carpet and position the burlap *(above, right)*; apply a thin layer of carpet glue on the backing of any flap you cut and press it down onto the burlap. Apply a layer of carpet glue on the backing of the patch and position it, aligning the pile direction; then, press the patch down firmly onto the burlap. Run a dull knife along the patch edges to free any stuck threads.

RESECURING A WALL-TO-WALL CARPET

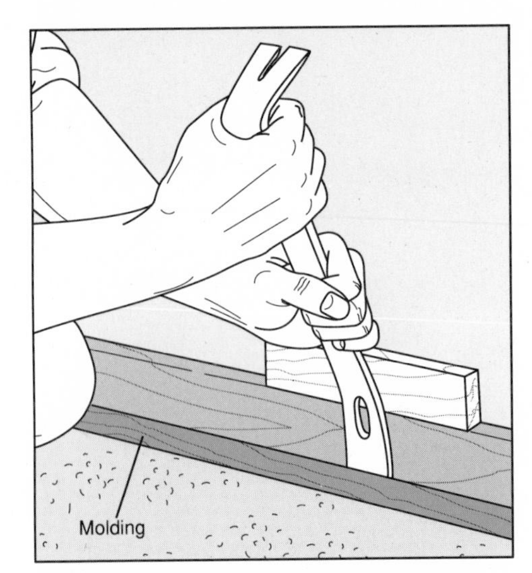

1 Prying off the molding. Pry off the molding along the wall nearest the buckled, wrinkled or loose carpet. Starting at the center of the molding, fit the blade of a putty knife between it and the baseboard; tap the handle of the putty knife with a hammer, if necessary. Insert the flat end of a small pry bar behind the blade of the putty knife, then pull out the putty knife. Using a wood block for leverage, work along the molding with the pry bar, easing it out a little at a time *(above)*. If an end of the molding is caught behind an adjoining piece of molding, gently pull from the center of the molding to free it.

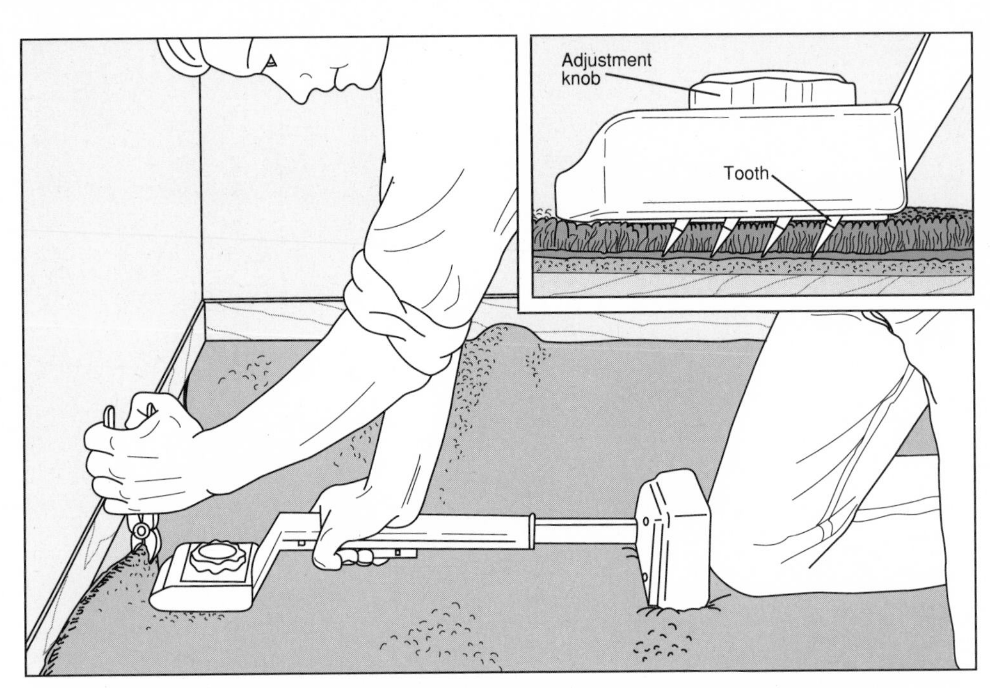

2 Smoothing and flattening the carpet with a knee-kicker. Rent a knee-kicker at a tool rental center *(page 128)*; set it up according to the manufacturer's instructions. Positioning the knee-kicker about 2 inches from the wall without the molding, turn the adjustment knob until the teeth are set to the depth necessary to bite into the carpet backing—but not the underpadding *(inset)*. Press the extension release trigger of the knee-kicker to extend the shaft to its full length. Placing one knee against the kick pad, hold the shaft with one hand while you use pliers to lift the edge of the carpet along the wall off the tacks under it *(above)*. As you free the edge of the carpet, thrust your knee sharply against the kick pad, carrying the carpet toward the wall to catch on the tacks. Continue along the length of the wall as necessary to smooth and flatten the carpet; if necessary, have a helper hold it in place as you go to keep it from unhooking again as you thrust your knee against the kick pad.

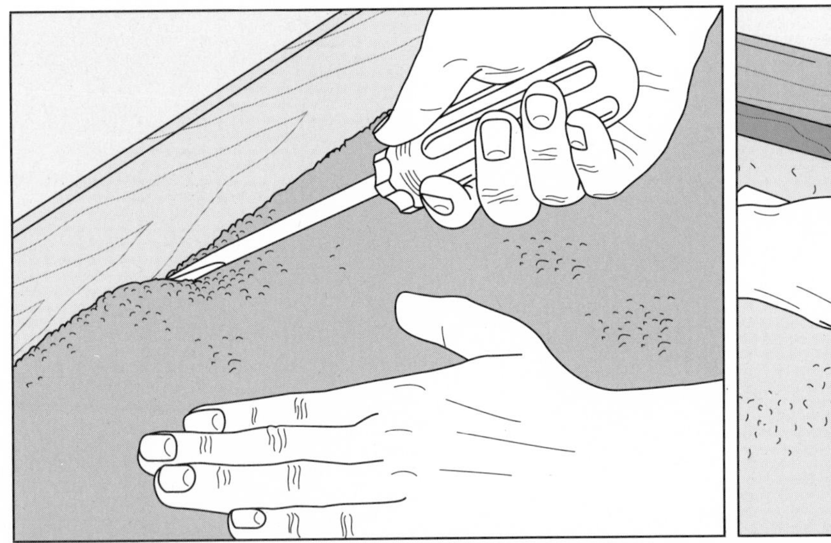

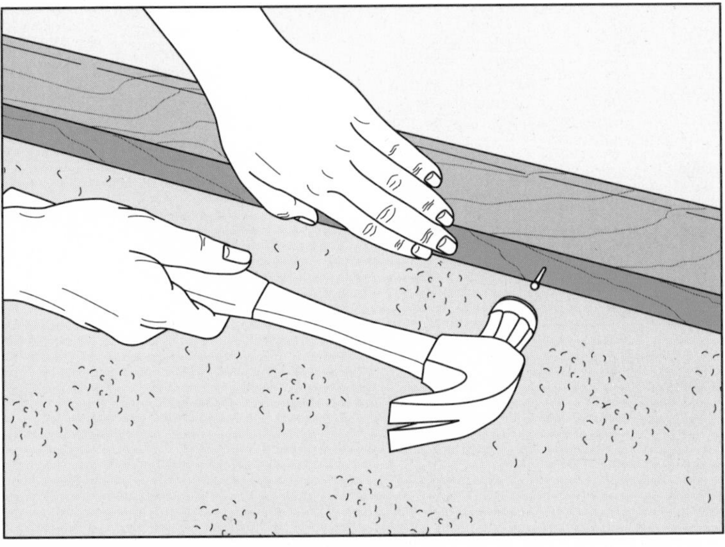

3 Resecuring the carpet edge. Once the carpet is smooth and flat, use a flat-head screwdriver to press down the edge along the wall *(above, left)* ensuring that it is securely hooked onto the tacks under it. Before reinstalling the molding, pull the nails out of it with pliers. If you damaged the molding when you removed it, glue it back together with wood glue or buy identical replacement molding at a building supply center. Holding the molding in place against the baseboard and the carpet, use a hammer to drive finishing nails at an angle through it and into the floor at 16-inch intervals *(above, right)*. Countersink the nail heads with the hammer and a nail set, setting them just below the surface. Cover the nail heads and fill any holes with a putty stick as you would to repair any wood surface *(page 44)*. Paint or finish the molding as you would any wood trim *(page 51)*.

SPOT-CLEANING A WOOD FLOOR

Removing stains from a waxed floor. Thoroughly buff the stained area with a clean, dry cloth. If the stain remains, wear work gloves and use fine steel wool to rub liquid or paste wax for wood floors into the stained area *(above)*. Apply the wax in a circular motion, then buff it with a clean, dry cloth. Continue applying wax and buffing it the same way until the stain is gone. If the stain is large or cannot be removed by waxing and buffing, rejuvenate the floor *(step below)*.

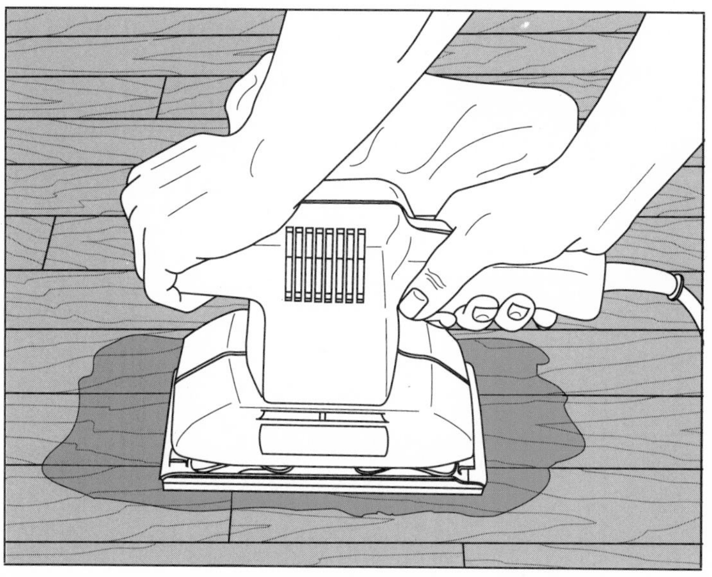

Removing stains from a polyurethaned floor. Rub the stained area using a clean cloth dampened with a solution of 1 tablespoon of vinegar per cup of water. If the stain remains, lightly sand the stained area using an orbital sander *(above)* or a sanding block fitted with fine-grit sandpaper; remove only a fine layer of wood. Wipe or brush off the dust, then apply polyurethane using a 2-inch trim paintbrush; to match the original wood color, you may have to apply a wood stain first.

REJUVENATING A WAXED WOOD FLOOR

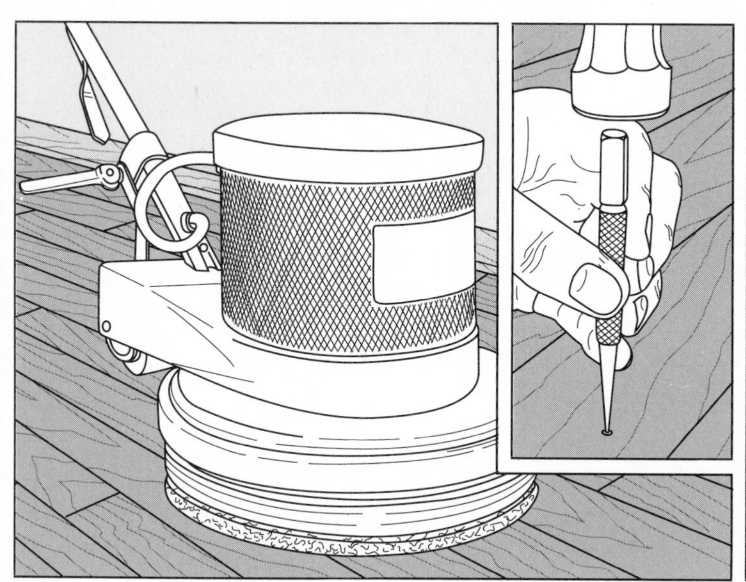

Reviving a waxed wood floor. Move the furniture out of the room, then vacuum the floor thoroughly. Check for protruding nail heads by wiping a cheesecloth over the floor; countersink any nail head that catches on the cloth using a nail set and a hammer *(inset)*. Rent a floor polisher *(page 128)* and buy a buffing pad as well as a wax removal pad at a tool rental center; set up according to the manufacturer's instructions. Before removing the old wax, try buffing the floor to bring out the shine. Attach the buffing pad to the floor polisher and begin buffing at the center of the room, working toward the edges of it and always polishing along the wood grain. If the floor still does not shine, strip off the wax using a wood floor wax stripper.

Replace the buffing pad on the floor polisher with the wax removal pad. Working on a 3-foot section of the floor at one time, apply the stripper according to the manufacturer's instructions, then remove the stripper-and-wax mixture with the floor polisher *(above, left)*; for hard-to-reach corners, use fine steel wool. Rewax the floor using liquid wax for wood floors, applying it with a sponge mop; begin in a corner of the room and work in sections toward a door. Pour a small pool of wax onto the floor and spread it in a thin, even film, always mopping along the wood grain *(above, right)*. Let the wax dry according to the manufacturer's instructions. Reinstall the buffing pad on the floor polisher and buff the floor until it is smooth and shiny. Move the furniture back into place.

REJUVENATING A POLYURETHANED WOOD FLOOR

1 Removing the old polyurethane. Move the furniture out of the room, then vacuum the floor thoroughly. Check for protruding nail heads by wiping a cheesecloth over the floor; countersink any nail head that catches on the cloth using a nail set and a hammer. Revive a dull floor by applying a fresh coat of polyurethane *(step 2)*; if the old finish is marred or flaking, remove it first.

To remove the old finish, rent a floor polisher *(page 128)* and buy fine-mesh screening pads at a tool rental center; set up according to the manufacturer's instructions. Beginning at the center of the room and working in sections toward the edges, keep the polisher moving in the direction of the wood grain *(left)*. If a screening pad clogs and loses its effectiveness, replace it. To remove the old finish from hard-to-reach corners, use an orbital sander or a sanding block fitted with medium-grit sandpaper. Once all the old finish is removed, vacuum the floor again.

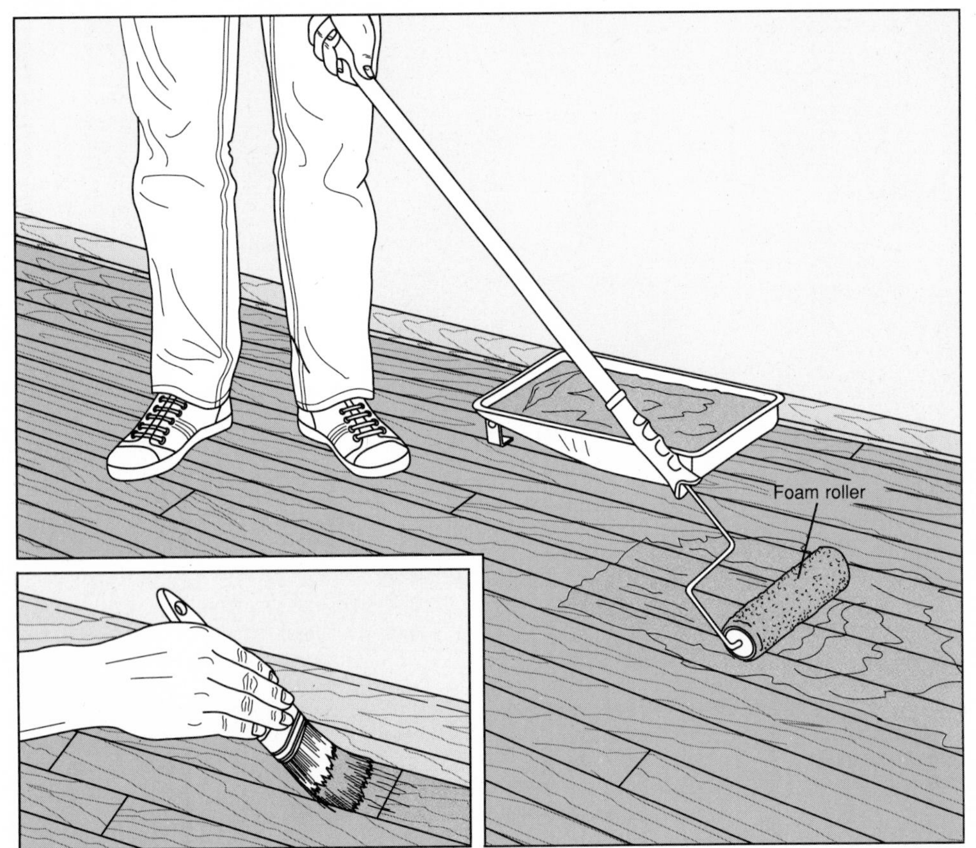

2 Applying new polyurethane. Apply polyurethane following the manufacturer's instructions; work in a well-ventilated room, opening windows and doors to the outdoors. On a bare wood floor, first apply a sealant of equal parts of polyurethane and mineral spirits. Otherwise, lightly sand the surface with fine-grit sandpaper and an orbital sander; a sanding block for hard-to-reach corners. After sanding, vacuum the floor thoroughly.

Begin applying polyurethane along the floor edges and in corners using a 2-inch trim paintbrush *(inset)*. Then, use a paint tray and a foam roller with an extension pole to apply polyurethane on the rest of the floor. Begin in a corner and work toward a door, rolling in the direction of the wood grain *(left)*. Let the polyurethane dry; then, lightly sand the floor with very fine-grit sandpaper, vacuum thoroughly and apply a second coat. Wait until the floor is completely dry before moving the furniture back into place.

SILENCING A SQUEAKY FLOOR BOARD

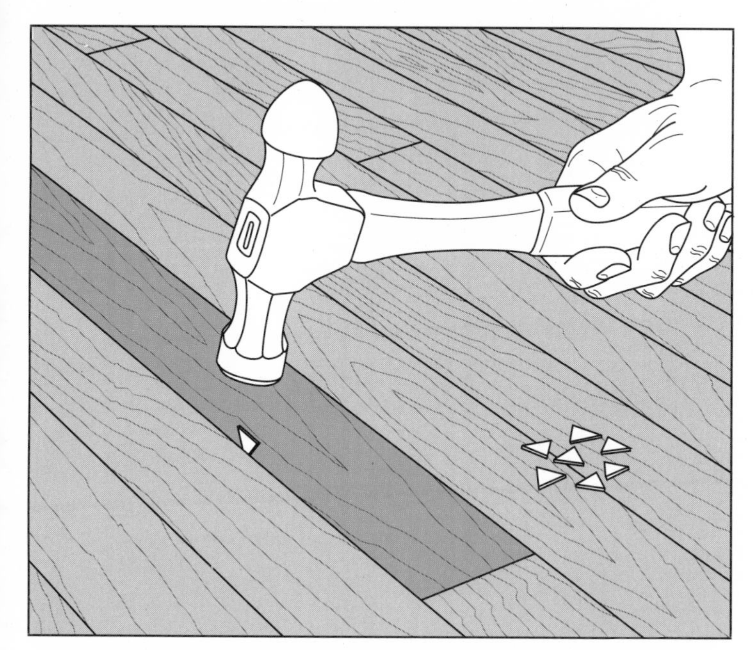

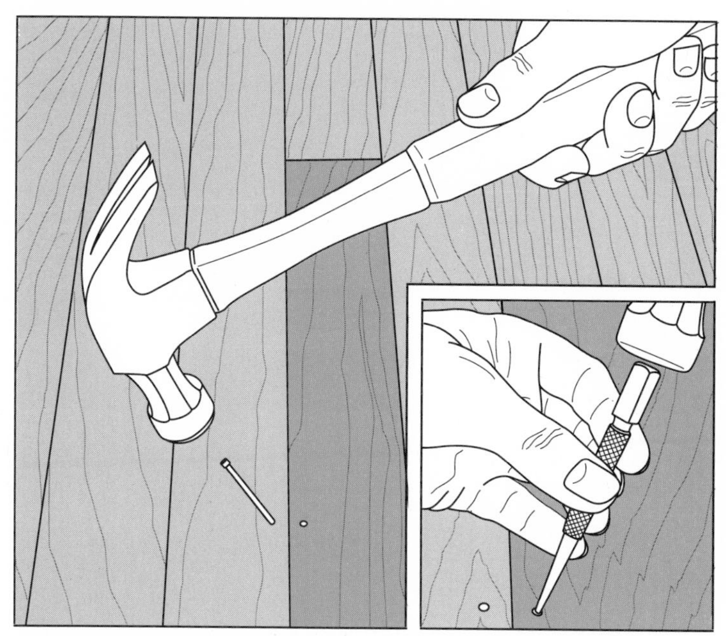

1 Curing a squeaky floor board with glazier's points. Locate the squeaky floor board by walking slowly across the floor. Insert into the joint along each side of the squeaky floor board a number of flat, triangular glazier's points—normally used to secure glass inside a window sash. Wearing safety goggles, gently tap each glazier's point below the surface of the floor with a hammer *(above)*. If the floor board still squeaks, secure it from below if you can reach the subfloor and joists *(step 3)*; otherwise, secure it from above *(step 2)*.

2 Securing a squeaky floor board from above. Nail the squeaky floor board together with the floor board along each side of it using 2-inch finishing nails. Drive one nail through an edge of the squeaky floor board at a 45-degree angle, then drive another nail through the edge of the floor board along it at the opposite 45-degree angle *(above)*—so that the two nails together form a V. Repeat the procedure on the other edge of the squeaky floor board. Countersink the nail heads using a nail set and a hammer *(inset)*, then cover them with a putty stick as you would to repair any wood surface *(page 44)*.

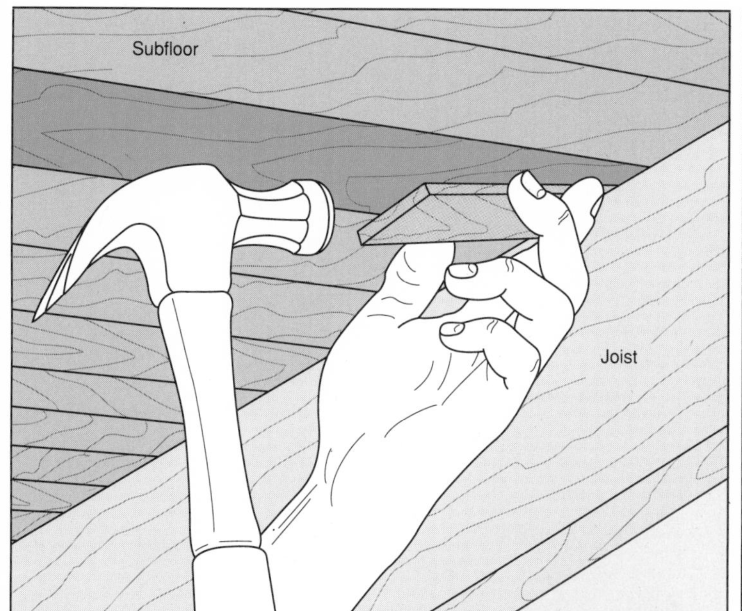

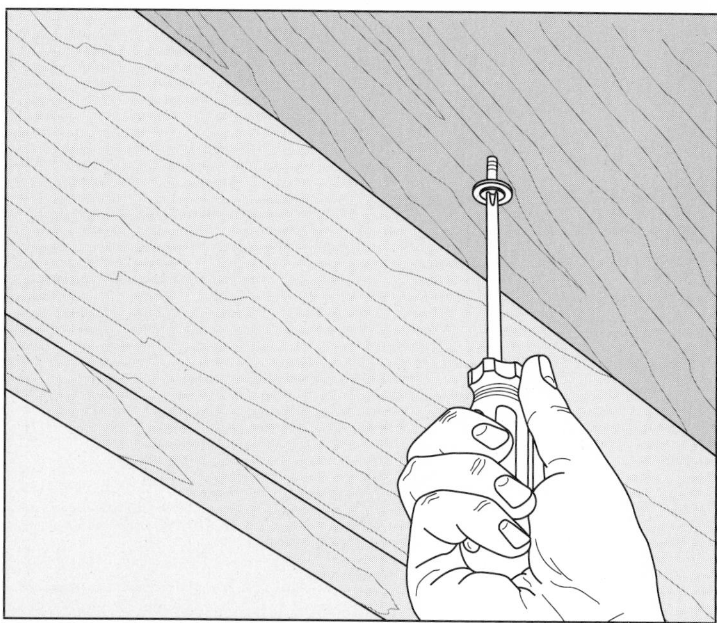

3 Securing a squeaky floor board from below. Shim the subfloor just below the squeaky floor board or draw the floor board down toward the subfloor with wood screws. Locate the squeaky floor board by standing below and listening carefully while a helper walks slowly across the floor above. To shim the subfloor, insert a 1/2-inch thick wood shim between the subfloor and the joist just below the squeaky floor board; use a hammer to tap it in until it is snug *(above, left)*. If the floor board still squeaks, continue to drive in shims along the joist as necessary the same way.

To draw the squeaky floor board down toward the subfloor, use wood screws 1 1/4 inches long; fit each screw with a washer to help ensure its holding power. Fit an electric drill *(page 129)* with a twist bit of the same diameter as a screw; wrap a small strip of masking tape around the bit 1 inch from the tip. Drill a pilot hole as near to the squeaky floor board as you can; stop drilling as soon as the tape touches the subfloor. Drive a screw into the pilot hole *(above, right)*, tightening it securely. If the floor board still squeaks, add more screws along the subfloor under it as necessary the same way.

SILENCING A SQUEAKY STAIR

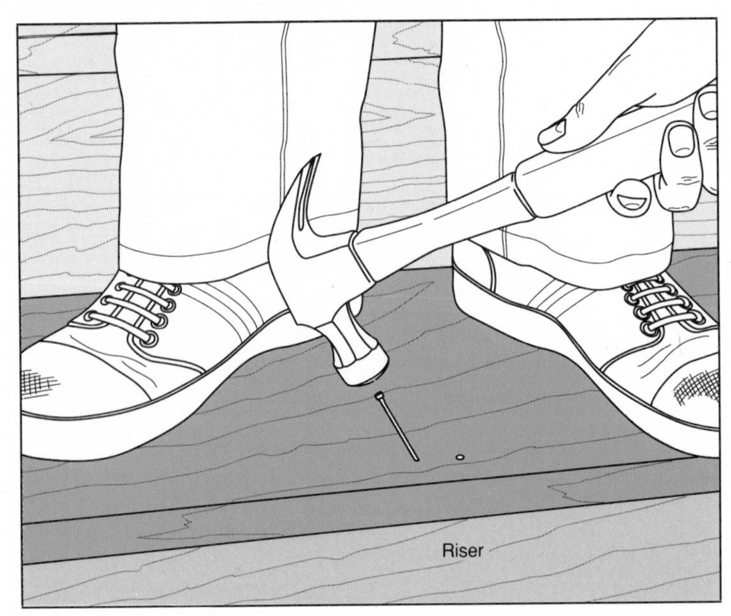

1 Securing a squeaky tread. Have a helper stand on the squeaky tread, then drive two 2-inch finishing nails at opposite 45-degree angles through it into the riser below it *(above)*—so that the two nails together form a V. Countersink the nail heads using a nail set and a hammer, then cover them with a putty stick as you would to repair any wood surface *(page 44)*. If the tread still squeaks, shim it *(step 2)* or pull it down using a wood block *(step 3)*; if there is a center stringer under the tread, draw the tread down to it with wood screws *(step 4)*.

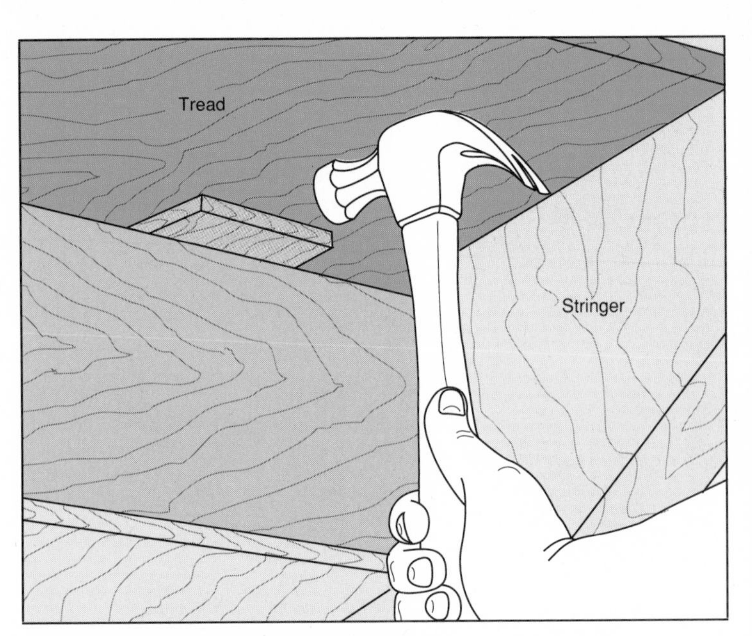

2 Shimming a squeaky tread. Work from under the stairs to shim a squeaky tread, installing a 1/2-inch thick wood shim every 4 to 6 inches into the joint between it and the riser. Position the first shim under the squeaky tread about 6 inches from one of the stringers and use a hammer to tap it into the joint until it is snug *(above)*. Continue installing shims along the squeaky tread the same way. Chisel off the end of any shim that protrudes from the front of the tread.

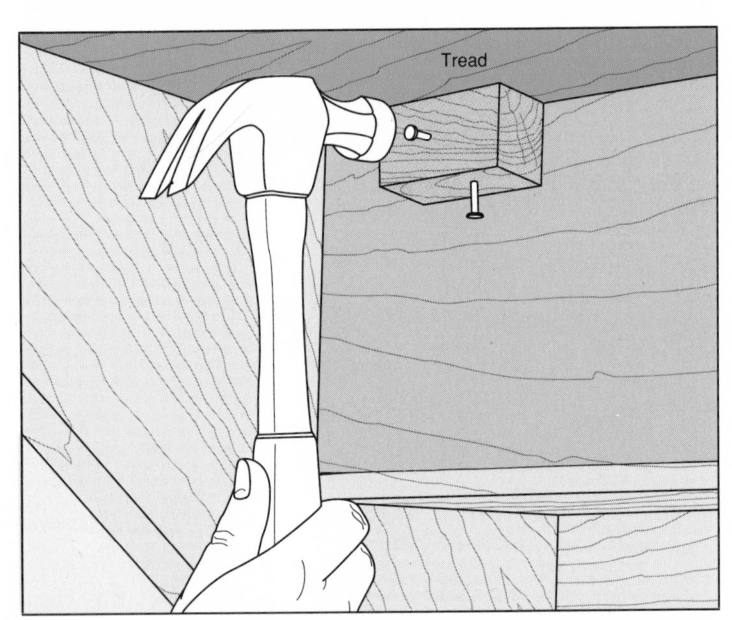

3 Securing a squeaky tread with a wood block. Drive a 2-inch nail into the long side of a 3-inch long 2-by-2 wood block until it just pierces the other side. Then, hammer a second 2-inch nail into the wood block at a 90-degree angle to the first until it just pierces the other side. Apply a liberal amount of wood glue to the sides of the wood block with the exposed nail tips. Having a helper stand on the squeaky tread, position the wood block with the glued sides pressed against the back of it and the riser below it; then, finish driving in the nails *(above)*. Wipe off any extruded glue using a cloth dampened with water.

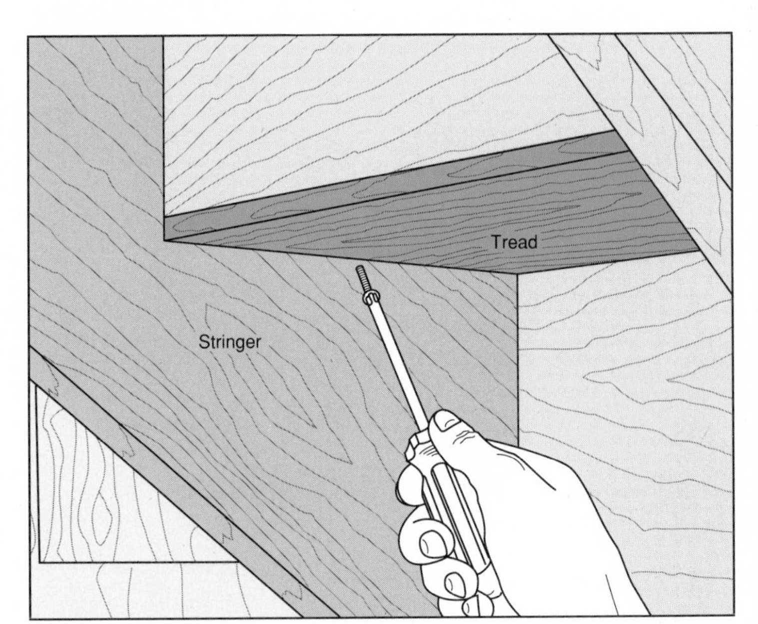

4 Securing a squeaky tread with wood screws. Having a helper stand on the squeaky tread, work from under the stairs to draw it down to the center stringer with 1-inch wood screws. Fit an electric drill *(page 129)* with a twist bit of the same diameter as a screw; wrap a small strip of masking tape around the bit 3/4 inch from the tip. Drill a pilot hole at a 30-degree angle into one side of the center stringer near the tread; stop drilling as soon as the tape touches the stringer. Drive a screw into the pilot hole *(above)*, tightening it securely. Install another screw on the other side of the center stringer the same way.

SECURING A NEWEL POST

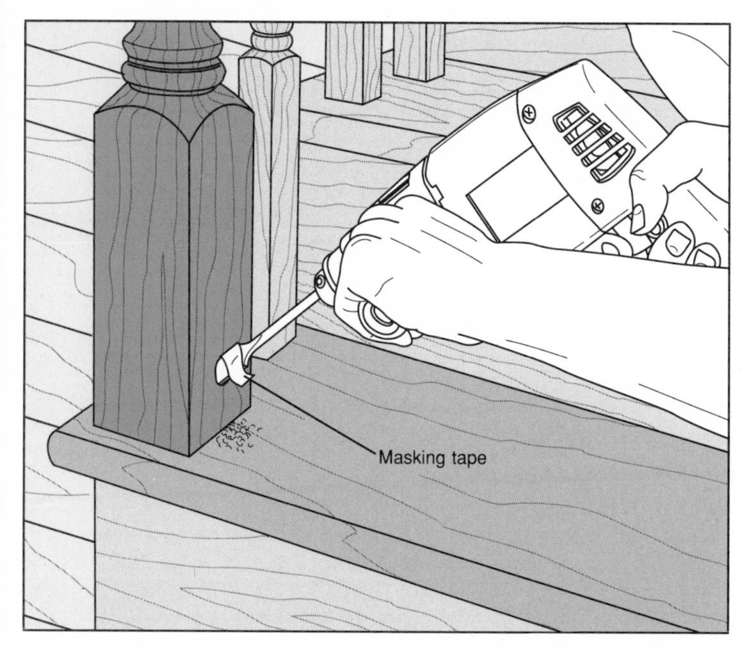

1 Counterboring into the newel post. To resecure a wobbly newel post, install a 4-inch lag bolt 2 inches above the base of it. Fit an electric drill *(page 129)* with a 3/4-inch spade bit; wrap a small strip of masking tape around the bit 3/4 inch from the tip. Position the bit at a 45-degree angle to the newel post on one side of it and bore a hole; stop drilling as soon as the tape touches the post *(above)*.

2 Installing a lag bolt. Fit the drill with a twist bit of the same diameter as the shank of the lag bolt; wrap a small strip of masking tape around the bit 3 1/2 inches from the tip. Position the bit in the counterbored hole, maintaining the 45-degree angle, then drill a hole through the newel post and into the tread or floor below; stop drilling as soon as the tape touches the post. Fit the lag bolt with a washer and insert it into the hole, tightening it by turning it clockwise with a socket wrench *(above)*. Cover the bolt head with wood patching compound and refinish the surface *(page 73)*.

SECURING A HANDRAIL

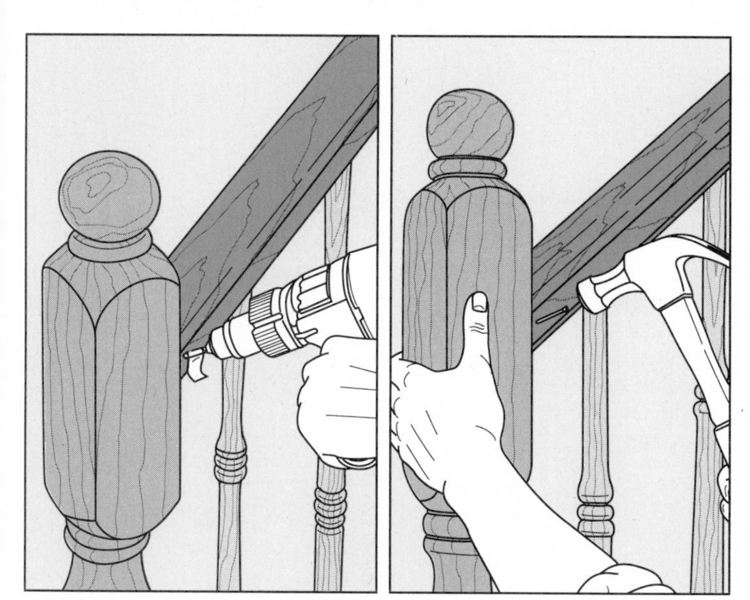

Securing a loose balustrade handrail. Secure a loose balustrade handrail using 3-inch finishing nails. Fit an electric drill *(page 129)* with a twist bit of the same diameter as a nail; wrap a small strip of masking tape around it 2 1/2 inches from the tip to mark the drilling depth. Drill a pilot hole into one side of the handrail at a 45-degree angle 1 inch from the newel post *(above, left)*; then, drive a nail into the pilot hole *(above, right)*. Repeat the procedure on the other side of the handrail. Countersink the nail heads using a nailset and the hammer; cover them with a putty stick as you would to repair any wood surface *(page 44)*.

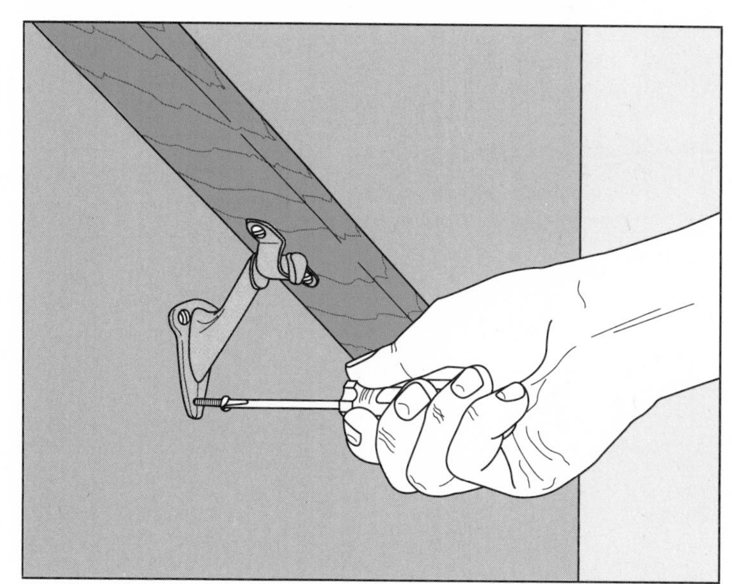

Securing a loose wall handrail. Inspect the support brackets; a wobbly wall handrail can often be corrected simply by tightening loose screws or replacing them with longer and thicker ones *(above)*. When a screw turns but does not tighten, remove it and plug the screw hole in the wall with a dowel. Buy a dowel of pine or other soft wood at a building supply center; using a utility knife, whittle it to the same diameter and cut it to the same length as the old screw. Fit the dowel through the support bracket into the screw hole in the wall, tapping it gently with a hammer. Then, reinstall the old screw.

REPLACING A BALUSTER

1 Removing a baluster and marking its replacement. If the baluster is only slightly damaged, repair it as you would any minor wood damage *(page 73)*. If the baluster is cracked or broken, replace it. To determine the length of the replacement baluster you need, measure the length of the old one and add 1/2 inch; for a stairway baluster, as shown, measure its tallest side. Note that to replace an old or ornate baluster you may require the special tools and skills of a professional carpenter.

To remove the baluster, use a compass saw first to cut it in half, then to cut through it at the top and bottom, protecting nearby surfaces with carboard *(far left)*. Take the baluster pieces to a building supply center and buy an exact replacement of the correct length. Using coarse-grit sandpaper on a sanding block, smooth the tread or floor and bottom of the handrail where the old baluster stood. Position the new baluster to mark it for cutting, orienting its contours to match adjacent balusters. Having a helper keep the baluster vertical using a carpenter's level, mark each side of the top of it with a sharp pencil *(near left)*. Use a backsaw to cut the baluster to size. Paint or finish the baluster to match the others as you would any wood trim *(page 51)*.

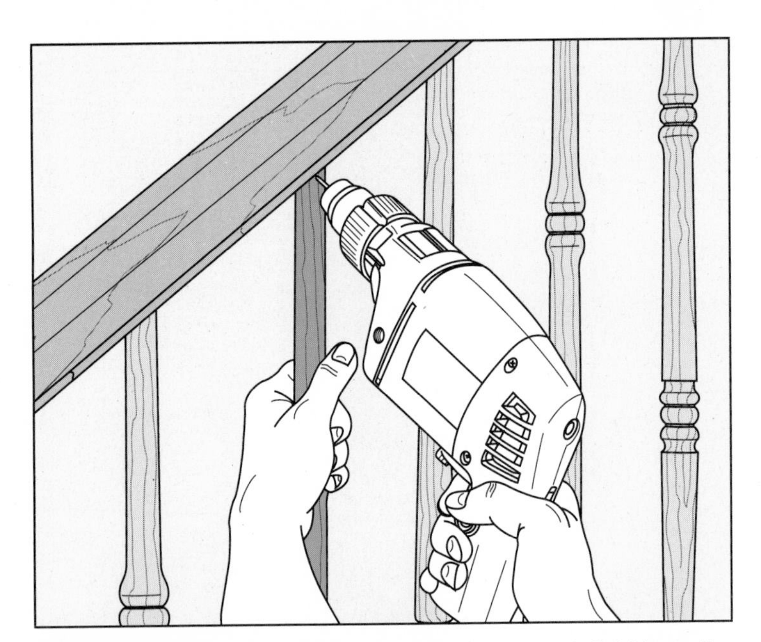

2 Drilling pilot holes. Install the baluster with 1-inch finishing nails. Using an awl, punch a starter hole 1/2 inch from each end of the baluster. Fit an electric drill *(page 129)* with a twist bit of the same diameter as a nail. Holding the baluster in place, position the bit against the top starter hole and drill a pilot hole at a 45-degree angle up through the baluster and into the bottom of the handrail *(above)*. Make a second pilot hole near the bottom of the baluster the same way, drilling down through it and into the tread or floor.

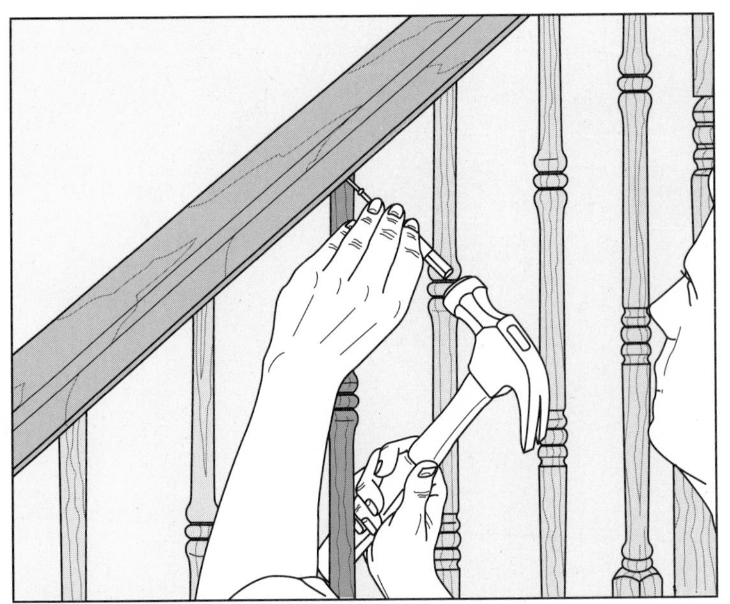

3 Securing the new baluster. Remove the baluster and drive finishing nails through the pilot holes in it, stopping when the nails just pierce the other side. Reposition the baluster and have a helper hold it securely in place, then finish driving the nails using a hammer and nail set *(above)*, countersinking the nail heads just below the surface. Cover the nail heads with a putty stick as you would to repair any wood surface *(page 44)*.

REPAIRING MINOR WOOD DAMAGE

1 Filling a small hole or crack. To patch a small hole or crack in a wood surface, use pre-mixed wood patching compound of a color that matches the wood; on painted wood, use white-colored compound. Load the tip of a putty knife with compound and smooth it over the damage *(above)*, overfilling the hole or crack slightly to allow for shrinkage. On curved surfaces such as balusters and newel posts, wear rubber gloves and press the compound into shape. Let the compound dry; if the patch shrinks below the surface level, fill it again.

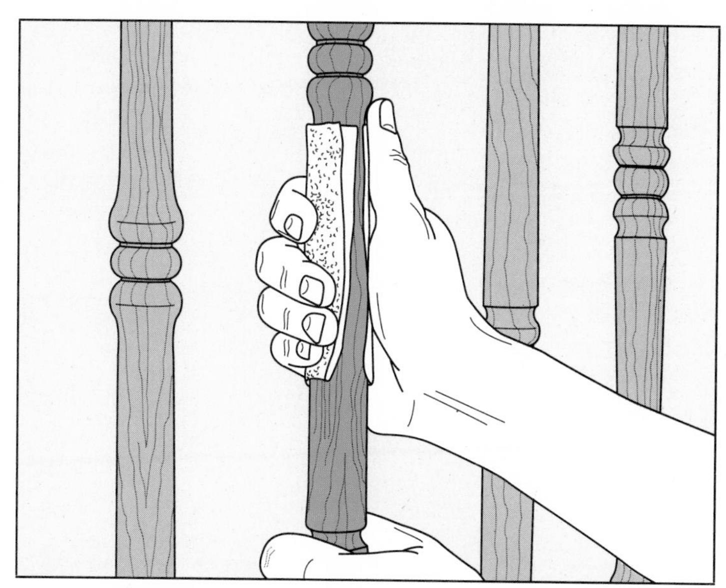

2 Sanding the patched wood. Use medium-grit sandpaper to sand the patch flush with the surrounding surface. Always sand in the direction of the wood grain. For a flat surface, fit the sandpaper onto a sanding block, then work back and forth with it. For a curved surface, fold a sheet of sandpaper in half once or twice and rub with it *(above)*. For grooves or intricate details, use the folded edge of a sandpaper sheet. After sanding, wipe or brush off any dust.

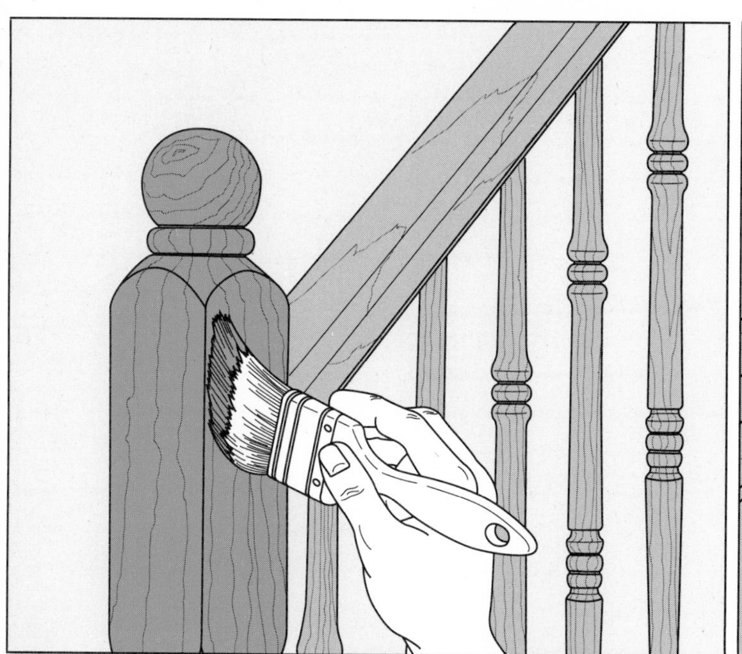

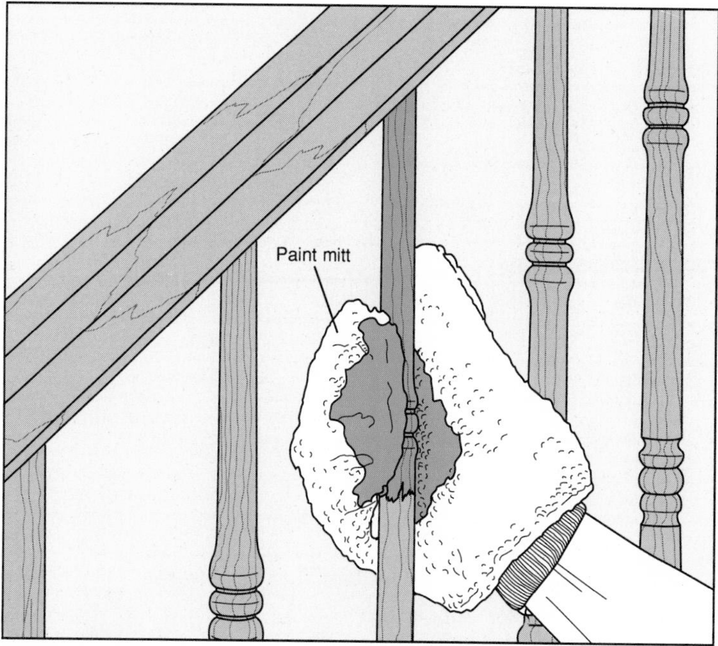

3 Painting or finishing the patched surface. Select a paint or finish; also any primer recommended by the paint manufacturer *(page 135)*. Protect adjacent surfaces with newspaper or drop cloths. Use a paintbrush to apply primer to any patched area; let it dry. To apply paint or finish on a small area, use a 2-inch trim paintbrush. Work slowly and carefully to avoid splatters and drips, applying the paint or finish in the direction of the wood grain as much as possible. On a newel post, begin at the top and work to the bottom in even strokes *(above, left)*. On intricate details, dab the wood with paint or finish to cover all edges and grooves; go over the surface with a dry brush, moving with the contours of the design. Use a paint mitt for surfaces that are difficult to reach with a brush; for extra protection wear a rubber glove under it. Dip your mitted-hand into the paint or finish, wiping the mitt on the inside of the can; avoid wetting the back of the mitt. Stroke the surface, moving with the wood grain when possible *(above, right)*. Let the paint or finish dry according to the manufacturers instructions; if necessary, apply another coat, sanding first with fine-grit sandpaper *(step 2)*. Safely dispose of leftover paint or finish *(page 141)*.

WINDOWS AND DOORS

Clean, smoothly-functioning doors and windows add to the resale value of your home. Before a visit from a potential buyer, go through your home, checking that each door and window opens and closes easily. Review the Troubleshooting Guide *(below)* and use the checklist diagram *(page 75)* to help you identify possible trouble spots. Wash windows until they sparkle and unstick those sealed shut by paint *(page 77)*; clean the tracks and lubricate stiff mechanisms *(page 76)*. Cracked window panes and torn screens detract enormously from a prospective buyer's impressions of your home. Remove shards of glass with care and install a new pane *(page 78, 79)*. Patch small holes in screens *(page 79)* and remove heavily-damaged screens. To fix a binding door, first diagnose the cause *(page 82)*; only then can the problem be corrected. Other door problems such as sticky locks *(page 81)* and loose doorknobs *(page 80)* are easily fixed in minutes.

Tour the exterior of your home, closely inspecting the condition of its doors and windows. Tighten loose shutter screws and replace damaged or unsightly glazing compound *(page 77)* as well as any damaged caulk *(page 84)*. A fresh coat of paint, carefully applied *(page 85)*, can dramatically enhance the look of your entire home. However, keep in mind that if you repaint one dingy-looking window or door, you may have to repaint all of them to maintain a uniform appearance. Consult the paint and primer chart in Tools & Techniques *(page 126)*. To paint door and window exteriors, refer to pages 36 and 37. Inside your home, use subdued colors on doors and around windows. Do not forget to inspect your garage door as well; silence a squeaky garage door and lubricate its parts *(page 81)*. For a more detailed checklist of problems to watch out for on the exterior of your home, read the chapter called Grounds And Exterior *(page 18)*.

TROUBLESHOOTING GUIDE

SYMPTOM	PROCEDURE
Window pane or sash dirty	Clean window *(p. 76)* □○
Screen dirty	Remove screen and wash with garden hose; for stubborn dirt, scrub gently with soft-bristled brush and solution of mild household detergent and water
Window does not open or close smoothly	Service window track and hardware *(p. 76)* □○
Painted window does not open	Break paint bond; strip sash channels *(p. 77)* □◒
Glazing compound around window pane dried out and cracked	Replace glazing compound *(p. 77)* ⬓○
Window pane cracked or broken	Replace pane: wood sash *(p. 78)* ⬓◒; metal sash *(p. 79)* ⬓◒
Screen wires bent	Straighten wires with tip of nail
Screen torn	Seal small hole with glue; patch large hole *(p. 79)* □○
Door swings with difficulty	Lubricate door hinges; sand painted or rusty hinge pins *(p. 80)* □○
Door squeaks as it swings	Lubricate door hinges *(p. 80)* □○
Door binds	Diagnose trouble spots *(p. 82)* □○ and repair as indicated
Closed door rattles	Shim door hinges *(p. 83)* ⬓◒
Door latch does not close properly	Adjust strike plate *(p. 83)* ⬓◒
Sliding door does not open or close smoothly	Service door hardware *(p. 80)* □○
Storm door swings with difficulty or slams shut	Adjust door closer *(p. 80)* □○
Storm door binds	Tighten door hinge screws
Doorknob loose or rattling	Tighten screws on escutcheon *(p. 80)* □○
Key does not turn in keyhole or turns stiffly	Lubricate keyhole and bolt *(p. 81)* □○
Garage door operates noisily or stiffly	Clean and lubricate door tracks, hinges and springs *(p. 81)* □○
Window sill or threshold soft or crumbling	Remove rot and patch *(p. 84)* □○; paint *(p. 85)* □○
Paint on window or door flaking, peeling, dingy or faded	Repaint *(p. 85)* □◒
Caulk around window or door exterior cracked or loose; air leaks through cracks	Replace caulk *(p. 84)* □○

DEGREE OF DIFFICULTY: □ Easy ⬓ Moderate ■ Complex
ESTIMATED TIME: ○ Less than 1 hour ◒ 1 to 3 hours ● Over 3 hours
(Does not include drying time)

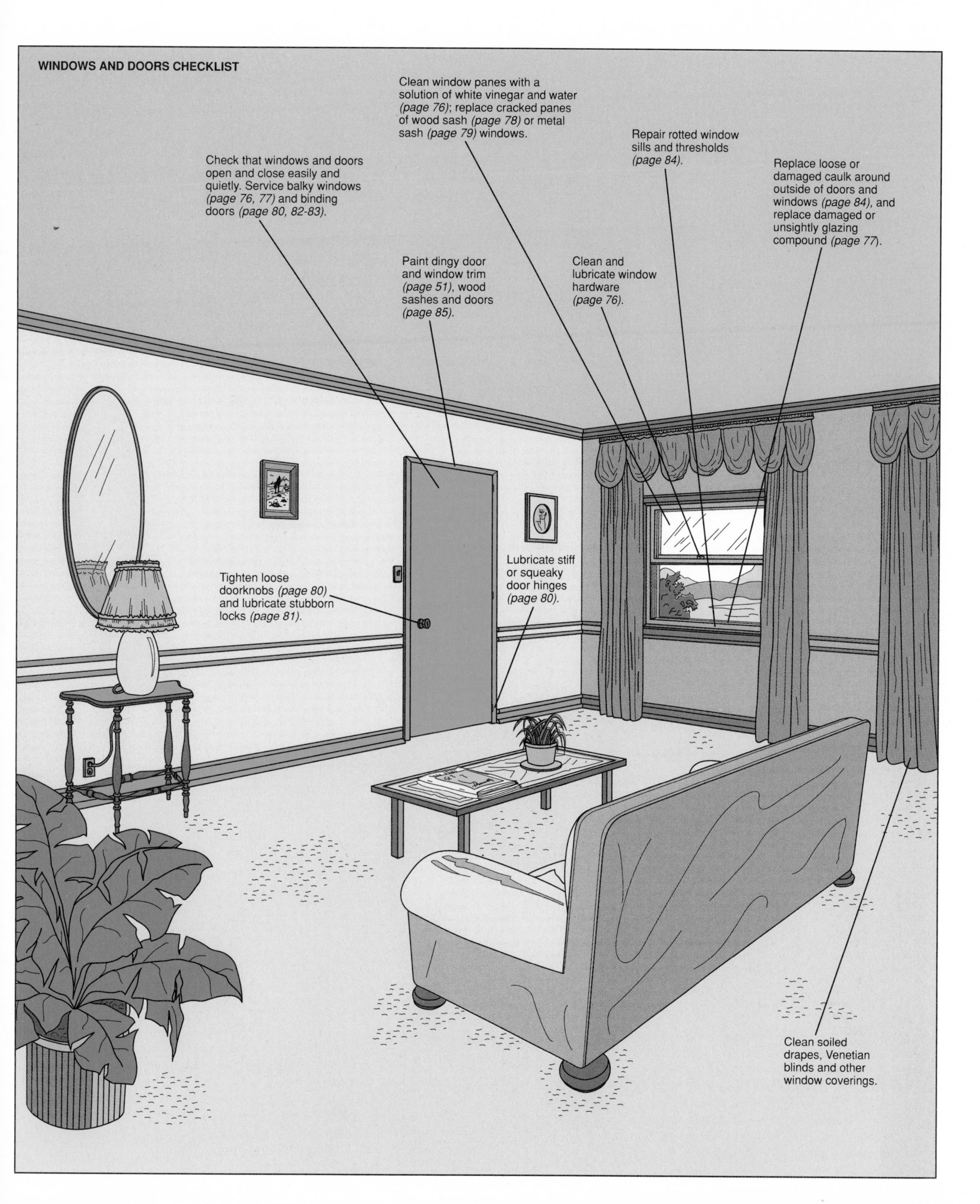
WINDOWS AND DOORS CHECKLIST
Clean window panes with a solution of white vinegar and water (page 76); replace cracked panes of wood sash (page 78) or metal sash (page 79) windows.
Repair rotted window sills and thresholds (page 84).
Check that windows and doors open and close easily and quietly. Service balky windows (page 76, 77) and binding doors (page 80, 82-83).
Replace loose or damaged caulk around outside of doors and windows (page 84), and replace damaged or unsightly glazing compound (page 77).
Paint dingy door and window trim (page 51), wood sashes and doors (page 85).
Clean and lubricate window hardware (page 76).
Lubricate stiff or squeaky door hinges (page 80).
Tighten loose doorknobs (page 80) and lubricate stubborn locks (page 81).
Clean soiled drapes, Venetian blinds and other window coverings.

CLEANING A WINDOW

Washing a window pane and sash. Wearing rubber gloves, use a squeegee and a solution of 1/2 cup of white vinegar per gallon of water to wash window glass. Washing one area at a time, scrub the glass with the sponge. Then, use the rubber blade to wipe off the solution *(left)*, angling it to force the solution to drip into a lower corner. To prevent streaks, dry the glass immediately with crumpled newspaper, wiping in a circular motion *(inset)*.

Use a clean cloth and the same solution to clean a wood sash and sill, taking care not to soak the wood with water. For heavily-soiled woodwork, clean with a solution of trisodium phosphate (TSP) *(page 54)* and wipe the woodwork dry with a fresh cloth. For mildew, wash with a solution of 2 cups of household bleach per gallon of water. Rinse thoroughly and wipe dry. Wash a metal sash with a solution of mild household detergent and water; avoid using an abrasive cleaner.

SERVICING WINDOW TRACKS AND HARDWARE

Cleaning and lubricating sliding window tracks. Slide open the window; if it is painted shut, break the paint bond *(page 77)*. Vacuum both window tracks using a nozzle attachment *(above)*. To remove stubborn dirt from the corners of a window track, scrub using an old toothbrush dipped in a solution of mild household detergent and water. Wipe dry with a clean cloth. If the window continues to balk, spray the tracks with a petroleum-based lubricant. Slide the window open and closed until it moves easily and smoothly.

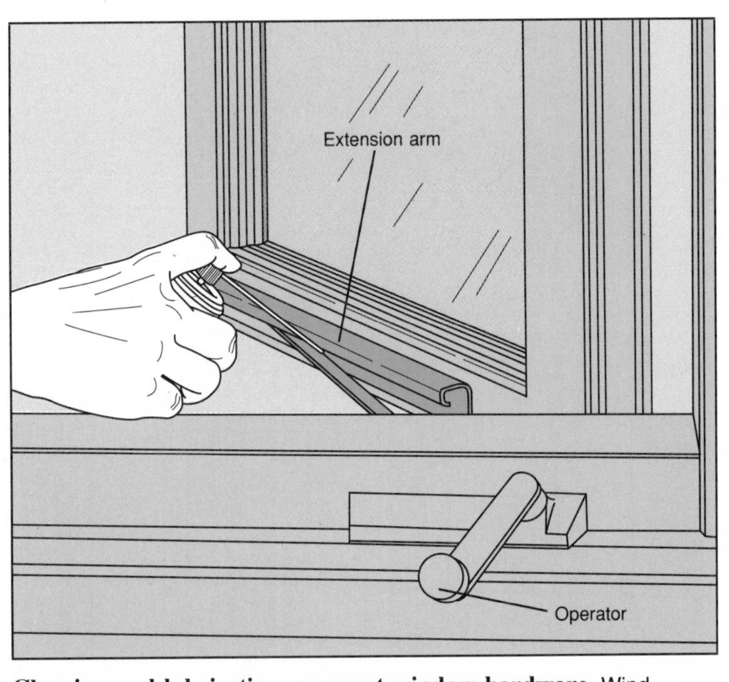

Cleaning and lubricating casement window hardware. Wind open the window; if it is painted shut, break the paint bond *(page 77)*. Use a wire brush to remove old paint and hardened grease from the extension-arm track, hinges and latch. Wipe all accessible metal parts with a clean rag dampened with rubbing alcohol. Lubricate a stubborn operator with petroleum-based lubricant. Insert a plastic straw into the sprayer nozzle and spray the lubricant along the extension arm *(above)* and its track, as well as on the hinges and latch.

UNSTICKING A PAINTED WINDOW

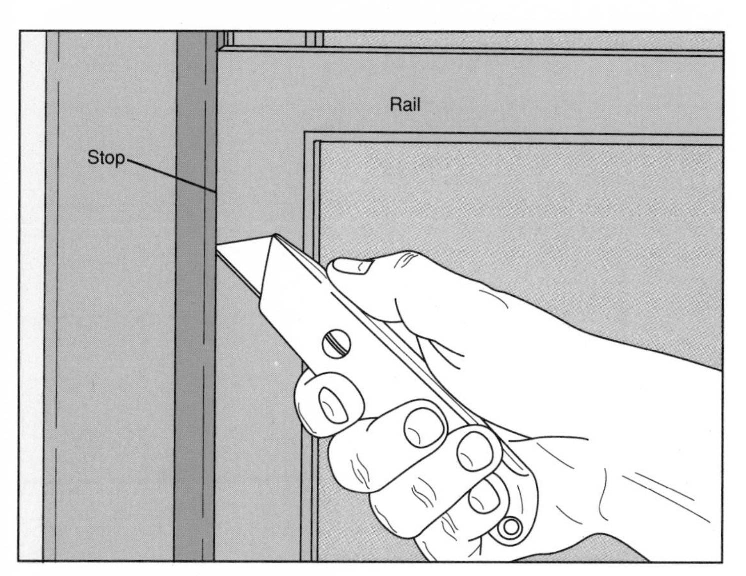

1 Breaking a paint bond. Carelessly-applied paint can seal a window shut. Use a utility knife to slice through the paint bond, drawing its blade between the window stop and sash *(above)*. Work the knife around the entire sash, taking care not to gouge the woodwork. Open the window; if it still does not budge, repeat the procedure on the exterior. On a double-hung window, paint may seal the rails together. Pass the utility knife between the rails several times. Once the paint bond is broken, raise the lower sash. If the sash of a double-hung window moves with difficulty, paint may have dripped along the jamb, building up the sash channels; if necessary, strip them *(step 2)*.

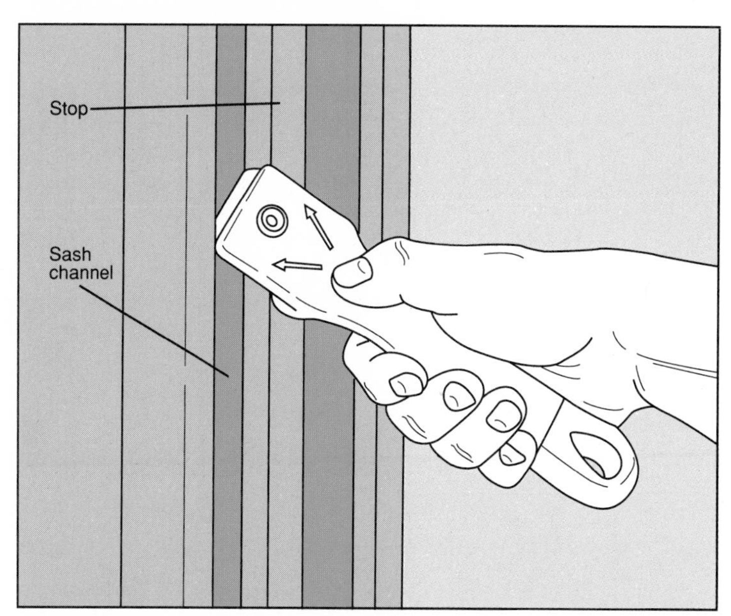

2 Stripping the sash channels. Raise the lower sash as high as possible. Use a paint scraper to remove thick, rough or bumpy paint caking the surface of the sash channels *(above)*; be careful not to gouge the wood. If the paint buildup is heavy, use a heat gun to soften the paint and a narrow putty knife to remove it. Sand the sash channels with medium-grit sandpaper and repaint them with a thin coat of paint *(page 85)*. Lubricate the sash channels with petroleum-based lubricant or rub them with paraffin wax.

REPLACING GLAZING COMPOUND

1 Removing old glazing compound. Using a rigid putty knife, pry out cracked or dried-out glazing compound between the window pane and sash. Hardened glazing compound may first require softening. To soften unpainted compound, coat it with linseed oil. After 30 minutes, remove the oil-saturated compound with the putty knife. Soften painted compound using a heat gun equipped with a deflector nozzle to protect the pane. Set the heat gun on its lowest setting. With the nozzle tip of the heat gun pressed gently against the window, work the softened compound free with an old screwdriver *(above)*. Push loose glazier's points back in until they protrude only halfway.

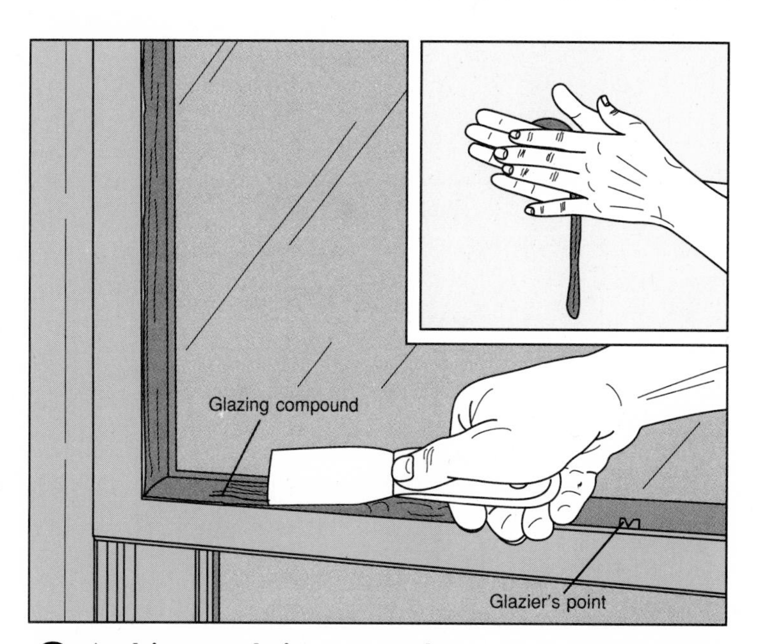

2 Applying new glazing compound. Buy a tin of putty-type glazing compound. Scoop out a little compound and roll it between your palms into a snake-like shape about 3/8 inch in diameter *(inset)*. Press the compound into the joint between the pane and sash, making sure the glazier's points are well covered. Trim off any excess compound with a putty knife. Wet the putty knife with water and draw it over the compound at a 45-degree angle *(above)*. Let the compound cure according to the manufacturer's instructions. Paint the sash *(page 85)*.

REPLACING A WINDOW PANE IN A WOOD SASH

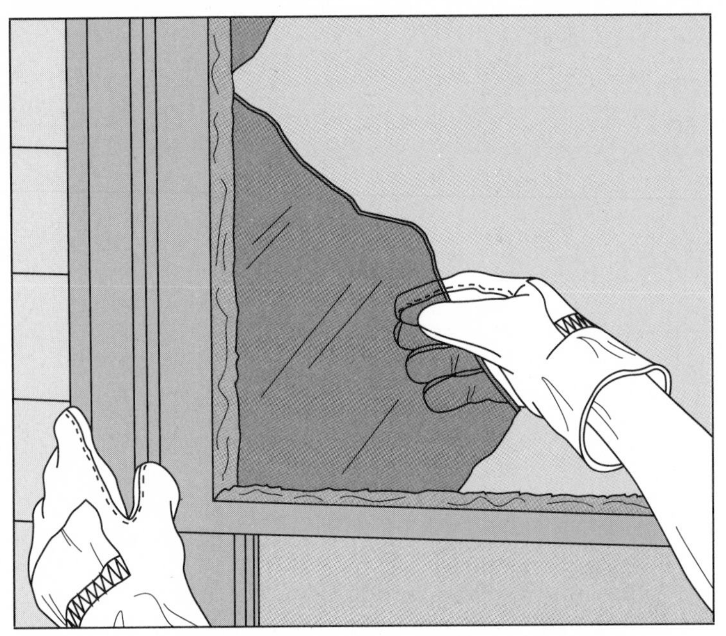

1 Removing the broken pane. Wearing heavy work gloves, safety goggles and thick shoes, start at the top of the window to remove shards of glass. Pull each piece of broken glass straight out of the window sash *(above)*; gently wiggle stubborn fragments free. Put the broken glass in a cardboard box for disposal. If the window has muntins—narrow strips of wood that divide the panes—take special care removing the glass; muntins are very delicate and their replacement requires the skill of a professional carpenter.

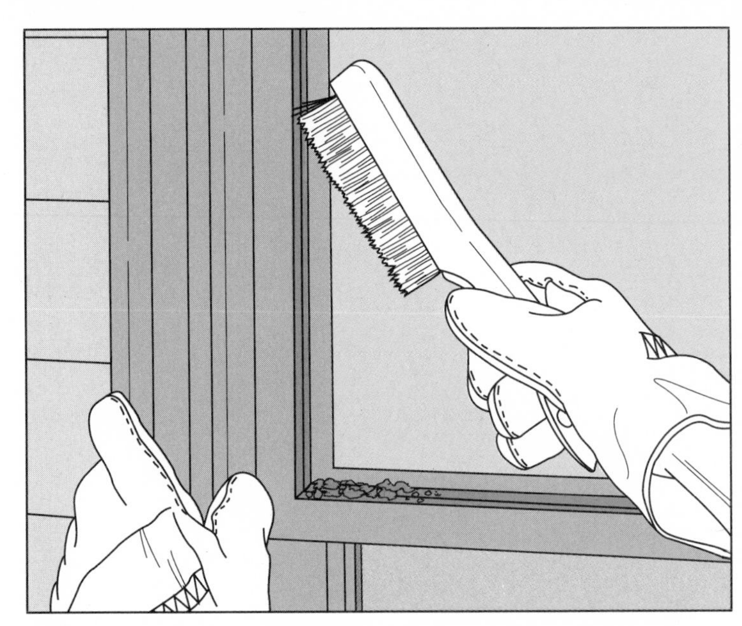

2 Preparing the groove. Remove the glazing compound from the sash *(page 77)*. Use long-nose pliers to pull out any remaining glazier's points. With a wire brush, gently clean the sash grooves *(above)*, using extra care around any muntins. Smooth any splintered wood with medium-grit sandpaper. Use a 1-inch trim paintbrush to prime the sash grooves with linseed oil. To fit a replacement pane, measure the opening inside the sash, including the depth of the sash grooves; then, subtract 1/8 inch from each measurement to allow for glass expansion. Buy a pane of glass cut to these specifications as well as a tin of putty-type glazing compound.

3 Applying the glazing compound. To provide a weatherseal and to ensure that the new pane of glass does not rattle in the window frame, line the sash grooves with a bed of glazing compound. Scoop out a small amount of compound and roll it between your palms into a snake-like shape about 3/8 inch in diameter. Carefully press the compound into the sash grooves *(above)*, making sure the corners are well covered.

4 Installing the new pane. While a broken pane may be removed from inside or outside, a new pane must be installed from outside; use a ladder *(page 137)* and work with a helper, if necessary. Wear work gloves and safety goggles, handling the pane carefully. Tilting the bottom edge of the pane in first, center it in the sash grooves *(above)*. Press glazier's points every 4 inches into the sash flush against the pane, then use a rigid putty knife to push them halfway in. Apply glazing compound along the joint between the pane and sash *(page 77)*.

REPLACING A WINDOW PANE IN A METAL SASH

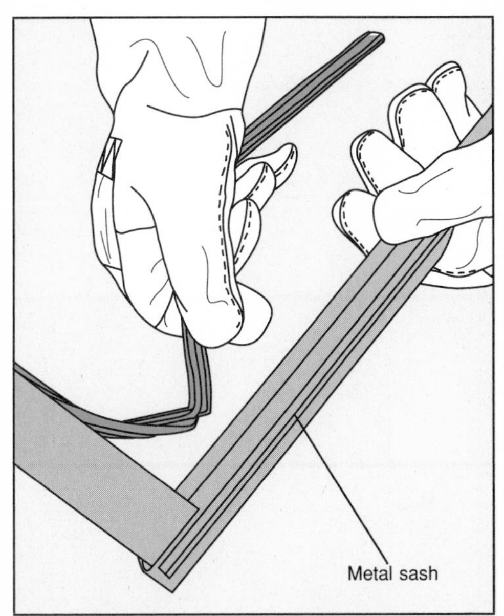

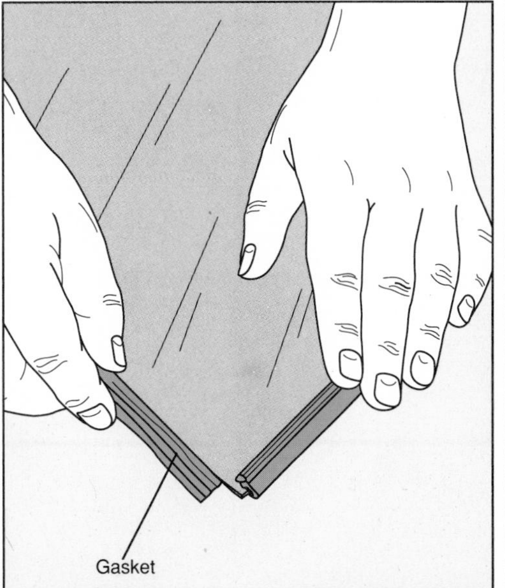

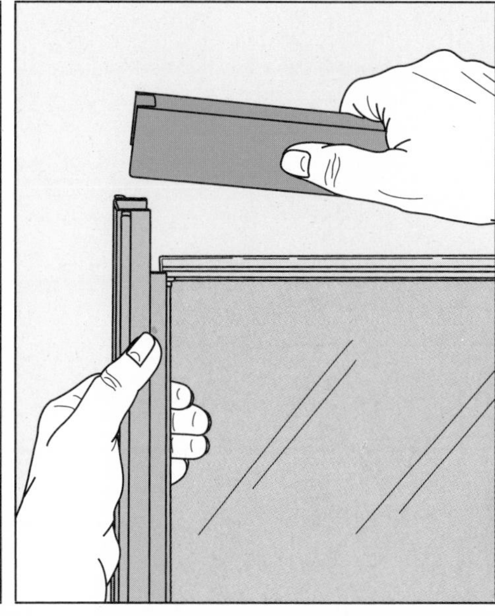

Replacing a broken pane of glass. Remove shards of glass as you would with a broken pane in a wood sash *(page 78)*. To install a new pane of glass, remove the sash from its metal frame by releasing the clips holding it in place. Lay the sash on a work table. To calculate the size of pane you need, measure the length and width of the opening from the inside edges of the sash, then pull out the rubber gasket *(above, left)* and measure its width; add twice the gasket width to the inside length and width measurements of the sash. Buy a replacement pane of glass at a hardware store or building supply center; if the gasket is cracked or damaged, also replace it. Most metal windows, such as the sliding type shown, must be disassembled to install a new pane of glass. To disassemble the sash, remove the framing screws and pull the sash apart. Fit the gasket around the edges of the new pane *(above, center)*; if you are using a new gasket, cut it at a 45-degree angle at the corners. Press the gasket firmly in place and reassemble the sash, reversing the steps used for disassembly *(above, right)*.

PATCHING A SCREEN

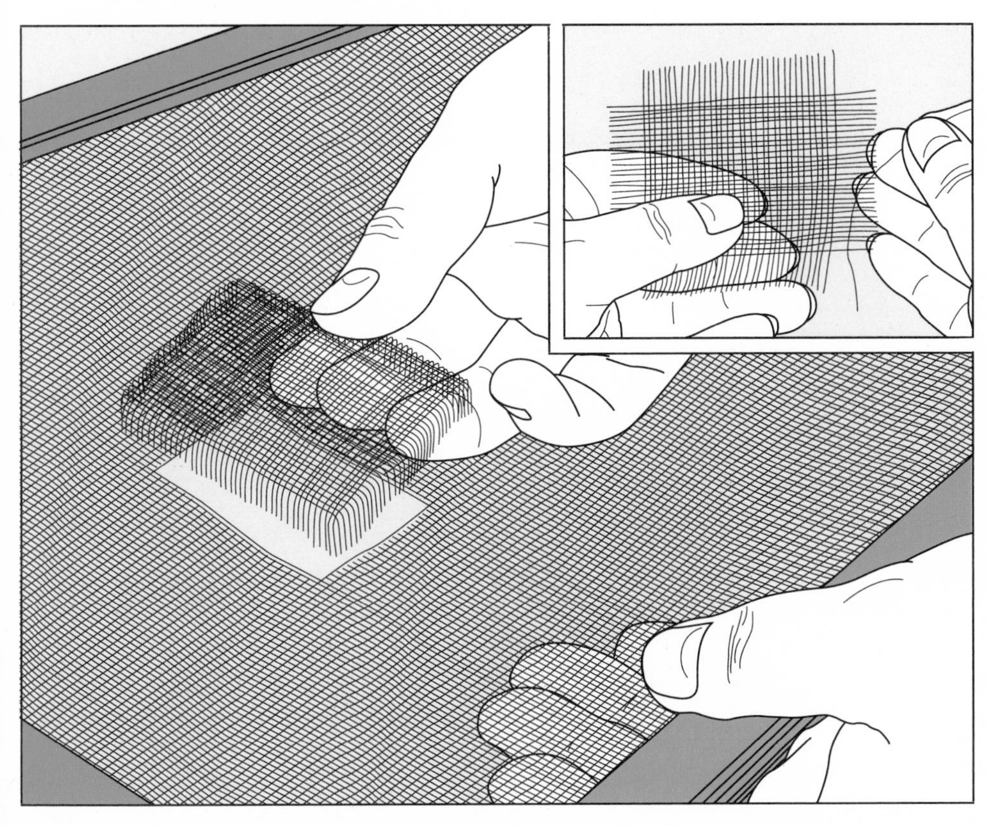

Patching a screen. Tiny holes in a metal screen can be sealed with a few drops of waterproof glue. Use a cloth to wipe away excess glue before it dries. To repair a larger hole, first remove the screen from the door or window by releasing the clips that hold it in place. Use scissors to cut the hole square. Buy a piece of matching screen at a hardware store or building supply center. Cut a patch in the new screen about 2 inches longer and wider than the hole. Pull out several strands of wire from each edge of the patch *(inset)*, keeping the central area larger than the hole. Neatly bend the pulled edges at right angles. Position the patch evenly over the hole *(left)* and work the wires through the screen remaining around it. Turn the screen over, pull the patch tight and bend the wires down against the screen. Reinstall the screen in the window or door.

To repair tiny holes in a nylon, plastic or fiberglass screen, straighten the broken ends with the tip of a nail and apply a few drops of epoxy. For a larger hole, cut a matching piece of screen and coat the edges of the patch and the area around the hole with a thin coat of epoxy. Press the patch in place and wipe off excess epoxy with a clean cloth.

SERVICING DOOR HARDWARE

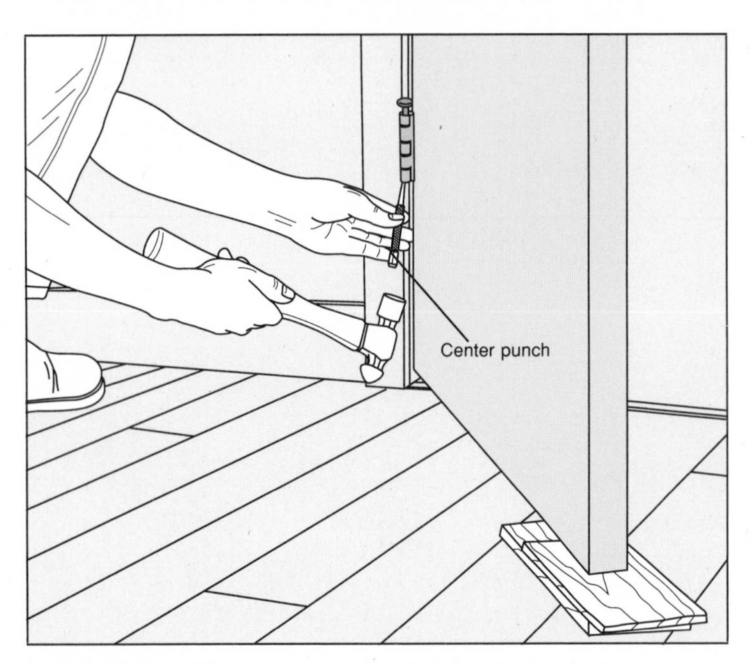

Lubricating a stiff or squeaky door hinge. Wedge the door open with shims and scrape any paint off the hinge pin. Position a center punch at the bottom of the pin and tap it with a ball-peen hammer *(above)*. Pull the pin out halfway and spray it with a petroleum-based lubricant. If the pin is covered with paint or rust, remove it and sand it lightly with medium-grit sandpaper, then lubricate it. Tap the pin back into place with the hammer. Repeat the procedure on the other hinge. Close and open the door a few times to work in the lubricant.

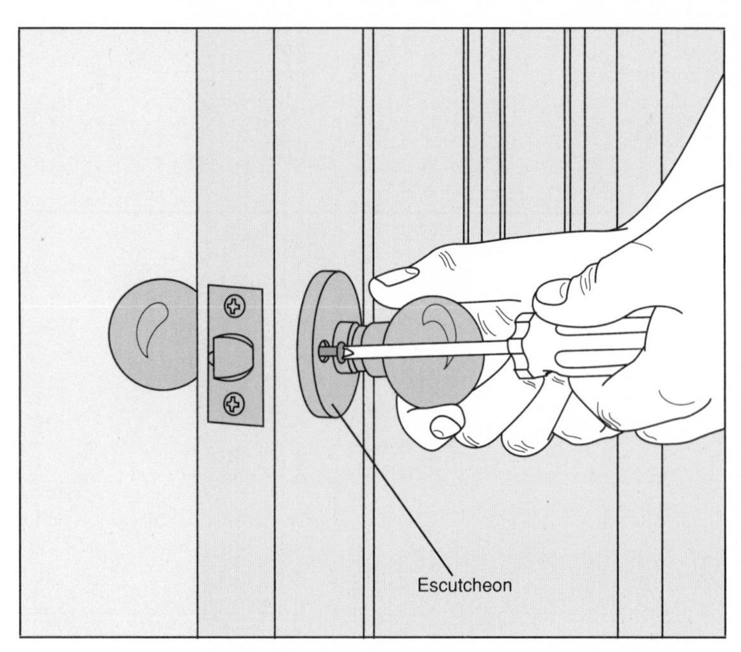

Tightening a loose doorknob. Resecure a loose doorknob by tightening the screws holding it to the door. On the popular model of doorknob shown, use a screwdriver to tighten the screws on the escutcheon *(above)*. On some models of doorknob, the escutcheon is secured to the door with setscrews; to tighten them use a hex wrench.

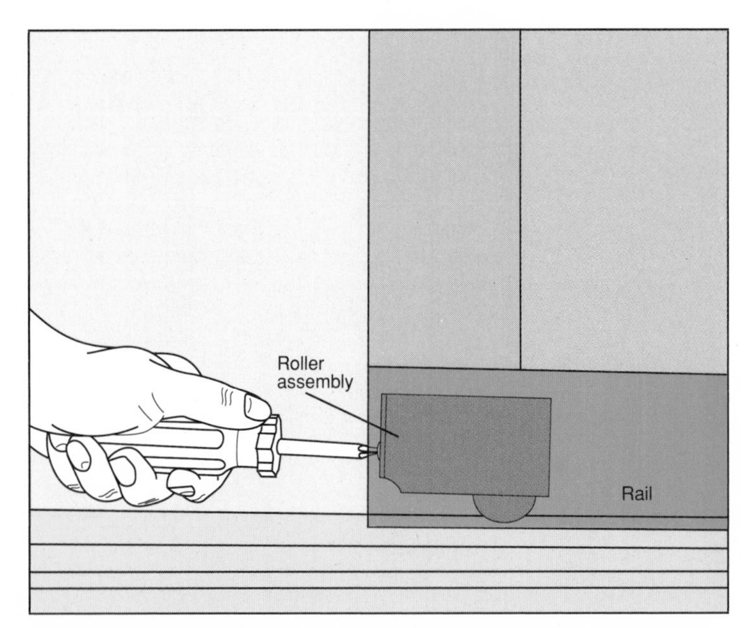

Fixing a balky sliding door. If a sliding door sticks, clean and lubricate the tracks as you would those of a sliding window *(page 76)*. If the door continues to stick, adjust the screw of the roller assembly in the bottom rail of the door. If the door drags in the track at the top, insert a screwdriver into the adjustment screw of the roller assembly *(above)* and turn counterclockwise; if the door rubs too tightly in the track at the bottom, turn clockwise. You may need help to raise the door slightly to take the pressure off the roller assembly so the screw can be adjusted.

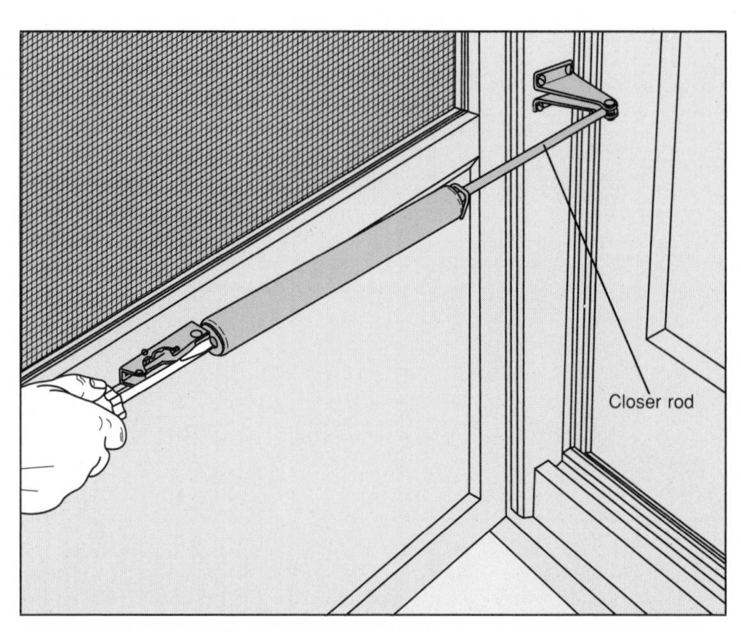

Servicing a storm-door closer. To clean dirt and grease off a storm-door closer, open the door and wipe the closer rod with a clean cloth. Then, lubricate the closer by spraying the rod with a petroleum-based lubricant. Adjust the closer to the desired closing speed by turning the screw at the end of it; adjust a slotted screw with a screwdriver *(above)* and a capped screw with pliers. If the door tends to slam shut, slow it down by turning the screw clockwise; if the door swings closed too slowly, speed it up by turning the screw counterclockwise. Tighten any loose bracket screws securing the closer to the door and the jamb.

SERVICING A DOOR LOCK

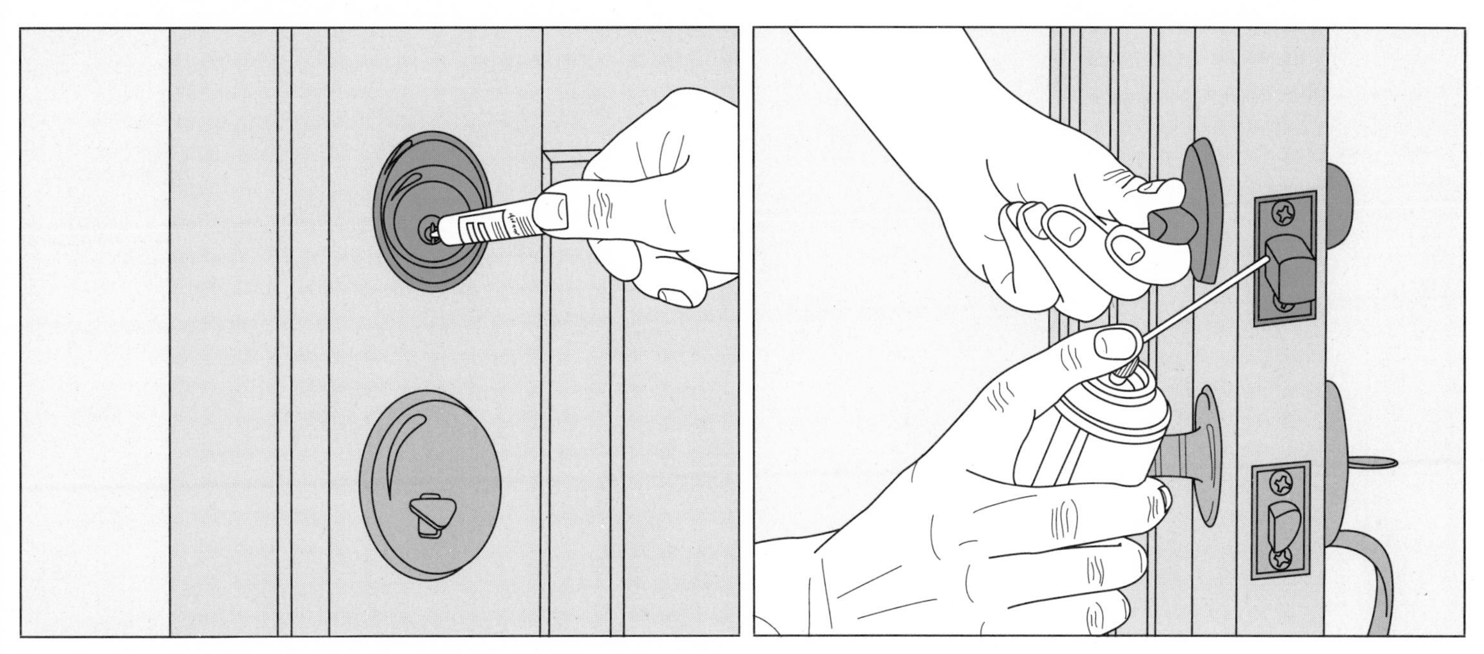

Lubricating a lock. Choose one type of lubricant and stick to it; mixing lubricants may gum a lock, requiring professional service. In general, use graphite powder to lubricate locks in a dry climate and a petroleum-based lubricant spray for locks in a humid region. To use graphite powder, press the nozzle of the container into the keyhole and squeeze once or twice *(above, left)*. Repeat the procedure in the cracks around the deadbolt. When applying a petroleum-based lubricant spray, first insert the plastic straw into the sprayer nozzle. Fit the straw into the keyhole and spray liberally. Open the door to spray around the latch and deadbolt *(above, right)*. Wipe off any excess lubricant with a clean rag. After applying any lubricant, insert the key into the lock and work the deadbolt back and forth several times to help distribute it.

SERVICING GARAGE DOOR TRACKS AND HARDWARE

1 Cleaning the tracks. Fix a balky garage door by cleaning its tracks. Spray degreasing solvent inside the tracks and use a cloth to wipe out dirt and grease *(above)*. Stand on a stepladder *(page 137)* to clean the upper reaches of the tracks.

2 Lubricating the moving parts. Lubricate all moving parts of a garage door with light machine oil. Squirt the oil on the metal axles, hinges and rollers *(above)* as well as the pivots and pulleys of the door mechanism. Wipe off any excess oil with a cloth. Open and close the door a few times to help distribute the oil through the parts.

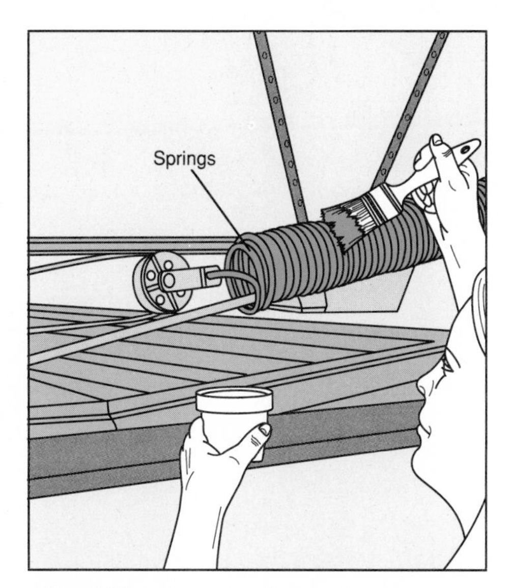

3 Oiling the extension springs. Lubricate the extension springs to stop squeaking and rusting. Open the door fully to release the tension in the springs. Standing on a stepladder *(page 137)*, dip an old paint brush into a container of light machine oil and coat each spring *(above)*. Use a cloth to wipe up any drips.

CORRECTING A BINDING DOOR

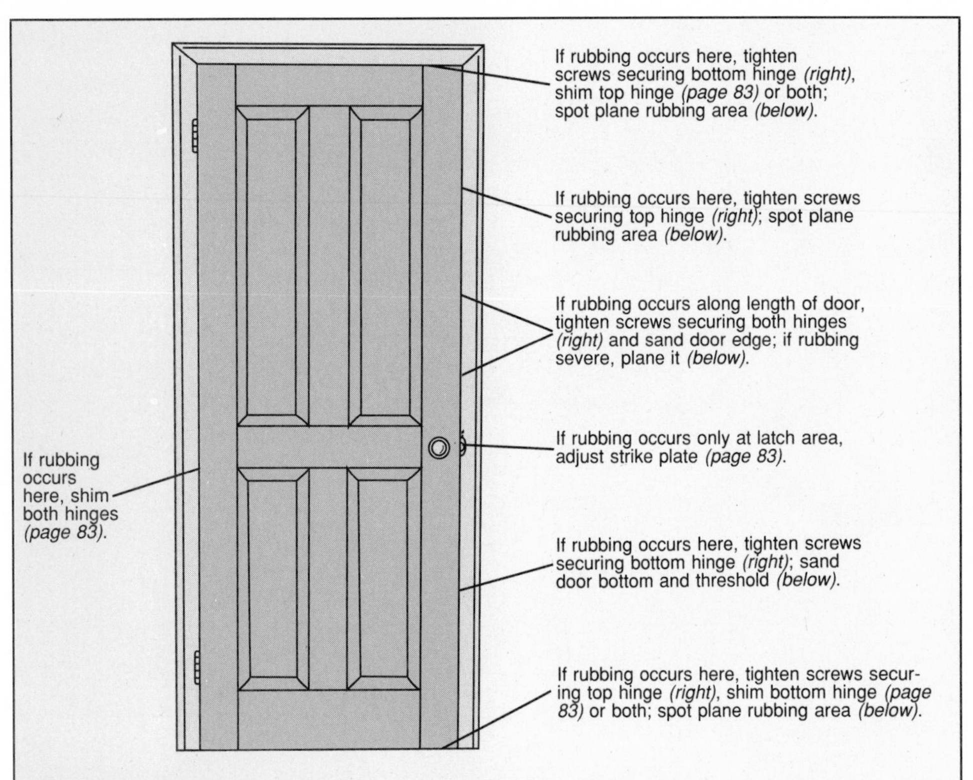

Diagnosing trouble spots. A binding door can often be corrected simply by tightening loose hinge screws on the door and jamb or using medium-grit sandpaper to remove paint buildup along the door edges. When a hinge screw turns but does not tighten, fix the worn screw hole. Wedge the door open with wood shims and remove the screw. Coat wood toothpicks with carpenter's glue and pack them into the screw hole. Once the glue has dried, use a utility knife to cut the toothpicks flush with the surface. Resecure the hinge with a new, longer screw of the same size head as the original.

If hinge screws are not the problem, adjust the door using the diagram at left as a guide. In most cases, rubbing can be corrected by shimming one of the door hinges *(page 83)*. If the door latch rubs against the strike plate, adjusting the strike plate may solve the problem *(page 83)*. If these repairs do not correct the binding, consider sanding the door and threshold *(step below, left)* or planing the door edge *(step below, right)*. Remove only small amounts of wood; a well-hung door has a 1/8-inch gap all around it to allow for expansion during humid weather.

Sanding the door and threshold. To sand the bottom edge of the door, open the door and slip a piece of medium-grit sandpaper under it at the spot that matches the rubbing marks on the threshold. Pull the sandpaper back and forth, sanding the problem area. Then, close the door; if it still binds, sand the threshold. Wearing safety goggles and a dust mask, use a small orbital sander fitted with medium-grit sandpaper to carefully remove a small amount of wood from the problem area *(above)*. Sand smoothly and evenly until the door can swing over the threshold without binding. Then, lightly sand the rest of the threshold and paint it *(page 85)*.

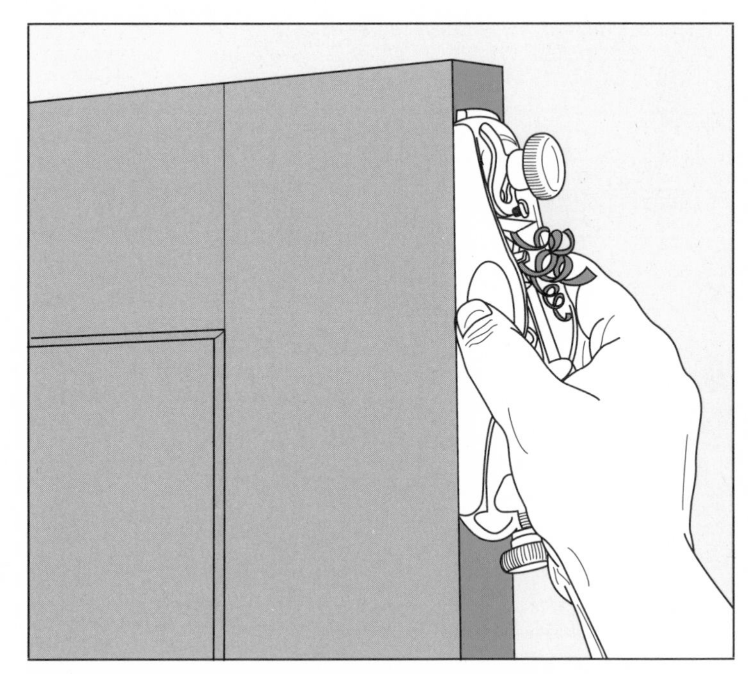

Planing a door. To remove paint buildup causing binding along the top or length of the door edge, open the door and sand smoothly over the paint using medium-grit sandpaper on a sanding block. If the door still binds, firmly wedge it open with wood shims. Then, work with a block plane to plane the rubbing area on the door *(above)*. Make long, even strokes with the plane, removing only a small amount of wood. If necessary, smooth any rough spots left by the plane using sandpaper. Paint the edge of the door *(page 85)*.

SHIMMING A DOOR HINGE

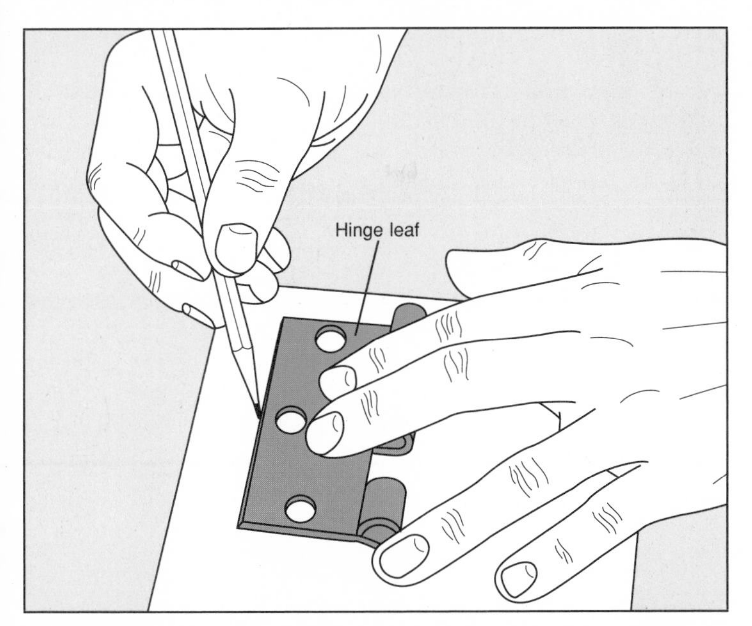

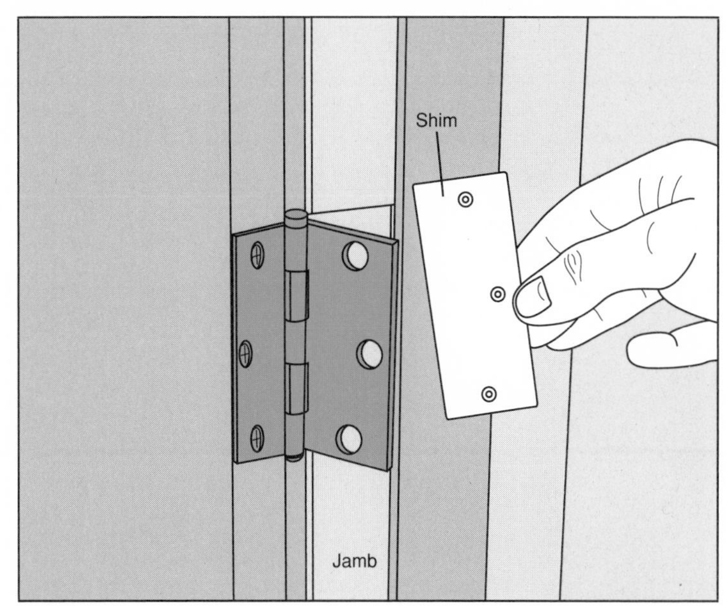

1 Making the shim. Wedge the door open with shims. Using a center punch and a ball-peen hammer, tap the hinge pin free of the hinge that requires shimming. Unscrew the hinge leaf from the jamb, then, place it on a piece of stiff cardboard and trace its outline with a pencil *(above)*; also mark the screw-hole openings. Cut out the shim using a utility knife or scissors and puncture it at the screw-hole markings with an awl. Make several shims in case you need more than one.

2 Installing the shim. Reinstall the hinge leaf with the hinge pin. Place a shim against the hinge mortise on the jamb *(above)* and press the hinge leaf over it. Resecure the hinge leaf to the jamb with longer screws of the same size head as the originals, then close the door; if it still binds, continue to add shims up to a maximum thickness of 1/16 inch. If shimming does not stop the door from binding, sand the door and threshold or plane the door *(page 82)*.

MOVING A STRIKE PLATE

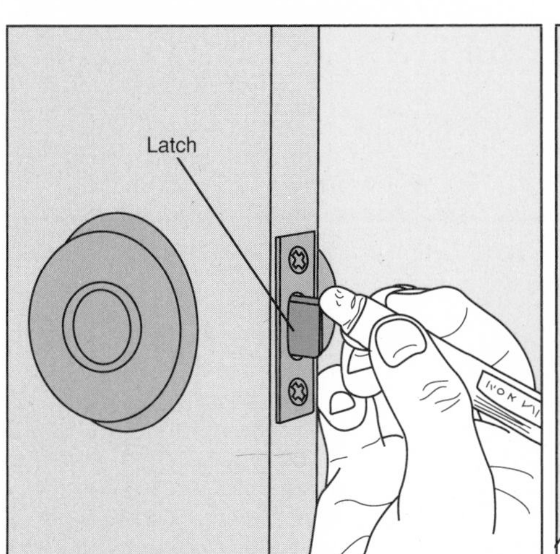

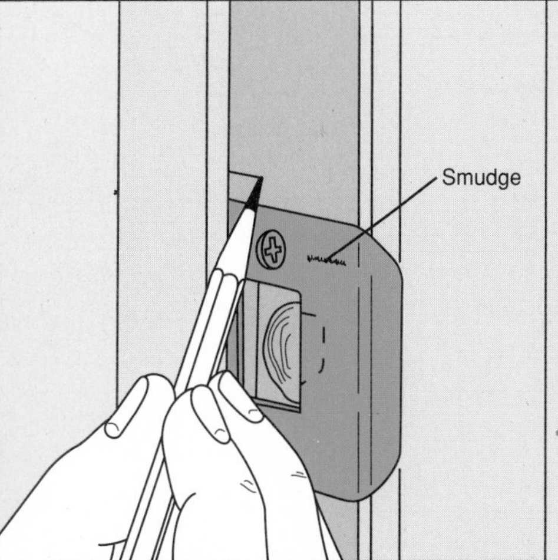

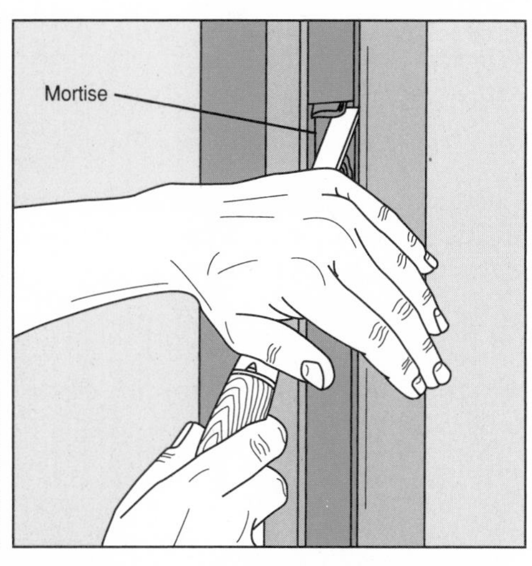

Curing an ill-fitting latch. When a latch hits the strike plate instead of extending into the strike hole, the door does not close properly. To determine whether to file or move the strike plate, rub a crayon on the edge of the latch *(above, left)* and close the door. Open the door and measure the distance between the strike plate opening and the crayon smudge. If the distance is less than 1/16 inch, file back the strike plate where the latch rubs it using a metal file. If the distance is greater than 1/16 inch, extend the strike plate mortise and move the strike plate. Mark an extension line on the jamb at a distance from the edge of the strike plate equal to the distance between the strike plate opening and the crayon smudge *(above, center)*. Unscrew and remove the strike plate from the jamb. Fill the screw holes by packing them with wood toothpicks coated with carpenter's glue. When the glue is dry, use a utility knife to cut the toothpicks flush with the surface. To extend the mortise, use a rubber mallet and a wood chisel to make a cut 1/8 inch deep in the jamb at the extension line. Then, chisel using hand force only to clean out the new mortise shape *(above, right)*. Seat the strike plate evenly in the mortise flush with the extension line and trace the outline of the new strike hole on the jamb. Remove the strike plate, then use the rubber mallet and wood chisel to carefully chip at the jamb, enlarging the strike hole. Reseat the strike plate and reinstall the top screw, making sure that the enlarged strike hole matches the strike plate opening. Close the door to check the latch. If the latch slides easily into the strike hole, reinstall the bottom screw of the strike plate; if it does not, enlarge the mortise and strike hole until it does. Fill any gaps around the strike plate with wood putty, applying it with a putty knife.

PATCHING A ROTTED SILL OR THRESHOLD

1 Removing rot. Look for rotted wood in a sill or threshold, at sash and frame joints, and under areas of peeling or chipped paint. Scrape away paint flakes and check for loose, graying wood fibers. Push an awl into the wood to test the area for softness. Wood that crumbles instead of splintering is weakened by rot. Use a paint scraper to scrape out softened wood down to healthy wood *(above)*. If the damage is slight, sand the area smooth with medium-grit sandpaper and a sanding block, then paint as you would for wood trim *(page 51)*; otherwise, fill the scraped area with wood putty *(step 2)*.

2 Filling with wood putty. Use a putty knife to fill the damaged area with pre-mixed exterior-grade wood putty *(above)*. For holes deeper than 1/4 inch, apply two or more layers of putty, letting each layer dry before applying the next. Let the putty dry according to the manufacturer's instructions. Smooth the repaired area with medium-grit sandpaper, then with fine-grit sandpaper. Wipe the area clean and paint as you would for wood trim *(page 51)*.

CAULKING A WINDOW OR DOOR

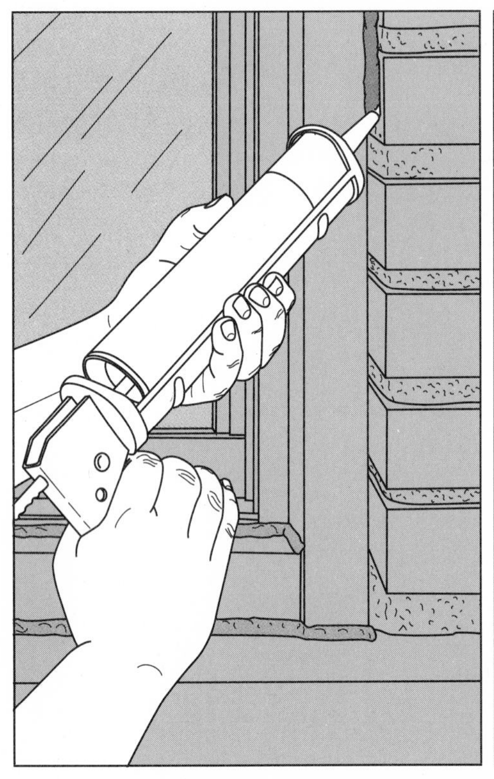

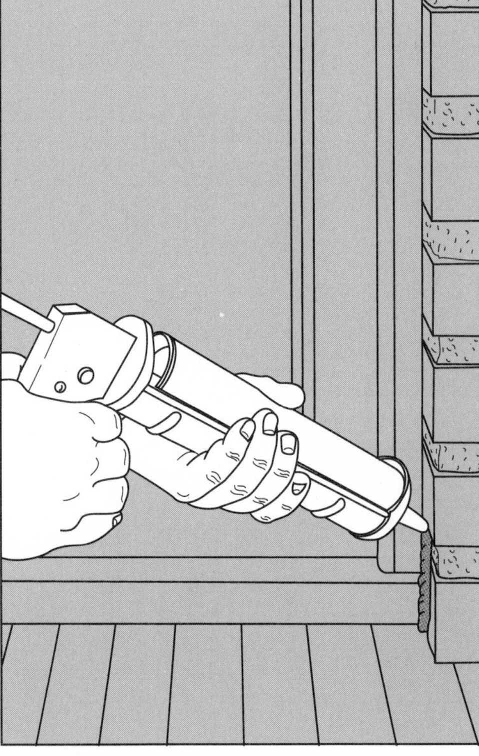

Applying caulk. Caulk the exterior joints of a window or door to prevent moisture problems and reduce air leaks, and for improved appearance. Look for loose, cracked or discolored caulk in the joints between the window or door frame and the trim, and between the trim and the wall. Remove damaged or unsightly caulk with a putty knife. Buy a cartridge of caulk *(page 133)* at a hardware store or building supply center and load it into a caulking gun. Cut off the cartridge tip at a 45-degree angle with a utility knife; make sure the opening is slightly narrower than the joint. Use a long nail or an awl to puncture the cartridge seal. Holding the caulking gun at a 45-degree angle to the joint, squeeze the trigger to eject a continuous bead of caulk along the joint at the window *(far left)* or door *(near left)*. If necessary, wear a rubber glove and run a wet finger along the bead to press it into place, smoothing and shaping it.

PAINTING WINDOWS AND DOORS

Painting a window. Make any necessary repairs to the window before painting, keeping in mind that any new glazing compound must be completely cured. Select a paint; for a patched surface, also a primer recommended by the paint manufacturer *(page 135)*. Prepare to paint *(page 49)*, using medium-grit sandpaper on a sanding block to smooth the surfaces, then wiping or brushing off any dust. Use a paintbrush to apply primer to any patched area; let it dry.

Open the window and paint first the sashes with a 1 1/2 inch sash paintbrush, then the jamb and trim with a 2-inch trim paintbrush; use the same technique described for wood trim *(page 51)*. To paint a double-hung window, raise the lower sash and pull down the upper sash. Paint as much of both sashes as you can reach *(above)*, leaving the bottom edge of the upper sash for exterior paint. Then, slide the sashes past one another, leaving them open a few inches at each end, and finish painting them. Paint the stool and apron. If the window has muntins, paint first the horizontal ones, then the vertical ones. Let the paint dry for a few hours, then lower both sashes and apply a thin coat of paint to the upper half of the channels. Let the paint dry, then raise both sashes and paint the lower half of the channels. Paint the outside of a window with exterior paint the same way. When the paint is dry, scrape paint off the window pane using a razor-blade tool—available at a hardware store or building supply center. Wash the window pane *(page 76)*.

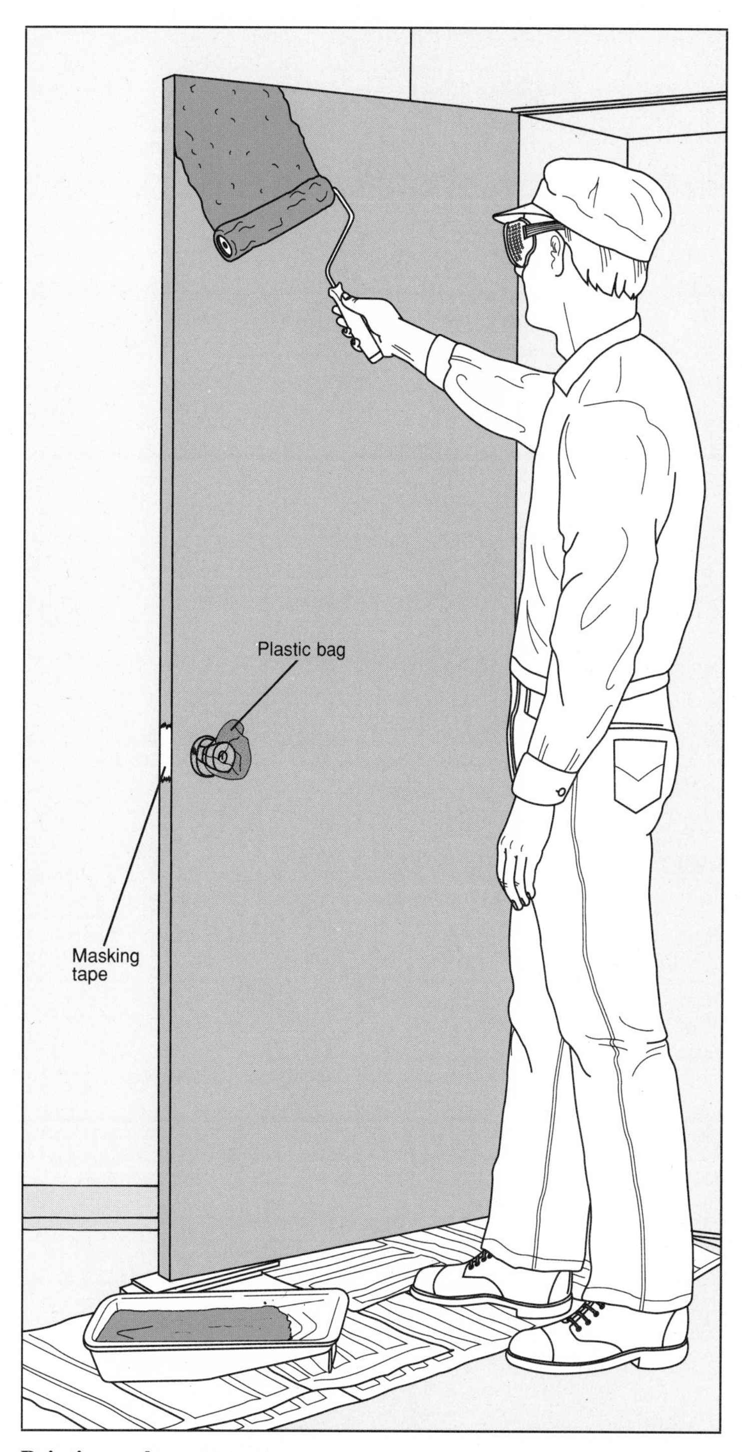

Painting a door. Make any necessary repairs to the door before painting. Select a paint; for a patched surface, also a primer recommended by the paint manufacturer *(page 135)*. Wedge the door open with wood shims. Prepare to paint *(page 49)*, covering the doorknob with a plastic bag and securing it with masking tape; protect the hinges and latch with masking tape. Use a paintbrush to apply primer to any patched area; let it dry. Paint a flat door with a roller after first using a paintbrush to paint the edges; wear safety goggles. Starting in an upper corner, paint a rough V pattern with the roller *(above)*, then fill in the area. Paint a door with recessed panels using a paintbrush, coating first the top panels, then the bottom panels and filling in the rest. Paint the exterior side of any door with exterior paint the same way. To paint the jamb and trim, use the same technique described for wood trim *(page 51)*.

BASEMENT AND GARAGE

An unfinished basement is not just a storage area; to the potential buyer, it may represent future living space, and to the trained eye of a house inspector, it is the bare bones of your house. Similarly, a clean, problem-free garage is evidence to any buyer of the care you have taken in looking after the entire house. Before putting your house up for sale, take the time to carefully inspect the basement and garage, and fix minor problems. Tidy up the basement and garage, eliminating clutter and organizing items stored in them neatly; wash any dirty windows and install high-wattage bulbs in lighting fixtures to brighten them up. Use the Troubleshooting Guide *(below)* and the checklist diagram *(page 87)* to help identify minor basement and garage problems; then, refer to the pages indicated to make the needed repair. Consult a housing professional if any major, structural repair is required.

If the concrete wall or floor of the basement or garage is dirty or stained, clean it *(page 88)*. If you have the time, follow up with a coat of paint *(page 93)*—a painted wall or floor can dramatically improve the appearance of an unfinished basement or a garage. Inspect any concrete surface for cracks. While most small floor cracks are usually superficial, a crack in a wall may indicate a serious structural problem. Evaluate any crack carefully, calling in a professional for a consultation, if necessary *(page 91)*. Make your own repairs only to small cracks *(page 91)*, and inform a potential buyer about any repair made.

If recurrent dampness or wetness is a problem in the basement or garage, take steps to minimize it. Dampness may simply be the result of excess moisture generated inside the house. Open windows and clear air vents for ventilation; set up a dehumidifier. Ensure that the clothes dryer is properly vented to the outdoors. Insulate any cold-water pipes on which condensation buildup is a problem. Outside the house, look for other problems that may be the cause of dampness or wetness. If you have brick exterior walls, check their weep holes and unclog any blocked holes *(page 89)*. If a downspout does not divert runoff water away from the house, install a splashblock or extend the downspout *(page 89)* to keep water away from the foundation and out of the basement. A more time-consuming, but surefire technique is to slope the ground so that surface water drains away from the foundation walls *(page 90)*. A sloped grade at the foundation is one of the first items on a house inspector's checklist. If necessary, steepen the ground at least 2 weeks before showing the house.

TROUBLESHOOTING GUIDE

SYMPTOM	PROCEDURE
Recurrent mustiness or clamminess	Increase ventilation; for example, open any windows, clear air vents and install a fan
	Decrease moisture; for example, vent clothes dryer to the outdoors, insulate cold water pipes and install a dehumidifier
Dirty or grimy concrete wall or floor	Wash concrete wall or floor *(p. 88)* □◒
	If desired, paint concrete surface *(p. 93)* ⬓◒
White, powdery mineral deposits (efflorescence) on concrete wall or floor	Wash concrete wall or floor *(p. 88)* □◒
Grease or oil stain on concrete wall or floor	Remove stain from concrete surface *(p. 88)* □○
Paint on concrete wall or floor faded or damaged	Paint concrete surface *(p. 93)* ⬓◒
Recurrent dampness or wetness around window	Caulk exterior window trim *(p. 74)*
Recurrent dampness or wetness on wall or on floor at base of wall	Evaluate any crack in concrete *(p. 91)*: caulk hairline crack *(p. 91)* □○ or patch small, open crack *(p. 92)* □○; for crack that indicates structural problem, consult a professional
	Improve above-ground drainage *(p. 89)* □◒
	Improve ground-level drainage *(p. 90)* ⬓●
	If dampness or wetness persists, consult a professional
Crack in concrete wall or floor	Evaluate any crack in concrete *(p. 91)*: caulk hairline crack *(p. 91)* □○ or patch small, open crack *(p. 92)* □○; for crack that indicates structural problem, consult a professional
Shallow surface hole (popout) in concrete floor	Repair concrete popouts *(p. 92)* □○
Metal pipe, duct or beam dull or rusted; paint on metal faded or damaged	Paint metal surface *(p. 94)* □◒
Uncovered basement insulation loose or damaged	Secure loose insulation or replace damaged insulation *(p. 94)* □○

DEGREE OF DIFFICULTY: □ **Easy** ⬓ **Moderate** ■ **Complex**
ESTIMATED TIME: ○ **Less than 1 hour** ◒ **1 to 3 hours** ● **Over 3 hours**
(Does not include drying time)

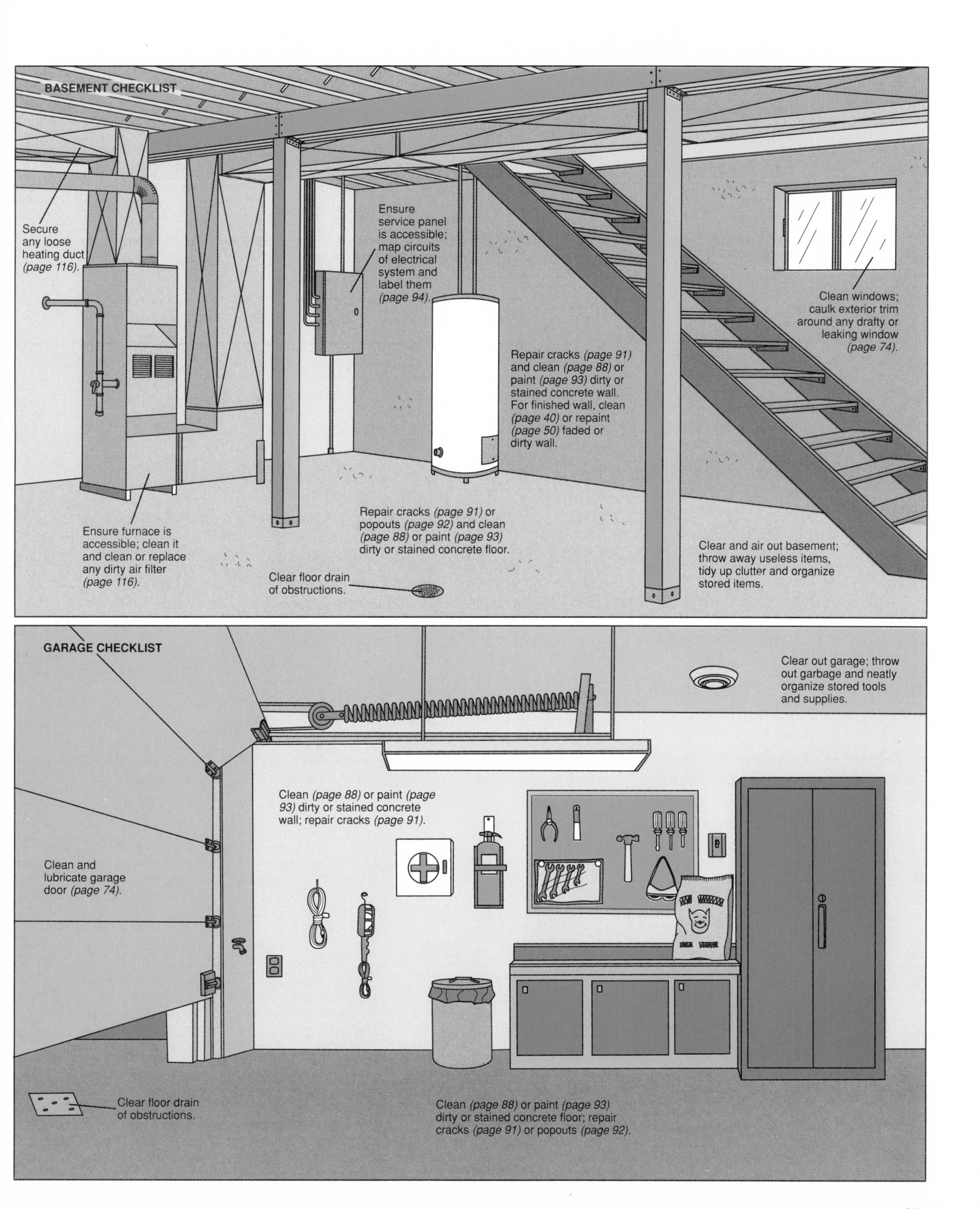
BASEMENT CHECKLIST
Secure any loose heating duct (page 116).
Ensure service panel is accessible; map circuits of electrical system and label them (page 94).
Clean windows; caulk exterior trim around any drafty or leaking window (page 74).
Repair cracks (page 91) and clean (page 88) or paint (page 93) dirty or stained concrete wall. For finished wall, clean (page 40) or repaint (page 50) faded or dirty wall.
Ensure furnace is accessible; clean it and clean or replace any dirty air filter (page 116).
Repair cracks (page 91) or popouts (page 92) and clean (page 88) or paint (page 93) dirty or stained concrete floor.
Clear and air out basement; throw away useless items, tidy up clutter and organize stored items.
Clear floor drain of obstructions.
GARAGE CHECKLIST
Clear out garage; throw out garbage and neatly organize stored tools and supplies.
Clean (page 88) or paint (page 93) dirty or stained concrete wall; repair cracks (page 91).
Clean and lubricate garage door (page 74).
Clear floor drain of obstructions.
Clean (page 88) or paint (page 93) dirty or stained concrete floor; repair cracks (page 91) or popouts (page 92).

CLEANING A CONCRETE WALL OR FLOOR

Washing off dirt and efflorescence. Protect any surface not to be washed with a drop cloth or sheet. To wash a wall or floor, wear rubber gloves and mix as many gallons of cleaner as needed in a plastic bucket. For light dirt, mix a little household detergent per gallon of water; for stubborn dirt and grime, mix a little scouring powder or 1/2 cup of trisodium phosphate (TSP) and 1/2 cup of household detergent per gallon of water. For light efflorescence, mix 1 cup of TSP per gallon of water; for heavy efflorescence, buy muriatic acid at a building supply center and wear safety goggles to mix it with water according to the manufacturer's instructions. **Caution:** Always pour acid into water; never pour water into acid.

To clean a concrete wall or floor with a solution of detergent or TSP, use a stiff-bristled scrub brush. Starting in a corner, vigorously scrub a small section; then, reload the brush. If the section is not clean, scrub it again; otherwise, scrub the next section. Continue *(left)* until the entire surface is clean; then, rinse it thoroughly with fresh water. To clean with muriatic acid, follow the same procedure, waiting for any fizzing action to stop and rinsing with fresh water before scrubbing the next section. Safely dispose of leftover cleaner *(page 141)*.

Removing a grease or oil stain. To remove a stain from a concrete wall or floor, work in a well-ventilated area at a temperature between 60 and 80 degrees Fahrenheit. Wearing rubber gloves, prepare a poultice. For a grease stain, buy an oil-dissolving solvent at a building supply center; then, using a sufficient amount of the solvent, mix in enough of a thickener such as talcum powder or fuller's earth to make a thick, smooth paste. For an oil stain, mix a sufficient amount of a solution of 1 part trisodium phosphate (TSP) and 6 parts water, then mix in enough of a thickener to make a thick, smooth paste. Wet the stain thoroughly with fresh water. Using a putty knife, spread a 1/2-inch layer of the poultice over the stain *(inset)*. Cover the wet poultice with plastic, taping it to the surrounding surface with duct tape. Let the poultice dry—if necessary, as long as 24 hours. Remove the plastic and scrape off the dry poultice with a putty knife. Wash the surface with fresh water, using a garden hose if there is a floor drain *(left)*; using a stiff-bristled scrub brush otherwise.

IMPROVING ABOVE-GROUND DRAINAGE

Unclogging a weep hole. If a wall or the floor is recurrently wet and an exterior wall above it is brick veneer, check for blocked weep holes; weep holes are open joints that drain moisture from the wall cavity behind bricks, usually spaced every 2 feet along the bottom course. To unclog a blocked weep hole, use a drill *(page 129)*, fitting it with a masonry bit slightly narrower than the hole and slightly longer than the brick width—usually 4 inches. Wearing work gloves and safety goggles, position the drill bit in the hole *(above)*, angling it to follow the angle of the hole; then, drill slowly into the wall cavity behind the bricks.

Installing a splashblock. If a wall or the floor is recurrently wet, check outside for pooling water from a faulty downspout or gutter and make any necessary repair *(page 18)*. If a short downspout elbow does not divert water away from the foundation, install a splashblock—but only if the ground slopes away from the foundation; otherwise, install an elbow extension *(step below)*. Buy a splashblock at least 18 inches long at a building supply center; lay it securely on the ground directly below the downspout *(above)*.

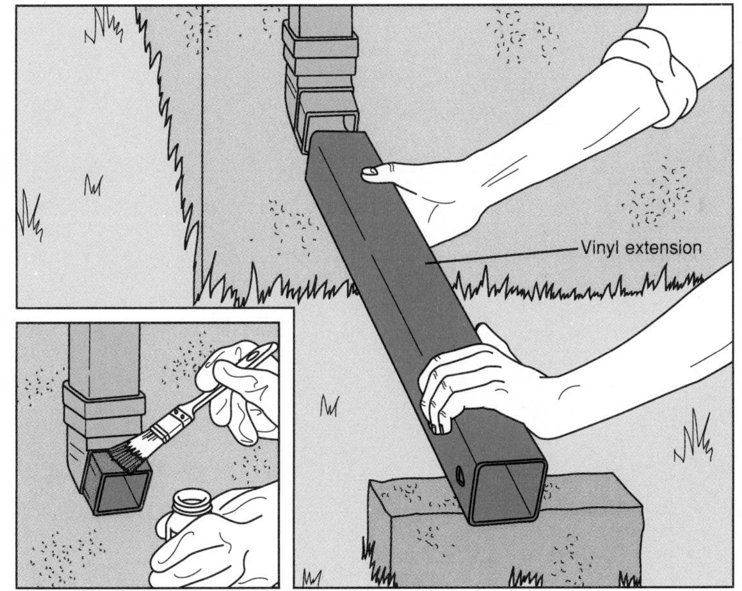

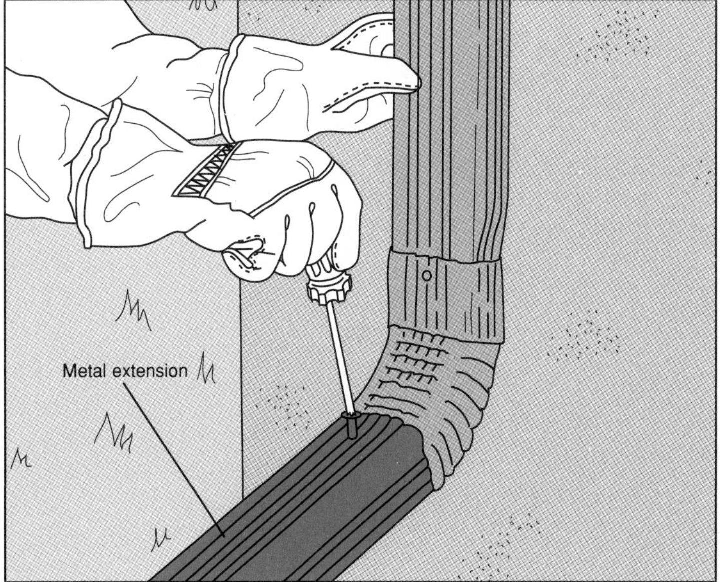

Installing a downspout elbow extension. If a wall or the floor is recurrently wet, check outside for pooling water from a faulty downspout or gutter and make any necessary repair *(page 18)*. If a short downspout elbow does not divert water away from the foundation, install a splashblock *(step above, right)* or extend the elbow. Buy a 3-foot length of downspout identical to the one on the house; as well, buy any connector, fastener or adhesive recommended by the manufacturer for installing it. To install an extension on the vinyl downspout shown, wear rubber gloves to brush PVC solvent cement onto the outside end of the elbow *(inset)* and an inside end of the extension. Then, supporting the extension on a block if necessary, push the cemented end onto the elbow *(above, left)*. To install an extension on the metal downspout shown, push the wider end of the extension snugly over the outside of the elbow; support the extension on a block if necessary. To secure the extension, use a drill fitted with a high speed bit *(page 129)* to bore a hole through the overlapped ends; then, drive a sheet metal screw into the hole *(above, right)*.

IMPROVING GROUND-LEVEL DRAINAGE

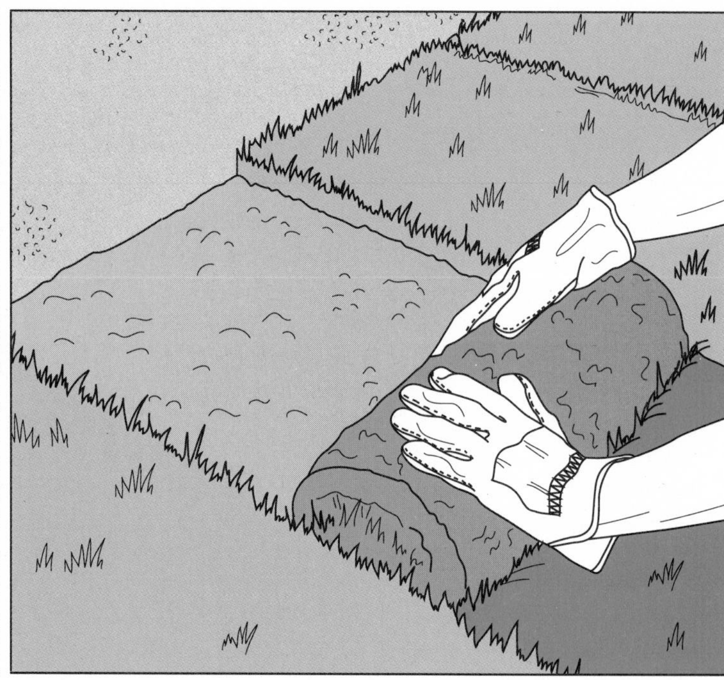

1 Removing the sod. If a wall or the floor is recurrently damp or wet and any sodded ground against the foundation outdoors is not at least 3 inches higher than the ground 3 feet from the foundation, steepen the ground slope along the wall to improve drainage. Water the area a day before working. Starting at one end of the wall against the foundation, use an edger or a spade to make a cut in the sod perpendicular to it about 2 inches deep and 3 feet long *(above, left)*. Repeat the procedure, making parallel cuts 1 to 2 blade widths apart until you reach the other end of the wall. Then, make a continuous cut in the sod along the foundation. To loosen and roll up each strip of sod, push the blade into the cut along one side of it and as far as possible horizontally under it; push no deeper than 1 inch. Then, work the blade along the cut under the strip. Repeat the procedure on the other side of the strip. Starting at the end of the strip against the foundation, lift it and roll it back slowly and tightly *(above, right)*. Cover the rolls of sod with wet burlap to keep them from drying out.

2 Steepening the ground slope and rolling back the sod. Buy enough topsoil to slope the ground away from the foundation 1 inch every foot—the ground at the foundation should be at least 3 inches higher than the ground 3 feet from the foundation. Using a spade, dig into and break up the soil along the foundation; then, spread on the new topsoil and use the spade to mix it in, pushing the soil up against the foundation *(above, left)*. With the back of the spade, firmly tamp down the soil to pack it level along the foundation and sloped evenly away from it. Sprinkle bone meal on the packed soil. Kneeling on a board, unroll the strips of sod *(above, right)*; move the board up behind the rolls as you go to help press the sod into the soil evenly. Continue, the same way until all the rolls of sod are set in place; ensure the strips are butted together at the edges as closely as possible.

3 Filling in gaps between sod strips. To prevent the sod from drying out, fill any gaps between the strips with topsoil *(above)*; fill any gaps at the end of the strips along the foundation the same way. Using a lawn rake, disentangle any packed grass. Then, use a sprinkler or a spray nozzle attachment on a garden hose to water the sod thoroughly; repeat the watering daily for 2 to 3 weeks until the sod is well rooted.

EVALUATING A CRACK IN CONCRETE

A crack in a basement or garage concrete floor, while unsightly, is usually not evidence of a structural problem; a crack in a concrete basement wall may be evidence of a serious structural problem and should be carefully evaluated. A crack is a sign of movement, whether from the settling of the house or the swelling and shrinking caused by temperature fluctuations. House settling, when it occurs uniformly, will usually not create structural problems; however, uneven settling, when one part of a house settles faster than another, can result in structural failure.

Take the time to evaluate any crack you find and to deal with it properly; if you have any doubt about a crack or your ability to evaluate it, contact a professional building engineer. Then, inform a potential house buyer of any problem found and remedied; as a seller, you can be liable for any defect found by a buyer.

Do not attempt to repair any long, wide or deep crack without a professional evaluation. A vertical crack with zig-zagging edges, or one that is wide at one end and tapers to a hairline at the other should be professionally evaluated. A crack that extends from the top to the bottom of a wall or that extends from a basement wall to a wall on the story above is evidence of a serious problem. A long, open horizontal crack in a basement wall may indicate excessive pressure on the foundation from surrounding earth and a stepped, pyramid-like crack may indicate damage to a foundation support below the wall; do not attempt to patch either type without first consulting a professional.

A short, narrow and stationary surface crack with edges of the same length is usually not a problem—even if it is active: expanding in cold weather as moisture in the concrete freezes. As long as a crack remains small, it is typically not a danger. Once you are sure that there is no structural damage, caulk a hairline crack *(step below)* or patch a small, open crack *(page 92)*.

REPAIRING A CRACK IN CONCRETE

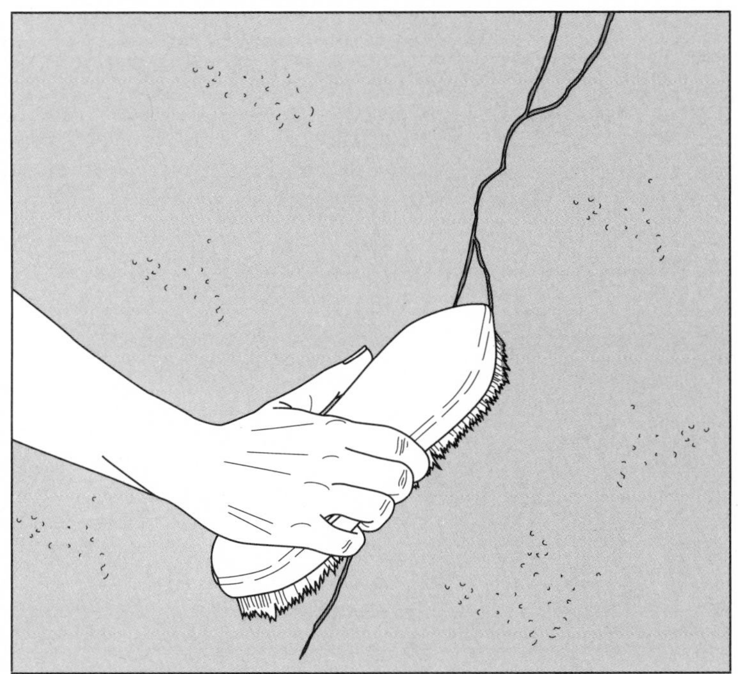

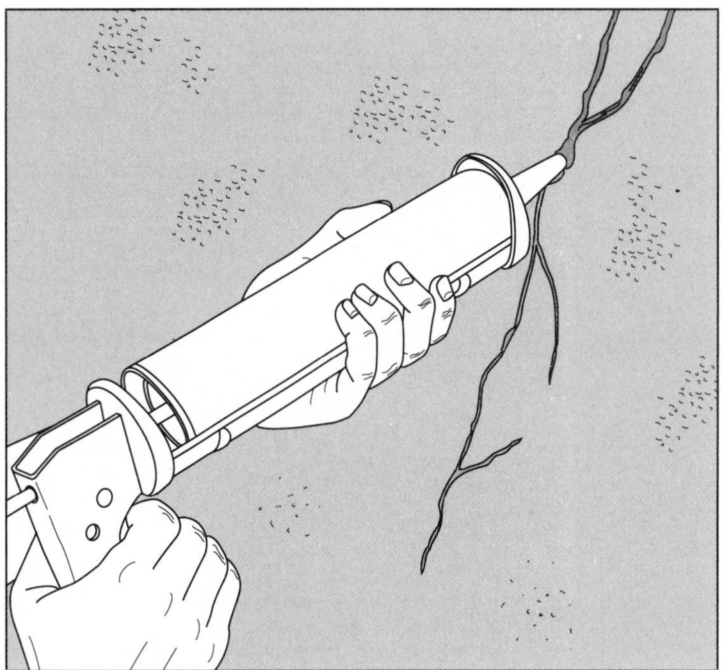

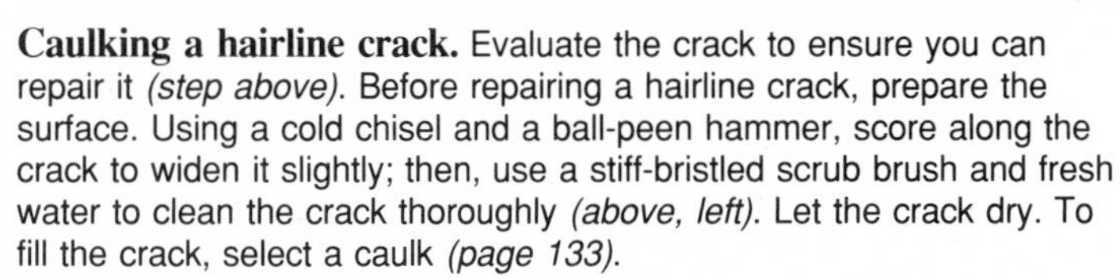

Caulking a hairline crack. Evaluate the crack to ensure you can repair it *(step above)*. Before repairing a hairline crack, prepare the surface. Using a cold chisel and a ball-peen hammer, score along the crack to widen it slightly; then, use a stiff-bristled scrub brush and fresh water to clean the crack thoroughly *(above, left)*. Let the crack dry. To fill the crack, select a caulk *(page 133)*.

Load a caulking gun with the caulk. Starting at one end of the crack and holding the gun at a 45-degree angle to the surface, squeeze the trigger to eject a continuous bead of caulk along the crack *(above, right)*. Then, wearing a rubber glove, run a wet finger along the caulk to press it into the crack, smoothing the edges flush with the surrounding surface. Let the caulk dry. If necessary, paint the surface *(page 93)*.

REPAIRING A CRACK IN CONCRETE (continued)

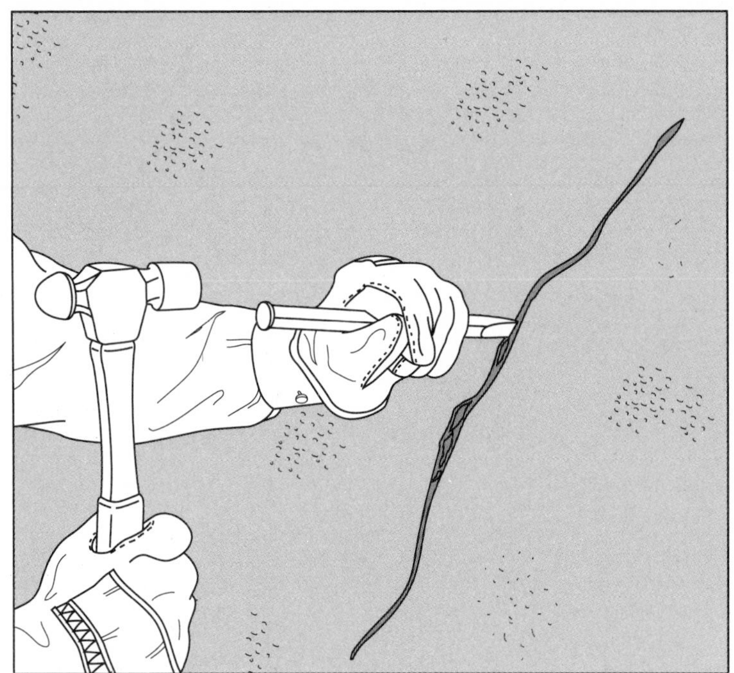

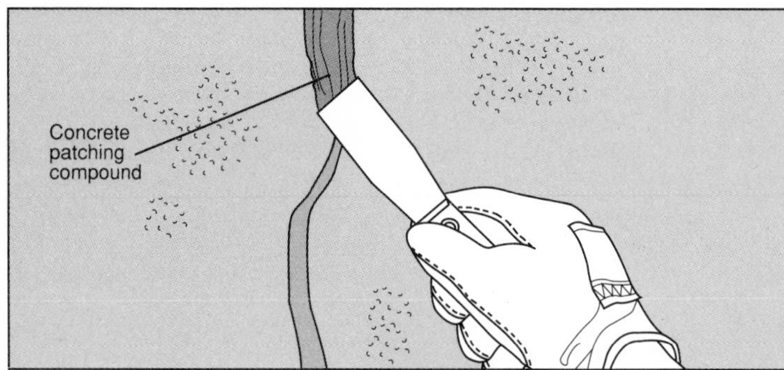

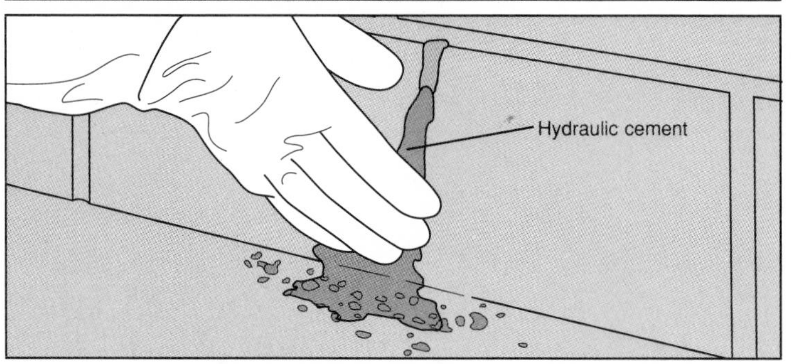

Patching a narrow crack. Evaluate the crack to ensure you can repair it *(page 91)*. Before repairing a narrow crack up to 1/4 inch wide, prepare the surface. Using a cold chisel and a ball-peen hammer, undercut the edges of the crack, widening it slightly *(above)*; then, use a stiff-bristled scrub brush and fresh water to clean the crack thoroughly. Buy the appropriate patching material for the crack: concrete patching compound for a dry crack and quick-setting hydraulic cement for a leaking crack. Prepare the concrete patching compound or hydraulic cement following the manufacturer's instructions.

To apply concrete patching compound, wear work gloves and use a putty knife. Wet the crack with water from a spray bottle; then, starting at one end, press in the compound *(above right, top)*, smoothing it flush with the surface. To apply hydraulic cement, wear rubber gloves and use your hand. Starting at one end, press the cement into the crack *(above right, bottom)*, filling it completely. Hold the cement in place until it sets—about 3 minutes; then, use a putty knife to smooth it flush with the surface. Let the compound or cement cure. Safely dispose of leftover material *(page 141)*. If necessary, paint the surface *(page 93)*.

REPAIRING CONCRETE POPOUTS

1 Patching the surface. To repair popouts—shallow surface holes in concrete—use concrete patching compound; if necessary, also a bonding agent recommended by the manufacturer. Wearing work gloves and safety goggles, use a bull-point chisel and a small sledgehammer to enlarge and deepen the popouts; then, use a stiff-bristled brush to clean them. Dampen the surface with water from a spray bottle. To apply any bonding agent necessary, use an old paintbrush, brushing on an even coat *(above, left)*; wait for the surface to become tacky—usually about 15 minutes. Prepare the concrete patching compound following the manufacturer's instructions. Using a pointing trowel, spread compound over the holes *(above, right)*.

2 Smoothing the patch. Using a rectangular trowel, smooth the wet patching compound flush with the surface *(above)*. Let the compound cure according to the label instructions. Safely dispose of leftover compound *(page 141)*. If necessary, paint the surface *(page 93)*.

PAINTING A CONCRETE SURFACE

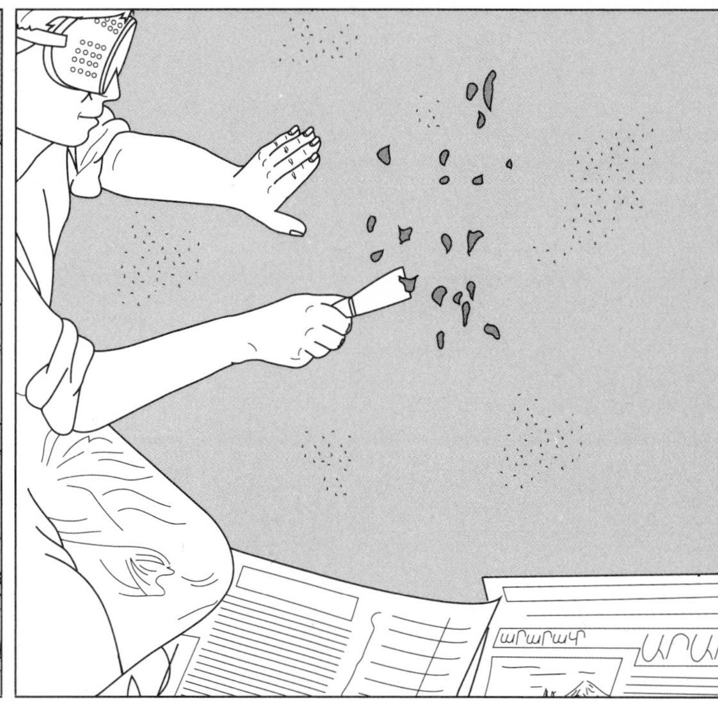

1 Preparing the surface. Prepare to paint *(page 49)*, protecting any nearby surface not to be painted with newspapers or drop cloths *(above, left)*. Wearing safety goggles and using a putty knife, scrape any peeling paint off the concrete *(above, right)*. Wash off any dirt or efflorescence and remove any grease or oil stain *(page 88)*; then, repair any crack *(page 91)* or popouts *(page 92)*. Before painting a concrete floor, etch it. Buy muriatic acid at a building supply center; wearing safety goggles and rubber gloves, mix it with water according to the manufacturer's instructions. **Caution:** Always pour acid into water; never pour water into acid. Starting in one corner of the floor, use a sponge mop to thoroughly wet a large section; then, use a stiff-bristled scrub brush to work in the solution. Wait 15 minutes, then rinse the section thoroughly with fresh water. Continue, section by section, until the floor is etched. Let the floor dry and safely dispose of leftover solution *(page 141)*.

2 Painting a concrete wall or floor. Select a paint; for unpainted concrete or any patched surface, also any primer recommended by the paint manufacturer *(page 135)*. If you are working overhead, wear a hat and safety goggles. Apply any primer as you would paint, then let the primer dry. To paint a wall or floor, use a 2-inch trim brush, a wall brush and a long-nap roller fitted with an extension pole. Use the trim brush to paint a 2-inch strip along any edge of the surface where it meets another surface or an obstruction. Use the wall brush to paint joints and depressions in the surface, forcing the bristles into gaps in the surface. Then, use the roller to complete the painting job. Starting in a corner, apply firm pressure to roll paint in overlapping strips onto a section of the surface, working it into the concrete pores; then, roll back over the paint to smooth it. Reload the roller and continue, section by section *(left)*, until the surface is painted; roll slowly to avoid splattering. Let the paint dry; if necessary, apply another coat. Safely dispose of leftover paint *(page 141)*.

PAINTING A METAL SURFACE

Painting metal. If rusted or dull metal pipes, ducts or beams detract from the appearance of a basement or garage, paint them. Prepare to paint *(page 49)*, protecting any nearby surface not to be painted with newspapers or drop cloths. Wearing safety goggles and using a wire brush, scrape rust and peeling paint off the surface. Select a paint compatible with the type of metal; for unpainted metal, also any primer recommended by the paint manufacturer *(page 135)*. For a cold water pipe, use only alkyd paint. If you are working overhead, wear a hat and safety goggles. Apply any primer as you would paint, then let the primer dry. To paint a metal surface, use a paintbrush. Starting at one end of the surface, use a steady back-and-forth stroke to brush paint onto a section *(left)*, then reverse the direction of the stroke to brush back over the paint and smooth it. Reload the brush and continue, section by section, until the surface is painted; smooth drips and streaks as you go. Let the paint dry. If necessary, apply another coat. Safely dispose of leftover paint *(page 141)*.

SECURING OR REPLACING INSULATION

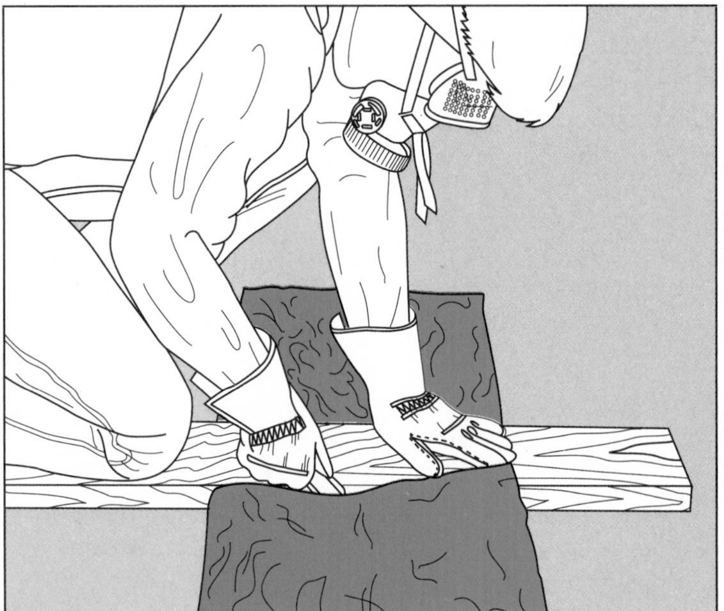

Repairing faulty insulation. Wear a respirator, safety goggles, work gloves and long sleeves to make any repair to fiberglass insulation. If the wire bracing that holds uncovered insulation between the joists of a ceiling is loose and the insulation is hanging out of position, use a staple gun to refasten the bracing to the joists *(inset)*.

If any insulation is damaged, replace it. Using tin snips, cut out any wire bracing that holds the damaged insulation in place; then, set the cut piece of bracing aside and pull out the damaged insulation. Measure the size of the open space and buy enough identical replacement insulation to fill it, ensuring the insulation has a vapor barrier backing. To cut a batt of insulation to size, lay it on the floor. Using a board as a guide, cut the insulation with a utility knife *(above, left)*; if necessary, make several passes with it. To install the insulation, push it snugly into the opening between the joists *(above, right)*, ensuring that the vapor barrier backing is against the ceiling. Fit the bracing back over the new insulation and use a staple gun to fasten it to the joists.

ELECTRICITY

Although virtually invisible, the electrical system is one of your home's most important features—and potentially its most hazardous. The network of cables and wires hidden behind the walls and ceilings is strictly regulated by codes and standards that safeguard against fire and shock, allowing for the efficient, convenient and safe delivery of electricity throughout the house. And however minor an electrical problem may seem, it should always be treated as serious and repaired immediately.

Before putting your house up for sale, carefully check the electrical system. Start your inspection at the service panel, making sure that each circuit in your home is correctly and clearly labeled *(page 96)*—one sign of a well-maintained system. Eliminate hazards, removing any octopus adapter or any extension cord used as permanent wiring and installing safety caps into unused outlet receptacles, for example *(page 97)*. Service the wire connections of any outlet, switch or lighting fixture that works intermittently *(page 97)*.

Replace any faulty duplex outlet *(page 99)*, single-pole switch *(page 102)*, indoor lighting fixture *(page 104)* or outdoor lighting fixture *(page 105)*. Consider upgrading a single-pole switch with a dimmer switch *(page 103)* or a duplex outlet located outdoors or in an area subject to moisture with a ground-fault circuit interrupter (GFCI) type *(page 101)*. Take down any lighting fixture you wish to keep and install another fixture *(page 104)* or a ceiling or wall plate *(page 105)* in its place.

Before servicing any component of your electrical system, shut off electricity to the circuit for it at the service panel *(page 96)*. Purchase any replacement part you need at a hardware store or a building supply center; ensure that it is listed by the Underwriters Laboratories (UL) and of the same voltage and amperage rating as the part you are replacing. If you are ever in doubt about the safety of your electrical system or your ability to service it, do not hesitate to consult a qualified electrician.

TROUBLESHOOTING GUIDE

SYMPTOM	PROCEDURE
Service panel labels missing, outdated or illegible	Map and label electrical circuits *(p. 96)* □●
Circuit breaker trips or fuse blows repeatedly	Redistribute electrical load on circuit
	If problem persists, call for professional service
Extension cord or octupus adapter plugged into outlet as permanent wiring	Eliminate electrical hazard *(p. 97)* □○
Outlet receptacle unused	Eliminate electrical hazard *(p. 97)* □○
Outlet, switch or lighting fixture works intermittently; sparks or shocks	Service wire connections *(p. 97)* □○
	Test and replace duplex outlet *(p. 99)* ⬓○, single-pole switch *(p. 102)* □○, indoor lighting fixture *(p. 104)* ⬓○ or outdoor lighting fixture *(p. 105)* ⬓○
	If problem persists, call for professional service
Duplex outlet does not work	Test and replace duplex outlet *(p. 99)* ⬓○; install GFCI outlet in garage, basement or bathroom or within 6 feet of a sink or other area subjected to moisture *(p. 101)* ⬓○
Duplex outlet in area subjected to moisture not ground-fault circuit interrupter (GFCI) type	Install GFCI outlet in garage, basement or bathroom or within 6 feet of a sink or other area subjected to moisture *(p. 101)* ⬓○
Single-pole switch does not work	Test and replace single-pole switch *(p. 102)* □○
Lighting fixture indoors does not work	Test and replace single-pole switch *(p. 102)* □○; test and replace indoor lighting fixture *(p. 104)* ⬓○
Lighting fixture indoors does not have dimmer switch	Install dimmer switch *(p. 103)* ⬓○
Lighting fixture indoors not included in sale of house	Replace indoor lighting fixture *(p. 104)* ⬓○ or install ceiling or wall plate *(p. 105)* □○
Lighting fixture outdoors does not work	Test and replace single-pole switch *(p. 102)* □○; test and replace outdoor lighting fixture *(p. 106)* ⬓○
Lighting fixture outdoors not included in sale of house	Replace outdoor lighting fixture *(p. 106)* ⬓○ or install ceiling or wall plate *(p. 105)* □○
Doorbell does not work	Service doorbell system *(p. 98)* □○

DEGREE OF DIFFICULTY: □ **Easy** ⬓ **Moderate** ■ **Complex**
ESTIMATED TIME: ○ **Less than 1 hour** ◒ **1 to 3 hours** ● **Over 3 hours**

LABELING YOUR SERVICE PANEL

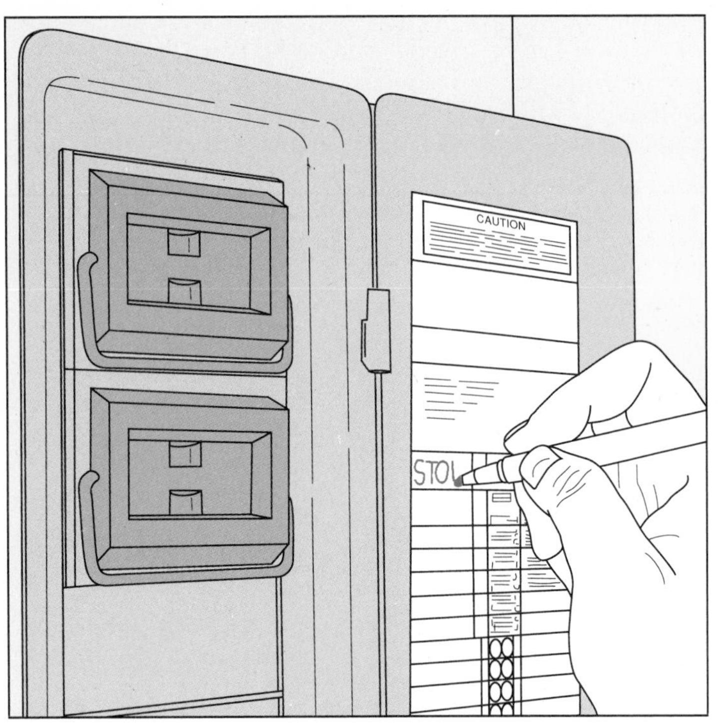

Mapping the circuits of your electrical system. Labels on service panels are often missing, outdated or illegible. Correctly and clearly label each circuit on the service panel of your home, providing evidence of a well-maintained electrical system—and enabling a quick response by anyone in the event of an electrical emergency. Begin by sketching a floor plan of your house, then walk around each room, mapping its outlets, switches, major appliances and other electrical fixtures. Turn off each switch and unplug each major appliance. At the service panel, post a new label for each circuit, then designate a number for each circuit and write it on the label. Shut off electricity to circuit number 1, shutting off the circuit breaker or removing the fuse *(step below)*.

To identify the electrical units on the circuit, find the outlets, switches, major appliances and other electrical fixtures that no longer receive electricity. Turn on each switch, plug in each major appliance and use a working lamp or a receptacle analyzer *(page 99)* to check the upper and lower receptacle of each outlet; those that do not work are on the circuit. (Note that a circuit can serve more than one room or floor.) On your map, write the circuit number beside each outlet, switch, major appliance and other electrical fixture on the circuit, then return to the service panel and restore the electricity to the circuit. Use the information recorded on your floor plan to characterize the circuit and write a short description of it on its label *(left)*. Then, shut off electricity to circuit number 2 and repeat the procedure, continuing the same way until you have mapped each circuit; include each 240-volt circuit controlled by a double circuit breaker or fuse block. Post your map at the service panel for future reference.

SHUTTING OFF AND RESTORING POWER

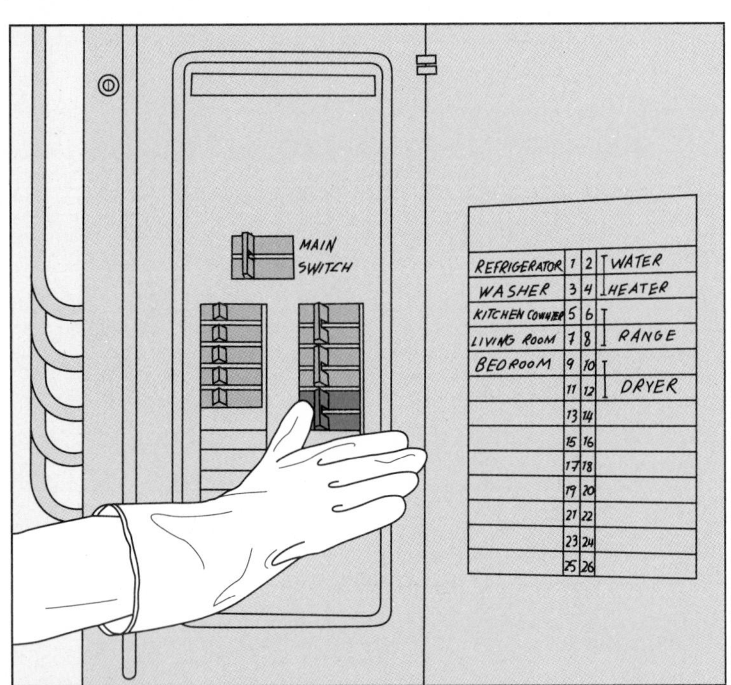

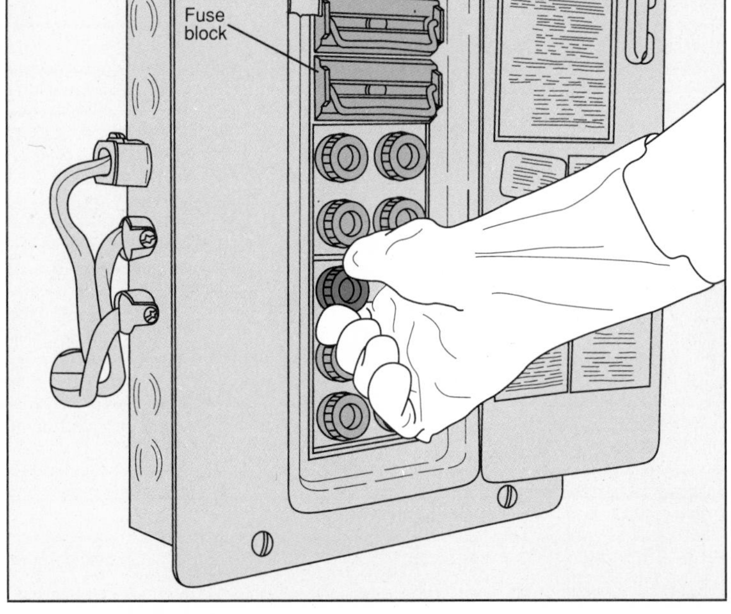

Shutting off and restoring electricity to a circuit. Take basic safety precautions when working at the service panel. If the area around the service panel is damp, stand on a dry board or wear dry rubber boots. To prevent your body from becoming a route for electricity, wear heavy rubber gloves and work with one hand; keep your other hand in your pocket or behind your back and avoid touching anything metal. Locate the circuit breaker or fuse controlling the circuit; if it is not labeled, shut off electricity at the main circuit breaker or fuse block *(page 10)*, then map the circuits of your electrical system *(step above)* after your repair.

As an added precaution when shutting off electricity at a circuit breaker, use your knuckle; any shock will jerk your hand away from the service panel. To shut off electricity at a circuit breaker, flip the circuit breaker to OFF *(above, left)*; to restore the electricity, flip the circuit breaker fully to OFF, then to ON. To shut off electricity at a plug fuse, grasp the fuse only by its insulated rim and unscrew it *(above, right)*; to restore the electricity, reinstall the fuse tightly. To shut off electricity at a cartridge fuse, grip the handle of the fuse block and pull it straight out; to restore the electricity, put back the fuse block.

ELIMINATING ELECTRICAL HAZARDS

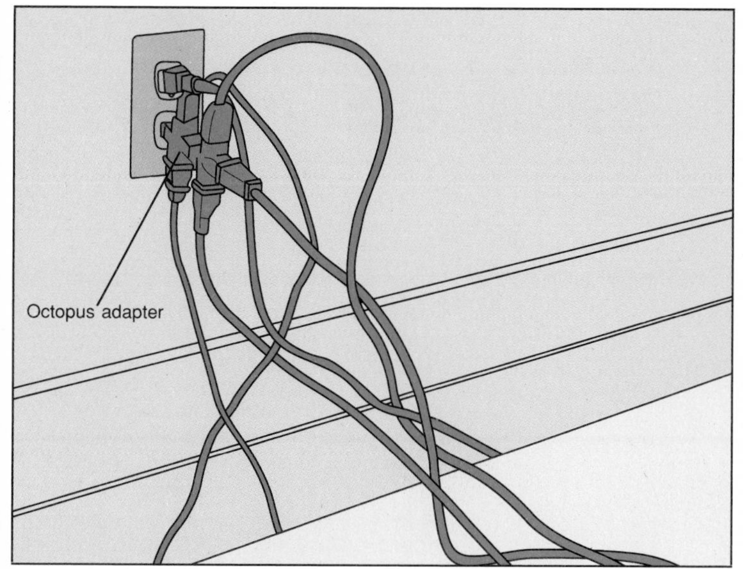

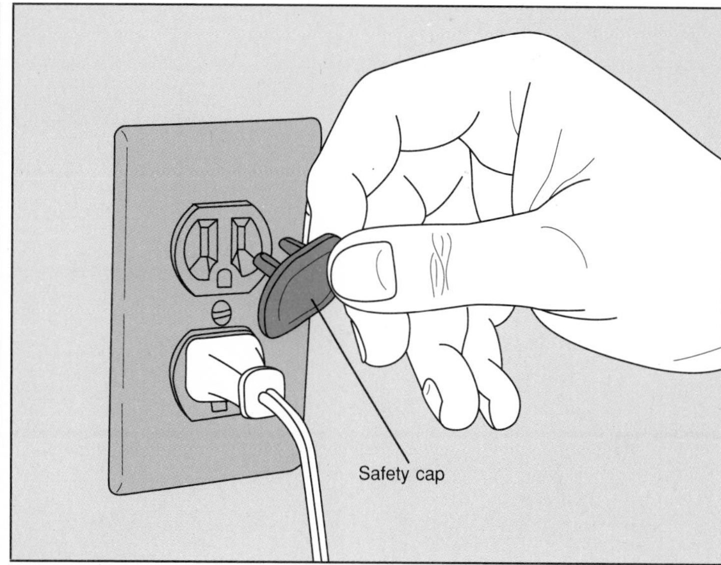

Living safely with electricity. Permanent use of extension cords and octopus adapters *(above, left)* is an indication that the wiring of your home is inadequate; plugging too many power cords or extension cords into one outlet can overload the electrical system. If necessary, move appliances, lamps and other electrical units to other circuits to distribute the electrical load or have a qualified electrician upgrade your electrical system. Cover any unused receptacle of an outlet with a plastic safety cap that fits tightly into the slots *(above, right)*. The safety cap protects curious fingers from electrical shock and also prevents dirt and dust from entering unused receptacles.

SERVICING ELECTRICAL BOXES

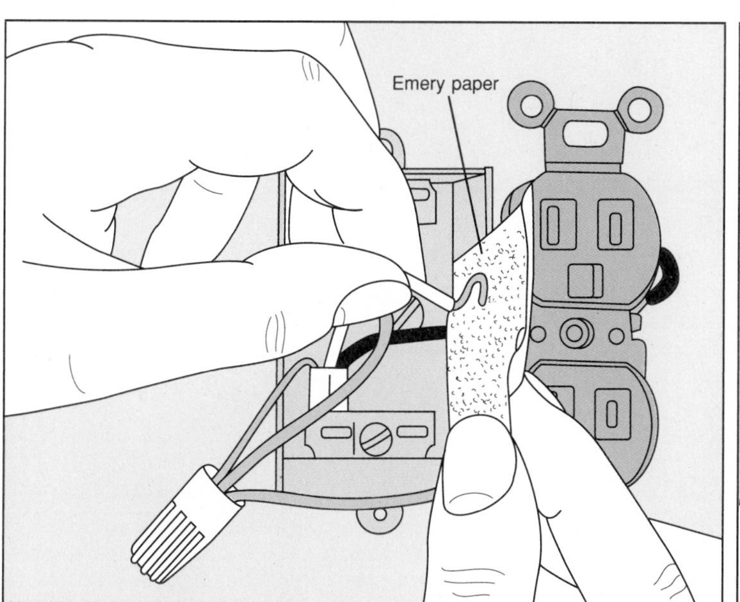

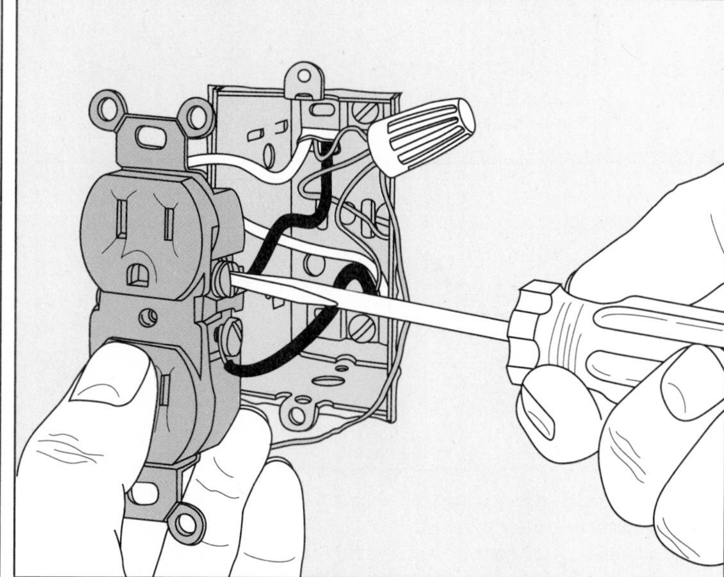

Servicing the wire connections. Dirty, corroded or loose wire connections or damaged wire ends in an electrical box can cause an outlet, switch or lighting fixture to work intermittently—and produce dangerous sparks or shocks. To check the wire connections in an electrical box, shut off electricity to the circuit at the service panel *(page 96)*, then expose the wires and test for voltage as you would at any duplex outlet *(page 99)*, single-pole switch *(page 102)* or lighting fixture *(page 104)*. **Caution:** Do not touch any wire or terminal screw until you have tested for voltage and confirmed that the electricity is shut off.

If a wire end is damaged, repair it *(page 139)*; if it is dirty or corroded, disconnect it and use fine emery paper to burnish it *(above, left)*. To reconnect a wire, hook it in a clockwise direction around its terminal screw: on the duplex outlet shown, each black wire around its brass terminal screw; each white wire around its silver terminal screw; any bare copper wire to its grounding terminal screw. Tighten each wire connection by turning its terminal screw clockwise with a screwdriver *(above, right)*. Then, reinstall the outlet, the switch or the lighting fixture along with its cover plate and restore the electricity to the circuit.

SERVICING THE DOORBELL

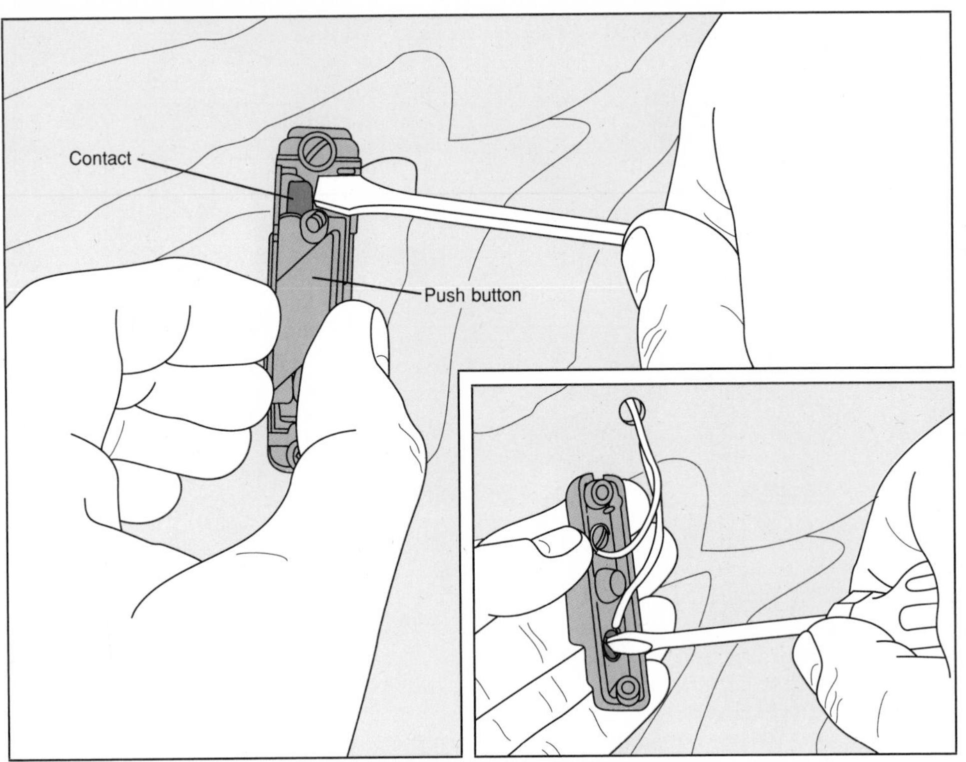

1 Servicing the push button. Shut off electricity to the circuit for the doorbell at the service panel *(page 96)*, then pry off or unscrew the cover of the push button. Burnish each metal contact using fine emery paper and pry it up slightly with an old screwdriver *(left)*; apply gentle pressure to avoid breaking it. Reinstall the cover of the push button and restore the electricity to the circuit. Press the push button to test the doorbell. If the doorbell sounds constantly, the contacts are bent up too far; use the same procedure to bend each contact down slightly.

If the doorbell does not sound, check the wire connections at the push button. Shut off electricity to the circuit, remove the cover of the push button and unscrew the push button from the wall or door frame. Pull out the push button enough to expose the wires behind it. If a wire end is damaged, repair it *(page 139)*. If a wire end is loose, hook it in a clockwise direction around its terminal screw and tighten it *(inset)*. Reinstall the cover of the push button and restore the electricity to the circuit to test the doorbell again; if it still does not sound, test the wires *(step 2)*.

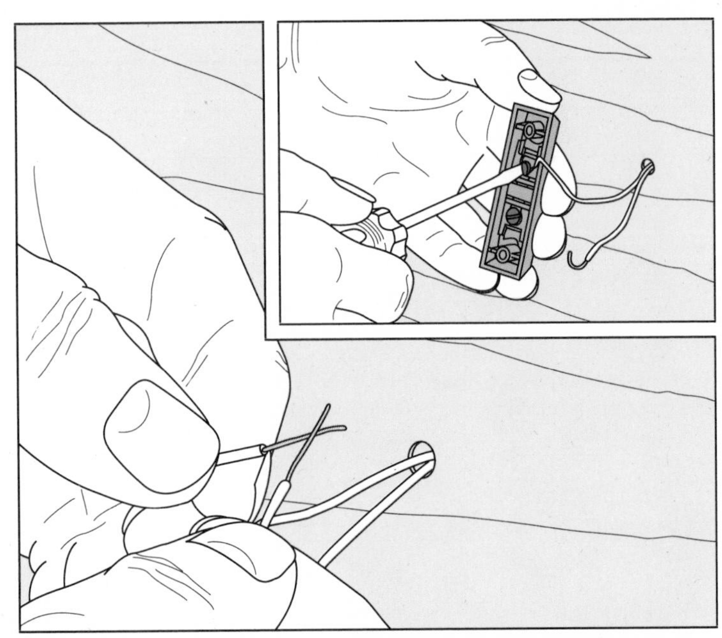

2 Testing the wires. Shut off electricity to the circuit *(page 96)*, remove the cover of the push button and unscrew the push button from the wall or door frame. Pull out the push button enough to expose the wires behind it. Loosen each terminal screw using a screwdriver and disconnect its wire, then twist the wire ends together *(above)* and restore the electricity to the circuit. If the doorbell does not sound, check the wire connections at the transformer *(step 3)*. If the doorbell sounds constantly, the push button is faulty; shut off electricity to the circuit and untwist the wire ends. Purchase a replacement push button at a hardware store or a building supply center. To install the push button, hook each wire in a clockwise direction around its terminal screw, then tighten it *(inset)*. Screw the push button onto the wall or door frame and install its cover, then restore the electricity to the circuit.

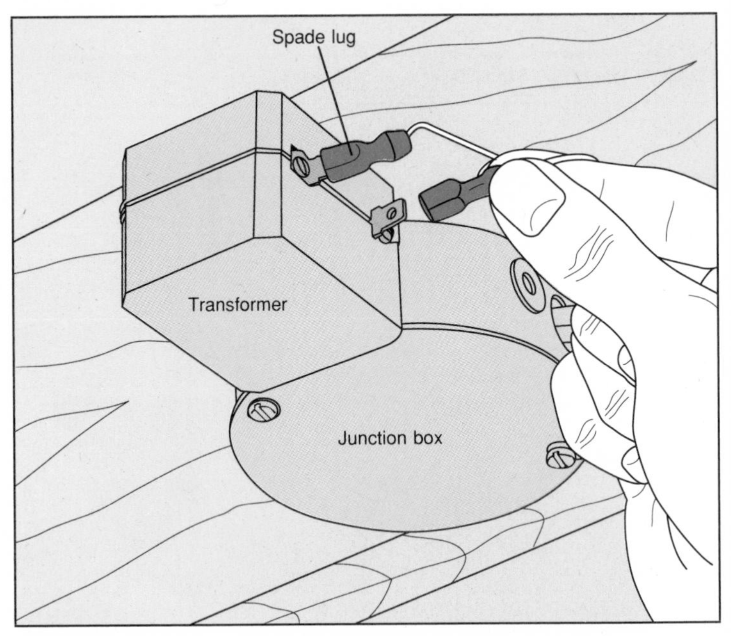

3 Checking the wires at the transformer. With the wire ends twisted together, shut off electricity to the circuit *(page 96)*. Locate the transformer, usually attached to a junction box in the basement or utility room. Check the low-voltage wire connections at the transformer; (120-volt wires are inside the junction box). If a wire end is damaged, repair it *(page 139)*. If a wire end is loose, reconnect it; push the spade lug onto its terminal *(above)* or hook the wire in a clockwise direction around its terminal screw and tighten it. Restore the electricity to the circuit. If the doorbell does not sound, shut off electricity to the circuit and have the doorbell serviced by a qualified electrician. Otherwise, shut off electricity to the circuit, untwist the wire ends and reconnect each wire to the push button. Screw the push button back onto the wall or door frame and reinstall its cover, then restore the electricity to the circuit.

TESTING AND REPLACING A DUPLEX OUTLET

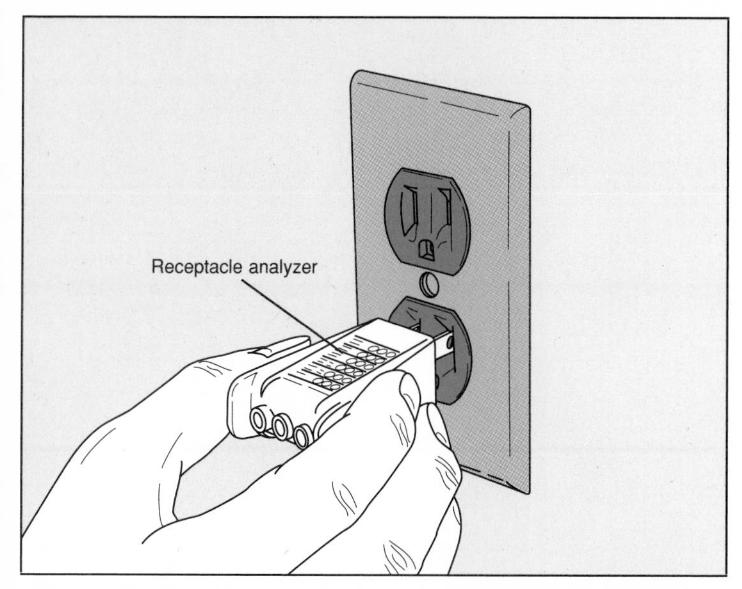

1 Testing the outlet. Test the receptacles of the outlet using a receptacle analyzer—available at a hardware store or a building supply center. The three prongs of the receptacle analyzer fit into the slots of a grounded outlet; three small display lights indicate if the outlet is faulty, if the black and white wires are connected to the correct terminal screws, and if the outlet is properly grounded. Without shutting off the electricity, plug the receptacle analyzer in turn into each receptacle of the outlet *(above)*. If the receptacle analyzer detects a problem, remove the outlet enough to expose the wires *(step 2)*.

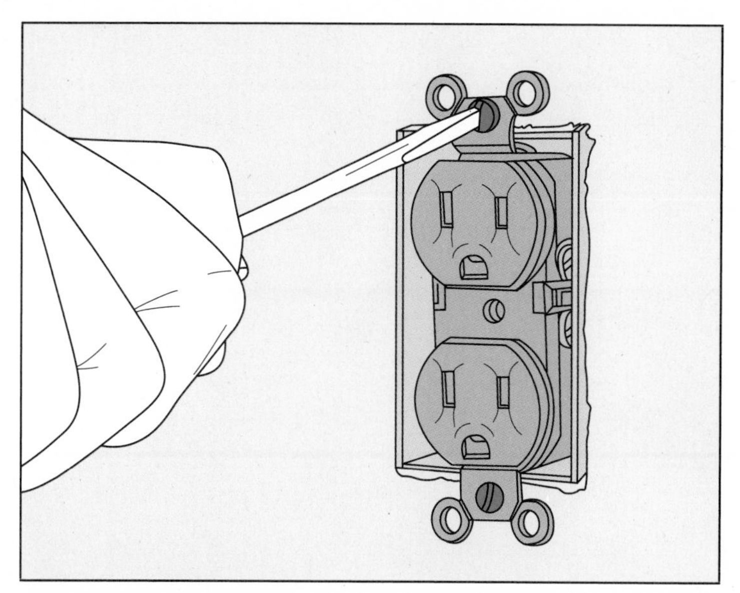

2 Exposing the wires. Shut off electricity to the circuit for the outlet at the service panel *(page 96)*. Unscrew the cover plate of the outlet and lift it away from the wall; if necessary, first score around it with a utility knife to free it from any paint or plaster. To release the outlet from the electrical box, remove the mounting screw at the top *(above)* and the bottom of the mounting strap, then grasp the mounting strap and pull the outlet out of the electrical box enough to expose the wires. **Caution:** Do not touch any wire or terminal screw until you have tested for voltage *(step 4)* and confirmed that the electricity is shut off.

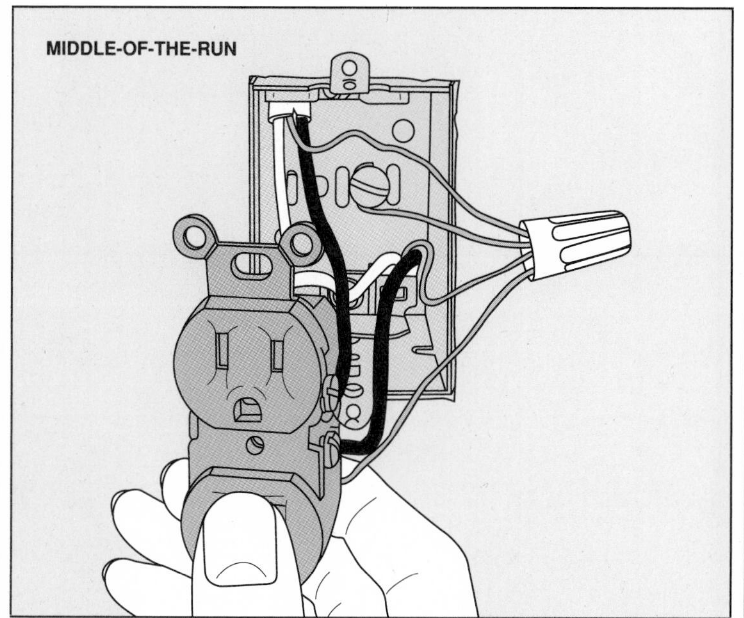

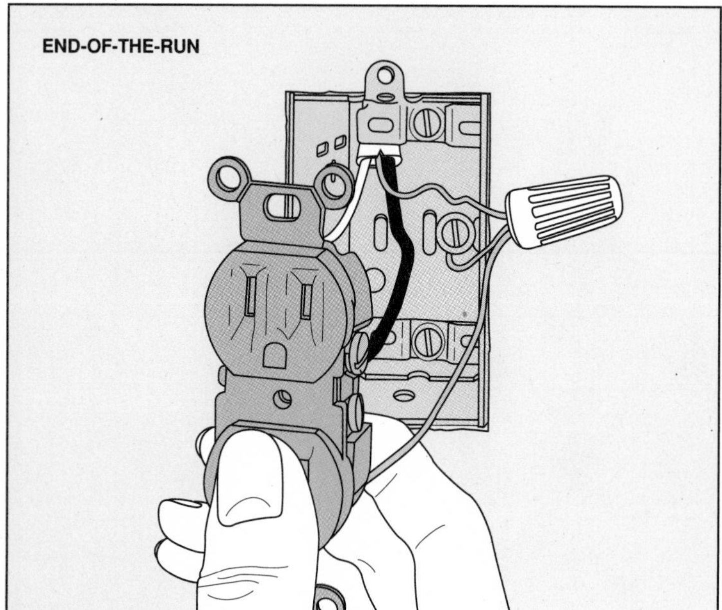

3 Inspecting the wires. Without touching any wire or terminal screw, check each cable entering the electrical box and the wire connections on the outlet. Each cable entering the electrical box should have three wires: a black wire, a white wire and a bare copper wire. If there are two cables entering the electrical box, the outlet is middle-of-the-run *(above, left)*; if there is one cable entering the electrical box, the outlet is end-of-the-run *(above, right)*. Each black wire should be connected to a brass terminal screw on the outlet; each white wire should be connected to a silver terminal screw on the outlet. Each bare copper wire is a grounding wire that should be connected inside a wire cap to a grounding wire running to the grounding terminal screw on the back of the electrical box; if there is a grounding terminal screw on the outlet, there also should be a grounding wire running from it connected inside the wire cap. Before servicing any wire connection, test for voltage *(step 4)* to confirm that the electricity is shut off.

TESTING AND REPLACING A DUPLEX OUTLET (continued)

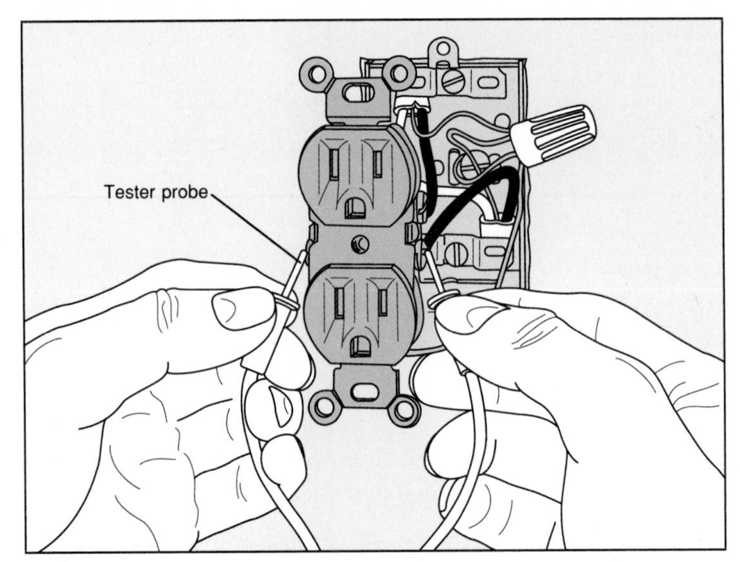

4 Testing for voltage. Use a voltage tester to confirm that the electricity is shut off. Touch one tester probe to a brass terminal screw and touch the other tester probe in turn to each silver terminal screw *(above)* and each grounding terminal screw. Then, touch one tester probe to the other brass terminal screw and repeat the procedure with the other tester probe. The tester should not glow in any test; if it does, shut off electricity to the correct circuit *(page 96)* and test again. When the electricity is shut off, service the wire connections *(page 97)*, then reinstall the outlet *(step 7)*. If the problem persists, replace the outlet *(step 5)*; if it is outdoors, in the garage, basement or bathroom, or in an area subject to moisture, replace it with a GFCI outlet *(page 101)*.

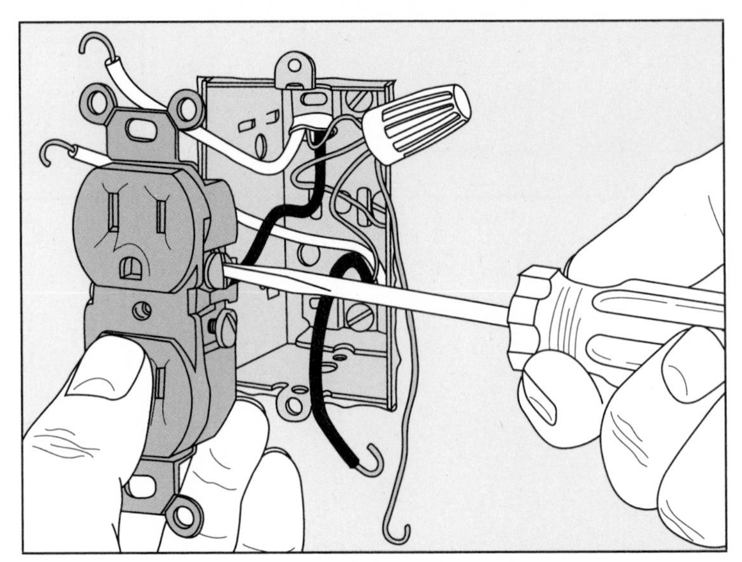

5 Replacing the outlet. Shut off electricity to the circuit *(page 96)* and expose the wires again *(step 2)*. Disconnect each wire from the outlet, loosening its terminal screw with a screwdriver. Purchase a replacement outlet at a hardware store or a building supply center. Hook each black wire in a clockwise direction around a brass terminal screw on the outlet and tighten it *(above)*. Connect each white wire to a silver terminal screw on the outlet the same way; also connect any grounding wire you disconnected to the grounding terminal screw on the outlet. If there is only a grounding wire running from the wire cap to the grounding terminal screw on the back of the electrical box, install a grounding jumper wire *(step 6)*; otherwise, install the outlet *(step 7)*.

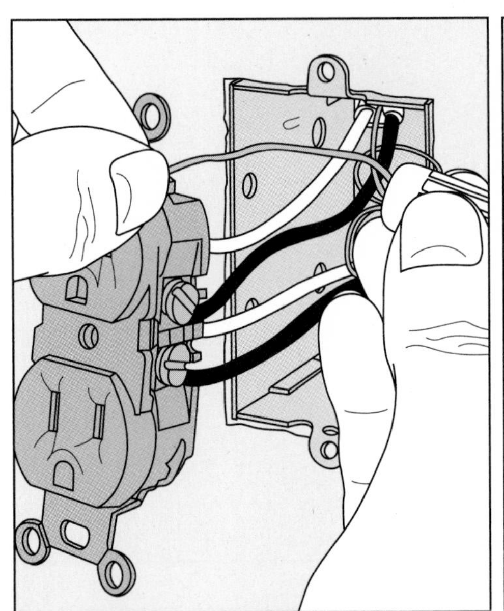

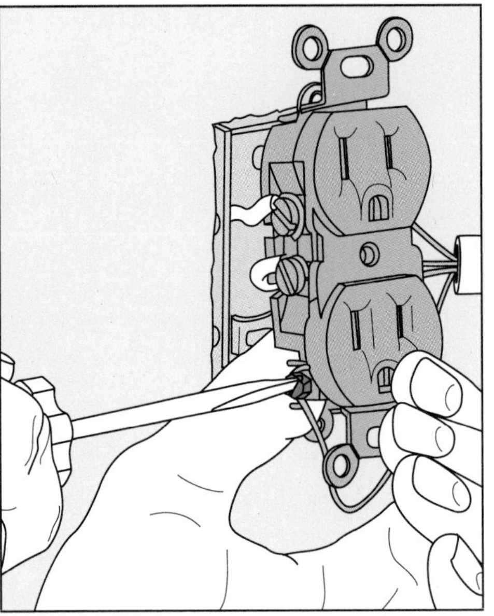

6 Installing a grounding jumper wire. Unscrew the wire cap and take it off the grounding wires. In a middle-of-the-run outlet, there are three grounding wires: one from each cable connected together with one running to the grounding terminal screw on the back of the electrical box; in an end-of-the-run outlet, there are two grounding wires: one from the cable connected with one running to the grounding terminal screw on the back of the electrical box. To run a grounding jumper wire from the grounding wires to the grounding terminal screw on the outlet, use bare copper wire or green grounding wire of the same gauge as the other grounding wires. Cut a grounding jumper wire about 4 inches long using wire cutters, then twist one end of it together with the ends of the other grounding wires and screw the wire cap onto them *(above, left)*. Hook the other end of the grounding jumper wire in a clockwise direction around the grounding terminal screw on the outlet and tighten it *(above, right)*.

7 Installing the outlet. Gently fold the wires into the electrical box and set the outlet into position on it. Ensuring the outlet is straight, install the mounting screw at the top and the bottom of the mounting strap, then screw the cover plate onto the outlet. Restore the electricity to the circuit for the outlet *(page 96)*. If you replaced the outlet and the problem persists, shut off electricity to the circuit and have the outlet serviced by a qualified electrician.

INSTALLING A GROUND-FAULT CIRCUIT INTERRUPTER (GFCI) OUTLET

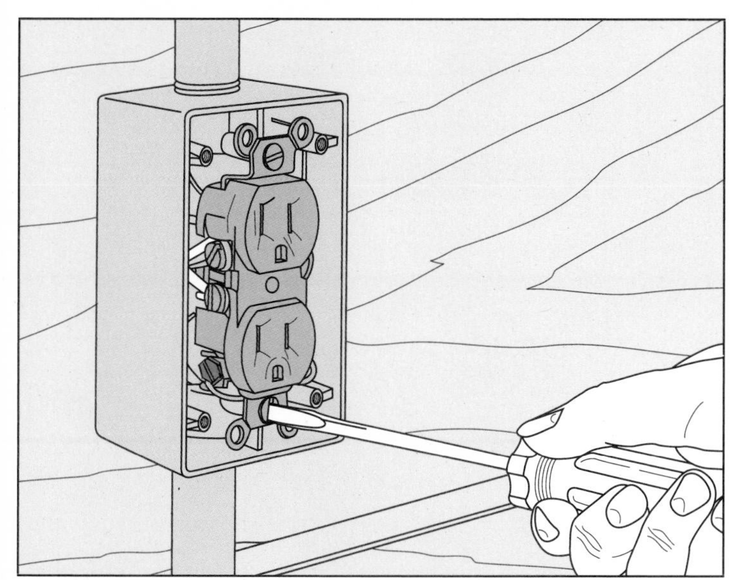

1 Removing the outlet. Any new outlet installed outdoors, in a garage, basement or bathroom, or within 6 feet of a sink or other area subject to moisture must be a ground-fault circuit interrupter (GFCI) outlet—required by the U.S. National Electrical Code. To upgrade a duplex outlet to a GFCI outlet, shut off electricity to the circuit *(page 96)*. Take the weatherproof cover or cover plate off the outlet. Unscrew the mounting strap *(above)*, then grasp it and pull the outlet out of the electrical box enough to expose the wires. **Caution:** Do not touch any wire or terminal screw until you have tested for voltage as you would at any duplex outlet *(page 100)* and confirmed that the electricity is shut off. Then, disconnect each wire from the outlet, loosening its terminal screw with a screwdriver.

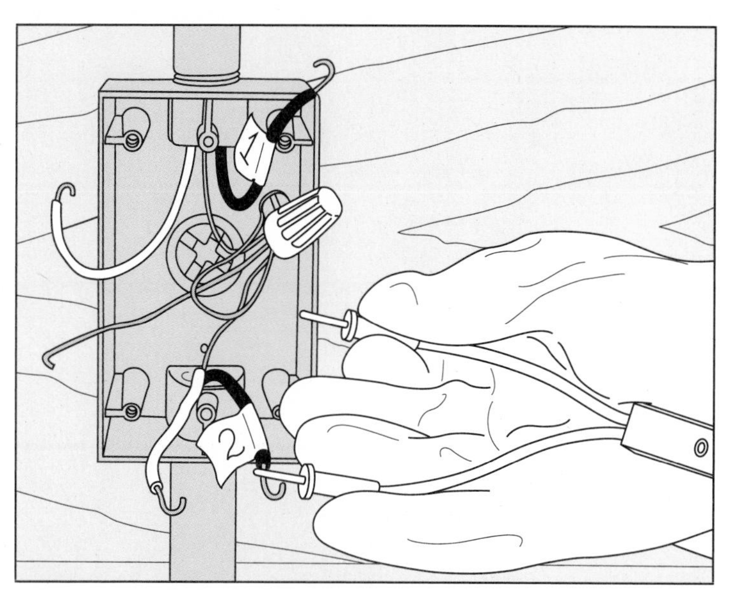

2 Identifying the hot black wire. If one cable enters the electrical box, install the GFCI outlet *(step 3)*. Otherwise, use a voltage tester to identify the black wire that is hot—carries current into the electrical box. Label each black wire by using masking tape to number it. Ensure the end of each black wire is isolated from contact with anything, then restore the electricity to the circuit *(page 96)*. **Caution:** Using only one hand, hold the tester probes by the insulated handles; wear a rubber glove and stand on a dry spot. Touch one tester probe to the grounded electrical box and touch the other tester probe in turn to the end of each black wire *(above)*; the tester will glow when its probe touches the hot black wire. Note the number of the hot black wire, then shut off electricity to the circuit.

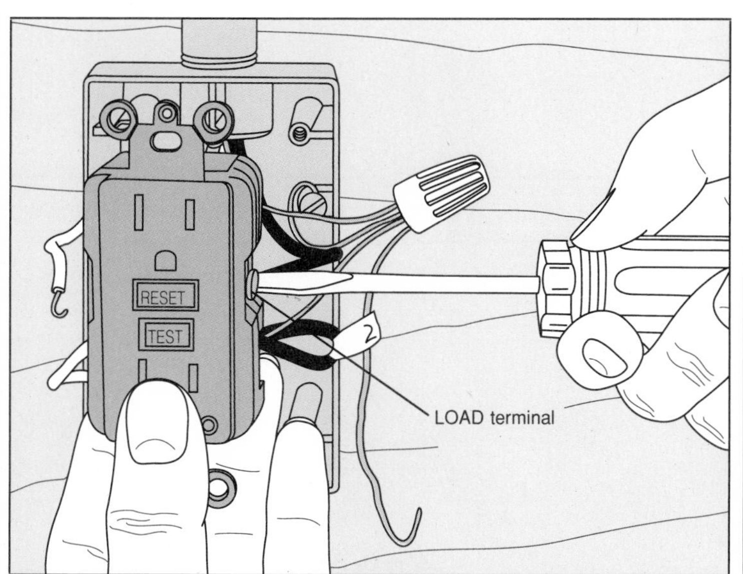

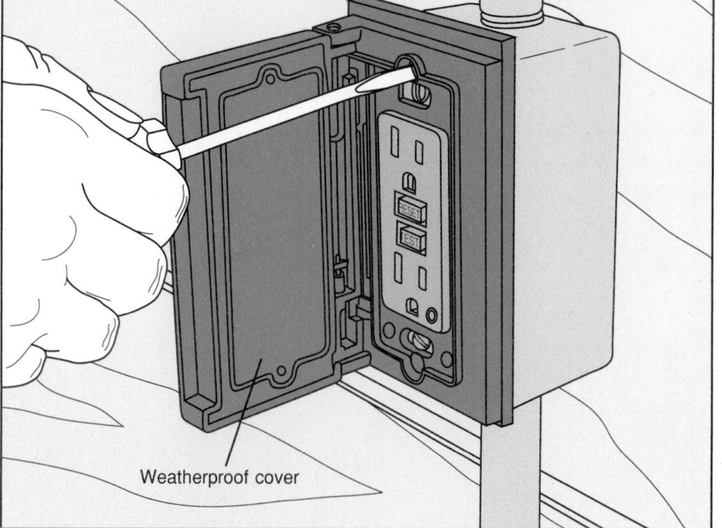

3 Installing the GFCI outlet. Purchase a receptacle-type GFCI outlet at a hardware store or a building supply center. If there are two cables entering the electrical box, hook the hot black wire in a clockwise direction around the brass terminal screw marked LINE and tighten it, then connect the white wire from the same cable to the silver terminal screw marked LINE the same way. Use the same procedure to connect the black wire and the white wire from the other cable to the terminal screws marked LOAD: the black wire to the brass terminal screw *(above, left)*; the white wire to the silver terminal screw. If there is one cable entering the electrical box, the black wire is hot—carries in current; connect it to the brass terminal screw marked LINE and the white wire to the silver terminal screw marked LINE. Also connect any grounding wire you disconnected to the grounding terminal screw on the outlet; if there is only a grounding wire running from the wire cap to the grounding terminal screw on the back of the electrical box, install a grounding jumper wire as you would for any duplex outlet *(page 100)*. Gently fold the wires into the electrical box and set the outlet into position on it. Ensuring the outlet is straight, screw the mounting strap to the electrical box, then screw the weatherproof cover *(above, right)* or cover plate onto the outlet. Restore the electricity to the circuit for the outlet *(page 96)*.

TESTING AND REPLACING A SINGLE-POLE SWITCH

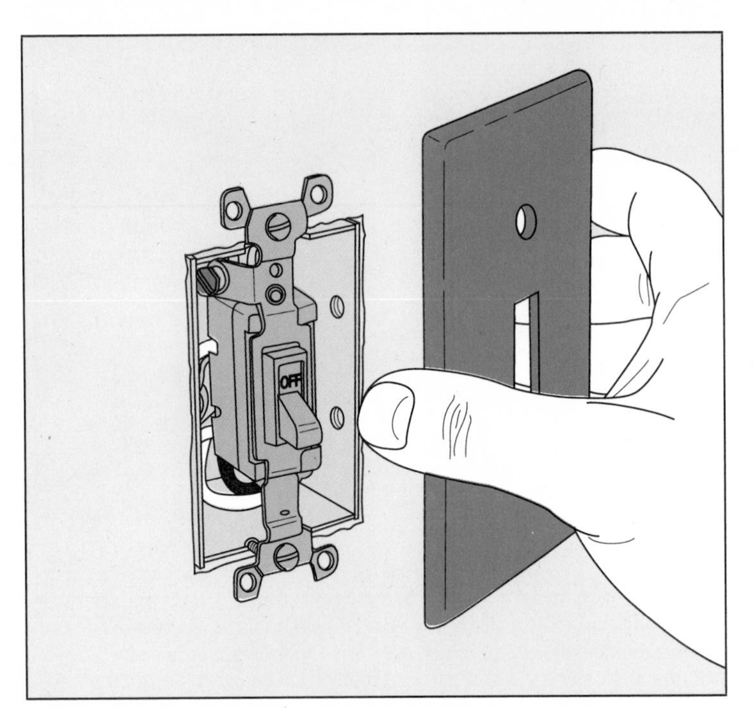

1 Exposing the wires. Shut off electricity to the circuit for the switch at the service panel *(page 96)*. Unscrew the cover plate of the switch and lift it off *(above)*; if necessary, first score around it with a utility knife to free it from any paint or plaster. To release the switch from the electrical box, remove the mounting screw at the top and the bottom of the mounting strap, then grasp the mounting strap and pull the switch out of the electrical box enough to expose the wires. **Caution:** Do not touch any wire or terminal screw until you have tested for voltage *(step 3)* and confirmed that the electricity is shut off.

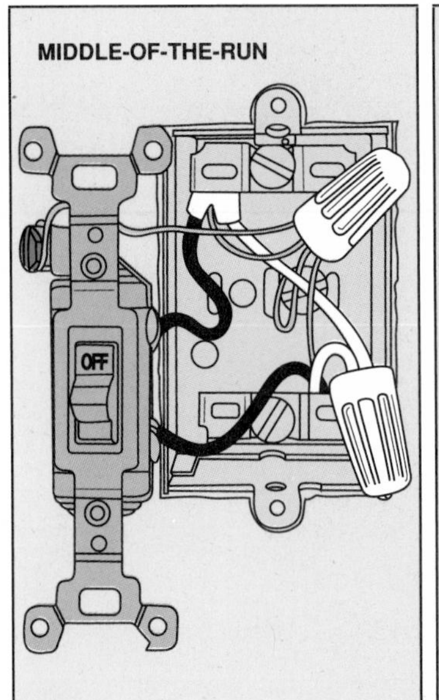

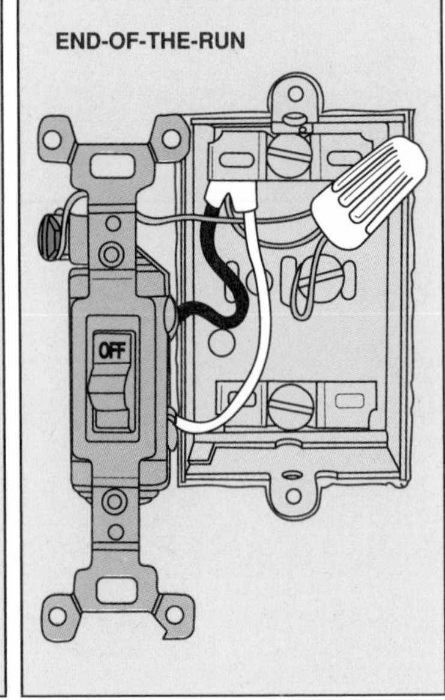

2 Inspecting the wires. If the switch is middle-of-the-run *(above, left)*, at least two cables enter the electrical box: each black wire should be connected to a brass terminal screw; the white wires should be connected inside a wire cap. If the switch is end-of-the-run *(above, right)*, one cable enters the electrical box: the black wire and the white wire should be connected to a brass terminal screw. Each bare copper wire is a grounding wire that should be connected inside a wire cap to a grounding wire running to the grounding terminal screw on the electrical box; if there is a grounding terminal screw on the switch, there also should be a grounding wire running from it connected inside the wire cap. Before servicing any wire connection, test for voltage *(step 3)* to confirm that the electricity is shut off.

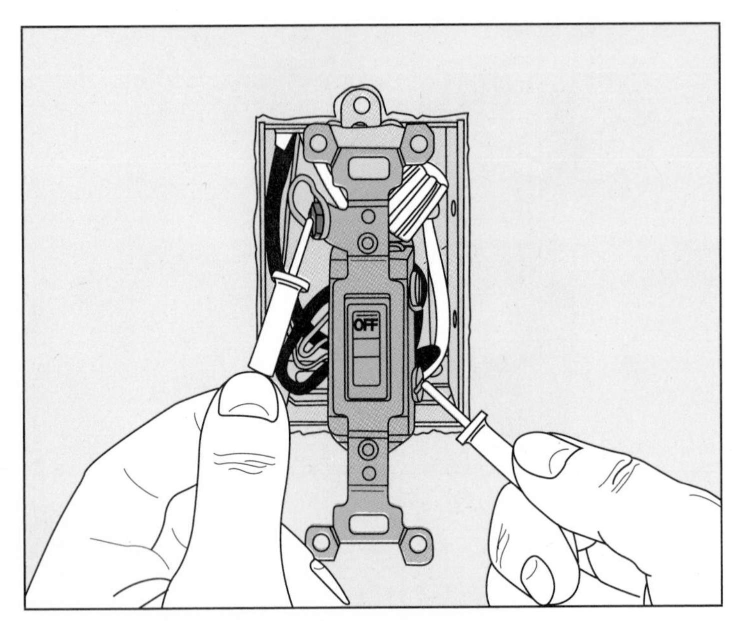

3 Testing for voltage. Use a voltage tester to confirm that the electricity is shut off. Touch one tester probe to the brass terminal screw and touch the other tester probe in turn to the silver terminal screw and each grounding terminal screw *(above)*. Then, touch one tester probe to the silver terminal screw and touch the other probe in turn to each grounding terminal screw. The tester should not glow in any test; if it does, shut off electricity to the correct circuit *(page 96)* and test again.

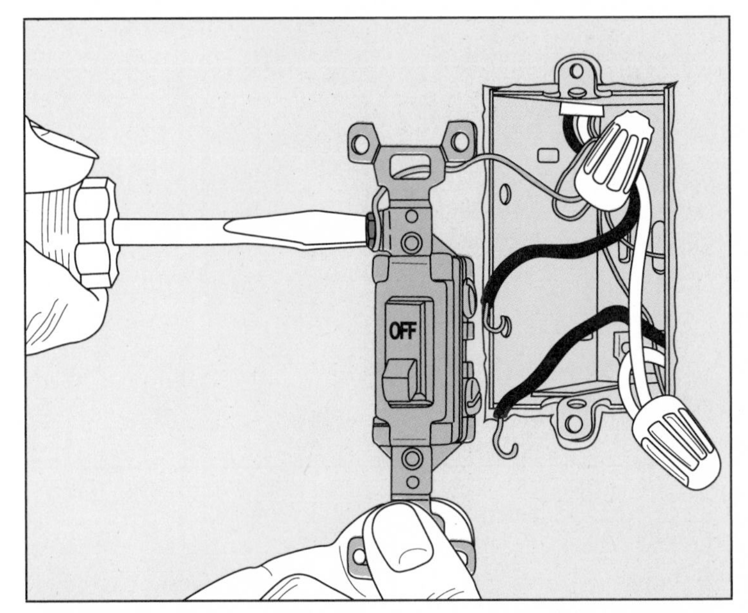

4 Removing the switch. When the electricity is shut off, check the wire connections; if the switch is end-of-the-run, also recode the white wire as black with electrical tape or paint. If you suspect the switch is faulty, disconnect each wire from it using a screwdriver *(above)*, then test it *(step 5)*. Otherwise, service the wire connections *(page 97)*, then reinstall the switch *(step 6)*; if the problem persists, expose the wires *(step 1)* and test for voltage *(step 3)* again, then remove the switch.

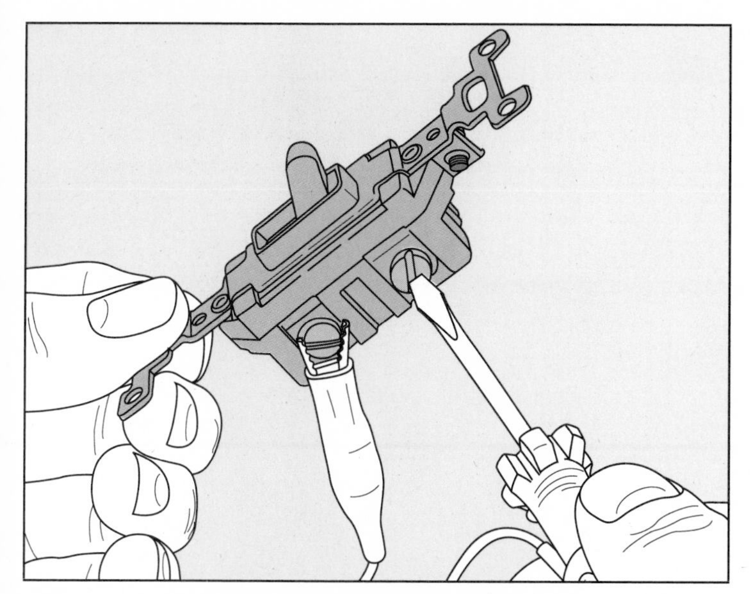

5 Testing the switch. Test the switch using a continuity tester, connecting the tester probes to the brass terminal screws that carry current—not to any grounding terminal screw. Place the alligator clip of the tester on one terminal screw and touch the other tester probe to the other terminal screw, setting the switch first to the ON position *(above)*, then to the OFF position. The continuity tester should glow when the switch is set to the ON position and should not glow when the switch is set to the OFF position. If the switch tests faulty, purchase a replacement switch at a hardware store or a building supply center. To install the switch, ensure it is set in the OFF position and hold it with its toggle pointing down.

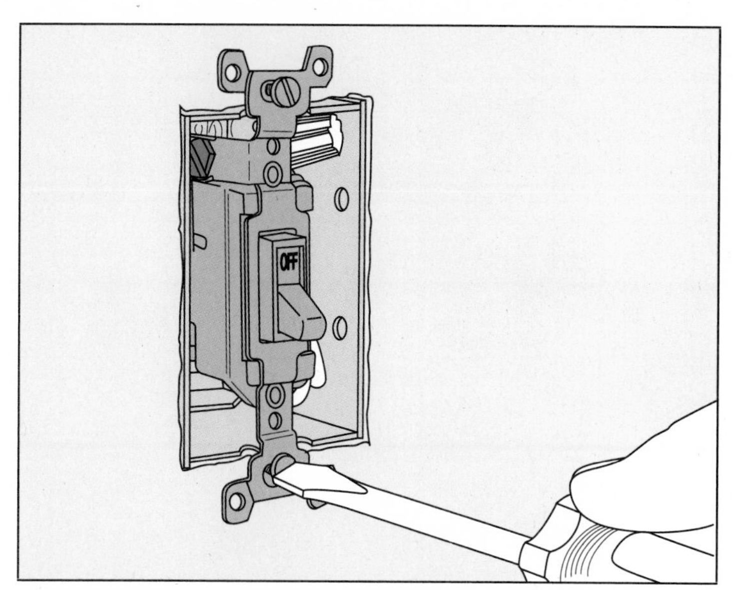

6 Installing the switch. Hook each black wire (or white wire recoded as black) in a clockwise direction around a brass terminal screw and tighten it. Also connect any grounding wire you disconnected to the grounding terminal screw on the switch; if there is only a grounding wire running from a wire cap to the grounding terminal screw on the back of the electrical box, install a grounding jumper wire as you would for any duplex outlet *(page 100)*. Gently fold the wires into the electrical box and screw on the mounting strap *(above)*, then screw on the cover plate and restore the electricity to the circuit *(page 96)*. If the problem persists, shut off electricity to the circuit and have the switch serviced by a qualified electrician.

INSTALLING A SINGLE-POLE DIMMER SWITCH

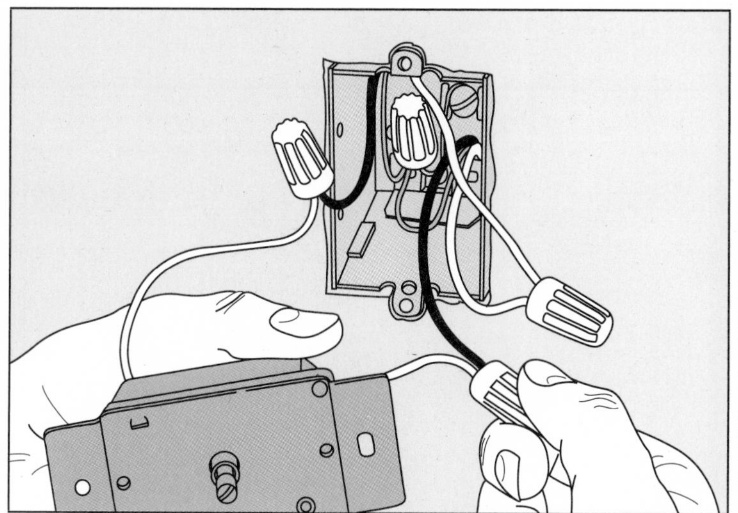

Removing a single-pole switch and installing a dimmer switch. A dimmer switch has a control knob that turns on and off a lighting fixture and adjusts the lighting level. To upgrade a single-pole switch with a dimmer switch, expose the wires and inspect them, test for voltage, then remove the switch *(page 102)*. If you disconnect a grounding wire from a grounding terminal screw on the switch, also take it out of the wire cap. Unscrew the wire cap, untwist the ends of the grounding wires and remove the grounding wire you disconnected, then twist the ends of the other grounding wires back together and screw on the wire cap.

Purchase a dimmer switch at a hardware store or a building supply center. To connect a standard single-pole dimmer switch, twist the ends of each wire on it in turn in a clockwise direction together with the ends of a black wire (or white wire recoded as black) entering the electrical box and screw on a wire cap *(above, left)*. Gently fold the wires into the electrical box and set the dimmer switch into position on it. Ensuring the dimmer switch is straight, screw the mounting strap to the electrical box *(above, right)*, then screw the cover plate onto the switch. Push the control knob into place and restore the electricity to the circuit *(page 96)*.

TESTING AND REPLACING AN INDOOR LIGHTING FIXTURE

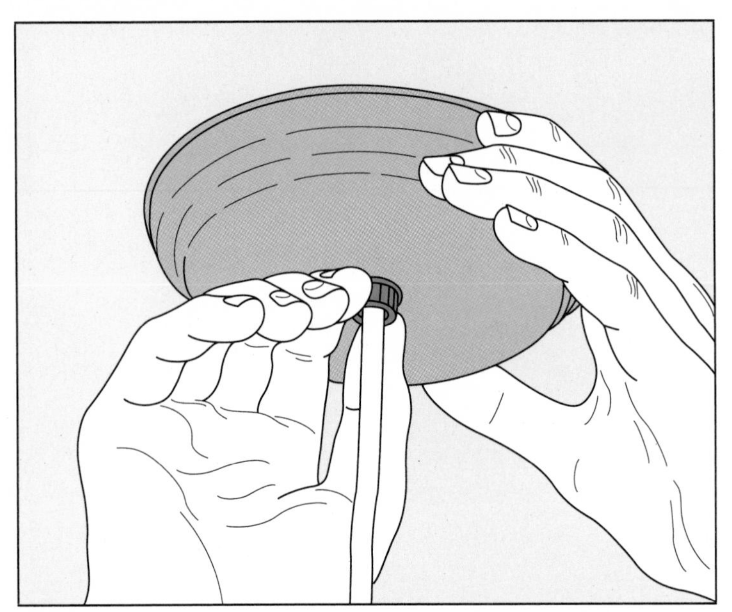

1 Exposing the wires. To test the fixture, turn off its switch and remove any globe. If the bulb is loose, tighten it and turn on the switch; if the bulb lights, turn off the switch and reinstall any globe you removed. If the bulb is not loose and does not light, replace it with one of the same wattage and turn on the switch; if the bulb lights, turn off the switch and reinstall any globe you removed. To service or replace the fixture, shut off electricity to the circuit at the service panel *(page 96)* and remove any globe and the bulb. Unscrew any cover plate or canopy *(above)* or the fixture and pull it off the electrical box enough to expose the wires.

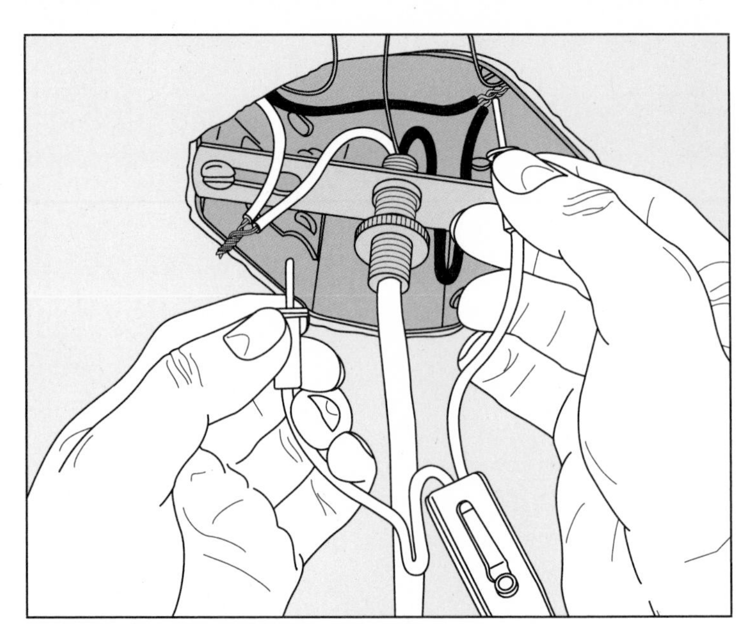

2 Testing for voltage. Carefully unscrew each wire cap, exposing the wire ends twisted together inside it. **Caution:** Do not touch any wire ends until you have tested for voltage using a voltage tester and confirmed that the electricity is shut off. Touch one tester probe to the black wire ends and touch the other tester probe in turn to the grounded electrical box *(above)* and the white wire ends. Then, touch one tester probe to the white wire ends and touch the other probe to the grounded electrical box. The tester should not glow in any test; if it does, shut off electricity to the correct circuit *(page 96)* and test again.

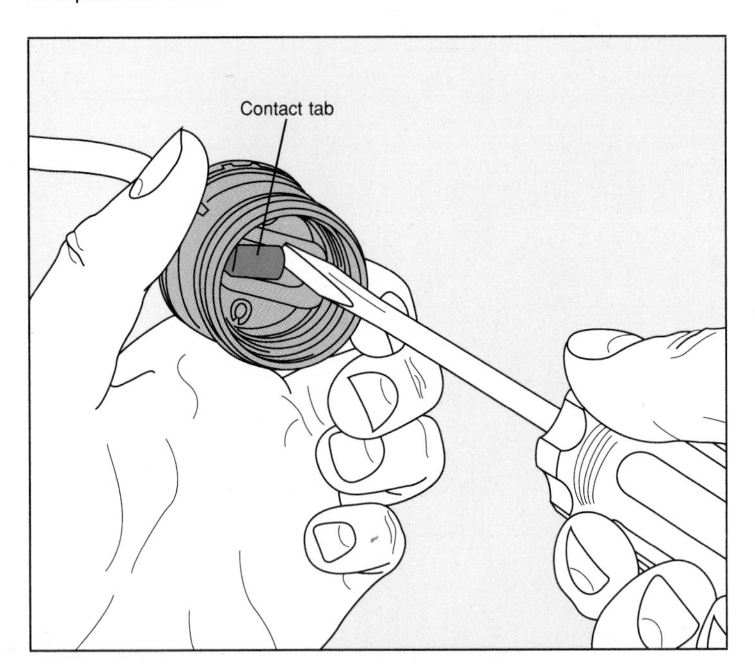

3 Servicing the fixture. To install a new fixture or a ceiling or wall plate *(page 105)*, remove the fixture *(step 4)*; otherwise, service it. Scrape any corrosion off the contact tab of the socket and pry it up slightly to improve contact with the bulb *(above)*. Screw the wire caps back onto the wire ends and reinstall the cover plate or canopy or the fixture, then restore the electricity *(page 96)*. Install a bulb and turn on the switch. If the bulb lights, turn off the switch and reinstall any globe you removed; if it does not light, turn off the switch, expose the wires *(step 1)* and test for voltage *(step 2)*, then remove the fixture.

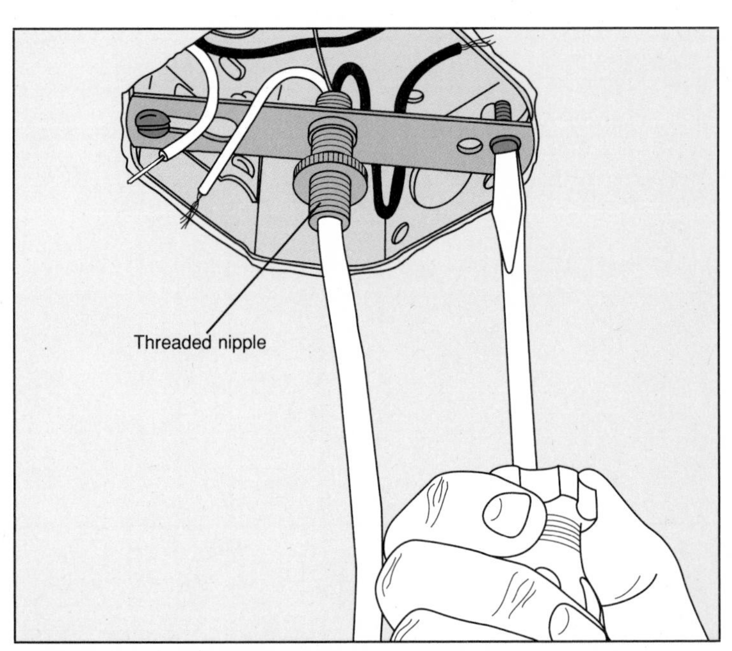

4 Removing the fixture. Have a helper support the fixture in position until you are ready to lower it, if necessary. Then, untwist each set of wire ends and carefully take the fixture off the electrical box; leave in place any grounding wire connected to a terminal screw on the electrical box. If the fixture is held by a mounting strap, remove the screw at each end of it *(above)*, then take down the fixture and feed the wires out through the threaded nipple. Purchase a replacement fixture at a hardware store or a building supply center and install it *(step 5)*; or, install a ceiling or wall plate on the electrical box *(page 105)*.

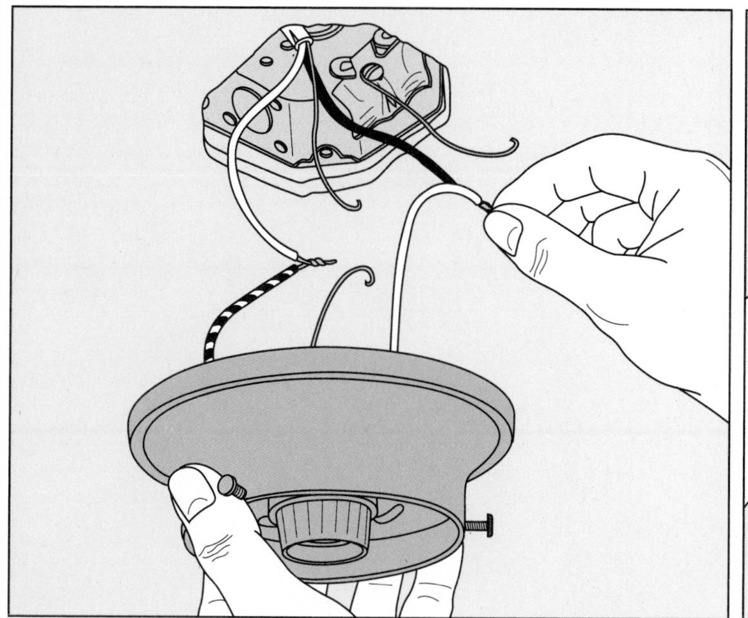

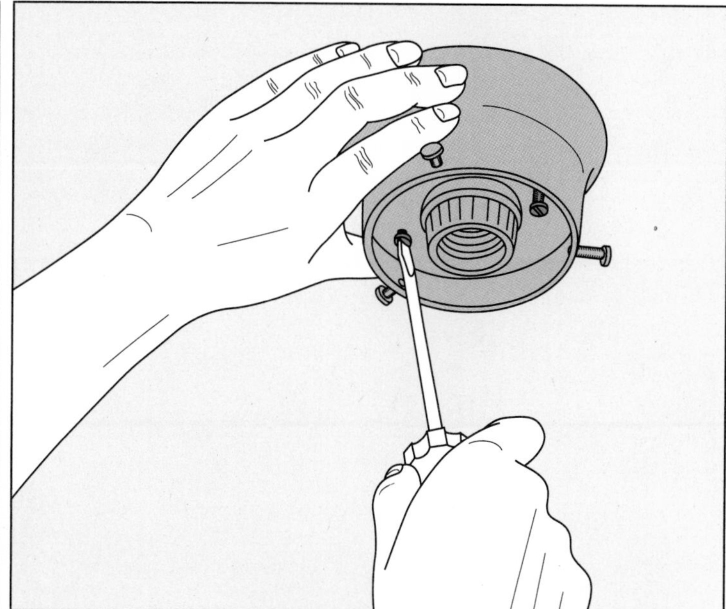

5 Installing the fixture. Have a helper support the fixture in position, if necessary; if it needs to be held by a mounting strap, feed the wires in through the threaded nipple. Connect the wires of the fixture to the wires of the cable entering the electrical box: the unmarked hot wire with the black wire; the marked neutral wire (white or gray insulation; threaded tracers in the wire strands; stripes, grooves or ridges) with the white wire; and the grounding wires with each other. Twist each set of wire ends together in turn in a clockwise direction *(above, left)*, then screw on a wire cap. If there is no grounding wire running from a grounding terminal screw on the back of the electrical box, use wire cutters to cut one about 4 inches long from bare copper wire or green grounding wire of the same gauge as the other grounding wires; twist one end together with the ends of the other grounding wires and screw on a wire cap, then hook the other end in a clockwise direction around a grounding terminal screw on the electrical box and tighten it. Gently fold the wires into the electrical box, then screw on the fixture *(above, right)* or screw on the mounting strap and install the cover plate or canopy. Screw in a bulb, install any globe and restore the electricity *(page 96)*.

INSTALLING A CEILING OR WALL PLATE

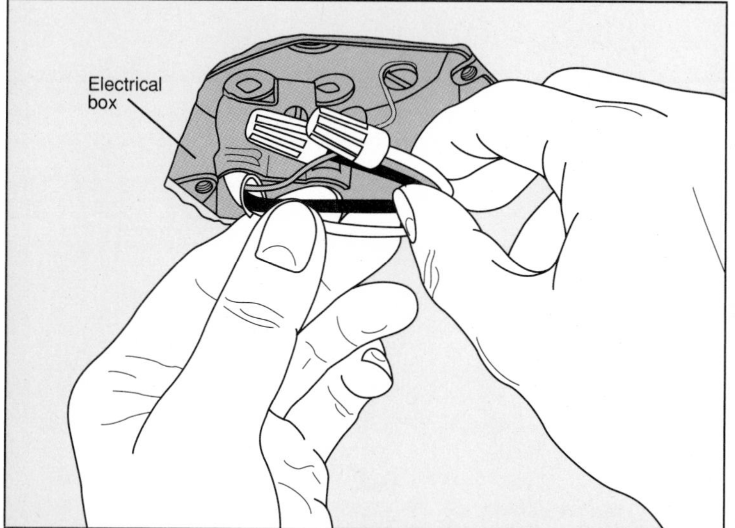

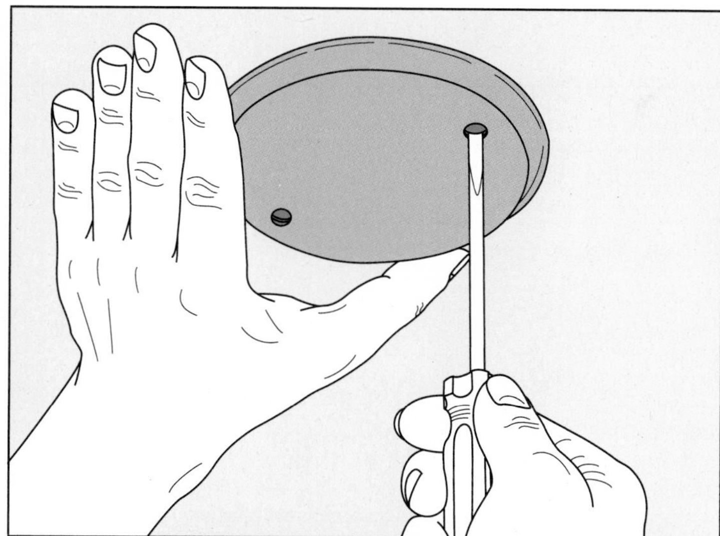

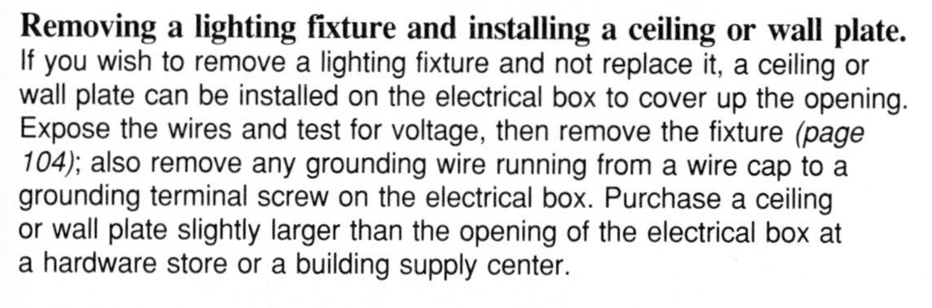

Removing a lighting fixture and installing a ceiling or wall plate. If you wish to remove a lighting fixture and not replace it, a ceiling or wall plate can be installed on the electrical box to cover up the opening. Expose the wires and test for voltage, then remove the fixture *(page 104)*; also remove any grounding wire running from a wire cap to a grounding terminal screw on the electrical box. Purchase a ceiling or wall plate slightly larger than the opening of the electrical box at a hardware store or a building supply center.

Wrap electrical tape around the ends of the black wire entering the electrical box and screw on a wire cap; isolate the ends of the white wire the same way. Hook the end of the grounding wire entering the electrical box in a clockwise direction around a grounding terminal screw on the electrical box and tighten it. Gently fold the wires into the electrical box *(above, left)* and set the plate into position on it. Ensuring the plate is straight, screw it to the electrical box *(above, right)*. Then, restore the electricity to the circuit *(page 96)*.

TESTING AND REPLACING AN OUTDOOR LIGHTING FIXTURE

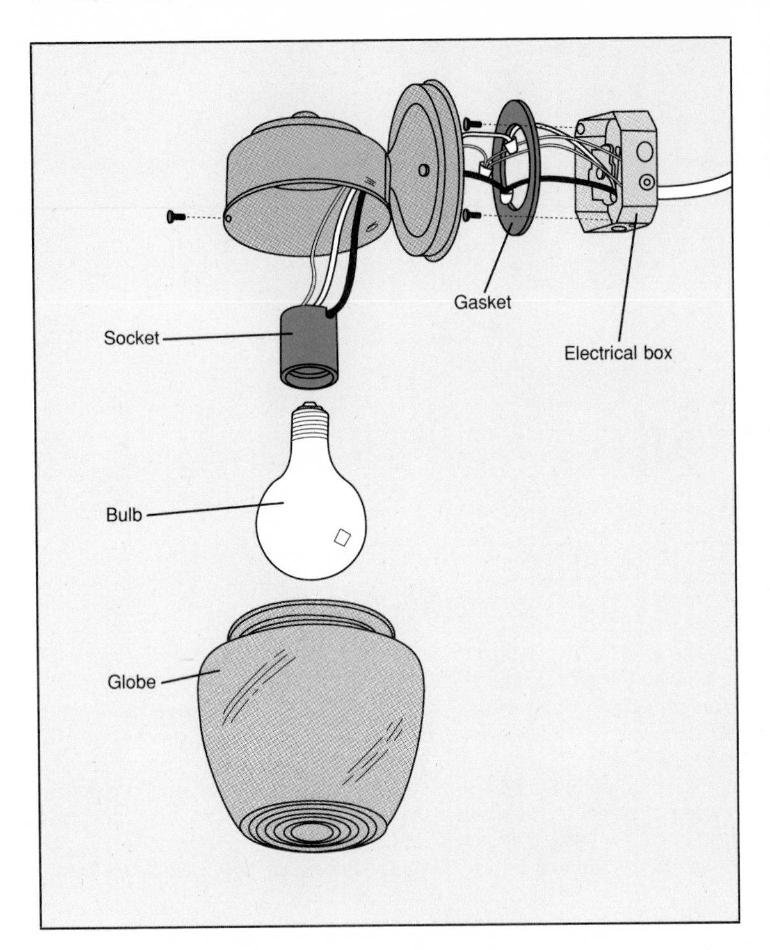

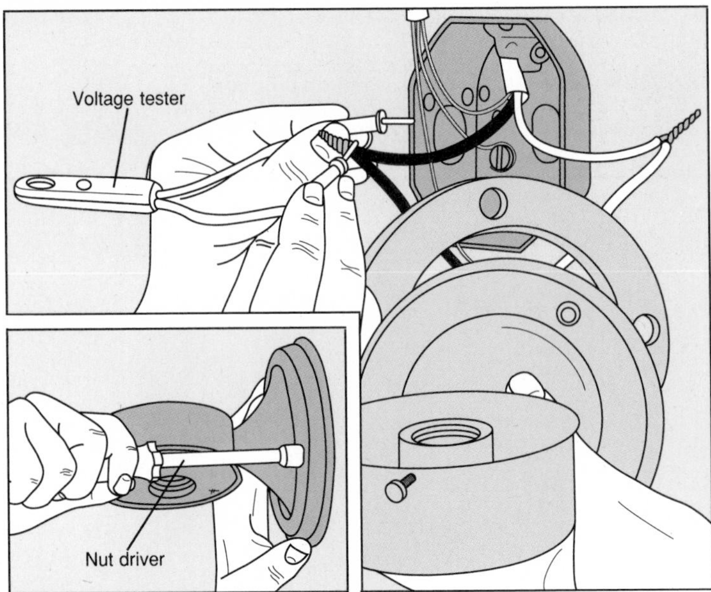

1 Exposing the wires. Shut off electricity to the circuit *(page 96)*, then remove the globe and the bulb. Unscrew the fixture *(inset)* and pull it out enough to expose the wires. Having a helper support the fixture, carefully unscrew each wire cap. **Caution:** Do not touch any wire ends until you have tested for voltage using a voltage tester and confirmed that the electricity is shut off. Touch one tester probe to the black wire ends and touch the other tester probe in turn to the grounded electrical box *(above)* and the white wire ends. Then, touch one tester probe to the white wire ends and touch the other probe to the grounded electrical box. The tester should not glow in any test; if it does, shut off electricity to the correct circuit and test again.

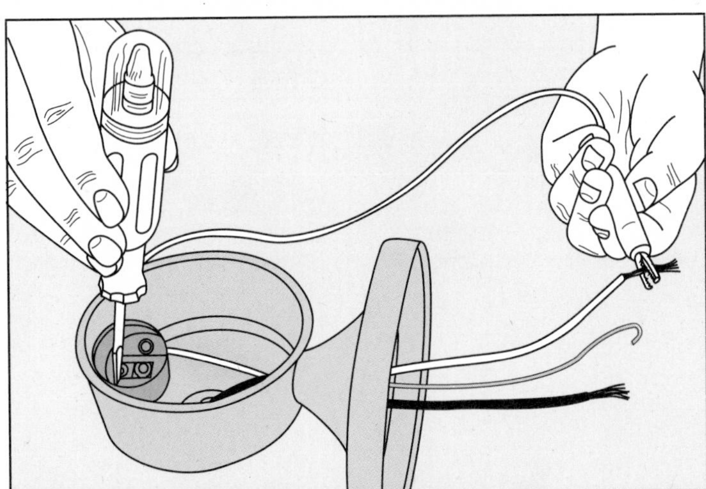

2 Testing the fixture. When the electricity is shut off, untwist each set of wire ends and take off the fixture and the gasket; leave in place any grounding wire connected to a terminal screw on the electrical box. To test the fixture, use a continuity tester. First, place the alligator clip on the black wire ends and touch the probe to the contact tab of the socket; then, place the alligator clip on the white wire ends and touch the probe to the threaded metal tube of the socket *(above)*. For each test, the tester should glow. Then, place the alligator clip on the white wire ends and touch the probe in turn to the black wire ends and the grounding wire; then test between the black wire ends and the grounding wire. For each test, the tester should not glow. If the fixture fails any test, replace it; purchase a new fixture at a hardware store or a building supply center.

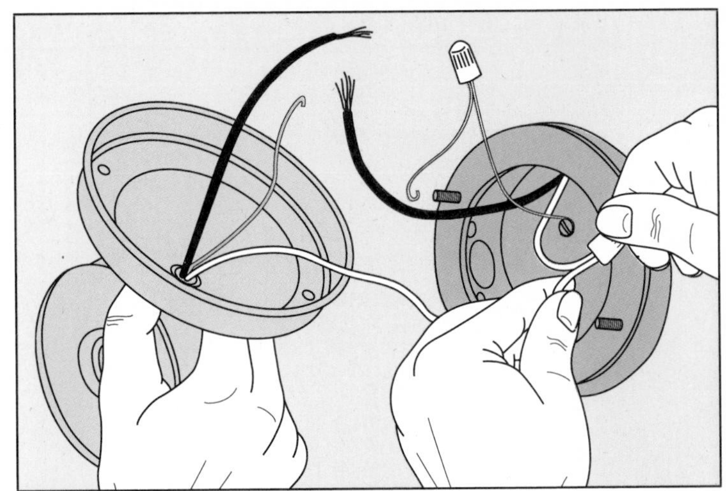

3 Installing the fixture. Having a helper support the fixture, connect the black wires together, the white wires together and the grounding wires together. Twist each set of wire ends together in turn in a clockwise direction, then screw on a wire cap *(above)*. If there is no grounding wire running from a grounding terminal screw on the back of the electrical box, use wire cutters to cut one about 4 inches long from bare copper wire or green grounding wire of the same gauge as the other grounding wires; twist one end together with the ends of the other grounding wires and screw on a wire cap, then hook the other end in a clockwise direction around a grounding terminal screw on the electrical box and tighten it. Gently fold the wires into the electrical box, then screw on the fixture. Screw in a bulb, install the globe and restore the electricity to the circuit *(page 96)*.

PLUMBING

Sound, secure plumbing is close to the top of every buyer's list of priorities in a prospective new home. Even the most inexperienced home buyer will make simple tests of your home's plumbing system, whether it be by turning on a faucet to check water pressure or by listening for the sound of telltale leaks and drips. A small problem such as a minor leak from a faucet, a slow-draining sink or a toilet that flushes improperly can lead to the false impression that your entire plumbing system is in need of costly repair. Before showing your house, make sure that all your kitchen and bathroom plumbing fixtures are in good working order. Use the Troubleshooting Guide below to help identify those small plumbing problems that can make all the difference in successfully selling your home; then, refer to the pages indicated to make the appropriate repairs.

Inspect your sinks, above and below. If a sink or bathtub drain is clogged or it empties sluggishly, clear it *(page 113)*. Under the sink, be on the lookout for minor drips and leaks; if necessary, tighten or replace any leaking fitting *(page 114)*. Check the operation of all sink faucets. Replace any damaged or leaking aerators on faucet spouts *(page 109)*. If a faucet leaks around the handle, collar or base, or the faucet spout drips, service the faucet, whether it is a double-handle type *(page 109)* or a single-lever type with a rotating ball *(page 110)* or a cartridge *(page 111)*. If a leak or drip persists after servicing a faucet, it is usually worth the small investment of time and money to replace the faucet set *(page 109)* before showing the house to a prospective buyer.

The source of a toilet problem may take a little longer to track down and clear up. If you have a toilet that runs continuously after flushing or that flushes incompletely or sluggishly, you can easily make small adjustments to the float assembly *(page 114)* or flush assembly *(page 115)* that will usually fix the problem. If minor adjustments do not work, it is not difficult to replace the toilet ball cock *(page 116)*.

Small plumbing repairs are not difficult, provided you work patiently and carefully. Before beginning a repair, ensure you know how to properly turn off and on the water supply *(page 108)*. Most repairs can be made with an adjustable wrench or channel-joint pliers and a screwdriver. Refer to Tools & Techniques *(page 126)* for advice on using any tools required. If you need to replace fittings or fixtures, note their makes, model numbers and exact sizes; if possible, bring old fittings with you to buy identical replacement parts. Shower heads, faucet sets, and toilet assemblies usually come with complete installation instructions; follow the manufacturer's directions carefully. After inspecting, servicing or replacing your plumbing fixtures, take the time to clean and polish them *(page 54)* so they will merit the attention a prospective house buyer is likely to give them.

TROUBLESHOOTING GUIDE

SYMPTOM	PROCEDURE
Faucet aerator leaks around edge	Clean or replace aerator *(p. 109)* □○
Shower head leaks around edge	Clean or replace shower head *(p. 109)* □◒
Water flow from faucet with aerator sluggish or erratic	Clean or replace aerator *(p. 109)* □○
Water flow from shower head sluggish or erratic	Clean or replace shower head *(p. 109)* □◒
Sink faucet under handle, collar or base leaks; faucet spout drips	Service faucet: double-handle compression type *(p. 109)* □○; single-lever rotating-ball type *(p. 110)* □○; single-lever cartridge type *(p. 111)* □○
	If leak or drip persists, replace faucet *(p. 112)* ⬓◒
Sink drain clogged or sluggish	Clear sink drain *(p. 113)* □○
	If blockage persists, clean sink trap *(p. 113)* ⬓◒
Bathtub drain clogged or sluggish	Clear bathtub drain *(p. 113)* □○
	If blockage persists, call a plumber
Fitting under sink leaks	Service leaking sink fitting *(p. 114)* □○
Toilet runs continuously after flushing	If tank fills too high, service toilet float assembly *(p. 114)* □○; if tank does not refill, service toilet flush assembly *(p. 115)* □○
	If problem persists, replace toilet ball cock *(p. 116)* ⬓◒
Toilet flushes incompletely or sluggishly	If tank fills to normal level, service toilet flush assembly *(p. 115)* □○; if tank fills only partially, service toilet float assembly *(p. 114)* □○
	If problem persists, replace toilet ball cock *(p. 116)* ⬓◒

DEGREE OF DIFFICULTY: □ **Easy** ⬓ **Moderate** ■ **Complex**
ESTIMATED TIME: ○ **Less than 1 hour** ◒ **1 to 3 hours** ● **Over 3 hours**

SHUTTING OFF THE MAIN WATER SUPPLY

Turning off the water supply to the house. The main water supply pipe provides water to the house; the main shutoff valve turns the water on or off. Locate the valve on the pipe where it enters the house—usually indoors, or in hot climates, outdoors, near the water meter; or, in the basement, crawl space or utility room. If your water comes from a well, the valve may be on the pipe near the pressure gauge or water pump. Tag the valve *(above)* for future identification. To turn off the water, close the valve by turning the handle fully clockwise; if there is a valve on each side of the water meter, close the valve on the supply side (before the water meter). Then, open all house faucets to drain the house pipes. To turn on the water, close all open faucets, then open the main shutoff valve by turning the handle fully counterclockwise; turn slowly to prevent a pressure surge. Wait several minutes, then open each house faucet in turn to release trapped air; let it run until water flows smoothly, then close it.

SHUTTING OFF THE WATER SUPPLY TO A FIXTURE

Turning off the water supply to a toilet. Locate the toilet shutoff valve on the supply pipe under the toilet tank. To shut off the water supply to the toilet, turn the handle fully clockwise *(above)*. If there is no valve or if the valve leaks, shut off the main water supply *(step above)*. Then, flush the toilet to drain the tank and bowl. Before restoring the water supply to the toilet, ensure the cover is installed on the tank. To restore the water supply, turn the shutoff valve handle fully counterclockwise; or, restore the main water supply.

Turning off the water supply to a sink. Locate the shutoff valve for each sink faucet on its water supply pipe under the sink. To shut off the water, turn the valve handle fully clockwise *(above)*. If there is no valve or if a valve leaks, shut off the main water supply *(step above)*. Then, open each faucet to drain its supply pipe. To restore the water supply, close each faucet and turn its shutoff valve handle fully counterclockwise; or, restore the main water supply. Wait several minutes, then open each faucet; let it run until water flows smoothly, then close it.

SERVICING A SPOUT ATTACHMENT

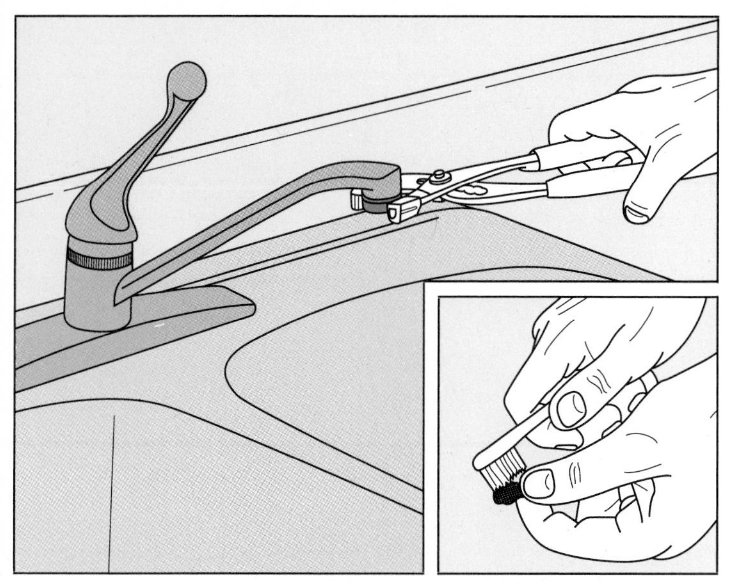

Cleaning or replacing an aerator. Close the faucet and the drain. Fit the taped jaws of a pair of channel-joint pliers onto the aerator *(above)*, and give the pliers a sharp clockwise turn to loosen it; then, unscrew the aerator from the faucet by hand. Take the washer and screen out of the aerator, noting their order for later reassembly. If any part is worn, replace it. Soak a dirty screen in vinegar for a few minutes; then, scrub it with an old toothbrush *(inset)* and rinse it. Reassemble the aerator and screw it onto the spout by hand; then, use the pliers to tighten it.

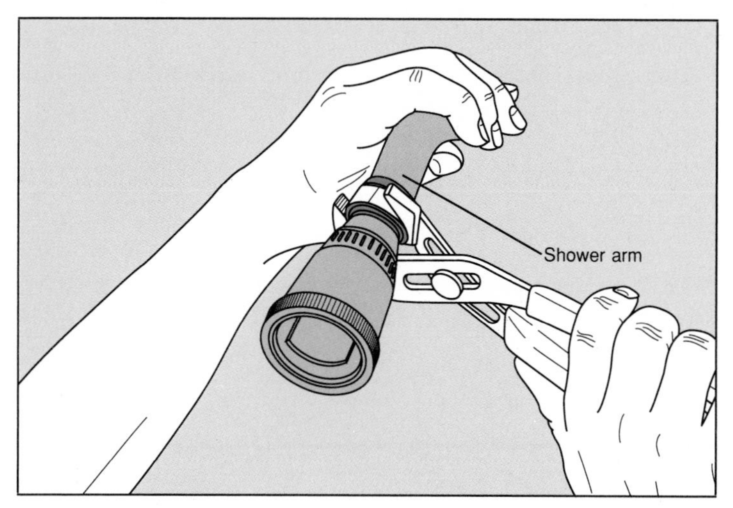

Cleaning or replacing a shower head. Close the faucet and the drain. Wrap the shower head collar with masking tape. Steadying the shower arm, use channel-joint pliers to loosen the collar *(above)*. Then, unscrew the shower head and disassemble it, noting the positions of parts for reassembly. If a part is damaged, replace it, if possible. If a part is mineral-encrusted, soak it in vinegar; then, scrub it with an old toothbrush and rinse it. Reassemble the head. Use the toothbrush to scrub out the pipe threads on the shower arm, then wrap them with pipe tape. Screw the head back onto the arm and use the pliers to retighten the collar on the head. If the problem persists, replace the head; if it still persists, call a plumber.

SERVICING A FAUCET (DOUBLE-HANDLE COMPRESSION TYPE)

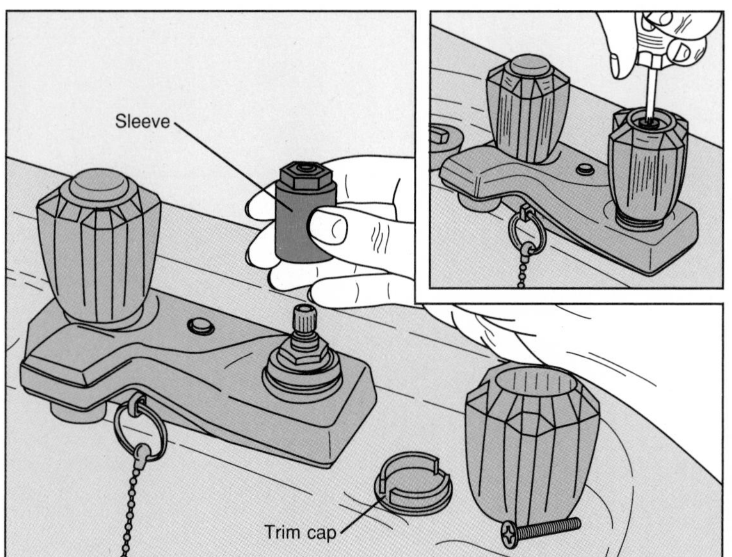

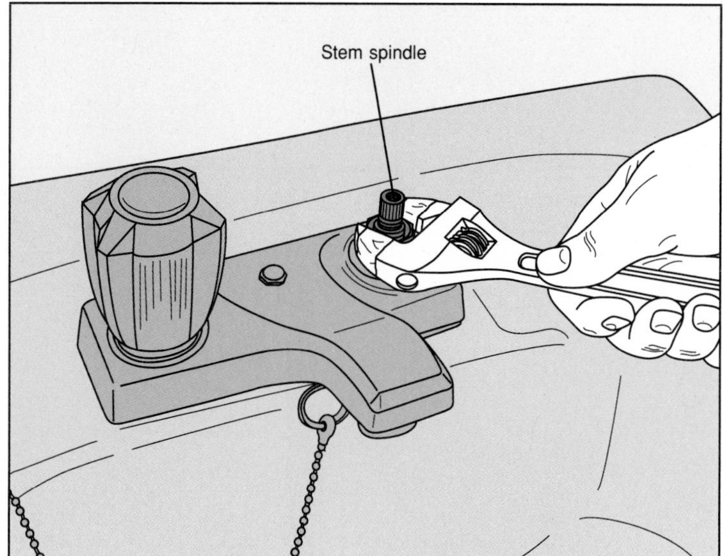

1 Disassembling the faucet. If a double-handle compression faucet leaks from under a handle, the likely cause is a worn O-ring on the handle stem. If the faucet has a dripping spout, the likely cause is a worn washer on the stem of one handle: the hot-water handle if warm water is dripping; the cold-water handle if cold water is dripping. To confirm that a particular handle is faulty, close the shutoff valve on the water supply pipe to the handle under the sink *(page 108)*; the leak or drip should stop. Then, close the shutoff valve for the other handle to shut off the water supply to the sink.

Cover the drain. Using the tip of a blunt knife, carefully pry the trim cap off the top of the faulty handle; then, use a screwdriver to loosen and remove the screw from the top of the handle *(inset)*; if the screw will not turn, apply penetrating oil and try again. Lift off the handle, then lift off the sleeve *(above, left)*. Fit the taped jaws of an adjustable wrench onto the locknut at the base of the stem spindle *(above, right)* and give the wrench a sharp turn to loosen the locknut. Then, grasp the tip of the stem spindle firmly and carefully pull up to lift the stem assembly out of the faucet body. Replace the washer *(step 2)* or the O-ring *(step 3)*.

SERVICING A FAUCET (DOUBLE-HANDLE COMPRESSION TYPE) (continued)

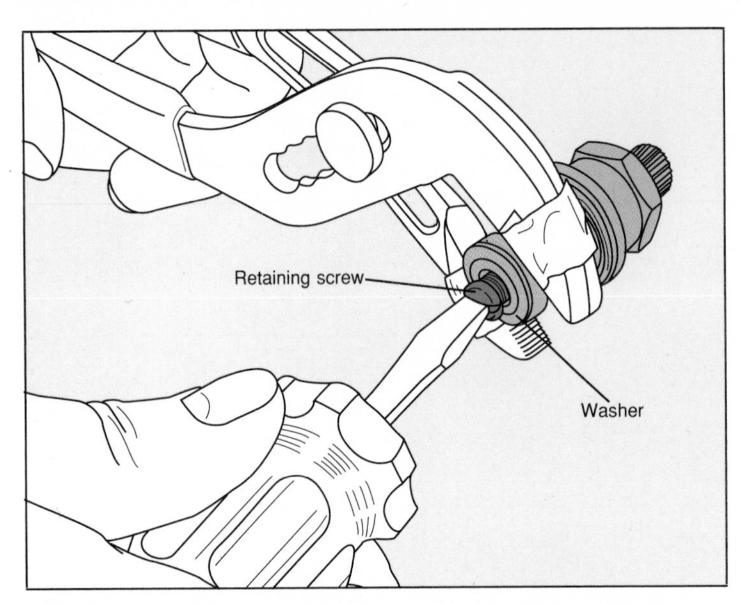

2 Replacing the washer. Hold the stem assembly between the taped jaws of a pair of channel-joint pliers and use a screwdriver to remove the retaining screw that holds the washer to the base *(above)*; then, remove the washer. To install an identical washer, place it with its flat side against the base and reinstall the retaining screw. Reassemble the faucet, reversing the procedure used to disassemble it *(step 1)*. Restore the sink water supply *(page 108)*. If the faucet still drips, replace any faulty washer in the other handle; otherwise, replace the faucet *(page 112)*.

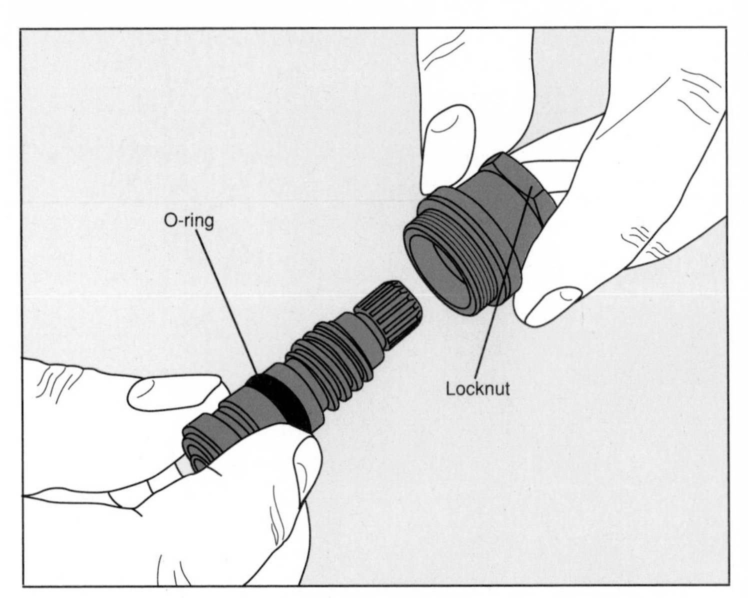

3 Replacing the O-ring. Unscrew and remove the locknut from the top of the stem spindle *(above)*; then, use long-nose pliers to pull the O-ring out of its grooved seat and off the top of the spindle. To install an identical O-ring, roll it down the spindle until it is firmly seated in its groove. To lubricate the ring, dab on petroleum jelly with a finger. Screw the locknut back onto the stem spindle. Reassemble the faucet handle, reversing the procedure used to disassemble it *(step 1)*. Restore the water supply to the sink *(page 108)*. If the faucet still leaks, replace it *(page 112)*.

SERVICING A FAUCET (SINGLE-LEVER ROTATING-BALL TYPE)

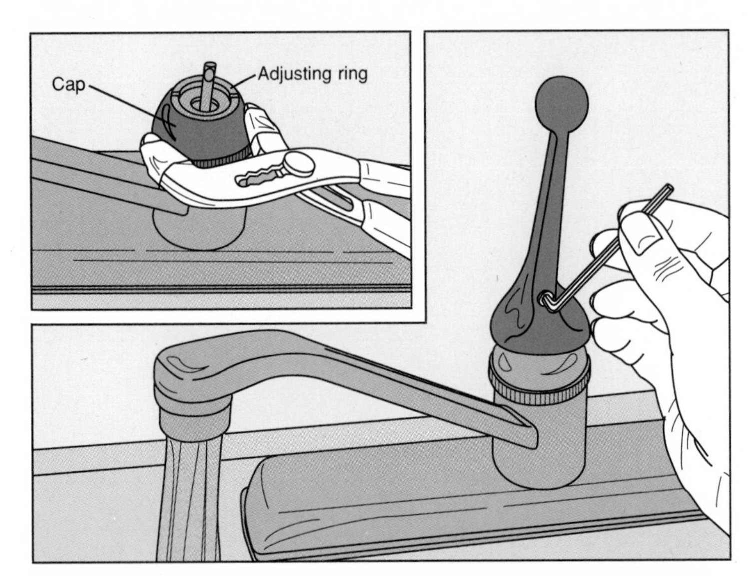

1 Disassembling the faucet. Raise the handle. Use a hex wrench to loosen the setscrew *(above)*; then, lift off the handle. To fix a leak from under the handle, use a screwdriver tip to turn the adjusting ring slightly clockwise. If water stops leaking, reinstall the handle; if not, continue as you would to fix a spout collar leak. To fix a leak from under the spout collar, shut off the sink water supply *(page 108)* and cover the drain. Fit the taped jaws of a pair of channel-joint pliers onto the cap *(inset)* and turn clockwise to loosen and remove it. For a spout collar leak, replace the O-rings *(step 2)*. For a handle leak, replace the washer, the ball or the seats and springs *(step 3)*.

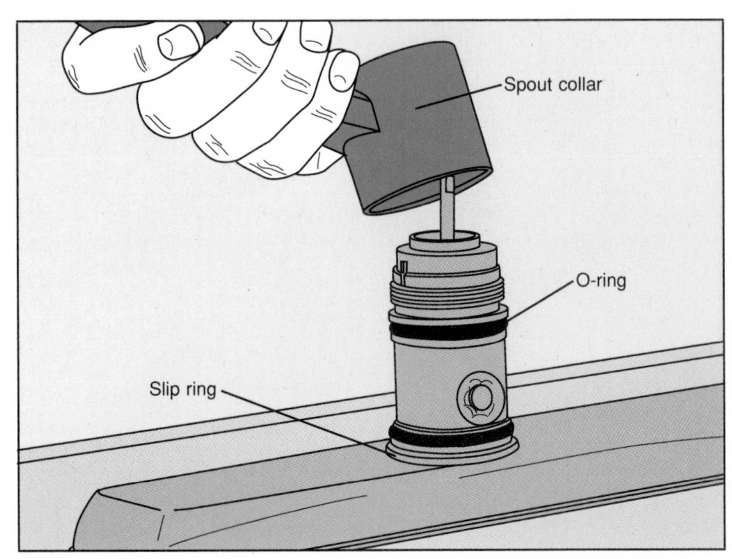

2 Replacing O-rings. Remove the spout collar by giving it a twist to loosen it; then, lift it off the faucet body *(above)*. To remove a faulty O-ring, use a screwdriver tip to pry it from its grooved seat and up off the faucet body. To install an identical O-ring, roll it down the faucet body until it is seated in its groove. Lubricate the ring by dabbing on petroleum jelly with a finger. Reinstall the spout collar on the faucet body, fitting it snugly over the plastic slip ring so the bottom is flush with the faucet deck. Reassemble the faucet, reversing the procedure used to disassemble it *(step 1)*. Restore the water supply to the sink *(page 108)*. If the faucet still leaks, replace it *(page 112)*.

SERVICING A FAUCET (SINGLE-LEVER ROTATING BALL TYPE) (continued)

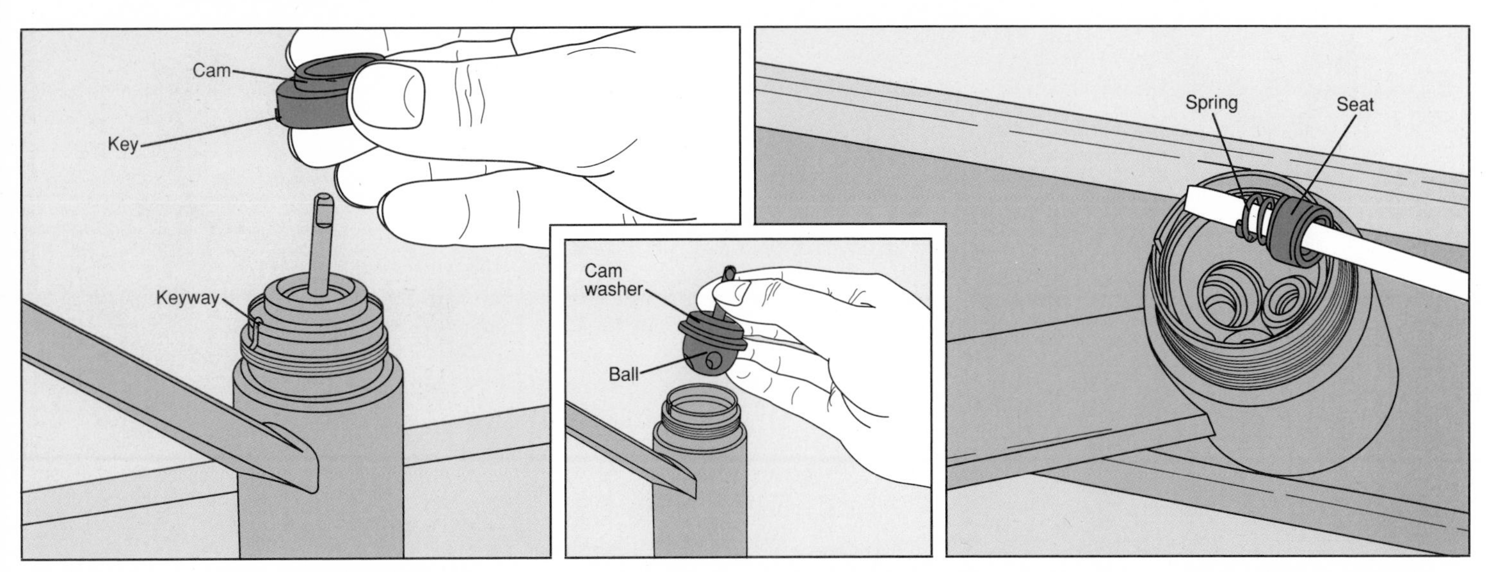

3 Replacing a washer, ball, seat or spring. Lift the plastic cam off the top of the faucet body *(above, left)*; then, lift the rotating ball and attached cam washer out of the faucet body *(inset)*. Using a screwdriver tip, carefully lift out one seat-and-spring set from its hole in the base of the faucet body *(above, right)*; then, lift out the second set. Inspect all parts carefully. If the rotating ball is damaged, buy an identical replacement for your faucet model; if a cam, cam washer, rubber seat or metal spring is damaged, buy a repair kit for your model that contains all these parts. To reassemble the faucet, follow the instructions that come with the replacement parts. On the model shown, carefully reinstall any springs and seats in the base of the faucet body. To seat the rotating ball, fit the slot in back of the ball over the pin in the base of the faucet body; then, seat the cam washer on top of the ball. Fit the plastic cam onto the faucet body, ensuring that the key on the side of the cam slips snugly into the keyway in the top edge of the faucet body. Reassemble the faucet, reversing the procedure used to disassemble it *(step 1)*. Restore the water supply to the sink *(page 108)*. If the faucet still leaks, replace it *(page 112)*.

SERVICING A FAUCET (SINGLE-LEVER CARTRIDGE TYPE)

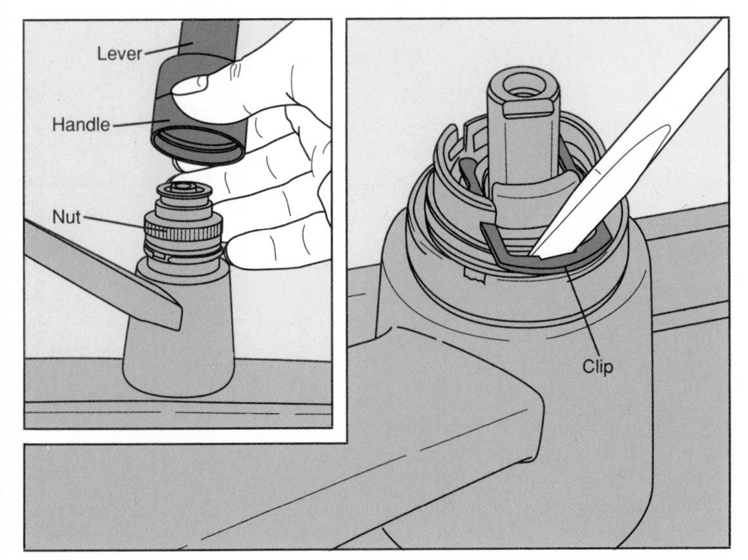

1 Disassembling the faucet. Shut off the sink water supply *(page 108)* and cover the drain. Use the tip of a knife to pry the trim cap off the handle top; then, use a screwdriver to remove the screw from the handle. Pull the handle lever sharply forward to detach the handle from the retainer nut and lift off the handle *(inset)*. Fit the taped jaws of a pair of channel-joint pliers onto the retainer nut and give the pliers a sharp turn to loosen and remove it. To fix a leak from under the spout collar, remove the collar and replace any faulty O-rings as you would for a rotating-ball faucet *(page 110)*. To fix a dripping spout or a leak from under the handle, use a screwdriver tip to pry the retainer clip out of the collar *(above)*; then, replace the cartridge *(step 2)*.

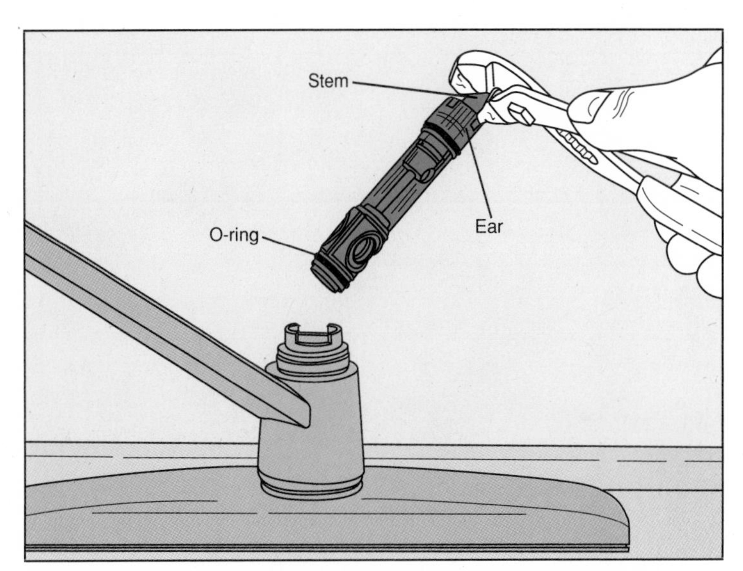

2 Replacing the cartridge. Fit the taped jaws of a pair of channel-joint pliers onto the cartridge stem and pull it out of the faucet body *(above)*. If the cartridge or its O-rings are worn, replace the cartridge with an exact duplicate. To install a cartridge, follow the instructions that come with it. On the model shown, fit the cartridge into the faucet body, ensuring that the plastic ears on the cartridge top are aligned with the notches in the top edge of the faucet body and that the notched side of the cartridge stem faces the sink. Reassemble the faucet, reversing the procedure used to disassemble it *(step 1)*. Restore the water supply to the sink *(page 108)*. If the faucet still leaks, replace it *(page 112)*.

REPLACING A FAUCET

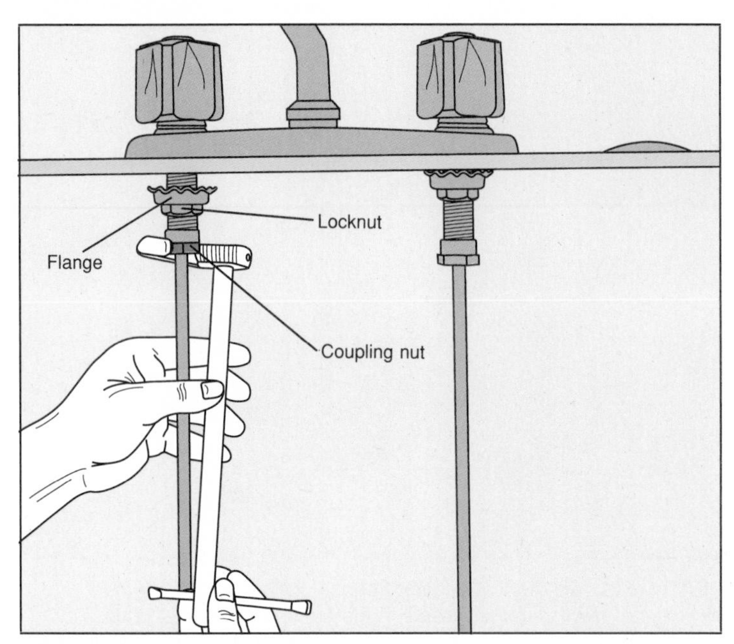

1 **Removing the faucet.** Shut off the sink water supply *(page 108)*. Cover the drain. Working under the sink, use a basin wrench to loosen the locknut at the top of a faucet tailpiece, and the coupling nut between the tailpiece and supply pipe *(above)*. If a nut is stuck, apply penetrating oil and wait overnight; then, try again. Thread the loose nuts down the tailpiece, then slide them and any flange down the supply pipe. Repeat the procedure for the nuts and flange on the other tailpiece. Working above the sink, raise the faucet out of the sink deck. Use a putty knife to scrape old sealant off the deck; clean the surface with fine steel wool. Working under the sink, slide the old locknuts and flanges off the supply pipes.

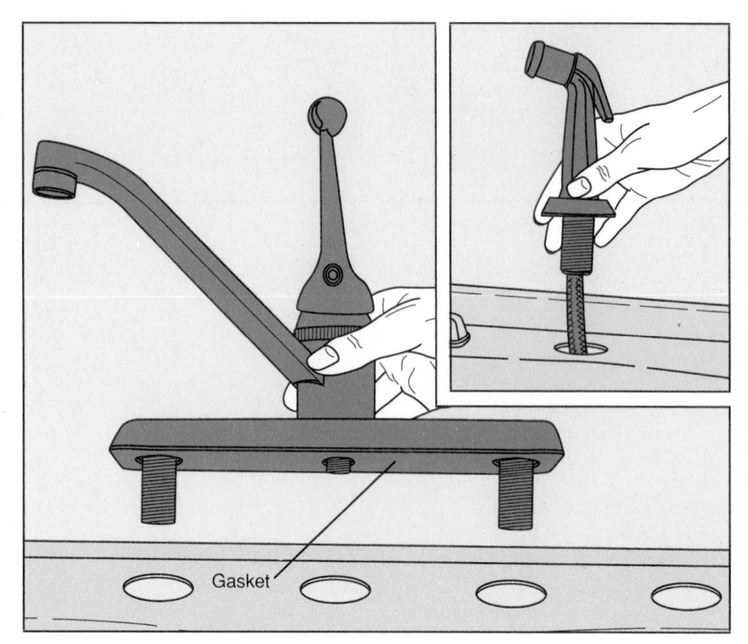

2 **Installing a new faucet.** Buy a popular single-lever faucet with the same number, spacing and length of tailpieces as the old faucet; for a kitchen, also buy a spray attachment if there is an extra hole for one in your sink deck—a metal plate may cover the hole. To install the faucet, follow the manufacturer's instructions. Working under the sink, slide any new locknuts and flanges onto the supply pipes. Working above the sink, ensure that any gasket is snugly seated in the faucet bottom; then, aligning the faucet tailpieces with the sink seating holes *(above)*, lower the faucet onto the sink deck. To install a spray attachment, feed its hose through the seating hole *(inset)* and rest it firmly on the sink deck.

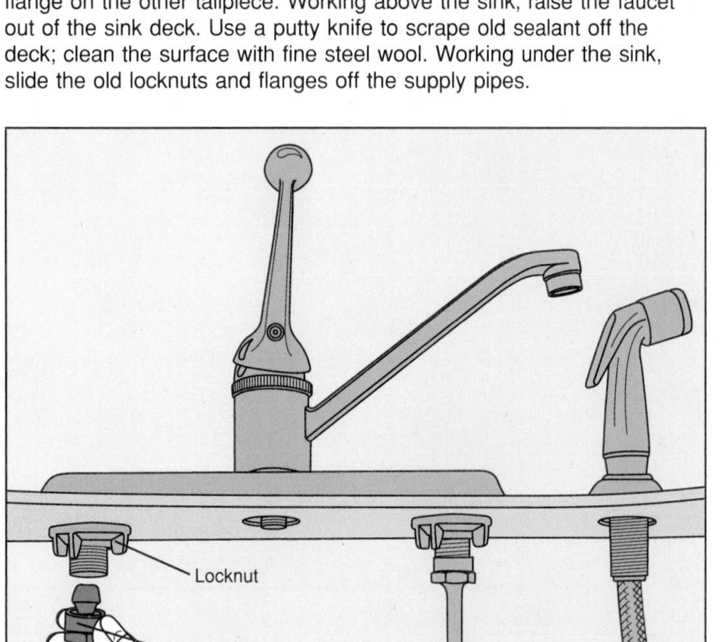

3 **Connecting the faucet.** Slide any new flanges (not on the model shown) and locknuts up the supply pipes, then thread them up the tailpieces and tighten them: with a basin wrench for a metal nut; by hand for a plastic nut. Slide the coupling nuts up the supply pipes and thread them onto the tailpieces *(above)*, then use a basin wrench to tighten them. If you installed a spray attachment, connect it *(step 4)*. Otherwise, restore the water supply *(page 108)*. To flush the faucet, remove the aerator *(page 109)* and fully open the faucet to hot, then cold, for one minute. Reinstall the aerator and tighten any leaking nut.

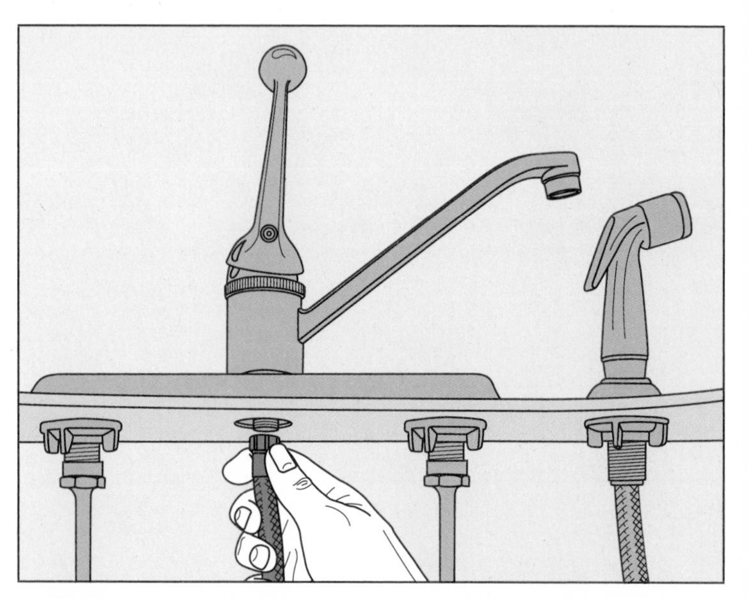

4 **Connecting the spray attachment.** Working under the sink, slide a locknut up the hose of the spray attachment and thread it up the tailpiece of the attachment: tighten a metal nut with a basin wrench; a plastic nut by hand. Then, connect the hose coupling nut to the spout tailpiece on the faucet *(above)*. Restore the water supply to the sink *(page 108)*. To flush the faucet, remove the aerator *(page 109)* and fully open the faucet to hot, then cold, for one minute. Reinstall the aerator. Inspect the coupling nuts; if a nut is leaking, use a basin wrench to tighten it.

CLEARING A CLOGGED DRAIN

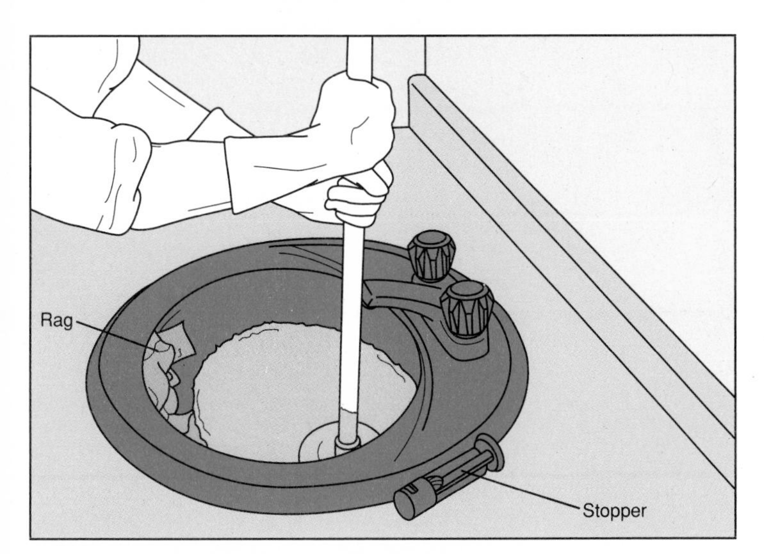

Clearing a sink drain. If the sink has a drain stopper, inspect it. To remove a stopper, open it, then pull it out or turn it and lift it out; if you cannot pull it out, first remove any retaining nut holding it under the sink. Clean a clogged stopper, then reinstall it. If the stopper is not clogged or the sink has no stopper, use a plunger. With any drain stopper removed, block the overflow hole in the sink with a wet rag. If you are clearing a double sink drain, close the drain of the second sink. Fill the sink with 4 to 6 inches of water—enough to cover the cup of a plunger. Wearing rubber gloves, fit the plunger cup over the drain opening, angling it slightly to avoid trapping air. Holding the cup against the sink bottom, pump the plunger up and down vigorously 8 to 10 times *(above)*, then lift it out. If the sink drains freely, reinstall any drain stopper. If plunging does not work, clean the trap *(step below)*.

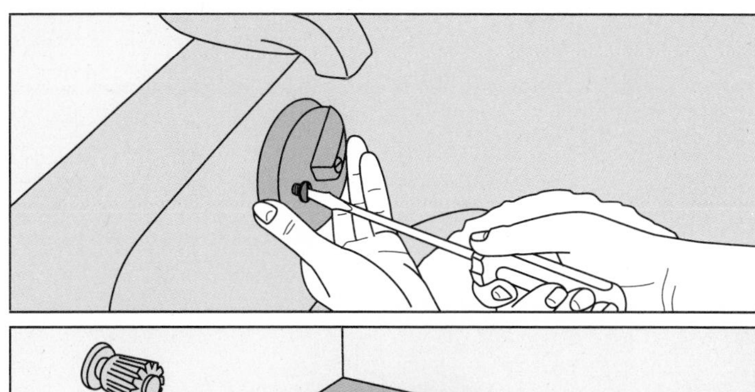

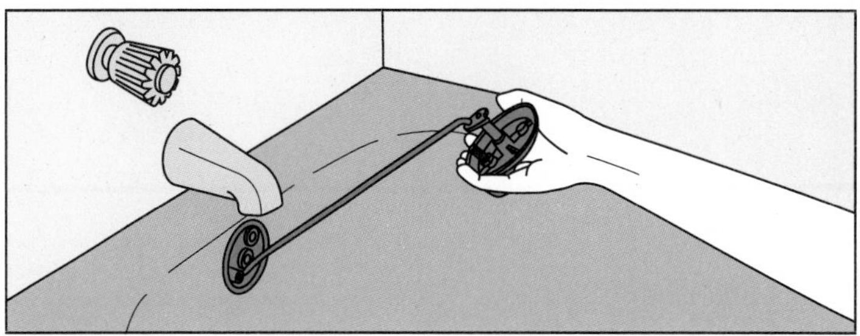

Clearing a bathtub drain. If the tub has a drain stopper, inspect it. To remove a stopper, open it and pull it out, working its rocker arm free of the drain opening; note the orientation of the rocker arm for reassembly. Clean a clogged stopper, then reinstall it. If the drain stopper is not clogged or if the tub has no drain stopper, inspect the overflow hole. Unscrew the overflow plate *(above, top)*, then remove it, pulling the lift assembly out through the overflow hole *(above, bottom)*. Use fine steel wool dampened with vinegar to clean debris off the assembly and plate, and the hole; then, lubricate the lift assembly with petroleum jelly. Reinstall the assembly and plate. If the blockage remains, use a plunger *(step left)*. If plunging does not work, call a plumber.

CLEANING A SINK TRAP

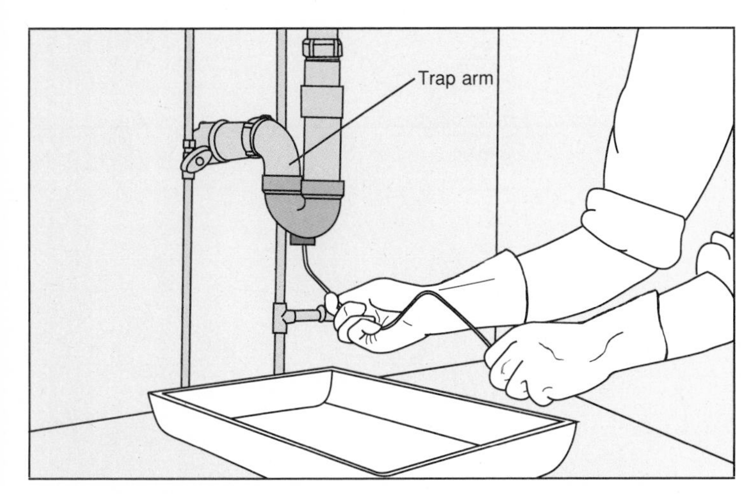

Removing the cleanout plug. If the trap bend below the sink does not have a cleanout plug, remove the trap bend to clean the trap *(step right)*. Otherwise, set a pan or pail under the trap bend to catch water and debris; have rags on hand to wipe up spills. Wearing rubber gloves, use an adjustable wrench to loosen the cleanout plug, then unscrew and remove it by hand. Using a straightened wire coat hanger, probe through the opening into the trap arm to snag and dislodge any debris *(above)*, catching it in the pan or pail. Then, reinstall the cleanout plug and open the sink faucet to flush the trap. If the drain remains blocked, call a plumber.

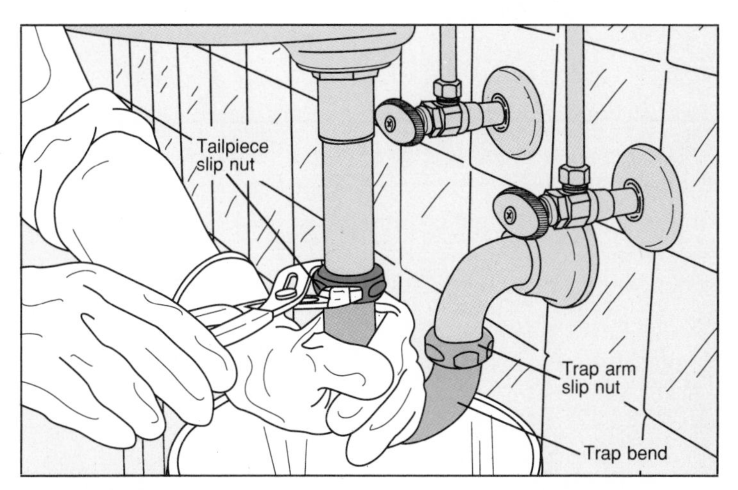

Removing the trap bend. If the trap bend has a cleanout plug, remove it to clean the trap *(step left)*. Otherwise, set a pan or pail under the bend; have rags on hand for spills. Wearing rubber gloves, support the bend with one hand and loosen the tailpiece slip nut with channel-joint pliers *(above)* or an adjustable wrench; then, loosen the trap arm slip nut. If a nut is stuck, apply penetrating oil, wait 15 minutes, and try again. Then, unscrew each nut by hand. Pull off the bend and empty it of water. If necessary, replace the bend or tailpiece *(page 114)*. To clean the bend, scrub it with a bottle brush and rinse it. Then, reinstall the bend and open the sink faucet to flush the trap. Inspect the slip nuts and tighten any leaking nut. If the blockage remains, call a plumber.

SERVICING LEAKING SINK FITTINGS

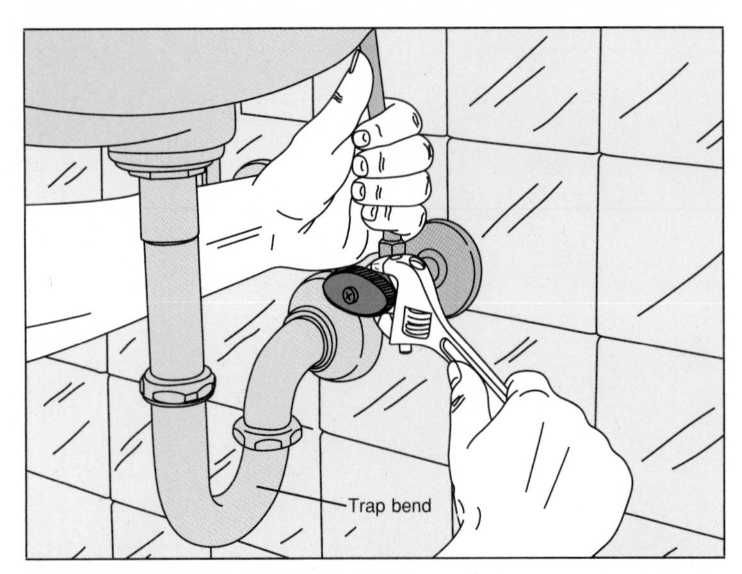

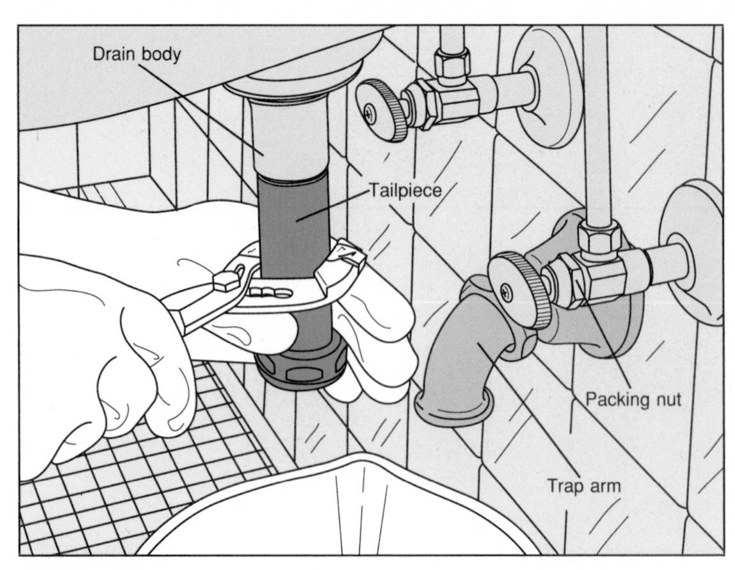

1 Tightening a loose fitting. Inspect the fittings under the sink. If the sink drain body, the trap arm or a water supply pipe is damaged or leaking, call a plumber. If the trap bend or tailpiece is damaged or leaking, replace it *(step 2)*. For a small leak from behind a shutoff valve handle, fit the taped jaws of an adjustable wrench onto the packing nut behind the handle *(above)* and turn slightly clockwise to tighten the nut; take care not to overtighten it. Do the same for a small leak from under a slip nut on the tailpiece or trap arm. If a leak from a tightened nut persists, call a plumber.

2 Replacing a damaged fitting. To replace a damaged trap bend or tailpiece, remove the trap bend *(page 113)*; if the tailpiece is damaged, loosen it with channel-joint pliers *(above)* or an adjustable wrench, then unscrew it by hand from the drain body. Buy an identical replacement tailpiece or trap bend. If you are replacing the tailpiece, install it first, reversing the procedure used to remove it. To install a trap bend, reverse the procedure used to remove the old one. Open the sink faucet to test the drain. Inspect the slip nuts; if a nut leaks, use the pliers or wrench to tighten it.

SERVICING A TOILET FLOAT ASSEMBLY

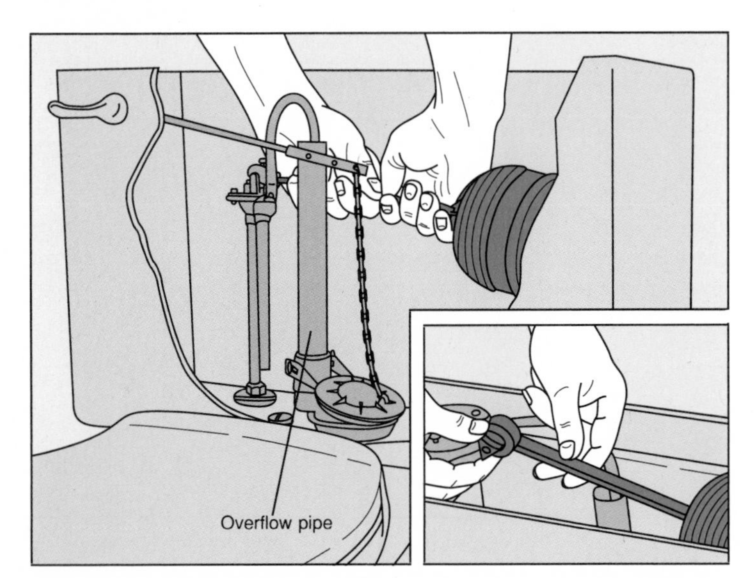

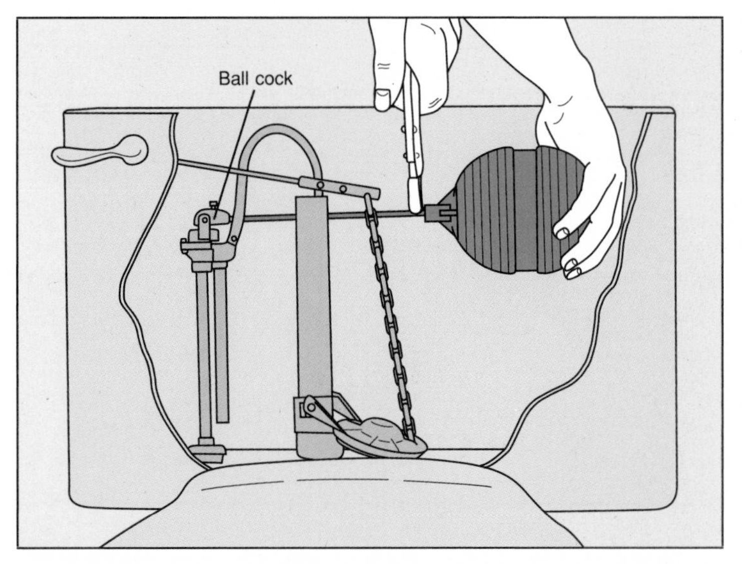

Adjusting the float arm. Remove the tank cover. The water level should be 1/2 to 1 inch below the top of the overflow pipe. If the water is too low, causing an incomplete flush, adjust the float arm to raise the water level. If the water is too high, running down the pipe and into the toilet continuously, inspect the float ball; if it is more than half submerged in water, replace it *(step right)*. Otherwise, adjust the float arm to lower the water level. To adjust a metal float arm, bend the end of the arm down to lower the water level *(above)*; up to raise the water level. To adjust a plastic float arm, turn the adjusting knob at the ball cock *(inset)* to lower or raise the arm. Put back the tank cover. If the problem persists, replace the float assembly *(page 116)*.

Replacing the float assembly or float ball. Shut off the water supply to the toilet *(page 108)*. Remove the tank cover. To remove the float ball, use locking pliers to hold the float arm steady and unscrew the ball from it *(above)*; if you cannot unscrew the ball, remove the float assembly. To remove the float assembly, follow the manufacturer's instructions for your toilet to detach the end of the float arm from the ball cock; then, lift out the arm and float ball. To replace the float assembly or float ball, buy an identical part; then, install it by reversing the steps used to remove it. Restore the water supply to the toilet *(page 108)*. Check the tank water level; if necessary, adjust the float arm *(step left)*. Put back the tank cover.

SERVICING A TOILET FLUSH ASSEMBLY

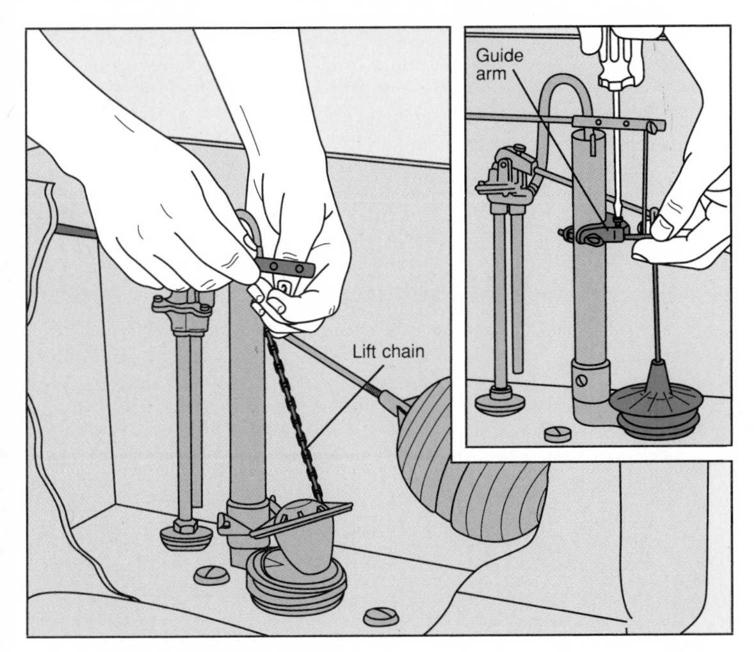

Adjusting the lift chain. Remove the tank cover. The lift chain should hang straight with 1 inch of slack at the bottom. Straighten a tangled chain. If the chain is too short and water runs continuously, replace it; unhook the old chain from the trip lever and flapper valve, buy a new chain of the correct length, and hook it in place. If the chain is too long, causing a slugggish or incomplete flush, shorten it; unhook the chain from the trip lever hole and hook it to a higher hole in the lever *(above)*. Or, replace the chain with one of the correct length. To adjust the length of the lift wire on an older toilet, loosen the guide arm screw and slide the guide arm *(inset)*: up to shorten the wire; down to lengthen it. Then, retighten the screw and put back the tank cover.

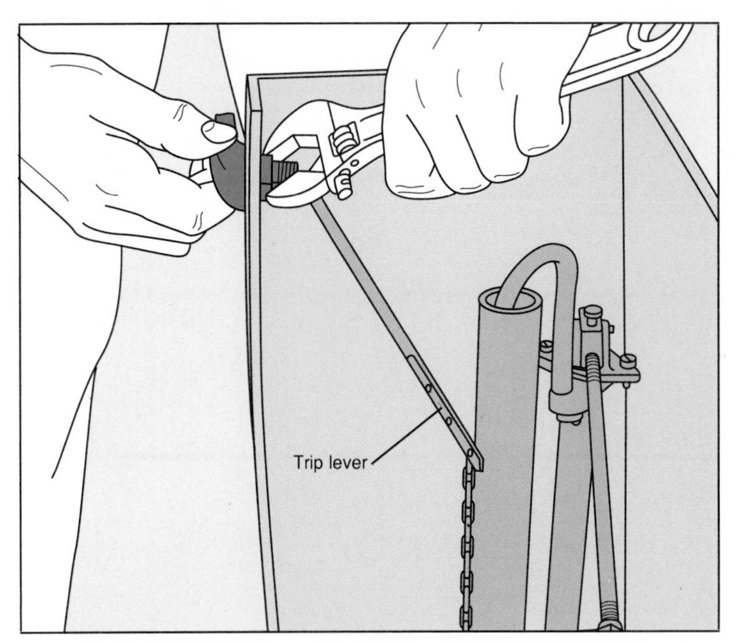

Adjusting the handle. Remove the tank cover. If the handle is loose, tighten it; if it sticks due to a buildup of deposits, remove and clean it. To tighten the handle, use an adjustable wrench to turn the locknut counterclockwise *(above)* until it is flush with the tank wall; if you cannot turn it, apply penetrating oil, wait 15 minutes, and try again. To remove and clean the handle, unhook the lift chain from the trip lever; then, use an adjustable wrench to turn the locknut clockwise to loosen it. Unscrew the locknut from the handle threads and slide it off the trip lever. Pull the handle and trip lever out of the tank. Use an old toothbrush dampened with vinegar to scrub the handle threads, then reinstall the handle. Put back the tank cover.

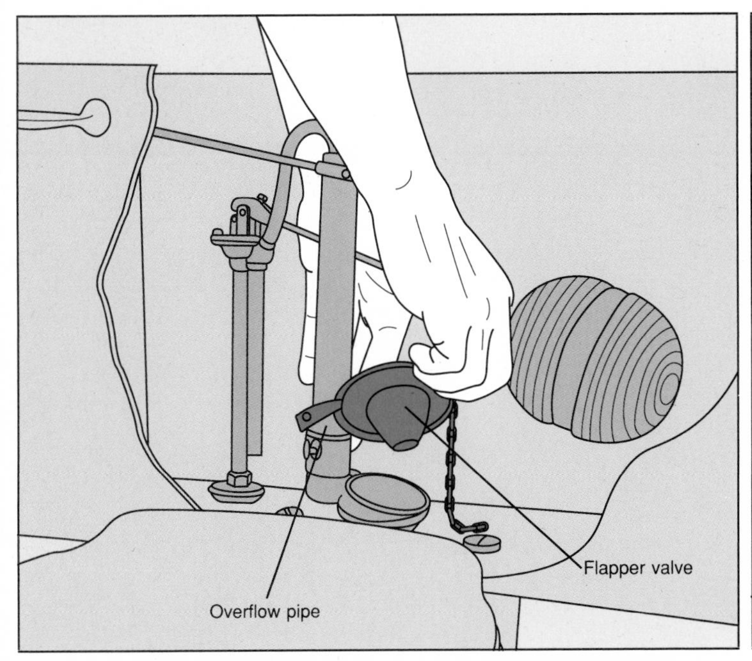

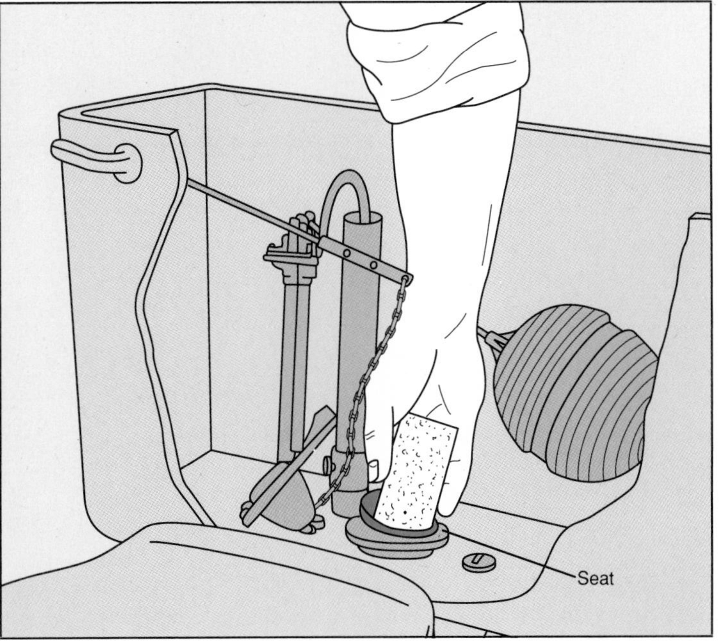

Servicing the flapper valve. Remove the tank cover. If the flapper valve is damaged, replace it; if the valve seat is encrusted with deposits that prevent the flapper valve from closing, clean it. Shut off the toilet water supply *(page 108)*. To replace the flapper valve, unhook the lift chain from the trip lever; then, following the instructions for your model of toilet, unhook the valve from the overflow pipe *(above, left)*. Buy an identical replacement valve and chain, and install them by reversing the steps used to remove the old ones. To clean the valve seat, unhook the valve from the overflow pipe. Gently scrub deposits from the seat with emery cloth *(above, right)* or fine steel wool; then, reattach the valve. If the valve still does not close snugly, replace it. Restore the water supply to the toilet and put back the tank cover *(page 108)*.

REPLACING A TOILET BALL COCK

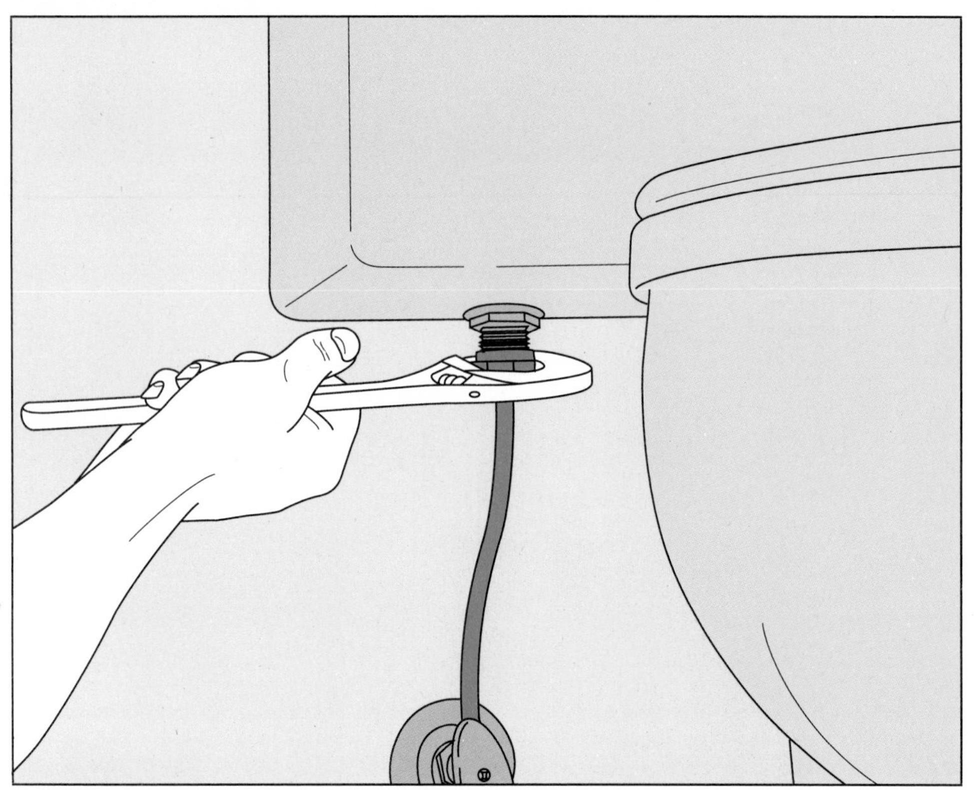

1 Loosening the coupling nut. If the toilet continues to run continuously or flush incompletely after servicing the float assembly or flush assembly, replace the ball cock. Shut off the water supply to the toilet *(page 108)*. Remove the tank cover. Set a pan or pail under the water supply pipe to catch water and debris. Using a sponge, sop up any water left in the bottom of the tank. Working below the tank, use an adjustable wrench to loosen the coupling nut between the ball cock tailpiece and the supply pipe *(above)*; if you cannot turn the nut, apply penetrating oil, wait overnight, and try again. Slide the loosened nut down the supply pipe and gently bend the supply pipe to one side.

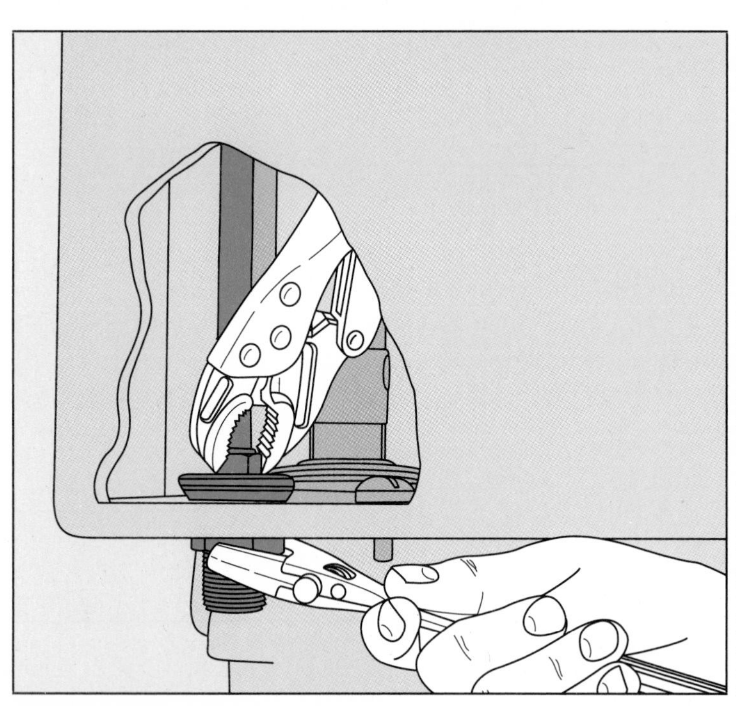

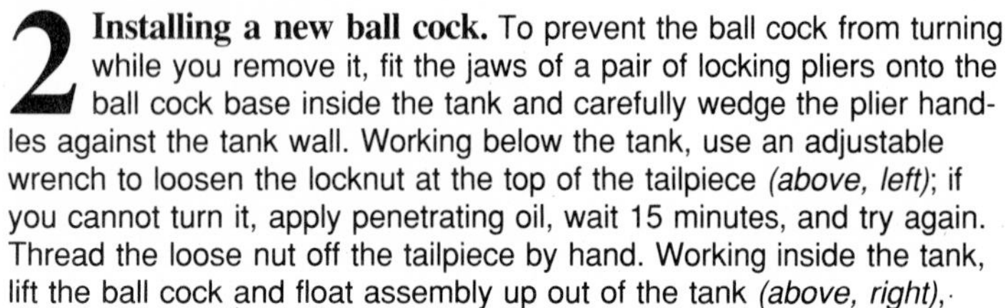

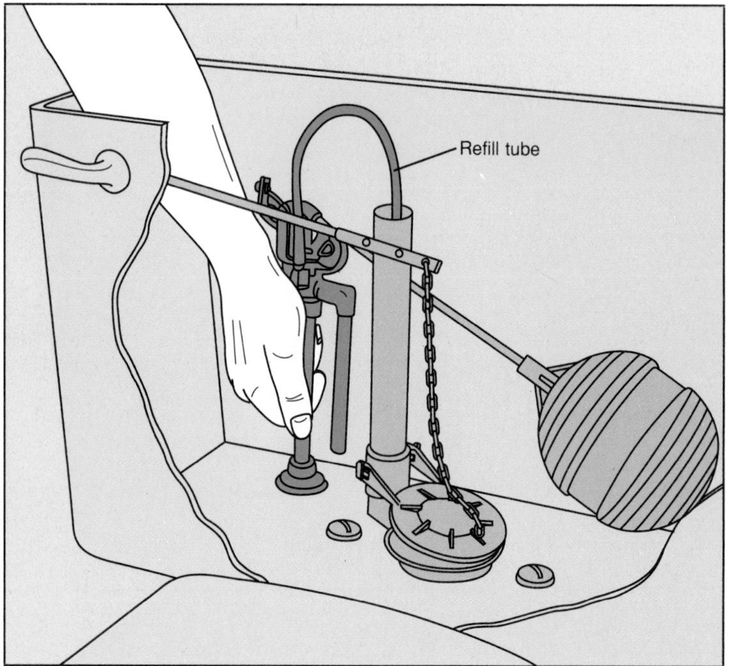

2 Installing a new ball cock. To prevent the ball cock from turning while you remove it, fit the jaws of a pair of locking pliers onto the ball cock base inside the tank and carefully wedge the plier handles against the tank wall. Working below the tank, use an adjustable wrench to loosen the locknut at the top of the tailpiece *(above, left)*; if you cannot turn it, apply penetrating oil, wait 15 minutes, and try again. Thread the loose nut off the tailpiece by hand. Working inside the tank, lift the ball cock and float assembly up out of the tank *(above, right)*, pulling the refill tube out of the overflow pipe. Then, following the instructions for your model, detach the float assembly and refill tube from the ball cock. Buy an identical replacement ball cock and install it by reversing the steps used to remove the old ball cock; then, reinstall the refill tube and float assembly. Reconnect the supply pipe to the ball cock tailpiece. Put back the tank cover and slowly restore the water supply to the toilet *(page 108)*. Flush the toilet, then check the water level and adjust the float arm, if necessary *(page 114)*.

HEATING AND COOLING

Heating and cooling costs represent some of the highest operating expenses that a homeowner faces. While your heating or cooling system may not be the focal point of a potential buyer's interest, a well-maintained system, no matter its type or age, signifies care and efficiency—qualities that can earn notice as translating into low monthly bills.

Central heating systems have three basic components: the heat producer—the furnace where energy is converted to heat; the heat exchanger—the furnace or boiler where heat is transferred to air or water; and a distribution system of ducts and registers, or pipes and radiators or convectors. Central cooling sytems may use a heat pump or a central air conditioning unit to cool the home, using the same distribution system employed by the heating system. This chapter focuses on servicing the most accessible areas of each system—such as the furnace *(page 121, 122)*, the air ducts *(page 119)* and radiators or convectors *(page 121)*. For other areas that require servicing, consult a heating and cooling professional.

Use the Troubleshooting Guide below as a checklist as you inspect the various units that make up your heating and cooling systems. Clearly label the main shutoff valves and any unit disconnect switch *(page 118)*. Look behind panels, vacuum dust and wipe surfaces clean. In some instances, you may not notice a problem until you actually remove a covering panel—as in the case of a dirty blower compartment on the furnace *(page 121)*. But a thorough home inspector will be alert to signs of neglect or deterioration.

Replace a worn furnace blower belt *(page 122)*, wash or replace a dirty furnace filter *(page 122)*, and clean the evaporator pad and water tray in a central humidifier *(page 123)*. If a window air conditioner is included in the sale of the house, clean or replace the filter, straighten bent vent fins and remove any debris *(page 124)*. Get your heating and cooling systems operating at their peak level of performance and avoid unpleasant surprises when a home inspector comes in on behalf of a would-be buyer.

TROUBLESHOOTING GUIDE

SYMPTOM	PROCEDURE
Air duct register or boot dirty	Clean register and duct boot *(p. 119)* □○
Air duct register vanes bent	Straighten vanes of register *(p. 119)* □○
Air duct hanger loose	Resecure duct hanger *(p. 119)* □○
Air duct joint leaking	Seal duct joint *(p. 119)* □○
Air duct rattles or shakes	Resecure duct hanger and seal duct joint *(p. 119)* □○
Baseboard heater dirty	Clean baseboard heater *(p. 120)* ⬓○
Convector dirty	Clean convector *(p. 120)* □○
Water pipe, radiator or convector emits gurgling sound	Bleed radiator or convector *(p. 121)* □○
Radiator or convector not bled since end of last heating season	Bleed radiator or convector *(p. 121)* □○
Furnace generates dusty air, musty odor	Clean furnace *(p. 121)* □○; service filter *(p. 122)* □○
Furnace dirty	Clean furnace *(p. 121)* □○
Furnace squeals slightly	Service blower belt *(p. 122)* ⬓○
Furnace filter dirty or damaged	Service filter *(p. 122)* □○
Humidifier generates dry air	Service humidifier *(p. 123)* □○
Humidifier dirty	Service humidifier *(p. 123)* □○
Fireplace dirty; bricks stained	Clean fireplace *(p. 124)* □○
Window air conditioner filter dirty or damaged	Clean or replace filter *(p. 124)* □○
Window air conditioner vents clogged or damaged	Service vents *(p. 124)* □○
Heat pump (outdoor unit) condenser coil fins clogged or bent	Service heat pump *(p. 125)* □○
Central air conditioner (outdoor unit) condenser coil fins clogged or bent	Service central air conditioner *(p. 125)* □○
System shutoff valve unlabeled	Label shutoff valve *(p. 118)* □○
Unit disconnect switch unlabeled	Label unit disconnect switch *(p. 118)* □○

DEGREE OF DIFFICULTY: □ **Easy** ⬓ **Moderate** ■ **Complex**
ESTIMATED TIME: ○ **Less than 1 hour** ◒ **1 to 3 hours** ● **Over 3 hours**

LABELING SYSTEM SHUTOFF VALVES

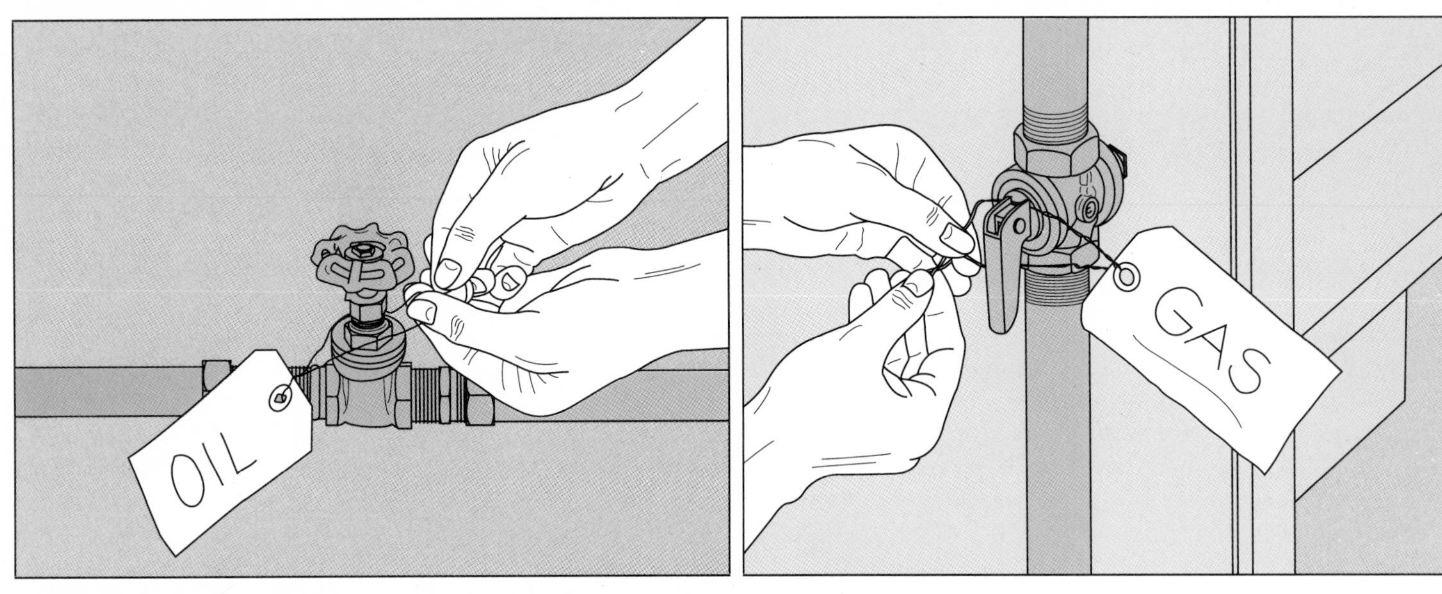

Locating and tagging shutoff valves. All system shutoff valves should be clearly labeled, evidence of a well-maintained system—and enabling a quick response by anyone in the event of an emergency. To label a shutoff valve, write the name of the system on a tag with a waterproof marker and tie the tag around the valve handle or lever. Oil furnace and boiler shutoff valves are operated by faucet-type handles *(above, left)*; gas shutoff valves are operated by levers *(above, right)*. Locate an oil system's shutoff valve on the oil supply pipe at the bottom of the furnace or boiler near the oil filter bowl. Locate a gas system's shutoff valve on the gas supply pipe next to the furnace or boiler. If the heat in your home is distributed by water, locate the water system's shutoff valve on the water supply pipe leading to the boiler.

SHUTTING OFF POWER TO A HEATING OR COOLING UNIT

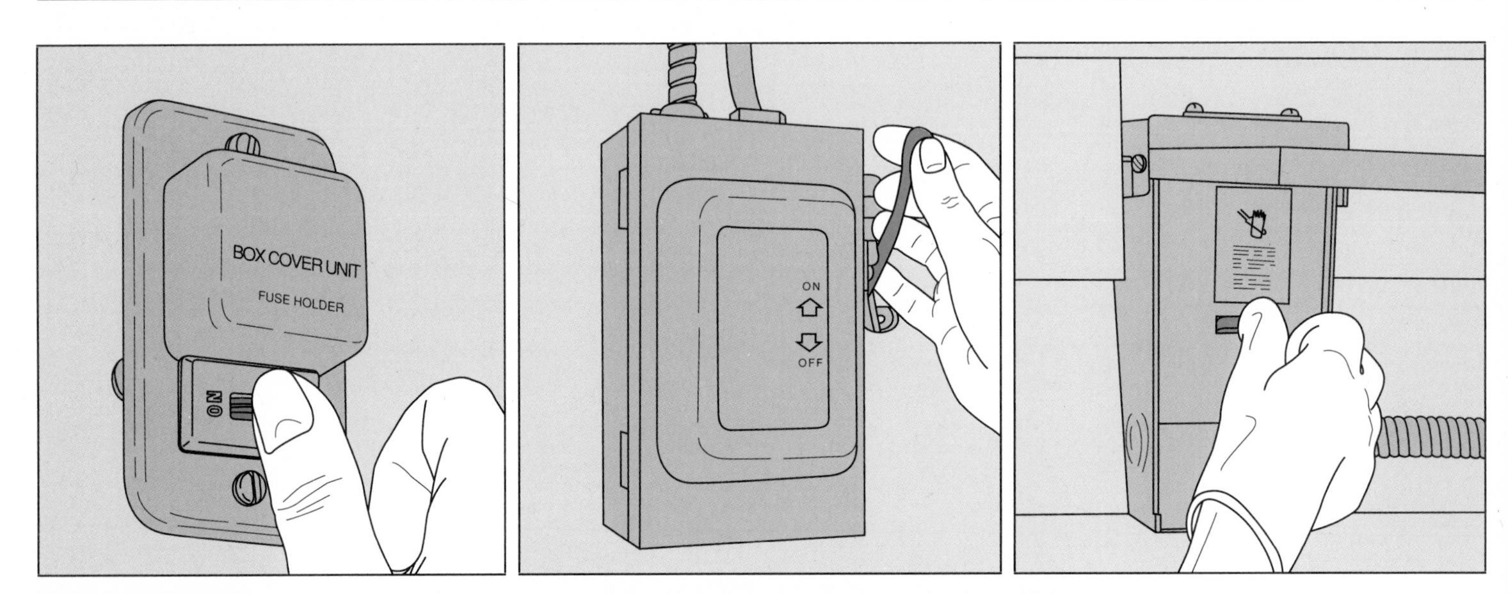

Turning off the power. Turn off the electrical power to the heating or cooling unit first at the main service panel *(page 96)*, then at the disconnect switch—if the unit has one. Locate the disconnect switch on or near the unit: for a furnace or boiler, typically indoors; for a heat pump or central air conditioning unit, often outdoors. If the area around the disconnect switch is wet or damp, stand on a dry board or wear rubber boots; also wear rubber gloves. At an indoor disconnect switch, use one hand to flip the toggle *(above, left)* or shift the lever *(above, center)* to OFF. At an outdoor disconnect switch, lift up the weatherproof cover, then use one hand to flip the toggle to OFF *(above, right)*. After servicing the heating or cooling unit, restore the electrical power first at any disconnect switch and then at the main service panel; ensure that the weatherproof cover of an exterior disconnect switch is closed securely. If the disconnect switch is not clearly labeled, write the name of the system on a tag with a waterproof marker and stick the tag to the box of the disconnect switch.

SERVICING AN AIR DUCT

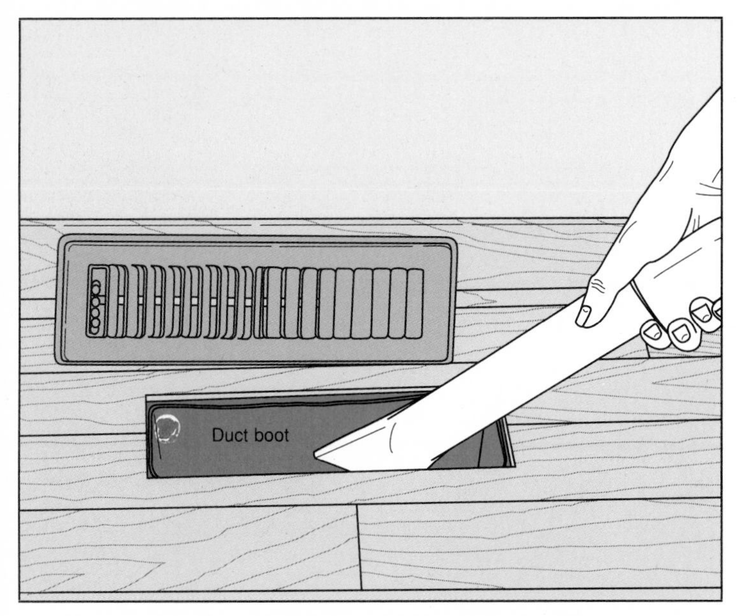

Cleaning a register and duct boot. If the heating system is in operation, lower the thermostat and allow the register to cool before you touch it. Use a vacuum cleaner with a narrow attachment to remove dust and dirt from the top of the register. To vacuum the bottom of the register and the walls of the duct boot, unscrew and remove the register; reach as far as you can into the duct with the vacuum attachment *(above)*. Reposition the register on the duct opening and screw it in place securely. If a vane is bent or twisted, straighten it *(step right)*.

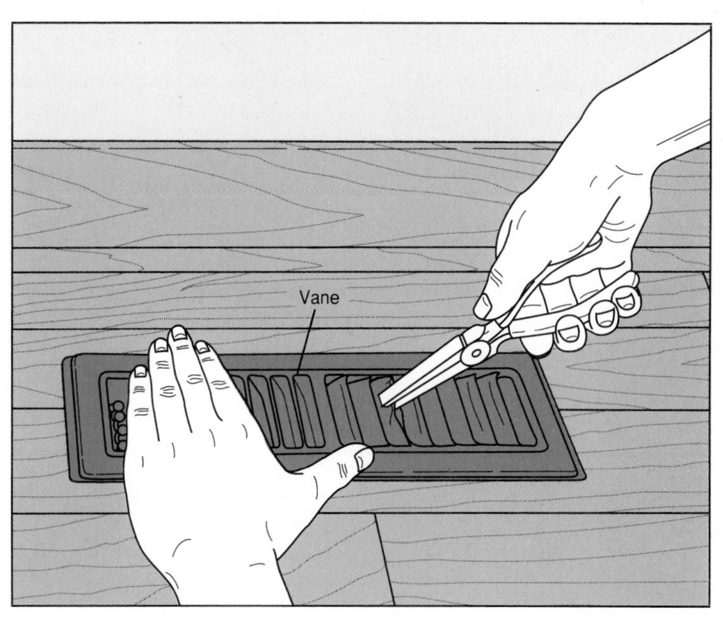

Straightening the vanes of a register. Inspect the vanes of a register for damage; if the heating system is in operation, lower the thermostat and allow the register to cool before you touch it. To straighten a bent or twisted vane, hold the register down with one hand and use long-nose pliers to gently bend the vane back into shape. Work from the outside edges of the vane toward the center of it *(above)* until it is aligned with the vane on each side of it. If the register or duct boot is dusty or dirty, clean it *(step left)*.

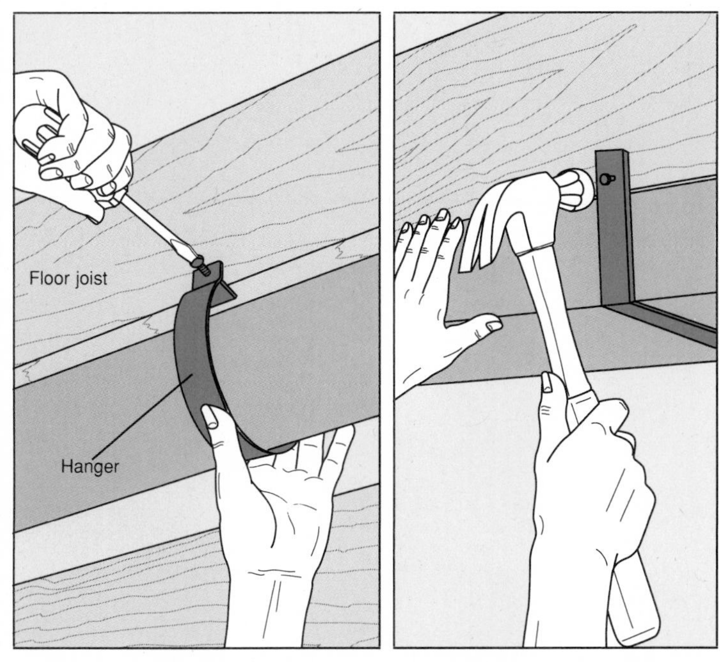

Resecuring a loose duct hanger. Air ducts are usually exposed in an unfinished basement. Look for loose or damaged duct hangers that may cause ducts to sag away from the joists. If a hanger on a round duct is loose, tighten the screws securing it to the floor joist *(above, left)*; use a stepladder *(page 137)*, if necessary. Resecure a loose hanger on a rectangular duct by nailing it back to the floor joist *(above, right)*.

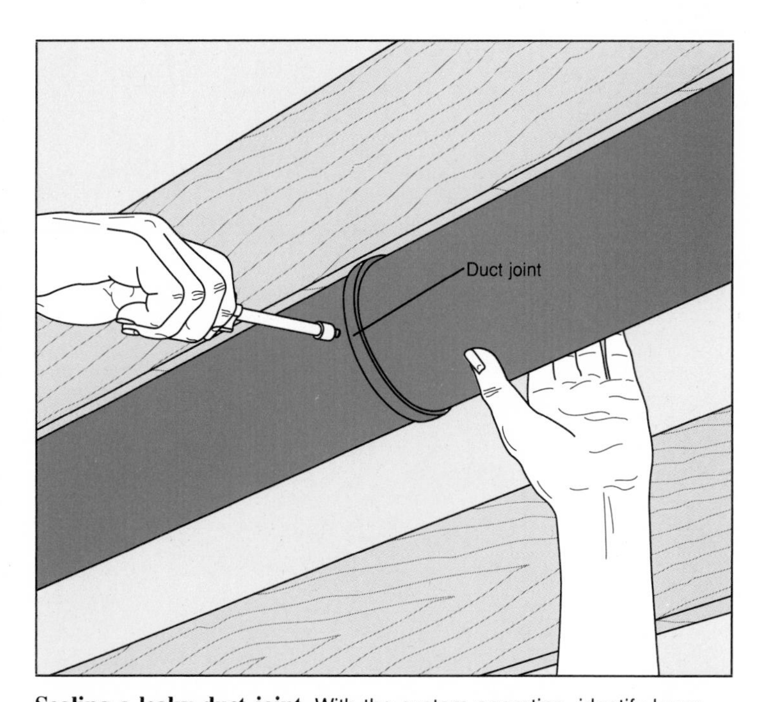

Sealing a leaky duct joint. With the system operating, identify loose or noisy duct joints in the basement. If air is leaking from a rectangular duct joint which is secured by sheet metal cleats, wrap several layers of duct tape neatly around the joint to seal it. If air is leaking from a round duct joint, first tighten any loose screws at the joint with a nutdriver *(above)*, then wrap duct tape neatly around the joint to seal it.

CLEANING A BASEBOARD HEATER OR A CONVECTOR

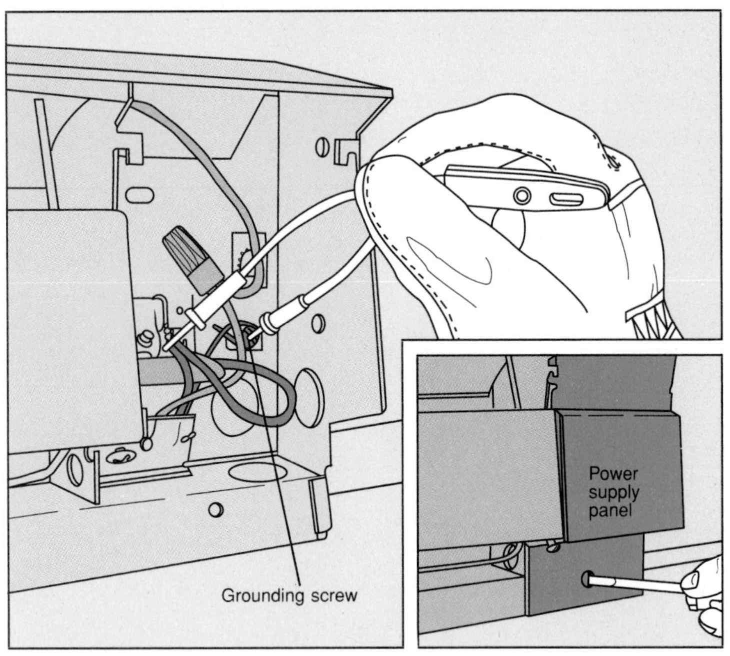

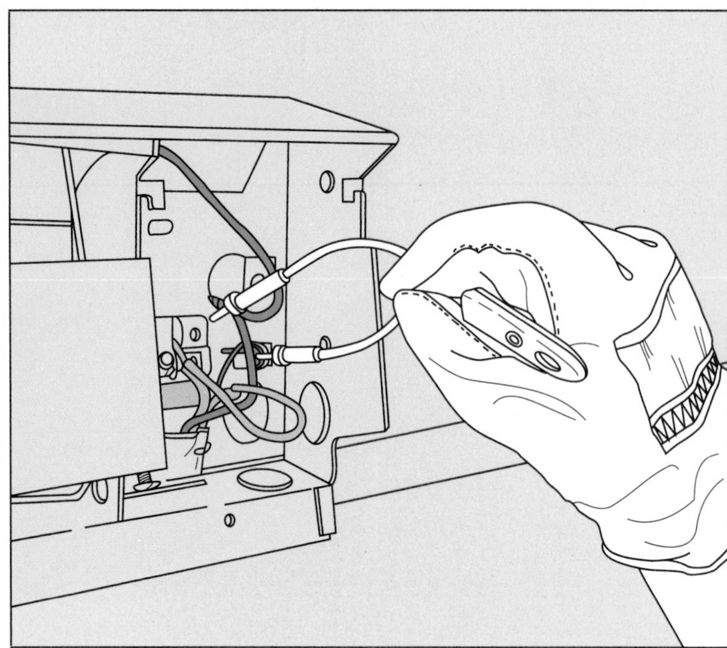

1 Testing to confirm the power is off. To clean a convector, remove the front panel *(step 2)*. Before cleaning a baseboard heater, turn off the electrical power to the circuit for it at the main service panel *(page 96)*. Then, unscrew and remove the power supply panel at one end of the heater *(inset)*. Using a voltage tester, conduct three tests to confirm that the power to the heater is off; wear insulated gloves. First, unscrew the wire cap connecting the black line-voltage wire to one of the heater element wires. Working with one hand, hold the tester by the insulation and carefully touch one probe to the uncapped wires and the other probe to the grounding screw *(above, left)*. Next, remove the other wire cap and repeat the test with its wires and the grounding screw *(above, right)*. Finally, touch a probe to each uncapped wire connection. If the power is off, the tester will not glow in any test. If the tester glows, shut off power to the correct circuit and repeat the tests. When you confirm that the power is off, reinstall the wire caps and the power supply panel.

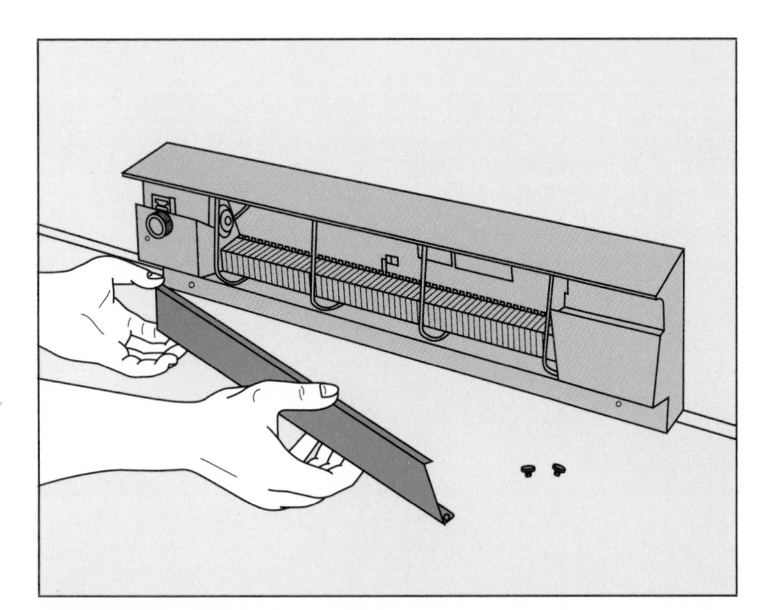

2 Removing the front panel. Remove any retaining screws holding the front panel of the heater in place; on the model of heater shown, use an offset screwdriver. If the heater has a separate control box panel and power supply panel at the ends of it, leave them in place. If the heater has retaining clips instead of retaining screws, remove them and set them aside. Lift the front panel off the heater carefully to avoid bending it *(above)*. Remove the front panel of a convector the same way, then stand it against the wall.

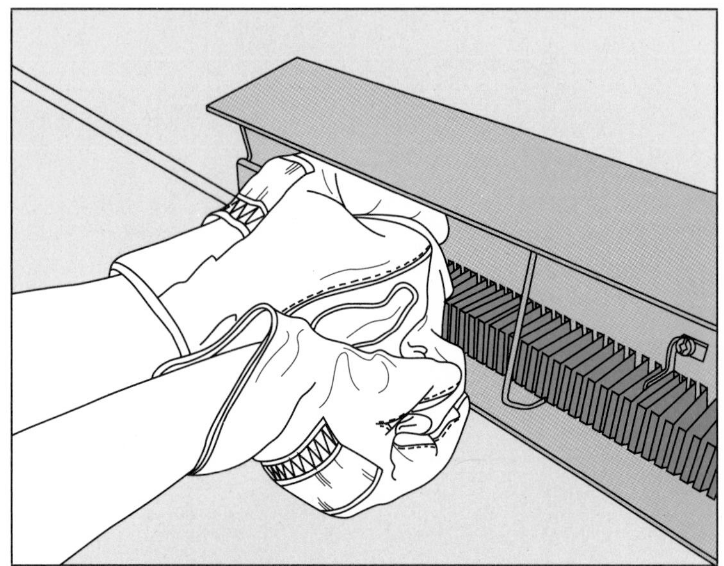

3 Cleaning the heat transfer fins. Wearing work gloves, gently brush the heat transfer fins with a dry paintbrush to loosen accumulated dust and dirt. Use a vacuum cleaner with a narrow attachment to remove dislodged particles. If the dust and dirt buildup is heavy, wipe the surface of each fin with a damp rag *(above)*. Use broad-billed pliers to carefully straighten any bent fin. Reinstall the front panel; for a baseboard heater, then restore the electrical power to the circuit for it at the main service panel *(page 96)*.

BLEEDING A RADIATOR OR A CONVECTOR

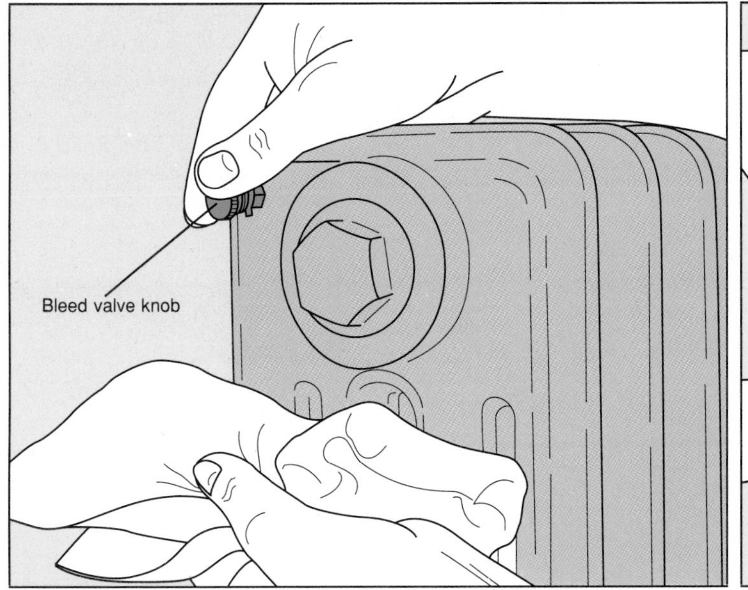

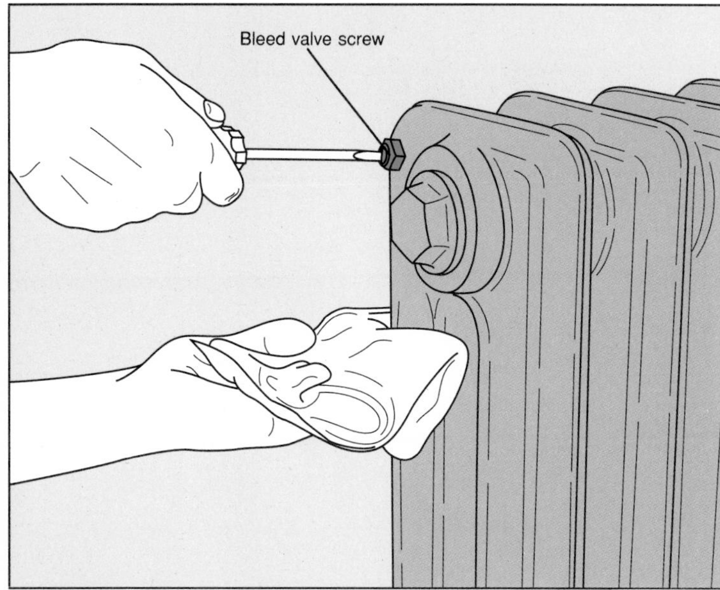

Clearing a bleed valve. Opening the bleed valves on radiators and convectors allows any trapped air to escape. Begin with the radiators or convectors on the top floor of your house and work down. Have an absorbent rag handy; when the air is vented, water will escape from the valve. Radiator bleed valves are on top of the radiator; reach convector bleed valves by unscrewing and removing the front panel. If a bleed valve is sealed with paint, wear rubber gloves and use a clean cloth moistened with mineral spirits to remove the paint. If there is a bleed valve knob, turn it counterclockwise to open the valve *(above, left)*. On other models, use a screwdriver to turn the screw and open the valve *(above, right)*. As soon as water escapes in a steady stream, the air has been bled; close the valve. Put back any front panel you removed.

CLEANING A FURNACE

1 Cleaning the furnace housing. Turn off power to the furnace *(page 118)*. If the furnace has been operating, allow it to cool. Wearing rubber gloves, use a clean cloth and a solution of 1/2 cup trisodium phosphate (TSP) per gallon of water to wash the furnace housing *(above)*. Wipe the housing dry with a soft cloth. Clean the exhaust stack of a gas furnace the same way. Wash the floor around the furnace with a solution of 1 cup household detergent per gallon of water; for stains, use the TSP solution. For any stubborn stain, use a solution of a higher TSP concentration. Clean off any rust spots with steel wool.

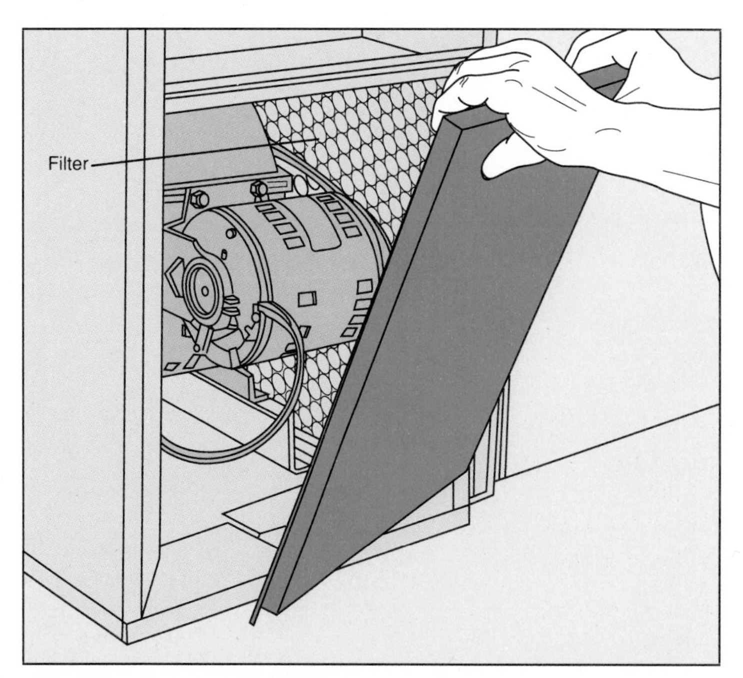

2 Cleaning inside the furnace. Remove the blower access panel at the bottom of the furnace—usually there is a maintenance label on it. On some models, the panel may be pulled off; on other models, it must be unscrewed, then pulled off *(above)*. Using a vacuum cleaner with a brush attachment, clean the blower housing and motor, if accessible, as well as the floor and walls of the blower compartment. Service the blower belt and air filter *(page 122)*. Otherwise, put back the panel and restore the power to the furnace *(page 118)*.

SERVICING A FURNACE BLOWER BELT

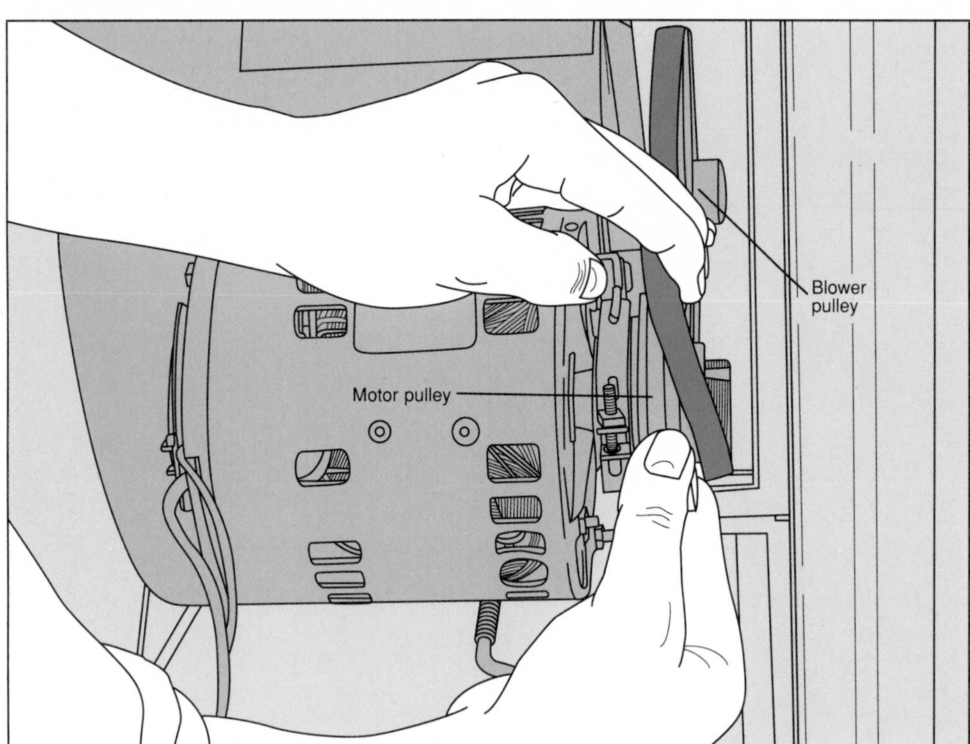

Inspecting and replacing the blower belt. Turn off power to the furnace *(page 118)* and remove the blower access panel as you would to clean inside the furnace *(page 121)*. Inspect the blower belt and test its tension. Push down on the belt midway between the pulleys until it is taut; it should slacken about 1 inch. If the belt slackens more than 1 inch or it is cracked, brittle or worn, replace it.

To remove the belt, push it over the top of the outer lip on the motor pulley with your thumb; if the belt is hard to remove, use your other hand to turn the pulley counterclockwise. Purchase a replacement belt at a building supply center; take the old belt with you. To install the new belt, place it over the blower pulley. Holding the belt in the top groove of the motor pulley with one hand, turn the pulley counterclockwise with the other hand to slip the belt onto it *(left)*. Reinstall the panel and restore the power to the furnace *(page 118)*.

SERVICING A FURNACE FILTER

Servicing an electronic filter. Turn off power to the furnace *(page 118)*. Locate the filter door panel at the bottom of the furnace and pull it open *(inset)*. Slide the filter out of its retainer sleeve *(above)*, pushing aside any retaining spring tabs. If the filter is dirty, wash it using a solution of mild household detergent and water; rinse it and let it dry. Or, wash the filter in a dishwasher, removing it before the drying cycle; run the dishwasher empty through another cycle before you use it again. If the filter is damaged, buy an exact replacement at a building supply center. Slide the filter into place, close the door panel and restore the power to the furnace.

Servicing a non-electronic filter. Turn off power to the furnace *(page 118)*. Locate the filter in the slot between the return duct and the blower, then slide it out *(above)*. On some furnaces, you may have to remove the blower access panel as you would to clean inside the furnace *(page 121)*, then pull out the filter. Clean a metal or foam filter with water, using a high-pressure nozzle on a garden hose; let the filter drip dry. Replace a dirty fiberglass filter. If a metal, foam or fiberglass filter is damaged, buy an exact replacement at a building supply center. Slide the filter into place, reinstall any access panel you removed and restore the power to the furnace.

SERVICING A CENTRAL HUMIDIFIER

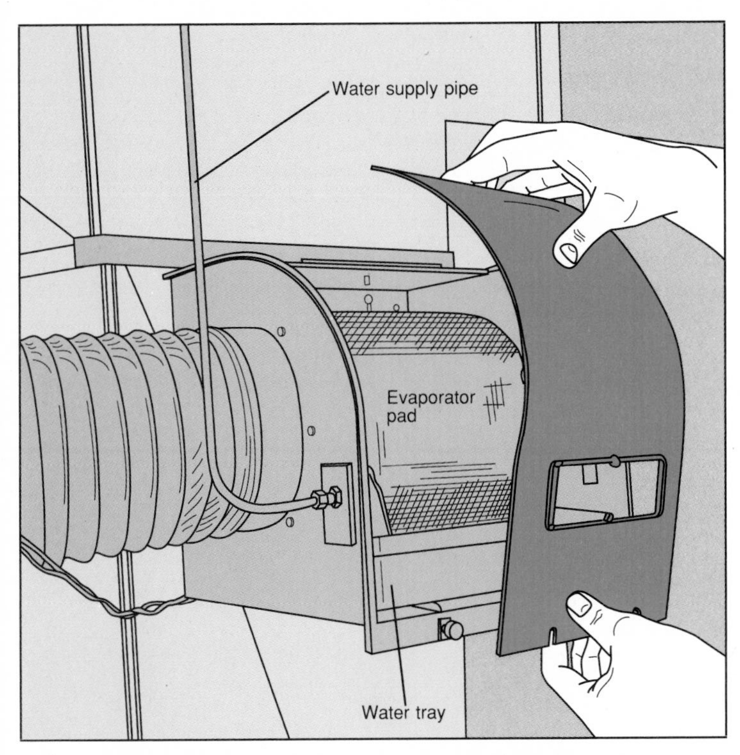

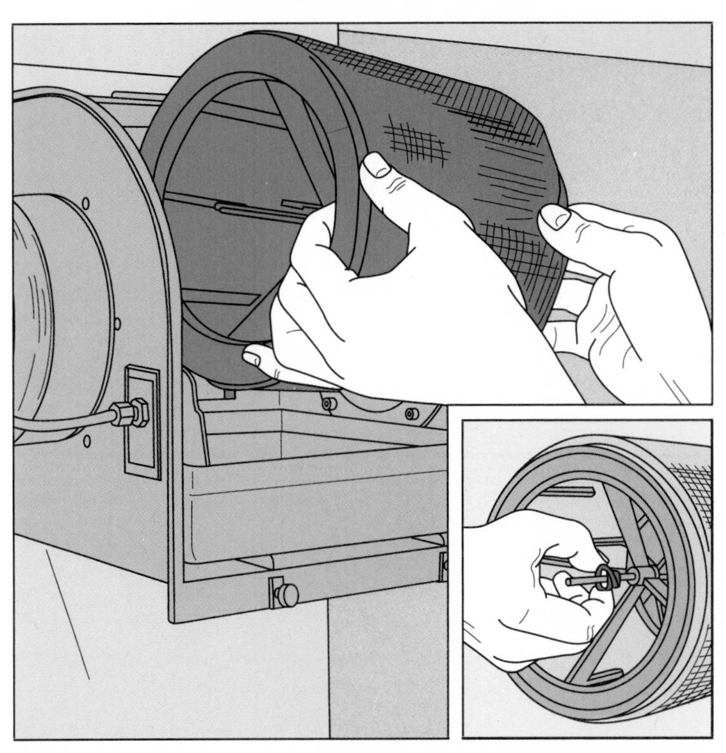

1 Removing the humidifier cover. Central humidifiers are usually mounted on ducts near the furnace. Turn off power to the furnace *(page 118)*, then locate the water pipe that supplies the humidifier and close the shutoff valve on it. Loosen the retaining nuts on the bottom of the humidifier cover and lift off the cover *(above)*. To clean or replace the evaporator pad or clean the water tray, take out the evaporator drum *(step 2)*.

2 Taking out the evaporator drum. To remove the evaporator drum, grasp both ends and lift the shaft out of its slots in the humidifier housing *(above)*. Release the evaporator pad from the drum by pinching the drum-shaft retaining clip *(inset)*; slide the pad off the shaft. Pull apart the drum section and evaporator pad. If the pad is slightly hardened, soak it in a solution of 3 parts vinegar and 1 part water until it softens, squeezing the solution through it. If the pad does not soften or has deteriorated, buy an exact replacement at a building supply center. Reassemble the evaporator drum.

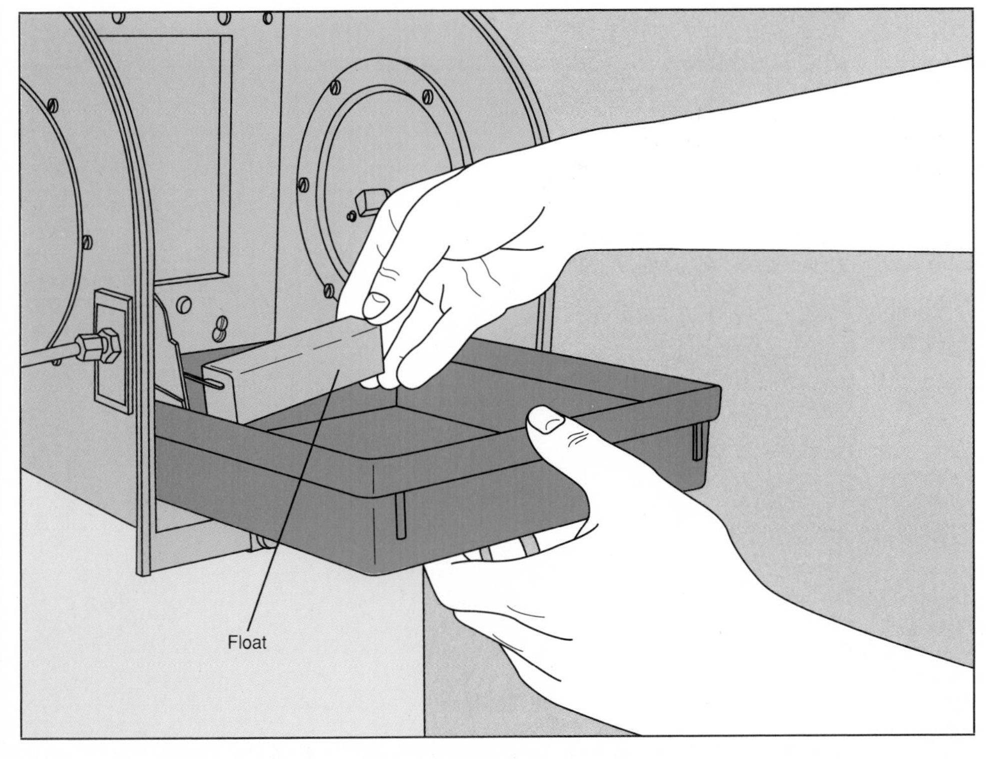

3 Cleaning the water tray. Lift the float at the back of the water tray and pull out the tray *(left)*. Wash the tray using a stiff-bristled brush and a solution of 3 parts vinegar and 1 part water; rinse it thoroughly. To inhibit mineral buildup and bacterial growth in the water, add a water-treatment preparation, available in either a liquid or tablet form at a hardware store or building supply center; follow the manufacturer's instructions. Reinstall the tray and the evaporator drum, then put back the humidifier cover. Open the shutoff valve on the water supply pipe to the humidifier and restore the power to the furnace *(page 118)*.

CLEANING A FIREPLACE

Sweeping the hearth. Before cleaning a fireplace, make sure that any fire is completely extinguished and the ashes are cool. Lift the log rest out of the fireplace. Use a fireplace broom to sweep ashes onto a metal shovel *(left)*. Place the ashes in a metal container, then cover the container and store it outdoors until it can be disposed of. To clean dirt, grime and smoke stains off the fireplace bricks, first protect the surrounding floor with newspaper. Wearing rubber gloves and safety goggles, scrub the bricks with a stiff-bristled brush and a household scouring powder; for stubborn stains, use a solution of 1/2 cup trisodium phosphate (TSP) and 1/2 cup household detergent per gallon of water. After sweeping the hearth and cleaning the bricks, put back the log rest and lay a fire; if prospective buyers are viewing your home on a cold winter day, consider lighting the fire before they arrive.

SERVICING A WINDOW AIR CONDITIONER

Inspecting and cleaning the air filter. Unplug the air conditioner, then unscrew and remove the front panel; if it is secured by clips, grip its sides and snap it off *(above)*. The filter is usually located in front of the evaporator coils or on the back of the front panel; unfasten the retaining clips and remove it. If the filter is damaged, buy a replacement at a building supply center; replace a dirty fiberglass filter. Clean a dirty panel and plastic or metal filter by vacuuming dirt with a brush attachment, then washing with a solution of mild household detergent and water; rinse the filter thoroughly and shake it dry. Fit the filter into place and reinstall the panel, then plug in the air conditioner.

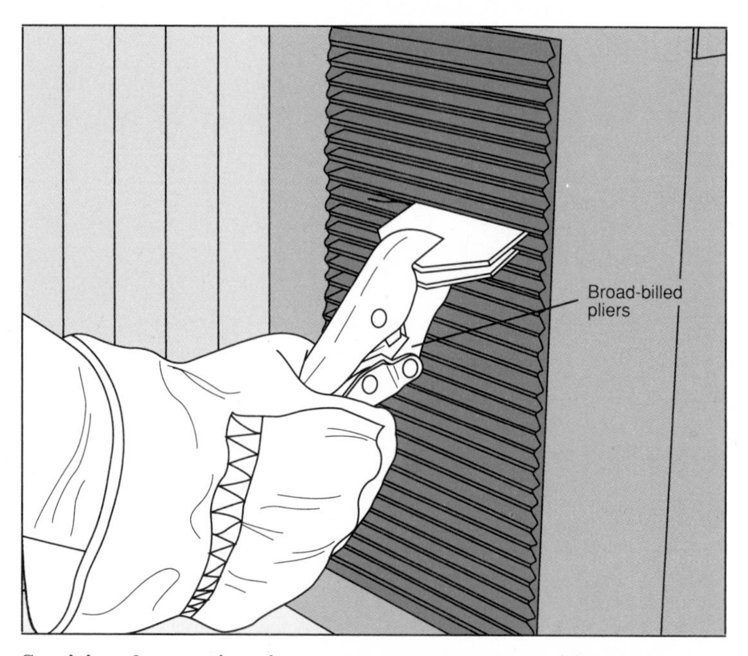

Servicing the exterior air vents. Unplug the air conditioner, then go outdoors to clean out its air vents. Remove leaves, twigs, dust and debris caught in the slots between the air vents with long-nose pliers; if the air conditioner is in the window of an upper story, use a ladder *(page 137)* to reach it. Wearing work gloves, use broad-billed pliers to straighten any bent air vents on the back panel *(above)*; if there is no back panel and the condenser coil fins are exposed, straighten any bent fins using a multi-headed fin comb—available at a building supply center. Go back indoors to plug in the air conditioner.

SERVICING A HEAT PUMP OR A CENTRAL AIR CONDITIONER

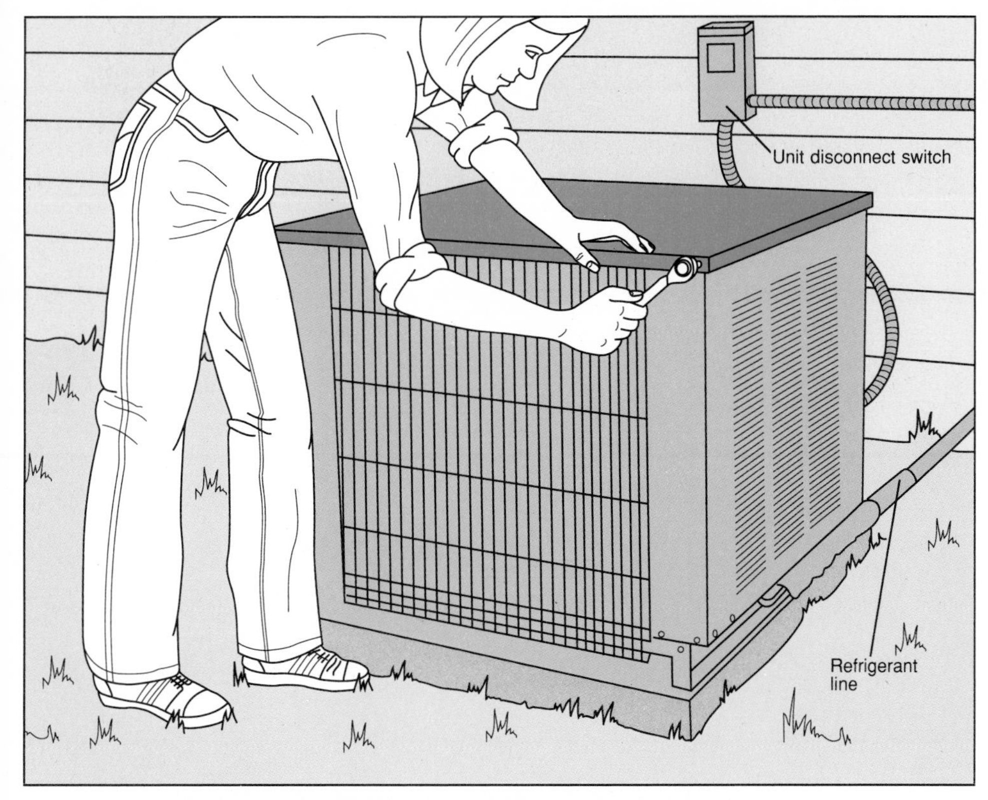

1 Removing the top panel. Turn off power to the unit *(page 118)*, then clear the area around it of any dirt and debris. Use long-nose pliers to remove any leaves or twigs from the unit. To clean the coils, first remove the top panel. On the heat pump shown, use a socket wrench *(left)*; on some models, you may require a screwdriver or nut driver to remove screws. Loosen stubborn bolts or screws with a few drops of penetrating oil. Wearing work gloves, lift off the top panel. If your unit has side panels, remove each one of them in turn—except the service panel, distinguished by the manufacturer's label on it. Pull each panel away from the unit, making sure to place it clear of the refrigerant line.

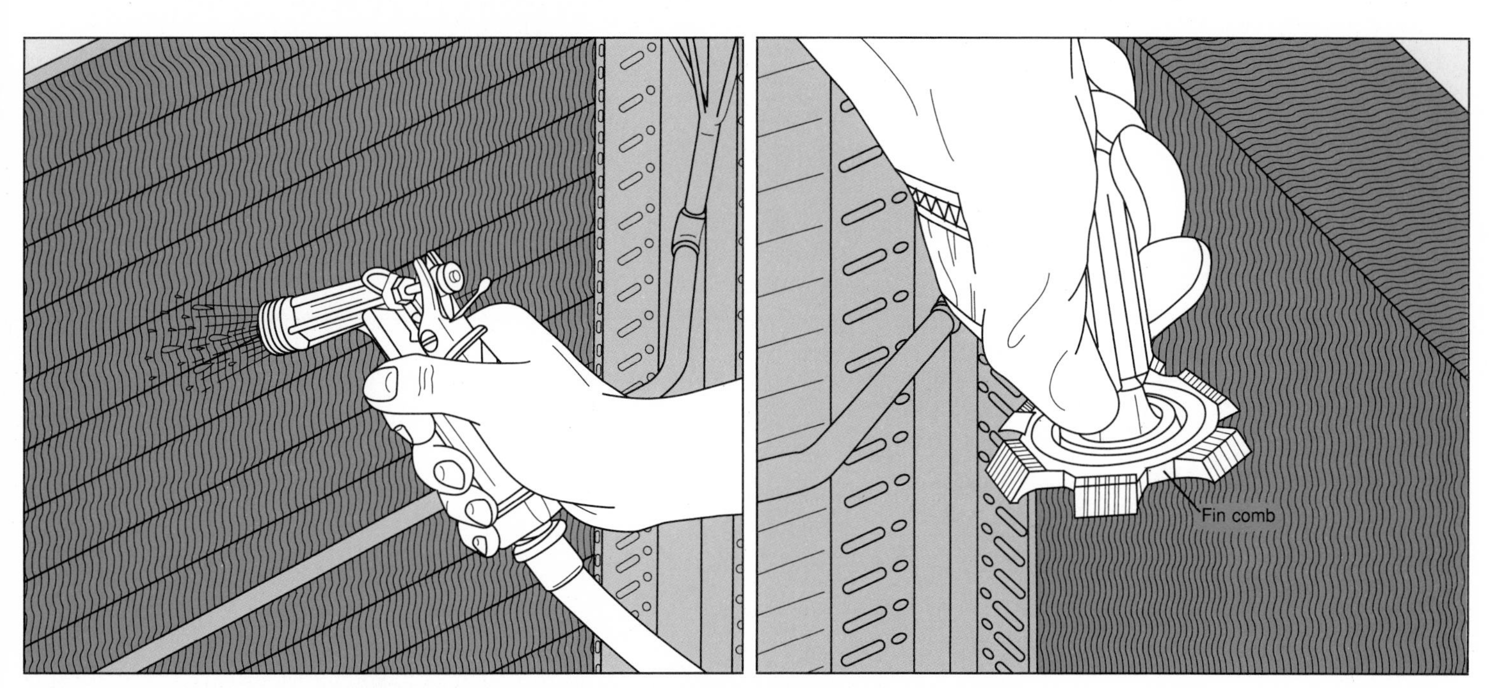

2 Servicing the condenser coil fins. Use a soft brush and a portable cordless vacuum cleaner to clean the coil fins. To remove stubborn dirt buildup, reach inside the unit and spray water through the fins, using a trigger nozzle on a garden hose *(above, left)*. To straighten any bent fins, wear work gloves and use a multi-headed fin comb—available at a building supply center. Do not use a knife or screwdriver to dislodge dirt from or straighten fins; a sharp edge can puncture the coils. Determine which end of the comb corresponds to the spacing of the fins; the comb teeth should fit easily between them. Gently fit the comb teeth between the fins in an undamaged section near the section to be straightened. Pull the comb up, sliding it through the damaged section *(above, right)*. Sweep debris accumulated at the bottom of the unit into a dustpan. Reinstall each panel you removed, reversing the procedure used to take it off *(step 1)*, then restore the power to the unit *(page 118)*.

TOOLS & TECHNIQUES

This section introduces tools and techniques that are used when fixing your house to sell, such as drilling *(page 129)*, sanding *(page 130)*, planing and sawing *(page 131)* and caulking *(page 133)*. As well, charts on fasteners *(page 132)*, caulks and sealants *(page 133)*, cleaners *(page 134)*, paints and finishes *(page 135)* and pest control *(page 140)* are designed for easy reference. Detailed instructions are also included on safely setting up and using ladders *(page 137)* and working on the roof *(page 138)*.

Fixing your house to sell typically requires only the basic kit of tools shown below. Special equipment, such as a pressure washer, an airless paint sprayer, a floor polisher or a water-extraction carpet cleaner, can be obtained at a tool rental center *(page 128)*. For the best results, always use the right tool for the job—and be sure to use the tool correctly.

Follow common-sense rules when you are working with power tools. Never use a faulty power tool and never operate a power tool in wet conditions. Always use grounded or double-insulated power tools; plug them into a grounded outlet or a portable ground-fault circuit interrupter *(page 129)*.

Take the time to care for your tools properly. Avoid laying tools down unprotected where they can be damaged or cause injury. Clean, sharpen and lubricate tools according to the manufacturer's instructions. Store tools on a shelf safely away

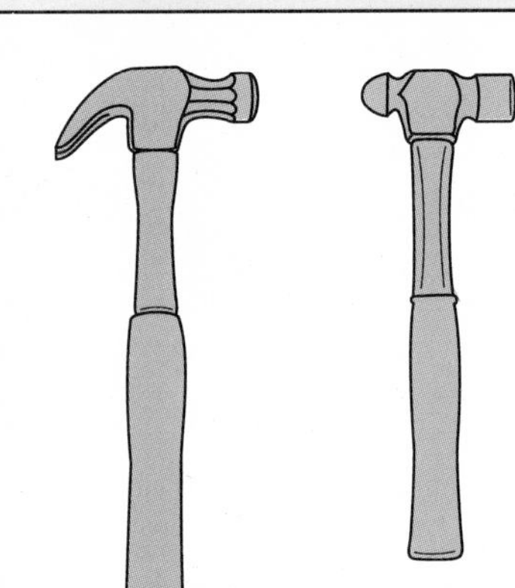

Claw hammer
To drive nails and strike nail sets; curved claw used to pull nails.

Ball-peen hammer
Hardened steel hammer for striking center punches and chisels.

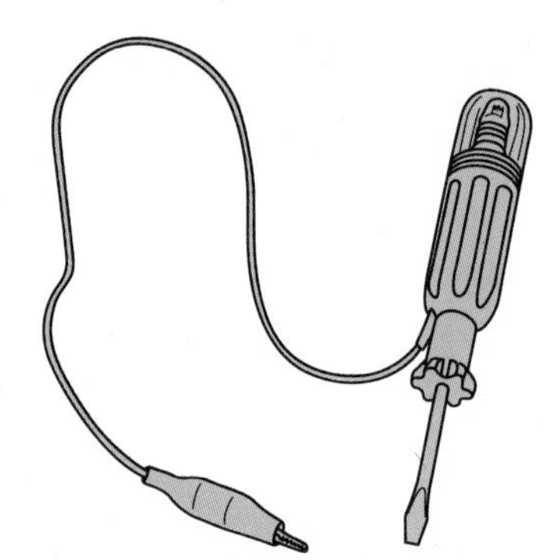

Continuity tester
To check that an electrical circuit is intact; use tester only on a circuit that has been turned off.

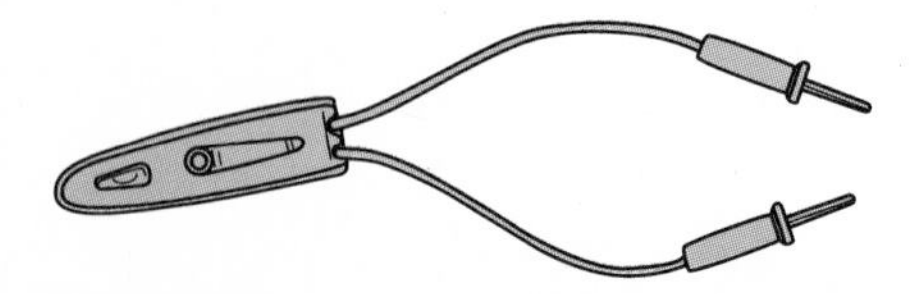

Voltage tester
To check that an electrical circuit has voltage; use tester only when wearing heavy rubber gloves.

Nail set
To set nail heads below a wood surface. Strike with a claw hammer.

Center punch
To dislodge door and window hinge pins. Strike with a ball-peen hammer.

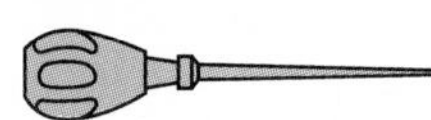

Awl
All-purpose tool used to mark cutting lines and to punch position holes for fasteners.

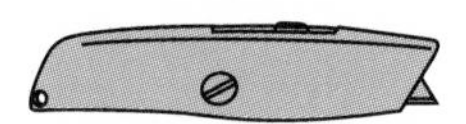

Utility knife
Used to score and cut various materials. Comes with range of blades, including hooked type.

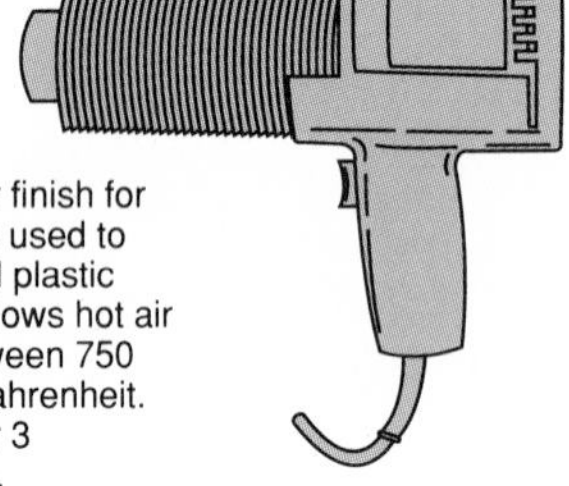

Heat gun
To soften old putty or finish for removal; can also be used to heat and reglue lifted plastic laminate surfaces. Blows hot air at temperatures between 750 and 1,200 degrees fahrenheit. Most types have 2 or 3 temperature settings.

Cold chisel
To chip concrete and mortar joints; struck with a ball-peen hammer.

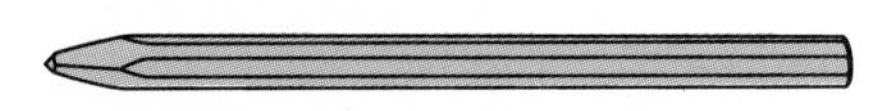

Bull-point chisel
To cut through or break up concrete, mortar and ceramic tile. Strike with a small sledgehammer or ball-peen hammer.

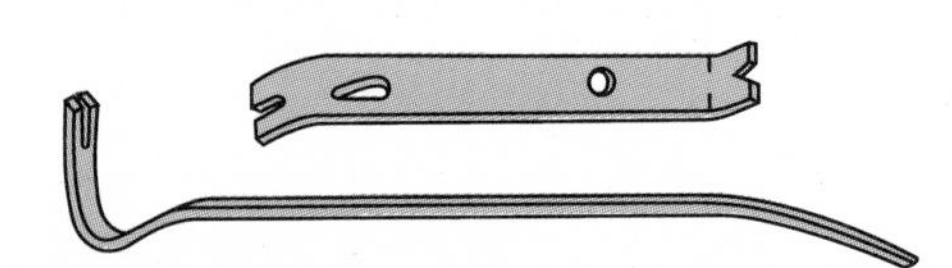

Pry bars
Flat end used for prying, wedging and lifting; curved end used to pull nails. Standard type *(bottom)* used for heavy work; utility bar *(top)* used for light work.

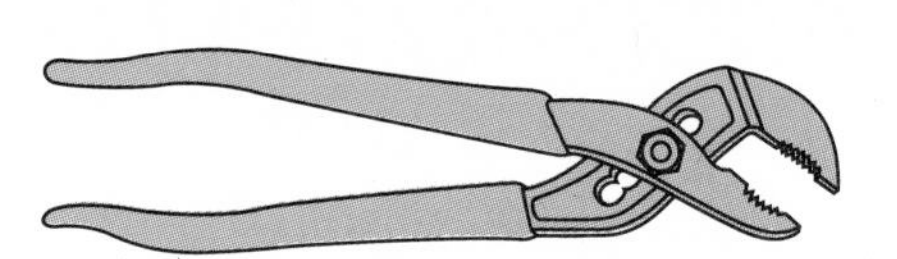

Channel-joint pliers
To install and remove bolts and plumbing fittings; adjustable jaws open to required size.

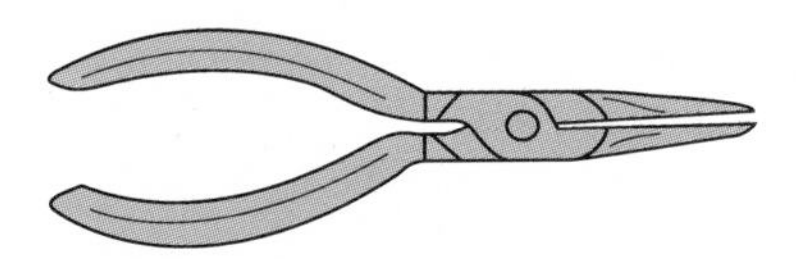

Long-nose pliers
Used for electrical work, and to hold small screws and bolts in tight spaces.

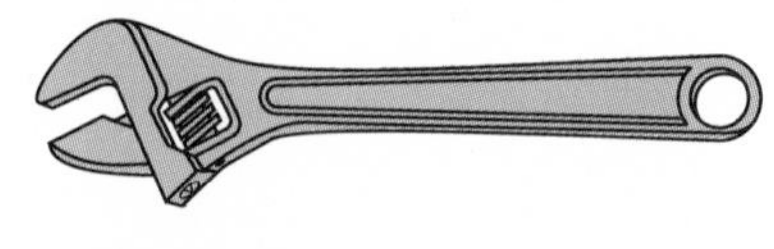

Adjustable wrench
To install and remove bolts and plumbing fittings; adjustable jaws open to required size. Always turn wrench so pressure is applied to the stronger fixed jaw.

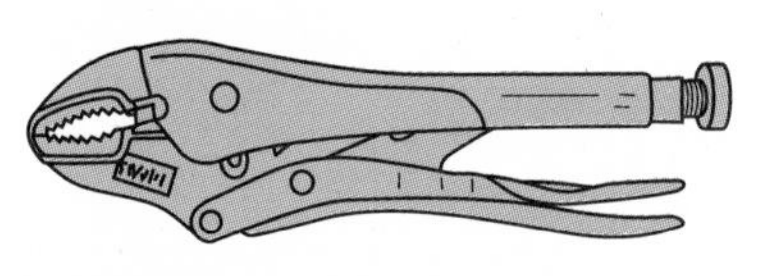

Locking pliers
Heavy-duty grippng and bending tool; jaws close around object, then locked by turning adjuster screw.

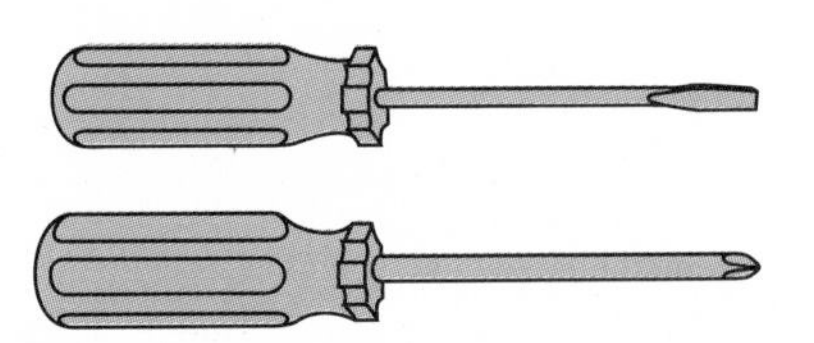

Screwdrivers
Flat-tipped screwdrivers in various sizes used to install and remove screws with slotted heads; Phillips screwdrivers used for cross-headed screws.

from children, in a locked metal or plastic tool box, or hang them well out of their reach.

Since many of the repairs you are likely to make when fixing your house to sell involve cleaning different types of household surfaces, keep an arsenal of cleaning tools—mops, sponges and cloths—and a good assortment of common household cleaning products on hand. Mild household detergent, trisodium phosphate (TSP) and bleach will do the trick for many cleaning jobs. Exercise caution when working with special cleaners. Never mix different cleaners together unless you are specifically instructed by the manufacturer; some combinations, such as ammonia and bleach, produce hazardous vapors. When you are finished a cleaning job, safely dispose of any leftover cleaner *(page 141)*.

Read and follow the safety information in the Emergency Guide *(page 8)*. Always wear the proper clothing and safety gear for the job: gloves when handling sharp, rough, dirty or hazardous materials; safety goggles for work that creates dust or flying debris or when there is a risk of chemical splash; and a dust mask or respirator when using dust-creating drilling or sanding tools or chemicals that emit hazardous vapors. Wear hearing protection when working with noisy power tools. If you are ever in doubt about your ability to complete a repair, do not hesitate to consult a professional.

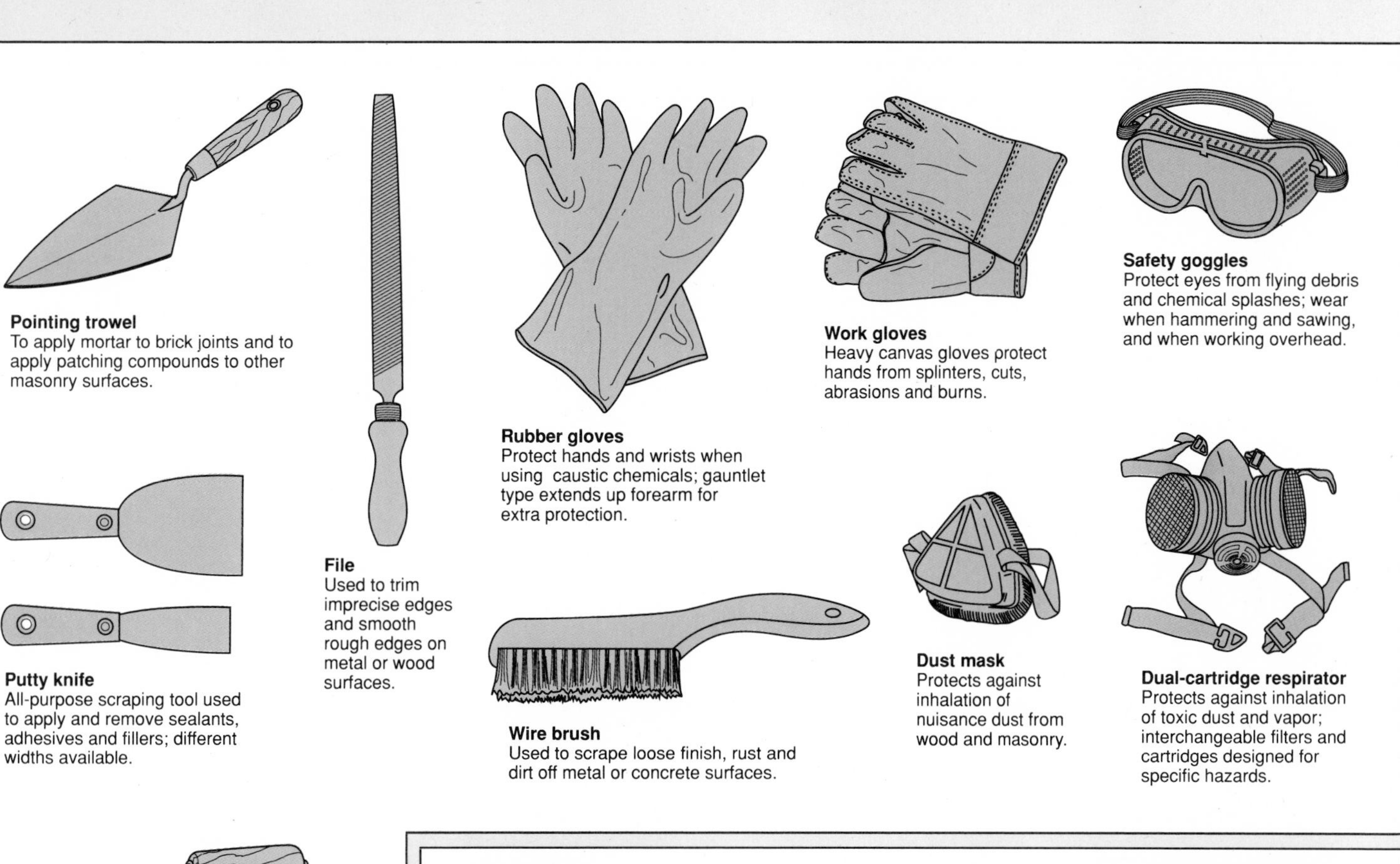

Pointing trowel
To apply mortar to brick joints and to apply patching compounds to other masonry surfaces.

File
Used to trim imprecise edges and smooth rough edges on metal or wood surfaces.

Rubber gloves
Protect hands and wrists when using caustic chemicals; gauntlet type extends up forearm for extra protection.

Work gloves
Heavy canvas gloves protect hands from splinters, cuts, abrasions and burns.

Safety goggles
Protect eyes from flying debris and chemical splashes; wear when hammering and sawing, and when working overhead.

Putty knife
All-purpose scraping tool used to apply and remove sealants, adhesives and fillers; different widths available.

Wire brush
Used to scrape loose finish, rust and dirt off metal or concrete surfaces.

Dust mask
Protects against inhalation of nuisance dust from wood and masonry.

Dual-cartridge respirator
Protects against inhalation of toxic dust and vapor; interchangeable filters and cartridges designed for specific hazards.

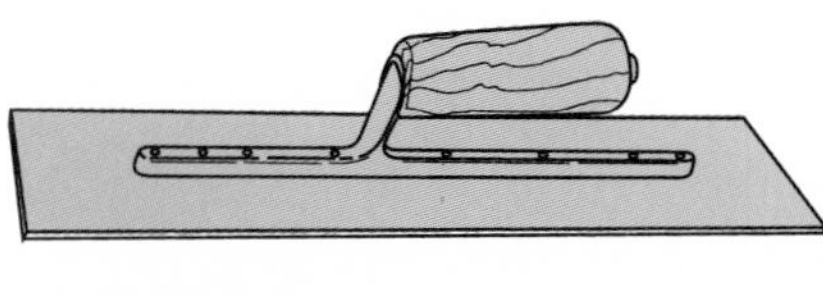

Rectangular trowel
For final smoothing of concrete and plaster patching compounds.

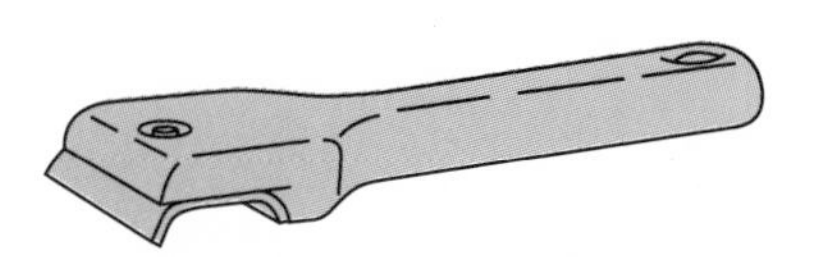

Paint scraper
Used to remove paint from flat wood surfaces; also used to scrape rot out of wood.

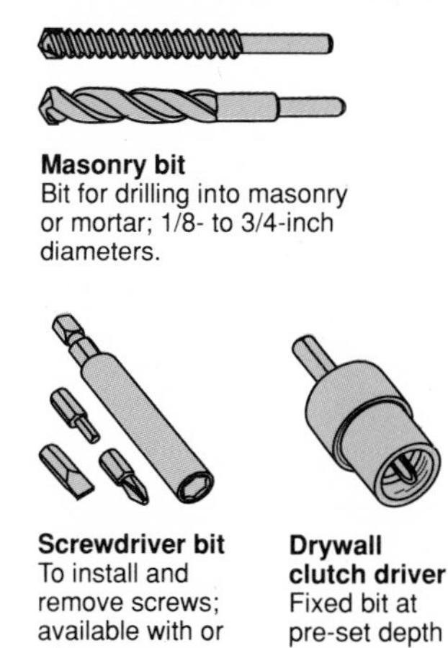

Masonry bit
Bit for drilling into masonry or mortar; 1/8- to 3/4-inch diameters.

Screwdriver bit
To install and remove screws; available with or without screw-holding collar.

Drywall clutch driver
Fixed bit at pre-set depth for driving a drywall screw.

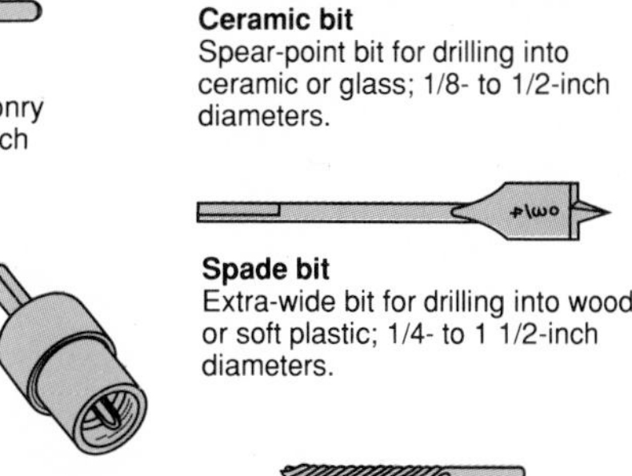

Ceramic bit
Spear-point bit for drilling into ceramic or glass; 1/8- to 1/2-inch diameters.

Spade bit
Extra-wide bit for drilling into wood or soft plastic; 1/4- to 1 1/2-inch diameters.

Twist bit
For drilling into wood or soft plastic; high-speed type for drilling into metal. Available in 1/16- to 1/2-inch diameters.

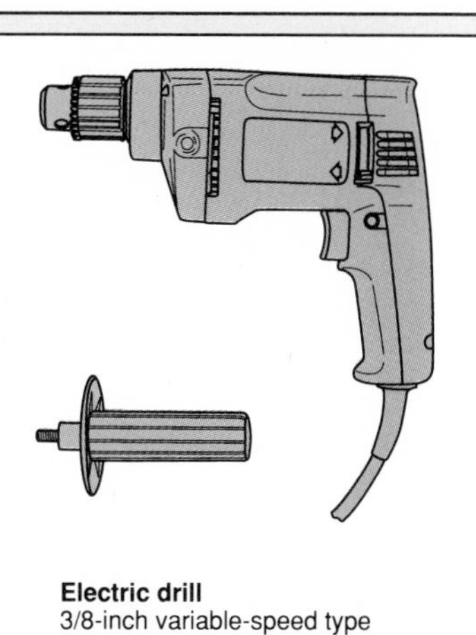

Electric drill
3/8-inch variable-speed type with reversing capability; optional side handle gives greatest control when drilling.

WORKING WITH RENTAL TOOLS

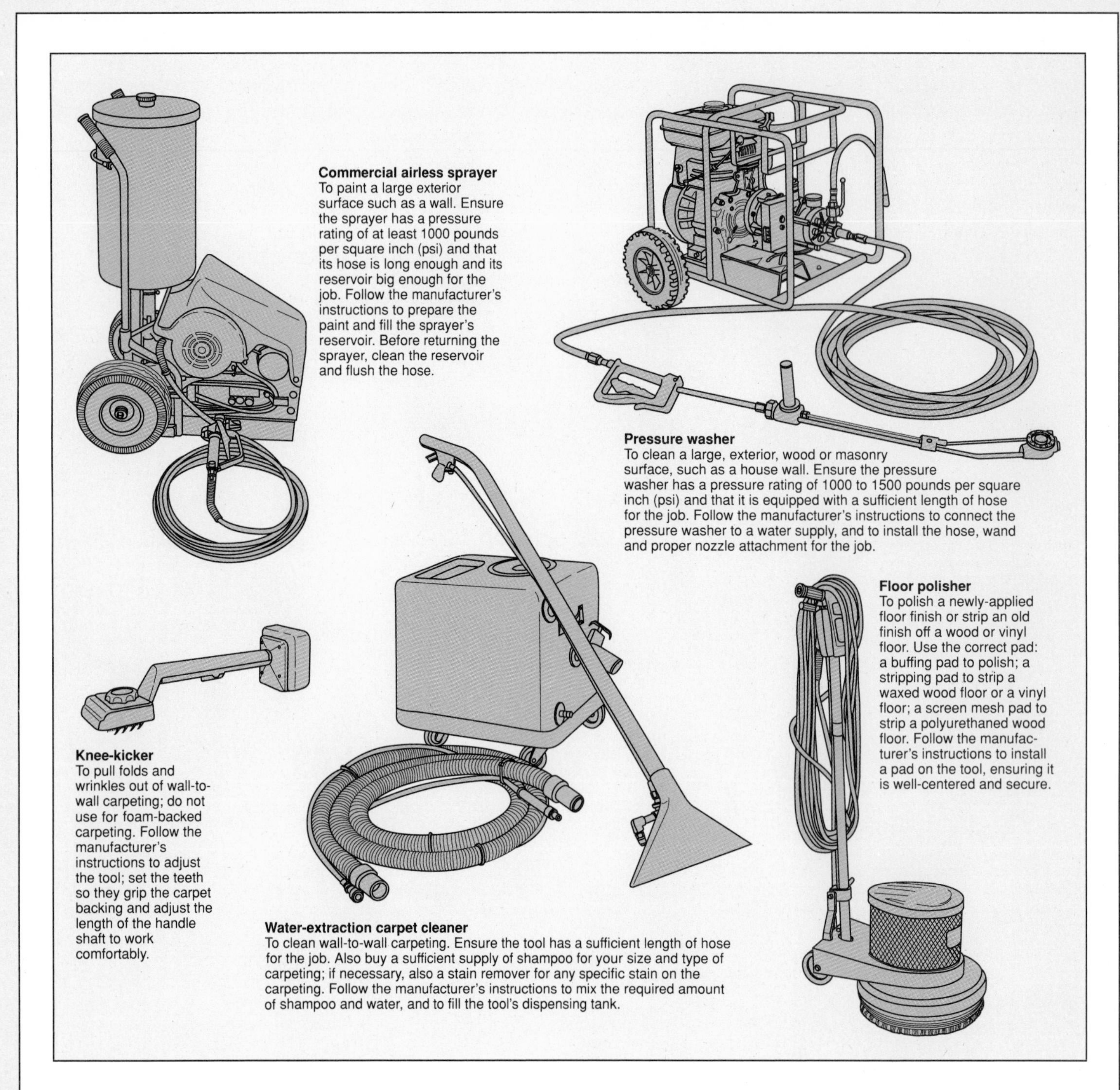

Renting special tools. Shop around when looking for a rental tool—prices and terms may vary. In most cases, insurance coverage is included in the rental price, but sometimes it is not; ask about your liability in the case of inadvertant damage to a rental tool. A rental center may include delivery and pick-up charges in the basic price; others will deliver and pick up a tool for an additional fee.

Rental tools are usually available by the hour or by the day. For cleaning wall-to-wall carpeting with a carpet cleaner or stripping or refinishing a floor with a floor polisher, plan to rent the tool for at least a day. To paint a house exterior with an airless sprayer or clean it with a pressure washer, you may need to rent the tool for several days. When you rent a tool, always inquire about conditions for returning the tool; generally, a carpet cleaner, a pressure washer or a paint sprayer must be emptied and cleaned before it is returned.

When renting a tool, always get a full range of accessories, attachments and supplies for it. In most cases, a tool rental center will let you return unused supplies and credit the amount against your final bill; make sure you check the center's policy on returns. Before renting a tool, ask to see the manufacturer's instructions for using it; if possible, ask for a demonstration before you take a tool home.

WORKING SAFELY WITH POWER TOOLS

Preparing to use a power tool. Before plugging in a power tool, ensure the electrical outlet is GFCI-protected *(step right)*; never use a power tool where it is wet or damp. Inspect a power tool before using it; if the plug or cord is faulty, have the tool serviced. If working at a distance from an outlet, use a heavy-duty extension cord; outdoors, ensure the cord is rated for outdoor use. Loop together an extension cord and the tool power cord loosely, as shown above, to prevent them from pulling apart while in use. When using a power tool, hold it firmly, ensuring you stand clear of the power cord and any moving tool part *(above)*.

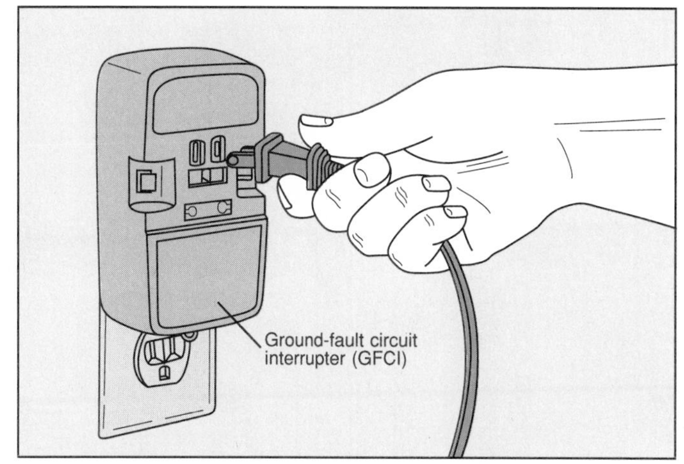

Using a gound-fault circuit interrupter (GFCI). A GFCI provides protection against electrical shock by monitoring the flow of current in an electrical circuit; the moment an irregularity in the current is detected, the GFCI automatically shuts off the electrical circuit. A home built or wired before 1975 is unlikely to have GFCIs permanently installed. If you do not have GFCIs permanently installed, use a portable GFCI when using a power tool at any outlet outdoors, or in a basement, utility room, kitchen, bathroom or garage. Plug the GFCI into the outlet following the manufacturer's instructions, then plug the power tool into the GFCI *(above)*.

DRILLING

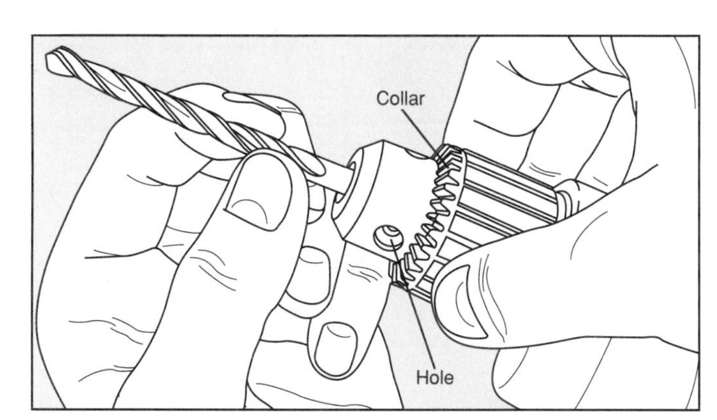

1 Setting up an electric drill. To change or install a drill bit, ensure the drill is unplugged. Choose a bit for the drill *(page 126)*. To remove a bit, fit the drill chuck key into a chuck hole and turn it counterclockwise to open the chuck jaws; then, slide out the bit. To install a bit, use the chuck key to open the chuck jaws wide enough to slide it in. Steadying the bit with one hand, turn the chuck collar to close the chuck jaws *(above)*. Tighten the chuck jaws with the chuck key, fitting it in turn into each chuck hole and turning it clockwise. If you are drilling to an exact depth, mark the drilling depth on the bit by wrapping a small strip of masking tape around it at the appropriate distance from the tip.

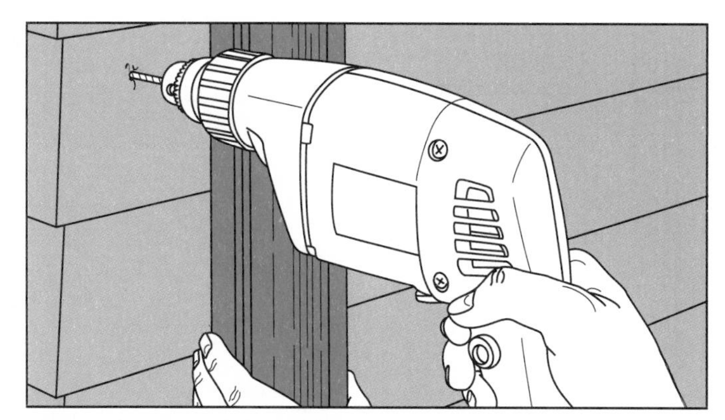

2 Using an electric drill. If necessary, measure and mark a position point for the hole. Prepare to work safely with a power tool *(steps above)*. Wearing safety goggles, plug in the drill and set any reversing switch to FORWARD. Set the tip of the drill at the starting point. Holding the drill steady, apply moderate pressure and depress the trigger switch slightly, running it at low speed. Keeping the bit straight, gradually increase the drill speed and your pressure as the bit starts to cut *(above)*. If the drill strains or the bit heats up, decrease your pressure. When the bit reaches the desired depth, withdraw it from the hole, and release the trigger switch. Unplug the drill and remove the bit *(step left)*.

SANDING

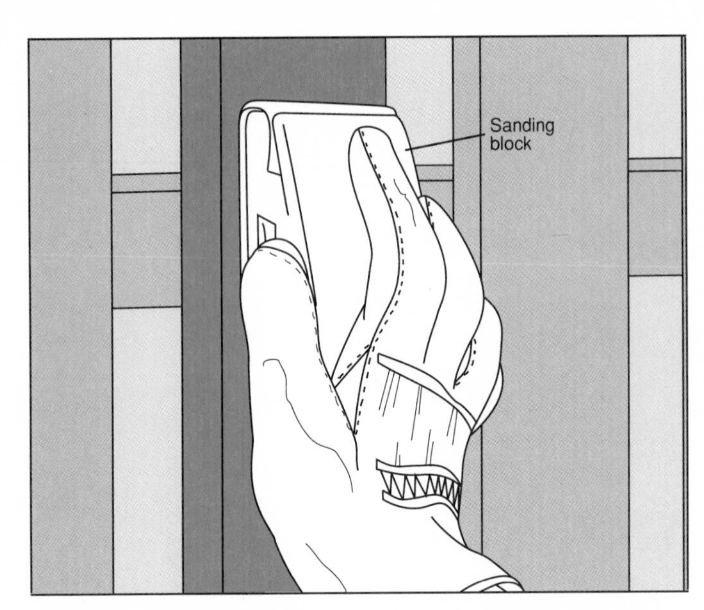

Using a sanding block. For a large surface, use an orbital sander *(step right)*. To smooth a small, flat surface, use a sanding block. Wear a dust mask, safety goggles and work gloves. Cut a sheet of sandpaper to fit the sanding block and install the sandpaper on the block. To use a sanding block, position it flat on the surface to be smoothed. Working in the direction of the wood grain, push the sanding block across the surface, applying even, moderate pressure *(above)*; then, reposition the sanding block and repeat. Continue until the surface is smooth, replacing the sandpaper when it clogs and cannot be cleared by tapping the sanding block on a hard surface. Use a soft brush to dust off the surface; then, wipe it thoroughly with a soft, clean cloth.

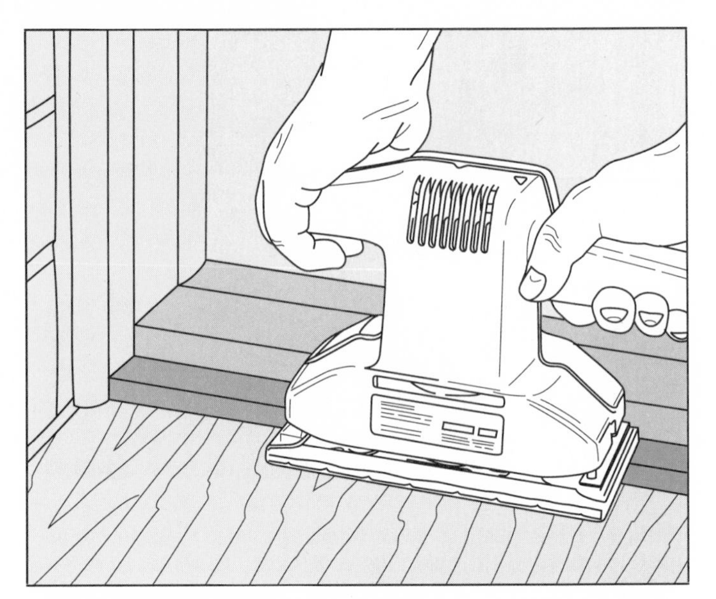

Using an orbital sander. For a large, flat surface, use an orbital sander. Prepare to work safely with a power tool *(page 129)*. Wear safety goggles and a dust mask. Cut a sheet of sandpaper to fit the sander and follow the manufacturer's instructions for your model to install it. To use an orbital sander, grip it with both hands, lift it, and switch it on. When the sander is running at full speed, gently set it on the surface; immediately move it slowly back and forth in long smooth, strokes *(above)* or circular strokes. Never let the sander rest in one spot. Continue until the surface is smooth, replacing the sandpaper when it clogs or wears. To stop, lift the sander and switch it off. Use a soft brush to dust the surface; then, wipe it thoroughly with a soft clean cloth.

LOCATING A STUD OR JOIST

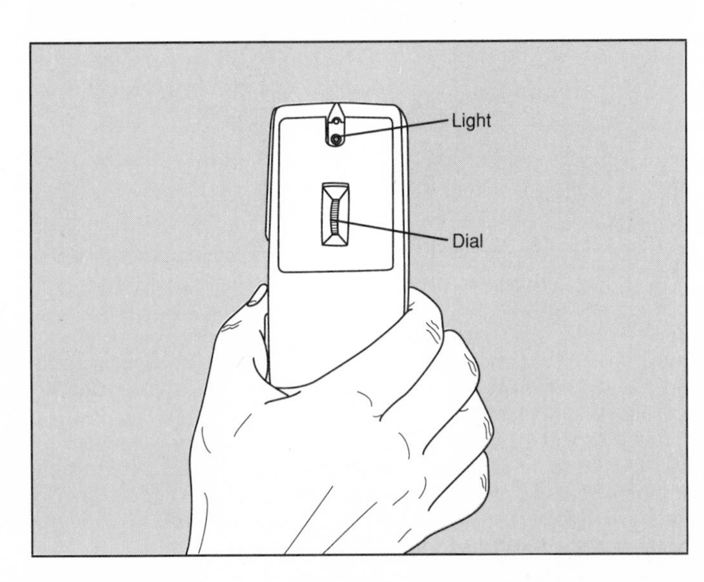

Using an electronic density sensor. An electronic density sensor can be used to accurately pinpoint the location of a stud or joist. Follow the manufacturer's instructions to operate your model. On the model shown, roll the dial upward to the "Start" position and place the tool flat on the surface *(left)*. Press the two buttons on the sides of the tool, turning on the red light, then slowly roll the dial downward until the green light comes on and the red light goes off. Still pressing the two buttons on the sides, slide the tool slowly along the surface. The edge of a stud or joist is indicated when the red light comes on; the other edge is indicated when the green light comes on and the red light goes off.

Alternately, you can often find a stud or joist by tapping along a wall or ceiling and listening for a change from a hollow to a solid sound about every 16 inches. Another method is to skim an electric razor along the surface and listen for a change in pitch. A magnetic compass needle may shift when passed over a nail in a stud or joist. Slight ridges or depressions at stud or joist positions can also be detected in the oblique glare of an exposed light bulb.

PLANING

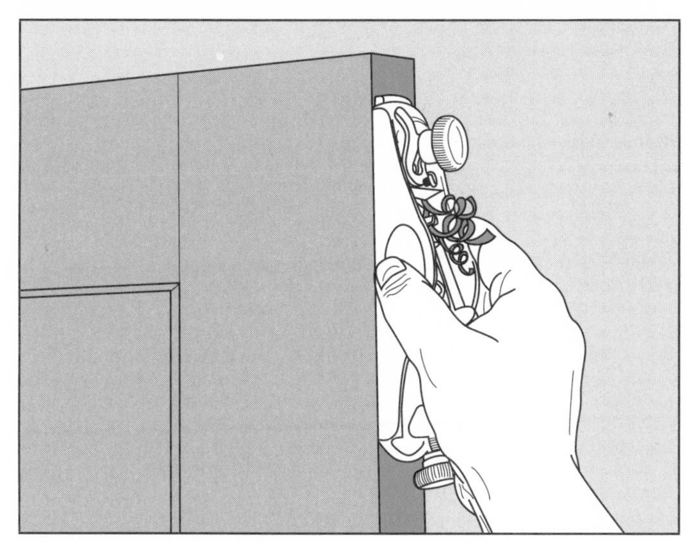

Using a block plane. Use a block plane to trim or smooth the edge of a piece of wood that is fastened in place. Inspect the plane before using it; if any part is damaged or the cutting iron is dull, have the plane serviced. Holding the plane upside down, adjust the cutting iron; turn the depth-adjustment knob until the cutting edge of the iron projects just slightly from the mouth; then, loosen the locking lever, move the lateral-adjustment lever sideways until the iron is aligned squarely within the mouth, and retighten the locking lever. Before trimming or smoothing the workpiece, make a test cut on a piece of scrap wood and, if necessary, readjust the cutting iron. To use a block plane, hold the plane in one hand, with your palm in back on the lever cap. Keeping the plane flat on the surface to be trimmed or smoothed, push the plane forward, putting pressure on the toe *(left)*; then, transfer pressure to the heel to raise the plane from the surface in a smooth motion. Reposition the plane and repeat until the surface is sufficiently trimmed or smoothed.

SAWING

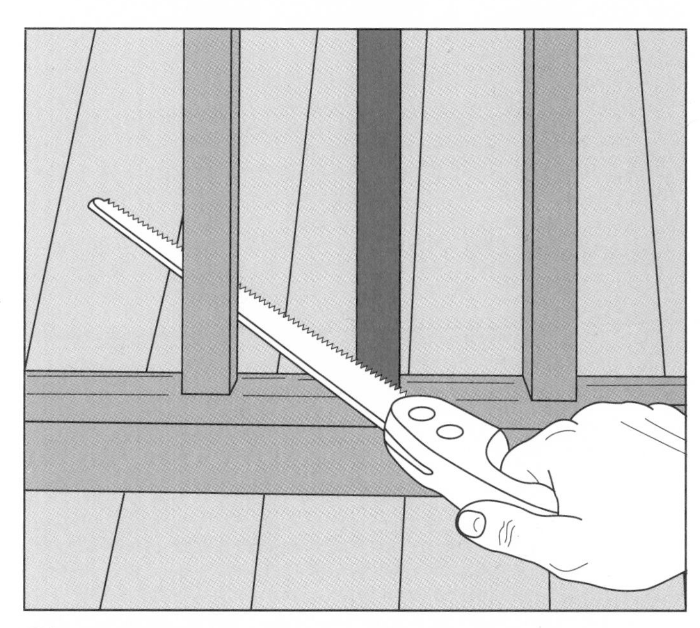

Using a compass saw. For cuts within the interior of a workpiece, in a tight corner or at an awkward angle, use a compass saw. Inspect the saw before using it; if any teeth are damaged or the blade is warped, have the saw serviced. Measure and mark the piece to be cut. If starting in the interior of the piece, drill a hole for the saw blade. To start the cut, hold the saw almost perpendicular to the piece and draw the blade slowly toward you a few times. Lower the angle of the saw to about 45 degrees and cut through the piece on the downstroke; use long, even strokes to keep the blade from buckling. In a tight corner or at an awkward angle, cut with the heel *(above)* or toe of the blade, using short, fast strokes.

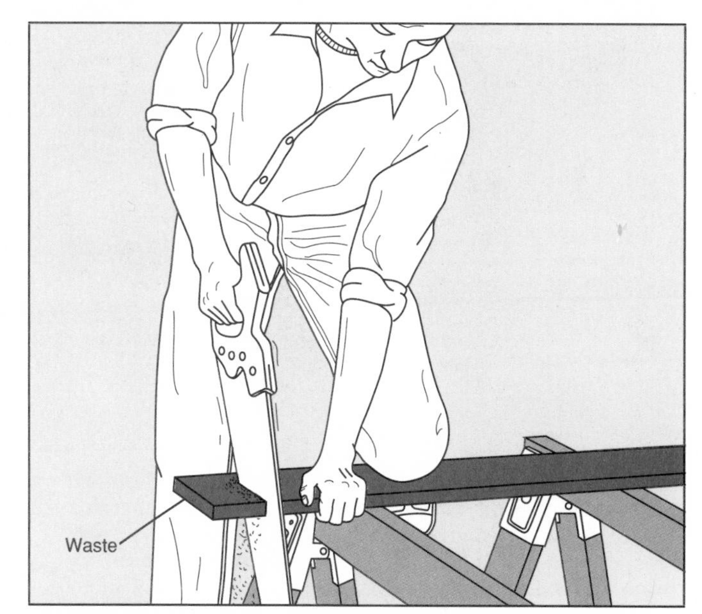

Using a crosscut saw. For quick, rough wood cuts across the grain, use a crosscut saw. Inspect the saw before using it; if any teeth are damaged or the blade is warped, have the saw serviced. Measure and mark the piece to be cut, and set it up securely on a work surface. To start the cut, hold the saw almost perpendicular to the piece, aligning your shoulder and arm with the cut mark, and draw the blade slowly toward you a few times. Lower the angle of the saw to about 45 degrees and cut through the piece on the downstroke *(above)* until the blade is 1 inch from the end of the cut. To finish the cut, grip the waste with one hand, hold the saw perpendicular to the piece and use short up-and-down strokes.

WORKING WITH FASTENERS

Common nail
Broad head and thick shank. Available in lengths up to 12 inches. Lengths expressed as "penny" ratings, written as a numeral followed by the letter "d". Used for general indoor and outdoor construction with wood.

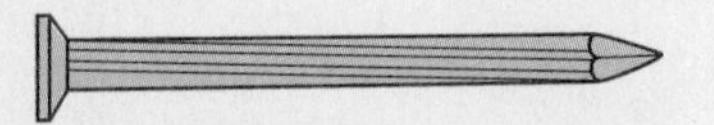

Masonry nail
Fluted type shown is made of hardened steel; flutes provide tight grip. Available in lengths up to 4 inches for fastening through wood to concrete block, concrete or mortar.

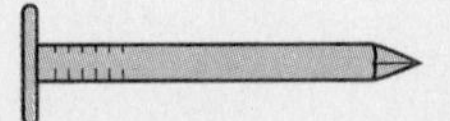

Roofing nail
Short shaft and broad, flat head provide good holding power for fastening thin, flexible roofing materials, such as asphalt shingles, to wood. Available in lengths up to 2 1/2 inches; galvanized for rust-resistance.

Spiral nail
Spiral shank twists into wood as nail driven; greater holding power than common nail. Available in lengths up to 4 inches. Special types of spiral nails are available for fastening hardwood siding or flooring, vinyl or aluminum siding and masonry.

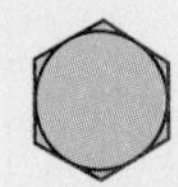
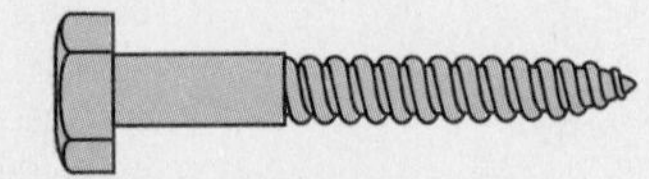

Lag bolt
Hexagonal head and threaded, screw-like shank. Used to fasten heavy wood or metal to wood or masonry; use with washer under head to fasten through wood, and with shield of matching diameter to fasten to masonry. Available in lengths up to 12 inches.

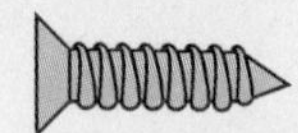
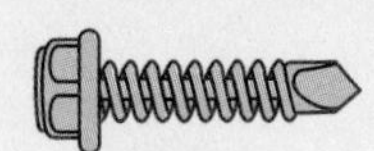

Sheet metal screw
Standard type *(above, left)* fastens light-gauge metals to each other. Self-tapping type *(above, right)* fastens heavy-gauge metals to each other or to wood; tip cuts through metal as head is driven. Common heads are slotted, Phillips (cross-headed) and hexagonal. Available in lengths up to 3 inches.

Finishing nail
Small, cupped head can be set below surface with a nail set to conceal nail. Available in lengths up to 4 inches. Used for interior and exterior light construction. Specially-hardened finishing nails are available for fastening through hardwood trim and molding.

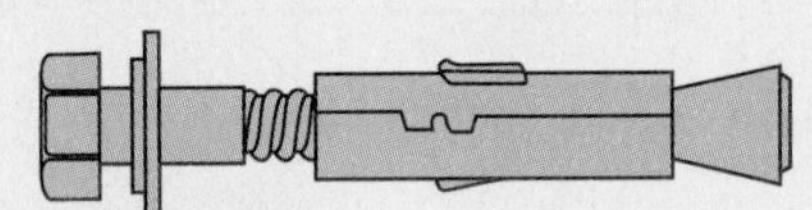

Expansion bolt
Bolt and lead shield fasten wood to masonry or concrete; shield expands as bolt is tightened. Drill hole of same diameter as shield; fit shield into hole, position object and drive bolt through it and into shield. Available in lengths up to 6 inches.

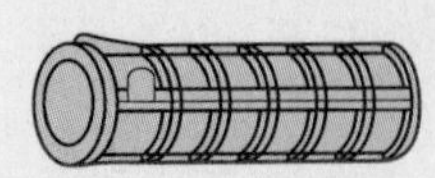

Lead or alloy shield
Used with wood screw or lag bolt to fasten through medium-weight or heavy material to masonry. Sized to match diameter and length of fastener. Drill hole of same diameter as shield; fit shield into hole, position object and drive screw through it and into shield.

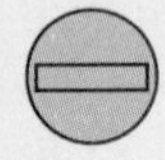

Flat-headed wood screw
Used to fasten through wood or plastic to wood. Threaded shank provides greater holding power than a nail. Common head recesses are cross-headed (Phillips), slot-headed and square-headed (Robertson). Can be driven flush or below surface. Available in lengths up to 6 inches.

Choosing a fastener. The chart above shows typical fasteners used for the many household repairs you may make when fixing a house to sell. Included are a variety of nails and screws used to fasten wood or metal objects to other surfaces—wood, metal, masonry or concrete. Use the chart to help you select the right fastener for a job. In general, choose a nail for rough work or for a job requiring many fasteners and a screw for finer work when good holding power is required or when the fastener may later have to be removed; use a lag bolt or expansion bolt for fastening large or heavy materials.

After choosing an appropriate fastener, determine if any special features are necessary. If the fastener is to be installed in a wet or damp location, use a rust-resistant fastener—a galvanized steel type indoors, a hot-dipped galvanized (HDG) steel type outdoors, and a stainless steel type in an area exposed to corrosive salt water. If you are fastening through or to metal, buy a fastener of the same metal to prevent a corrosive reaction.

Choose a fastener of a suitable length for the dimensions of the materials through and to which you are fastening. As a rough rule of thumb, the length of a nail or screw should be 2 to 3 times the thickness of the material through which you are fastening, and no less than 1/4 inch shorter than the combined thickness of the materials you are fastening.

If desired, drill a hole for a fastener before installing it to prevent damage to the materials. Use an electric drill to bore a hole in wood, metal or masonry, first fitting the drill with the proper drill bit for the material *(page 129)*. To install a fastener, always use the correct tool, ensuring that it is in good condition before using it. Use a claw hammer to install a nail and to strike a nail set to set a nail. To install a screw, use a screwdriver with a tip that matches the size and type of recess in the head of the screw—for example, a flat-tipped screwdriver for a slot-headed screw or a Phillips screwdriver for a cross-headed screw. To install a lag bolt or expansion bolt, use a wrench that fits snugly onto the bolt head.

WORKING WITH CAULKS OR SEALANTS

TYPE	USES AND CHARACTERISTICS
Acrylic latex caulk	Use to seal interior and exterior wood, metal, glass or masonry joints that undergo little movement (expansion and contraction), such as door and window frames, baseboards and trim. For kitchen or bathroom use, choose a waterproof type with a fungicide to prevent mold and mildew. Dries quickly and odorlessly. Available in a variety of colors; paintable with latex paint.
Silicone rubber caulk	Use to seal interior and exterior wood, metal, glass or masonry joints that undergo movement (expansion and contraction). For interior use, ventilate area during application to minimize strong vinegar-like odor. Not recommended for use on joints that must be painted. Available in a variety of colors including white, black, bronze, gray, brown and clear.
Vinyl latex caulk	Use to seal narrow interior joints that undergo very little movement (expansion and contraction), such as wood- or metal-to-glass joints in windows and wood-to-wood joints in baseboards and trim. Not as flexible as acrylic latex or silicone rubber caulk; dries fairly hard and may become brittle. Paintable with latex or alkyd paint.
Butyl rubber sealant	Use to seal exterior joints that undergo movement (expansion and contraction), such as wood- or metal-to-masonry joints around windows, doors and fixtures, and metal-to-metal joints of gutters and flashings. Messier application than silicone caulk, and may be sticky or stringy; not recommended for use where appearance is important. Available in white or gray; paintable with latex or alkyd paint.
Concrete latex caulk	Use to repair hairline cracks in concrete walkways, driveways, floors and walls. Available in gray; dries to match concrete. Paintable with latex or alkyd paint.
Asphalt crack sealant	Use to repair small cracks in asphalt driveways and walkways. Available in black; dries to rough-textured, matted finish to match asphalt surface.
Roofing cement (asphalt-based)	Use to seal torn, lifted or curled asphalt shingles and to seal loose flashing to other roofing materials. Available in black; some types paintable with alkyd paint.

Selecting a caulk or sealant. Caulks and sealants are used to fill joints between adjacent interior or exterior surfaces and act as a barrier against penetration by moisture, air, dirt and insect pests; they may also be used to patch small holes or cracks in interior and exterior surfaces. Use the chart above to help select the correct caulk or sealant for a job. Building supply centers carry a large variety of caulks and sealants that vary in price, flexibility and durability. Read the product's label carefully to ensure it can be used in your situation with the type of materials you are sealing. If sealing an exterior joint, make sure the product is marked for exterior use. If appearance is important, choose an appropriate-colored product or buy one that can be painted when cured. Carefully follow the manufacturer's instructions on the product label to prepare the surfaces and apply the caulk or sealant *(step below)*.

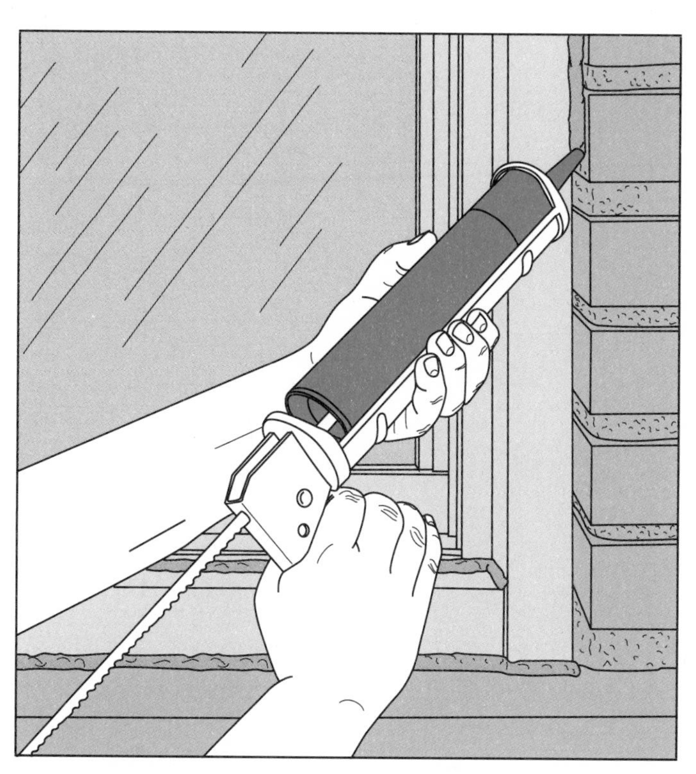

Using a caulking gun. Before caulking a joint, follow the manufacturer's instructions on the product label to prepare the surface. Remove old or loosened caulk with a putty knife, then brush or wipe clean the joint; if necessary, use any solvent recommended by the manufacturer. To apply caulk from a cartridge, use a drop-in type caulking gun, specifically made for disposable cartridges. Use a utility knife to cut off the cartridge tip at a 45-degree angle; then, load the cartridge into the caulking gun, rotating it so the cut in the tip faces down. Use a nail or an awl to puncture the seal in the cut tip. To apply the caulk, start at one end of the joint; on a vertical joint, start at the top. Holding the caulking gun at a 45-degree angle to the surface and ensuring the plunger is turned with its grooved side facing down, squeeze the trigger to eject a continuous bead of caulk along the joint *(left)*; at the end of the joint, release the trigger. Wearing a rubber glove, run a wet finger along the bead to press it into place, smoothing and shaping it; the finished bead should adhere to both sides of the joint and have a slightly concave surface. When finished, remove the cartridge from the caulking gun, pulling out the plunger to release it. To keep the leftover caulk from drying in the cartridge, cap the cartridge tip or insert a nail into it.

WORKING WITH COMMON HOUSEHOLD CLEANERS

Removing dirt, stains and deposits. To clean dirt and stains off interior and exterior household surfaces, a common household product can often suffice. Mild household detergent—or, for tough stains, trisodium phosphate (TSP)—can clean almost any surface if mixed and applied carefully. Other products typically found in the kitchen, bathroom or garage also make excellent cleaners; for example: bleach, hydrogen peroxide, baking soda, vinegar and rubbing alcohol. Use the chart below to determine whether you can quickly clean a surface with a common household product; for a special stain or surface not mentioned, consult the Troubleshooting Guide of the appropriate chapter in this book for further cleaning directions.

Exercise caution when cleaning with a common household product; keep it away from children and pets. Avoid mixing different products together unless instructed by the manufacturer. Wear rubber gloves when cleaning; if working overhead, also safety goggles. If you need to prepare a paste or poultice with a common household product, use a clean container. Start with a small amount of any dry ingredient, then slowly add liquid, stirring constantly until you achieve the consistency desired: batter-like for a paste and putty-like for a poultice. If you leave a poultice on a surface overnight, cover it with plastic; tape the plastic to the surface using duct tape or masking tape. When finished, safely dispose of any leftover cleaner *(page 141)*.

CLEANER	APPLICATION
Household detergent	For light dirt and grime on most household surfaces or for light stains on carpets, mix 1/4 cup detergent per gallon of water. Wipe clean a delicate surface with a cloth or sponge; scrub clean a sturdy surface with a stiff-bristled brush.
	For light dirt and grime on masonry surfaces, mix 1 cup detergent per gallon of water; scrub clean with a stiff-bristled brush.
Trisodium phosphate (TSP)	For stubborn dirt and light oil stains on masonry or asphalt, mix 1/2 cup TSP and 1/2 cup household detergent per gallon of water; scrub with a stiff-bristled brush.
	For stubborn oil stains on masonry or asphalt, mix a poultice of talcum powder or fuller's earth and a solution of 1 part TSP and 6 parts water. Apply with a rubber-gloved hand and leave overnight; then, scrape off by hand.
	For stubborn dirt and smoke stains on walls or ceilings, mix 3 tablespoons TSP per gallon of water; rub clean with a cloth or sponge.
	For smoke stains on furnaces or fireplaces and for stubborn dirt on exterior wood surfaces, mix 1/2 cup TSP per gallon of water; scrub with a stiff-bristled brush.
	For stubborn dirt on exterior metal surfaces and for light efflorescence on masonry, mix 1 cup TSP per gallon of water; scrub with a stiff-bristled brush.
Household bleach	For mildew and organic stains on exterior wood, metal, masonry or asphalt surfaces, mix 2 cups bleach per gallon of water; scrub with a stiff-bristled brush.
	For stubborn dirt and common stains on ceramic tile and grout, on porcelain and porcelain-enamel surfaces, or on metal plumbing fixtures, mix 2 cups bleach per gallon of water; rub clean with a sponge or scrub clean with a stiff-bristled brush.
	For stubborn stains on ceramic tile and grout, on porcelain and porcelain-enamel surfaces, and on metal plumbing fixtures, use a stiff-bristled brush dampened with undiluted bleach; scrub clean.
Hydrogen peroxide	For stubborn stains on porcelain and porcelain-enamel surfaces, use a sponge loaded with a paste of cream of tartar and hydrogen peroxide; rub clean.
Baking soda (sodium bicarbonate)	For common stains on rough interior and exterior wood surfaces, use a soft-bristled brush loaded with a paste of baking soda and water; scrub clean.
	For mineral deposits on porcelain and porcelain-enamel surfaces, use a stiff-bristled brush loaded with a paste of baking soda and white vinegar; scrub clean.
White vinegar	For mineral deposits on metal plumbing fixtures and for rust stains on stainless steel surfaces, use a stiff-bristled brush dampened with white vinegar; scrub clean.
	For stubborn mineral deposits on metal plumbing fixtures and stubborn rust stains on stainless steel surfaces, use a stiff-bristled brush loaded with a paste of baking soda and white vinegar; scrub clean.
	For stubborn dirt and filmy coatings on vinyl flooring or glass, mix 1/2 cup white vinegar per gallon of water; gently scrub clean with a soft-bristled brush or wipe clean with a cloth or sponge.
	For stubborn stains on ceramic tile and grout, mix 1/2 cup white vinegar or heavy-duty laundry detergent per gallon of water; scrub clean with a stiff-bristled brush.
	For stubborn stains on a polyurethaned wood floor, mix 1/2 cup white vinegar per gallon of water; scrub clean with a stiff-bristled brush.
Rubbing alcohol	For ink stains on plastic laminate surfaces, for dirt on metal hardware and for soap film on bathroom surfaces, use a sponge dampened with undiluted rubbing alcohol; rub clean.

WORKING WITH PAINT OR FINISH

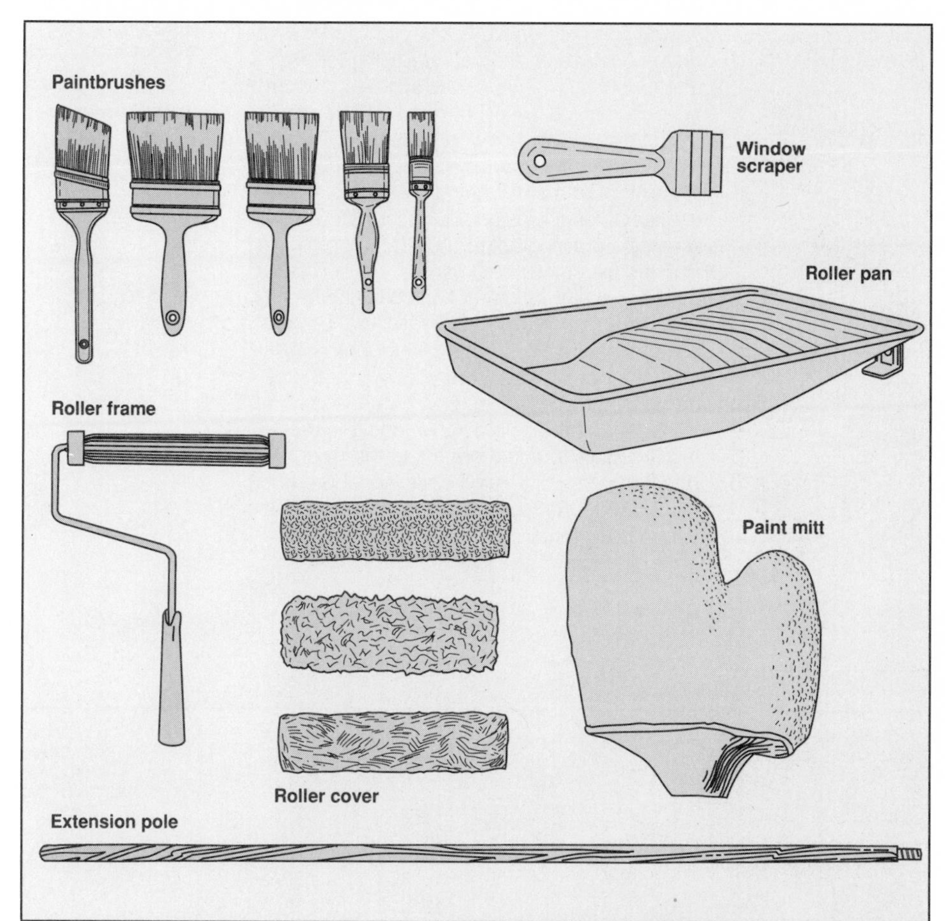

Selecting a paint or finish. Use the chart below to help you choose the best paint or finish for a job, choosing the type that can provide the appearance you want. If you are using leftover paint to touch up a surface, tint it, if necessary *(page 136)*, to match the old paint. If you are buying a new paint or finish, read the label carefully. Ensure the product is suitable for the surface; for an exterior surface, ensure the product is marked for exterior use. Check the surface coverage of a container of the paint or finish and buy enough for the job; if you are buying more than one container, choose containers with the same lot number to ensure that colors match. Also check the clean-up information on the label; buy enough of the paint or finish solvent to clean your tools and any accidental spills.

Once you have chosen a paint or finish, select the tool or tools for the job *(left)*, ensuring they are clean and in good condition. Then, follow the instructions on the paint or finish label for preparing the surface. After applying the paint or finish, clean your tools *(page 136)* and safely dispose of leftover paint or finish *(page 141)*.

PAINT OR FINISH	USE AND APPLICATION
Latex paint	Use on unfinished wood, masonry, metal, drywall or plaster surfaces, and over old latex or alkyd paint or wood stain. Available in flat or semi-gloss. Prime an unfinished or patched surface before applying latex paint. Thin and clean up latex paint with water. Dries in 2 to 4 hours.
Alkyd paint	Use on unfinished wood, masonry, metal, drywall or plaster surfaces, and over old alkyd paint, alkyd wood stain or polyurethane. Available in flat, semi-gloss or gloss. Prime an unfinished or patched surface before applying alkyd paint; prime a finished surface before applying gloss alkyd paint. Thin and clean up alkyd paint with mineral spirits. Dries in 6 to 8 hours.
Enamel paint	Use on unfinished wood and masonry surfaces subjected to heavy wear, such as porch, deck, basement and garage floors, and over old finish on these surfaces. Apply enamel paint directly to surface. Thin and clean up enamel paint with mineral spirits.
Aluminum paint (high-temperature type)	Use on unfinished metal surfaces subjected to high temperatures, such as a furnace exhaust stack or a radiator, and over old aluminum paint. Apply aluminum paint directly to surface.
Metal primer	Use on unfinished metal surfaces before applying a latex or alkyd paint; for unfinished galvanized steel surfaces, use a zinc-rich galvanized steel primer. Apply metal primer directly to surface. Thin and clean up metal primer with mineral spirits.
Polyurethane	Use on unfinished wood surfaces and over old polyurethane. Available in semi-gloss (satin) or gloss finish. Apply polyurethane directly to surface. Clean up polyurethane with mineral spirits.
Wood stain	Use on unfinished exterior wood surfaces and over old stain of the same type. Available in semi-transparent and opaque. Apply wood stain directly to surface. Thin and clean up alkyd types with mineral spirits; latex types with water.
Wood preservative	Use on unfinished exterior wood surfaces subjected to extreme weathering and moisture, and over old preservative of the same type. Apply wood preservative directly to surface. Clean up wood preservative with mineral spirits.

WORKING WITH PAINT OR FINISH (continued)

Tinting leftover paint. If a painted surface has darkened with age and you are using leftover paint to touch it up, use a tint such as raw umber or lampblack to adjust the paint color to match the surface. Ask at a paint store for a tint recommended for your paint type and color. To tint paint, pour a small amount of it into a clean container. Using a disposable stick, stir the paint, repeatedly drawing a figure-eight through it without striking the container; as you stir, add a few drops of tint *(left)* and continue stirring until the mixture is uniformly colored. Then, use the stick to smear some of the mixture onto white blotting paper—which will dry quickly and give you an instant paint chip. Compare the chip to the surface. If the chip color is too light, repeat the procedure to add more tint to the mixture to darken it; if the chip is too dark, add more leftover paint to the mixture to lighten it. When the mixture color matches the surface color, touch up the surface.

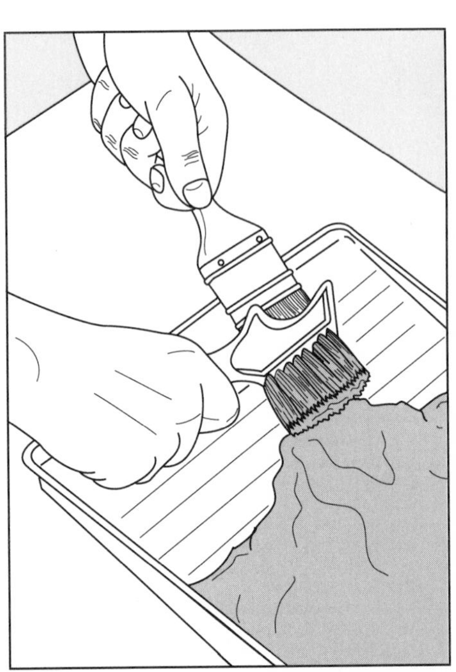

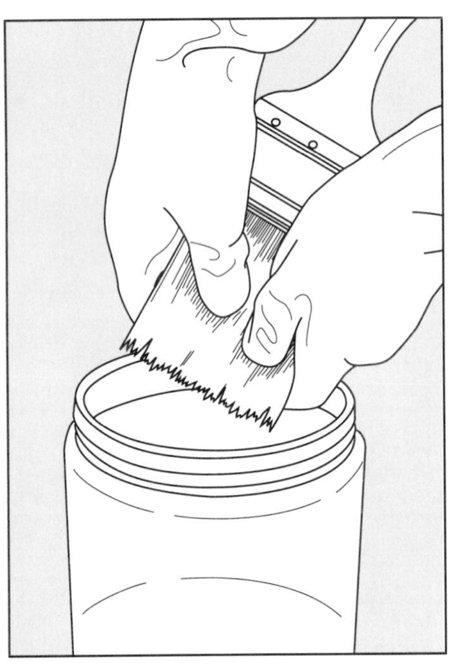

Cleaning finishing tools. Before cleaning finish off a tool, remove excess finish. For a paintbrush, draw the teeth of a brush comb through the bristles *(above, left)*; for a roller cover, draw the rounded edge of the comb along the cover. Squeeze out a paint mitt. To clean off a latex or water-based finish, wash the tool under running water, adding a few drops of liquid household detergent. Work the finish out of the tool with your fingers, continuing until the water runs clear. To clean off an alkyd or oil-based finish, pour the solvent recommended by the manufacturer into a container. Wearing rubber gloves, agitate the tool in the solvent, then lift it out and work in the solvent with your fingers *(above, right)*. If the solvent becomes cloudy, use a fresh batch, repeating the procedure as necessary. Rinse the tool with water, continuing until the water runs clear. Shake out excess liquid from the tool and let it dry; then, store the tool *(step right)*.

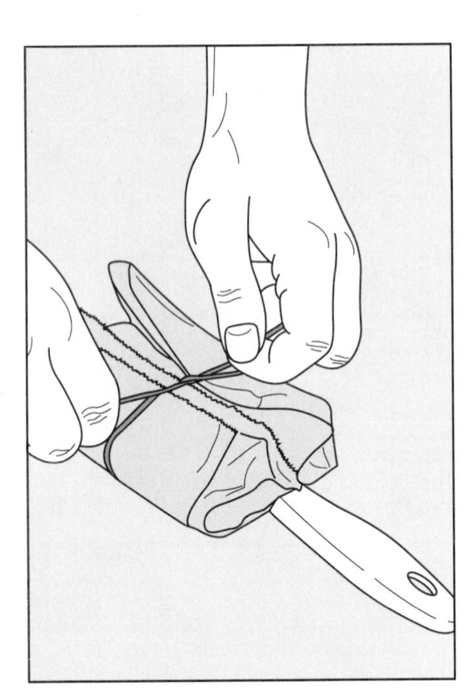

Storing finishing tools. Wrap a cleaned and dried finishing tool before storing it. To wrap a paintbrush, fold a piece of brown paper around the ferrule and bristles, then tie the wrapping with string *(above)*. To wrap a roller cover or a paint mitt, place it in its original package or in a plastic bag; then, puncture the bag with a few air holes to prevent mildew formation. Store a wrapped tool in a clean, dry location, easily accessible for the next time it is needed.

WORKING SAFELY ON A LADDER

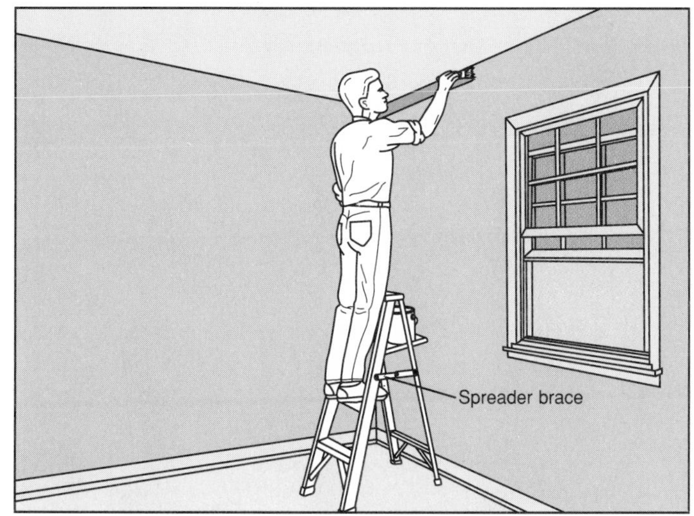

Setting up a stepladder. To work comfortably and safely up to 10 feet off the ground, set up a stepladder; use a stepladder at least 2 feet longer than the height at which you need to stand. Inspect the stepladder before using it; do not use it if a foot is worn, a step is loose or a spreader brace does not open fully. Set up the stepladder on a firm, level surface, opening its legs completely and locking its spreader braces. Indoors, set up a stepladder well away from stairs and overhead obstructions *(above, left)*; if the feet slip, place a non-slip rubber mat under them. Outdoors, if the ground is soft or uneven, place boards under the feet, as shown *(above, right)*; dig up the soil with a spade to level the boards, if necessary. Pull down the bucket tray and place any tools and materials on it before climbing the stepladder. To climb, face the stepladder and use both hands to grasp the steps rather than the siderails. To work from the stepladder, lean into it, keeping your hips between the siderails; do not stand higher than the third step from the top. Never overreach or straddle the space between the stepladder and another surface; climb down and reposition the stepladder.

Setting up an extension ladder. To work comfortably and safely more than 10 feet off the ground or on the roof, use an extension ladder. Calculate the length of ladder you need; to get off the ladder onto the roof, ensure that the ladder will extend 3 feet above the roof edge. Read the safety instruction label on the ladder siderail. Place the unextended ladder on the ground, perpendicular to the wall, with its fly section on the bottom and its feet out from the wall 1/4 of the height to which it will be raised. With a helper bracing the ladder bottom, raise the top of it above your head; then, walk under the ladder toward the bottom, moving your hands along the siderails to push it upright. With your helper holding the upright ladder, stand to one side, brace the bottom with your foot, and pull on the rope to release and raise the fly section *(above, left)*. When the fly section is extended to the height desired, gently release the rope to lock it. Carefully rest the ladder against the wall or roof edge. If the ground is soft or uneven, place a board under the feet; dig up the soil with a spade to level the board, if necessary. To stabilize the bottom of the ladder, drive a wooden stake into the ground between it and the wall, and tie each siderail to the stake. If you plan to get off the ladder onto the roof, stabilize the top of the ladder. Climb the ladder, using both hands to grasp the rungs. If the ladder is resting against a gutter, lay a 2-by-4 inside the gutter to keep it from crushing under the ladder weight. Then, install an eye screw in the fascia near each siderail and tie each siderail to the eye screw *(above, right)*. Before climbing onto a roof, ensure you know how to work safely on it *(page 138)*.

WORKING SAFELY ON THE ROOF

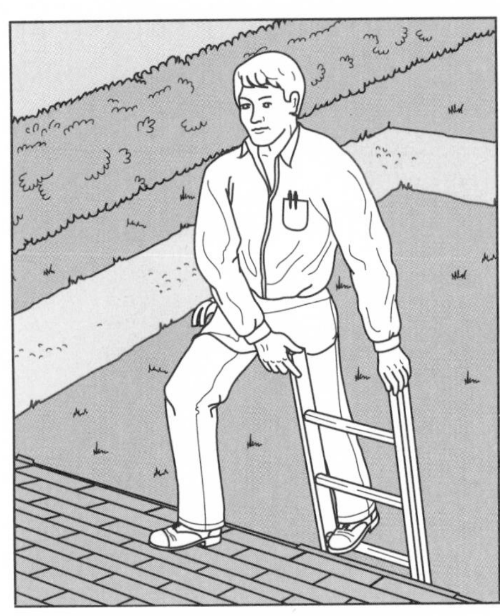

Getting on and off the roof. Never work on the roof in wet, cold, or windy weather. **Caution:** Do not work on a roof that slopes more than 6 inches per foot; have a professional roofer make the necessary repair. Set up an extension ladder *(page 137)*. Climb the ladder until your feet are on the rung level with or just below the eave. Holding firmly onto the top of the siderails with your hands, keep your left foot on the rung of the ladder and carefully step onto the roof with your right foot *(above, left)*, without leaning forward onto the top of the ladder. Grasp the right siderail with your left hand, then remove your right hand from the top of it and carefully step onto the roof with your left foot. When both feet are on the roof, let go of the ladder. Work safely on the roof, transporting tools and supplies up to it and traversing it as necessary *(step below)*.

Before getting off the roof, transport any tools and supplies transported up to it back to the ground. To get off the roof onto the ladder, stand to the left of the ladder, facing it, and grasp the top of the siderail closest to you with your right hand. At the same time, swing your left foot onto the center of the rung at or just below the eave and grasp the top of the other siderail with your left hand *(above, center)*, pivoting on your right foot. Then, swing your right foot onto the center of the rung below your left foot, still grasping the siderails with your hands *(above, right)*. Finally, step down one rung with your left foot and spread your legs slightly, keeping your feet against the siderails. Having a helper on the ground brace the bottom of the ladder, untie any ropes and remove any eye screws securing the top of the ladder to the fascia; also take any 2-by-4 out of the gutter. Then, climb down the ladder.

Working on the roof. To raise tools to the roof, have a helper on the ground with a bucket and a rope long enough to reach the roof. Have your helper tie one rope end to the bucket handle, place the tools in the bucket, and tie the other rope end to his belt loop. Then, have your helper climb the ladder, untie the rope end from his belt loop and pass you the rope end. Sitting on the roof with your feet planted firmly, pull up the rope to raise the bucket *(left)*. When the bucket reaches the eave, carefully pull it over the gutter or overhang onto the roof; hold the ladder for stability. Reverse the procedure to lower tools to the ground.

While on the roof, avoid walking along the edges. If the roof slopes less than 4 inches per foot, you may carefully walk up it diagonally to a desired point. If the roof slopes between 4 and 6 inches per foot, do not walk diagonally. Instead, walk straight up to the ridge; then, walk along the ridge to a point above the desired point and walk back down the roof to it. Reverse the procedure to walk back to the ladder.

WORKING WITH ELECTRICAL WIRING

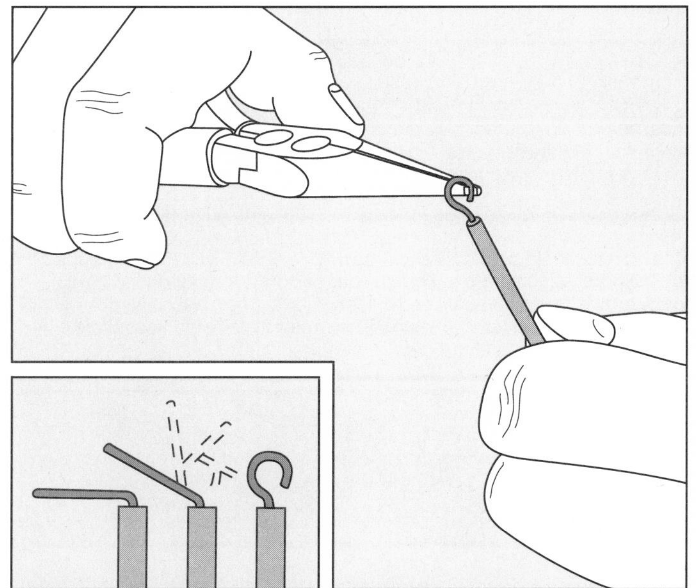

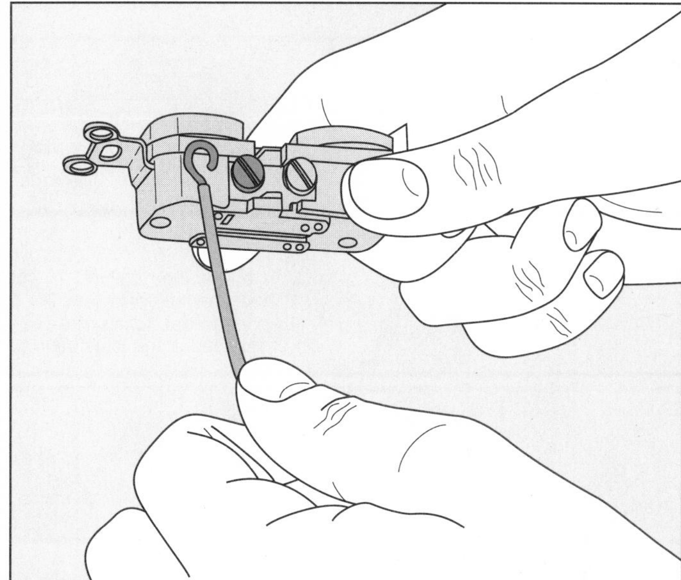

Making a terminal connection. To make a terminal connection, strip the wire *(step below, left)*, if necessary. Holding the wire, grip the bare end with long-nose pliers and bend it at a right angle to the length of the wire. Then, using the pliers to grip the bare wire just where it meets the insulation, make a slight upward bend in the wire; continue, moving the pliers along the bare wire to make one bend after another *(inset)*, until you form an open hook *(above, left)*. To connect the wire to a terminal, use a screwdriver to loosen, but not remove, the terminal screw. Fit the hooked wire end under the head and around the shaft of the screw, orienting the hook so it will close in the same clockwise direction as the screw *(above right)*. Ensure that the hook loops at least three-quarters of the way around the screw shaft. Using a screwdriver, tighten the screw until it grips the wire ends securely and flattens them slightly. If any bare wire protrudes from under the head of the terminal screw, loosen the screw and remove the wire, then start again.

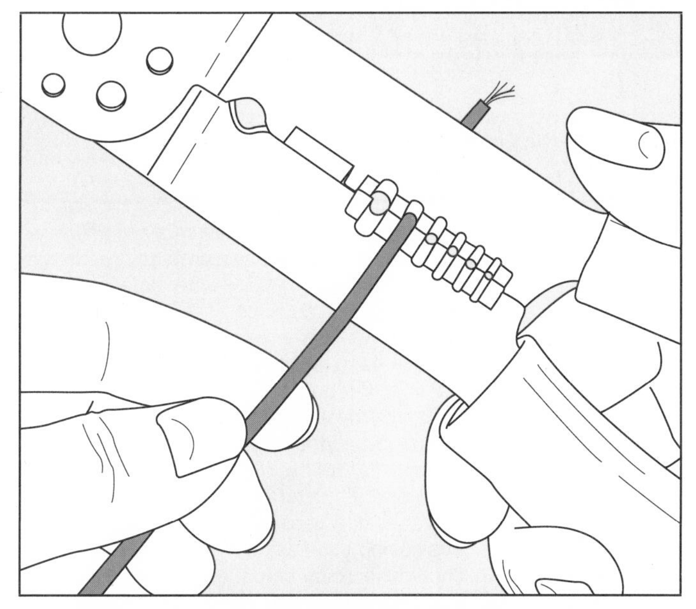

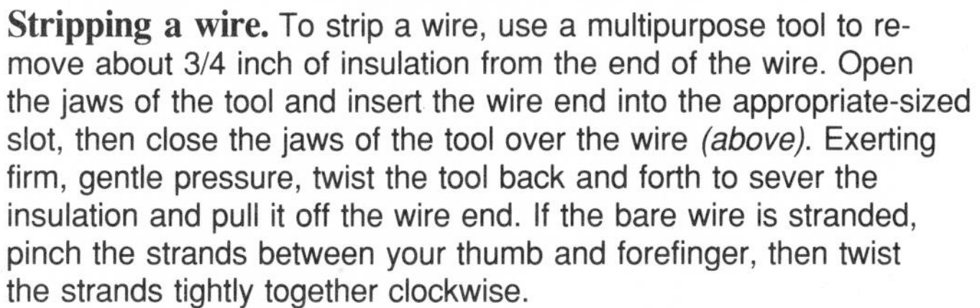

Stripping a wire. To strip a wire, use a multipurpose tool to remove about 3/4 inch of insulation from the end of the wire. Open the jaws of the tool and insert the wire end into the appropriate-sized slot, then close the jaws of the tool over the wire *(above)*. Exerting firm, gentle pressure, twist the tool back and forth to sever the insulation and pull it off the wire end. If the bare wire is stranded, pinch the strands between your thumb and forefinger, then twist the strands tightly together clockwise.

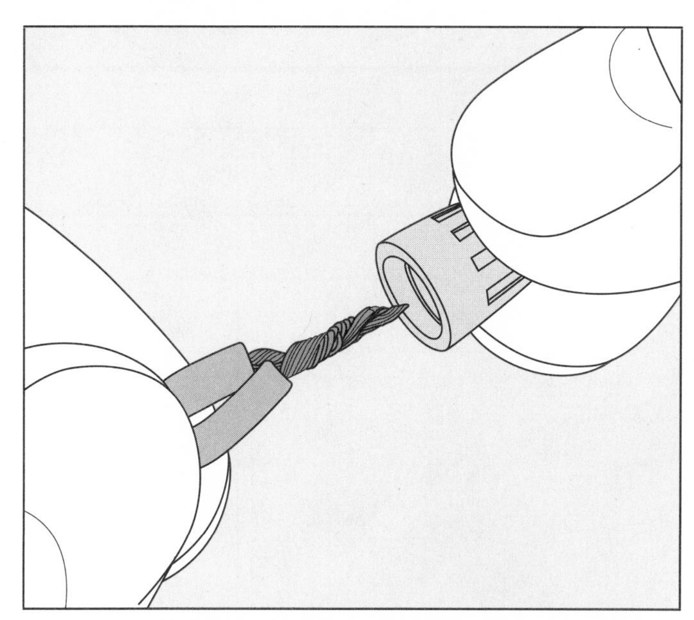

Making a wire cap connection. To make a wire cap connection, strip the wires *(step left)*, if necessary. Holding the wires side by side, grip the bare ends with pliers and twist them tightly together clockwise. Slip a wire cap over the connection *(above)* and screw the cap clockwise until it is tight and no bare wire remains exposed. Test the connection with a slight tug; if it is loose, unscrew and remove the wire cap, then untwist the wires and start again.

CONTROLLING PESTS

PEST	CONTROL
Ant 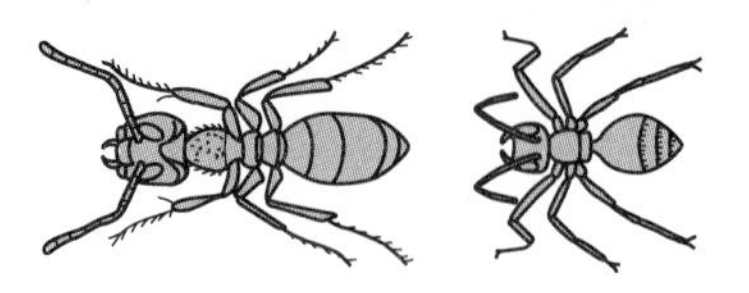	The carpenter ant *(far left)*, 1/4- to 3/4-inch long, burrows into exterior wood structures, causing serious damage; to control carpenter ants, call a pest control expert. The household ant *(near left)*, 1/16- to 3/16-inch long, can be a nuisance around the kitchen. To control household ants, track them back to their nest, then pour boiling water into it. Alternately, use a poison bait; spread jam on a piece of cardboard and sprinkle it with boric acid, then place the bait where ants congregate.
Flea 	The flea *(left)*, 1/25-inch long, infests household pets and any area where a pet sleeps, laying eggs on carpets and furniture. To control fleas, buy a commercial flea powder or spray recommended by a veterinarian and follow the manufacturer's recommendations to apply it to the pet; also buy a commercial, household flea-and-tick spray and follow the instructions to spray infested household surfaces. If the infestation continues, call a pest control expert.
Silverfish 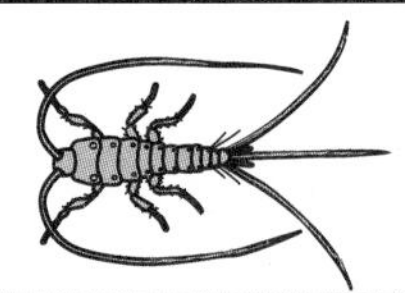	The silverfish *(left)*, 1/2-inch long, can be a nuisance in warm, dry interior household areas, such as an attic or storage room. Kill and dispose of an occasional silverfish. To control larger numbers, use boric acid; sprinkle the powder along wall, floor and cabinet edges where silverfish congregate. If the infestation continues, call a pest control expert.
Subterranean termite 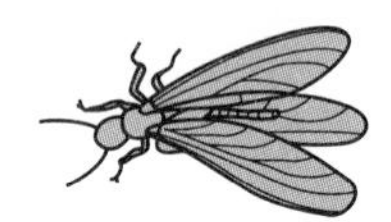	The subterranean termite *(left)*, up to 3/8-inch long, burrows into and eats away at house wood structures from the outside in and the ground up, causing serious damage. To control subterranean termites, call a pest control expert. If you have had an infestation treated, inform a house buyer; and write a clause into the sale contract stating that the infestation has been treated and that you are not responsible for future damage.
Wasp or hornet 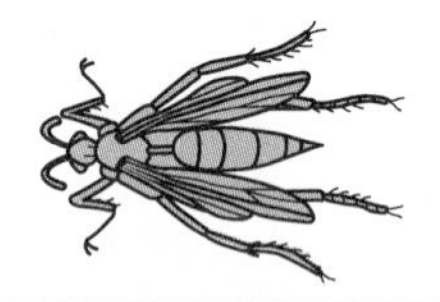	The black-and-yellow-striped yellow jacket may nest in the ground or in a house wall; the bald-faced hornet may build a football-shaped nest in a tree or under an eave. To control nesting yellow jackets and hornets, call a pest control expert. The paper wasp *(left)*, about 1-inch long, can be a nuisance if it builds its inverted, umbrella-shaped nest on or near the house. To control paper wasps, destroy the nest *(step below)*.

Destroying a wasp nest. Destroy a paper wasp nest, which has an inverted umbrella shape; for any other nest, consult a pest control expert. Determine whether the nest is active. After the first frost in a temperate region and during the winter in any region, a nest is inactive. At any other time, watch the nest. If wasps are present, the nest is active; if not, it is inactive. To destroy an inactive nest, knock it down using a broom *(far left)* or a board.

To destroy an active nest, buy a spray insecticide and follow the label instructions to apply it. Work at night when wasps are inactive and the air is calm. Wear rubber gloves and, if necessary, a respirator. Positioning yourself 10 feet from the nest, spray insecticide onto the nest *(left)* for a few seconds. If the wasps become active, stop; otherwise, continue spraying the nest until it is dripping wet. Watch the nest for several days; if it remains active, spray again. Once the nest is inactive, knock it down.

SAFELY DISPOSING OF CHEMICALS

Cleaning up safely. After a repair, exercise caution in handling any leftover cleaner, finishing product or pesticide used on the job; the substance may be poisonous, flammable, caustic or emit hazardous vapors. Take the time to minimize any danger to you, your family and your neighborhood by disposing of or storing it safely. Carefully follow the manufacturer's instructions on the label. Keep children and pets away from the area. Wear the proper safety gear—rubber gloves and long sleeves, safety goggles to protect your eyes from splashes, and a respirator for any substance that emits hazardous vapors. Work in a well-ventilated area; outdoors, work out of the wind. If a spill occurs, clean it quickly *(page 13)*. After a cleanup, wash yourself, your cloths and your tools thoroughly.

Neutralizing acids. Before disposing of leftover muriatic acid solution or any other acid solution or chemical, neutralize it, if possible; follow any instructions given on the product label. For example, to neutralize a bucketful of acid solution, wear rubber gloves and safety goggles, and add the contents of a 1-pound box of sodium bicarbonate (baking soda) to the solution; use a stick to stir the solution *(left)*. Dispose of a neutralized acid solution or chemical as you would any other liquid. If you cannot neutralize an acid solution or chemical, dispose of it safely *(step below, left)*.

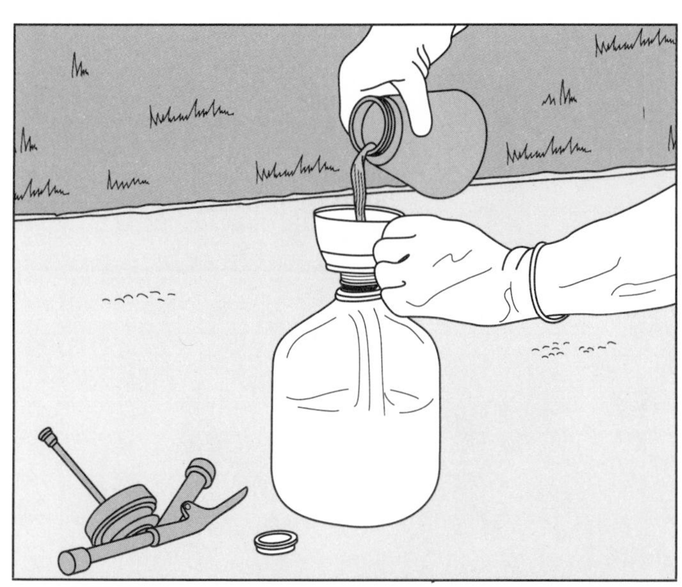

Safely disposing of chemicals. Follow the product label instructions to dispose of a cleaning or finishing product or pesticide. **Caution:** Never pour a hazardous product down a drain or throw it out with household refuse. If possible, return the product to its original container and cap it tightly. Otherwise, wear rubber gloves and safety goggles to funnel the chemical into a glass or plastic container *(above)*; then, label the container. Store the container out of reach in a cool, dry area until you can dispose of it safely. If your community does not have a designated Household Hazardous Waste Clean-up Day, consult your local department of environmental protection or public health for proper disposal procedures.

Safely storing chemicals. Follow any specific instructions on the product label to store a cleaning or finishing product or pesticide. If possible, store a product in its original container, tightly capped; do not remove the label. If you use another container, label it clearly. **Caution:** Never store a poisonous product in a container that might lead a child to mistake the contents for food or drink, and never store a caustic product in a container that might be corroded by it. Store chemicals well out of the reach of children and pets. If possible, use a lockable cabinet with sturdy shelves *(above)*. Ensure the storage site is located in a cool, dry area, away from sunlight and heat or ignition sources.

INDEX

Page references in *italics* indicate an illustration of the subject mentioned. Page references in **bold** indicate a Troubleshooting Guide for the subject mentioned.

H-I-J

K-L

M-N

P

R-S

T

V-W-Y

ACKNOWLEDGMENTS

The editors wish to thank the following:
Donald Allen, Paint Manager, D & G Materials, Montreal, Que.; John P. Bachner, Executive Vice President, ASFE-The Association of Engineering Firms Practicing in the Geosciences, Silverspring, MD; M. Barrett, Montreal, Que.; Harold Bedoukian, Ararat Rug Company, Ltd., Montreal, Que.; Roland Bertin, Coordinating Director, Brock Engineering Mfg. Co., Ltd., Montreal, Que.; Richard Boon, Deputy Director, Roofing Industry Educational Institute, Englewood, CO; Peter Bishin, Architect, Montreal, Que.; Charles Bradley, Owner, Bradley's Janitor Supply Co., Escondido, CA; Marcus Little, carpenter, Ottawa, Ont; Joe Bill Carter, Sales, Century 21 Ambassador Realty, Vista, CA; Martin Cooper, Martin Industries, Inc., Montreal, Que.; Laurie Craig, A Nu-World, Inc., St. Hubert, Que.; DAP Inc., Division of USG, Dayton, OH; Vitale Di Criscio, Manager, Gamma Rental Tools, Montreal, Que.; John Garavelli, Klean-Strip, Division of W.M. Barr Company, Memphis, TN; Stephen Greenford, Caninspect Building Inspections, Town of Mount Royal, Que.; Gennaro Guerra, Guertec Inc., Montreal, Que.; Michel Hamel, Quality Control Manager, Benjamin Moore & Co., Ltd., Montreal, Que.; Jay W. Hedden, Consultant, Leawood, KS; SC Johnson Wax, Racine, WI; Arthur M. Katz, President, Knockout Pest Control, Inc., Uniondale, NY; Mary Keller, Long & Foster Realtor®s, Lutherville, MD; Paul J. Koenig, Vice President, Marketing Services, Delta Faucet, Indianapolis, IN; Elissa Kuhlman, Realtor®s, Pro Consultants Partners, La Mesa, CA; Claude G. and Lucie Lamer, Metal Action, Montreal, Que.; Kenneth Larsen, President, G. Howard Simpkin, Montreal, Que.; Elliot Levine, B.Eng., Levine Brothers Plumbing, Montreal, Que.; Location d'Outillage ERA Inc., Montreal, Que.; Marvin Windows and Doors, Warroad, MN; Mark Monique, Chief Chemist, Savogran Company, Norwood, MA; Nicholas Harrison Munro, Montreal, Que.; National Association of Realtor®s, Public Relations Division, Chicago, IL; National Wood Flooring Association, St. Louis, MO; Norton Company, Worcester, Ma; Evan Powell, HomeTech Inc., Taylors, SC; C. Peter Prakke, Horticultural Consultant, "ORGANIX" Corporation, St. Eugene, Ont.; Paige Prentice, "In the Pink", Alexandria, VA; the technical advisors of Primeau Metal Inc., Montreal, Que.; George W. Rambo, Director of Research and Technical Resources, National Pest Control Association, Dunn Loring, VA; Red Devil, Inc., Union, NJ; William M. Rodgers, General Manager, SET Consumer Products, Cleveland, OH; Anthony C. Sillari, President, T.J. Sillari Plumbing, Inc., Somerville, MA; Stephen Skoda, President, Million Carpets and Tiles, Inc., Montreal, Que.; Society of Real Estate Appraisers, Chicago, IL; Robert L. Warren, Director of Technical Services, National Association of Plumbing, Heating and Cooling Contractors (NAPHCC), Falls Church, VA; Neil A. Wittet, President, Witco Industries, Hudson, Que.; Deborah J. Wright, Senior Product Planner, Melnor Industries, Inc., Moonachie, NJ; Martin Zaltzman, Purchasing, S. Albert & Co., Montreal, Que.

The following persons also assisted in the preparation of this book:
Lousnak Abdalian, Elizabeth Cameron, Maryse Doray, Francine Lemieux, Elizabeth W. Lewis, Jennifer Meltzer, Kelly Mulcair, Jean-Luc Roy, Gerry Wagschal, Katherine Zmetana